Born at the turn of the 20th century, in 1900, Vijaya Laksmi Pandit was the daughter of Motilal Nehru and his second wife, Swaruprani. She played a key role in India's freedom struggle. After Independence, Pandit entered the diplomatic service and served as India's ambassador to the Soviet Union, the United States, Mexico and Ireland. She was also the Indian High Commissioner to the United Kingdom. In 1953, she became the first woman President of the United Nations General Assembly. In India, she served as Governor of Maharashtra from 1962 to 1964, after which she was elected to the Lok Sabha. Her writings include *So I Became a Minister* (1939) and *Prison Days* (1945).

Also by Vijaya Lakshmi Pandit

So I Became a Minister (1939)

Prison Days (1945)

The Scope of Happiness

A Personal Memoir

Vijaya Lakshmi Pandit

SPEAKING TIGER PUBLISHING PVT. LTD
4381/4, Ansari Road, Daryaganj
New Delhi-110002

First published in the US by Crown Publishers Inc., New York, 1979
This edition published by Speaking Tiger in paperback, 2018

ISBN: 978-93-87693-63-0
eISBN: 978-93-87693-64-7

10 9 8 7 6 5 4 3 2 1

Typeset in Sabon Roman by SÜRYA, New Delhi
Printed at Sanat Printers, Kundli

To the memory of two men I loved,
my brother,
Jawaharlal Nehru;
my husband,
Ranjit Sitaram Pandit

They have 'awakened from the dream of life'.

Contents

Foreword

My mother was born in 1900. India was under British rule but patriots like Mohandas Karamchand Gandhi and other respected leaders of his generation believed in British justice. For them this meant that India was on the path to self-rule and equal status with Britain's white empire. In this belief they supported the empire during the First World War, only to be shocked by savage repression after it ended. With it ended all hope of progress toward self-rule. In 1921 Gandhi took the leadership of the Indian National Congress—until then an elite, upper-class body—and launched the revolution that brought the Indian masses into the fight for freedom. It was the first of its kind in history. It was non-violent. It called for breaking unjust laws, suffering persecution and imprisonments, and gladly bearing the hardships and personal sacrifice this commitment would involve. Indians responded in vast numbers to his call, among them, a young Jawaharlal Nehru who then brought his father, Motilal Nehru, and his whole family into the long hard fight for independence.

This was the background of my mother's girlhood, and her description of family life before and immediately after the decision to follow Gandhi is one of the most fascinating parts of this memoir. She writes of the family mansion where 'large numbers of servants (wore) wine and gold liveries, rooms decorated with glittering chandeliers and beautiful carpets, masses of flowers everywhere...' which was 'not the proper setting' for the Mahatma who came to stay for a few days in 1920 to explain the coming satyagraha movement to Motilal Nehru's family. 'To me, with his naked body and his big ears, by no means handsome, Gandhiji was, at that time, a strange new sight. He had by now shed his turban and his Gujarati clothes and begun wearing a loincloth to identify himself with the poorest Indian. His food was served in tin dishes—a plate, a bowl, and a mug—and these he carried everywhere with him.' Nothing could have been wider apart than these two lifestyles, and no transformation more dramatic than the one made overnight in Motilal Nehru's and his family's life when they resolved to follow Gandhi. In 1930, the mansion, Anand Bhawan, itself was given to the Congress party and re-named Swaraj Bhawan. The relationship with Gandhi grew beyond political mentor to close friend and advisor, and one who became a tower of strength and support in times of family tragedies.

My mother writes, 'It took a national revolution to start a revolution in my mind,' and once begun it was one that shaped the rest of her life. She believed she owed her achievements in later life, in India and on the international stage, to this grounding.

The memoir is also fascinating for its detailed description of the Nehru family from the time of Motilal's father, which can be found nowhere else, for its account of my mother's own childhood and youth—less known than her adult career as politician and diplomat—and the chapter where she writes of the remarkably gifted man, my father, Ranjit Sitaram Pandit, whom she married, and his family, distinguished for its Sanskrit scholarship.

She dedicated this memoir 'To the memory of two men I loved. My brother, Jawaharlal Nehru; my husband, Ranjit Sitaram Pandit.' They had been not only brothers-in-law but close friends and comrades in the fight for freedom, twice imprisoned in the same jail. The two great griefs in her life were her husband's death in 1944, of his fourth imprisonment under British rule, and her brother's in 1964 after a life of unremitting service to India. These two men were also the two who helped her become the woman she was.

April 2018 NAYANTARA SAHGAL
Dehradun

Introduction

My wife and I first met Nan Pandit when we went to India to negotiate the Transfer of Power in 1947, though there wasn't time to get to know her very well then because she was sent to take up her post as Indian Ambassador in Moscow twenty-four hours before the actual Transfer of Power took place at midnight on August 14/15, 1947. Her brother, Prime Minister Jawaharlal Nehru, had discussed the appointment with me, and I told him I could think of no one better suited to represent the views of India in the Eastern bloc. It was a bold and imaginative move that did much to enhance the prestige of free India.

I had met Jawaharlal Nehru when I was Supreme Allied Commander in Southeast Asia. In March 1946 he visited Singapore to study the conditions of the large Indian community there and meet the Indian forces. He had just been in prison for opposing our war effort, and one of the things in his programme was to lay a wreath on the memorial to the Indian National Army, which had fought against the Allies.

In my absence the local authorities had planned to cold-shoulder Nehru, hamper his movements, and restrict his contacts with the Indian troops. I realized this would be disastrous for future Anglo-Indian relations, since this man was clearly going to be Prime Minister of India. I lent him my car, we brought hundreds of Indian troops into Singapore to be able to see him, and I received him immediately at Government House.

I then drove with him through the streets, where he had a fantastic welcome, and I was able to persuade him not to lay the wreath on the pro-Japanese Indian National Army Memorial. In fact, his whole nine-day visit went extremely well, and this was the beginning of a deep friendship between Jawaharlal Nehru and Edwina and me.

What I did not know until I read this book was that Nan Pandit, too, had received help from my Command, but without my knowledge. She tells the story of how she met my Deputy Allied Air Commander, a great American, General George E. Stratemeyer, at a dinner party, and he subsequently arranged for her to fly to America in one of our allied aircraft to do propaganda for the British to quit India.

Nan Pandit has represented her country in a number of diplomatic and political posts, but I feel none was more important than that of Indian High Commissioner in London. It was during this time that Edwina and I got to know her extremely well. It is impossible to measure the immense amount of good she did, during her seven years in London, to cement Anglo-Indian relations. Her appointment was a brilliant piece of statesmanship, and she won the lasting affection of the British. Not only did they admire her intelligence and graceful but modest charm, but we all loved her for her great sense of fun and quick wit.

I remember the time she went to the Royal College of Physicians to receive an honourary degree. This was at the time when birth control was a very controversial subject, particularly in India, and she chose to tell the following story:

A young Indian wife had given birth year after year, and the time had come when she felt she could not cope with any more children. She went to see her doctor and explained that, although she did not wish to fail in her duty as a wife, would he please give her something that would prevent her conceiving any more children. The doctor listened sympathetically and then wrote out a prescription, which he handed to her.

The young woman thanked him profusely and got up to leave. As she got to the door she glanced at the prescription and saw he had written: One glass of cold water. 'Excuse me, doctor,' she said, 'I notice you have prescribed a glass of cold water. Do I take it before or after?' 'Neither,' the doctor replied. 'You take it instead.'

Nan Pandit's charming, well-written and informative autobiography gives an insight into a remarkable woman. Although born into a privileged background, her lifestyle changed completely in 1921, when her family decided to alter their lives completely and join Gandhi's National Movement. From then on she devoted her life to the cause of freedom in India. This involved her in great hardships, including terms in prison and the loss of her beloved husband, Ranjit, who died as a direct result of the conditions he suffered in prison. And yet this diminutive woman with a large heart never became embittered, and her love and affection for the British and her friendship with the British monarchy are beyond question.

I have personally always regretted that Jawaharlal Nehru did not persist in his decision to appoint her Vice-President of India. With her vast political and diplomatic knowledge, and her unique ability to make friends with all levels of people of all nations, no one was ever better suited to high office.

Hers is a story of selfless dedication not only to her mother country, India, but to the cause of freedom, peace, and understanding throughout the world. She has truly proved herself to be a good citizen of the world.

1979 LORD LOUIS MOUNTBATTEN

London

1. Maintenance of Internal Security Act.

1

Emergency

In June 1975 my daughter Nayantara and I had come to London from Padua where we had gone to attend the wedding of her son to an Italian girl. We spent the night at the Y.M.C.A. Indian Students' Hostel. Next morning, as I was getting breakfast at the cafeteria, a young man next in line to me said, 'I wonder if you know that about a dozen press people are waiting to meet you in the lounge? They say an emergency has been declared in India.' Breakfast no longer mattered and I went to meet the assembled journalists. They had no details, only the bare announcement by the Prime Minister that 'the government was forced to act because of the deep and widespread conspiracy which has been brewing ever since I began introducing certain progressive measures of benefit to the common man and common woman of India in the name of democracy.'

I told the journalists I could not comment on a situation of which I knew nothing. Comment in any case should come from the High Commissioner, but I was greatly distressed. I phoned India House and found they did not have too much information but that news was coming through all the time. Later in the day we went to the High Commissioner's residence and learned that Jayaprakash Narayan, Morarji Desai, and hundreds of others had been arrested at 2 a.m. and detained under MISA.[1] It was reminiscent of the midnight knock

1. Maintenance of Internal Security Act.

of forty years ago in Hitler's Germany. Civil liberties were being suppressed and censorship had been rigidly imposed on the press. The approach of High Commission officials, however, was jovial. 'What's all the fuss about? Everything is fine in India.' My obvious disapproval dampened the carefree atmosphere, and after an uncomfortable half hour my daughter and I left.

The English newspapers next morning reported that total censorship in India prohibited quotations and extracts from even the writings of Gandhi, Tagore, and Nehru, particularly any references to freedom. One report also said that the press response to censorship was to leave blank spaces for editorials and feature articles, but that these blank spaces had also been censored! We had meant to spend a few weeks in England visiting friends but now we decided we must return home immediately. If the country was to become a prison camp and all civil liberties were to be denied, our place was obviously there.

On the journey home my mind went over past events. The Emergency should not have come as a shock because it was the natural culmination of the shape things had been taking through the last few years...

In 1964, after my brother's death, Lal Bahadur Shastri had become Prime Minister through a consensus of the Congress party high command, and Indira Gandhi was named his Minister of Information. She had, I think, expected the Foreign Affairs portfolio but settled down to her new appointment. My brother's parliamentary constituency, Phulpur, was now vacant, and a by-election had to take place within six months, according to the rules. I was Governor of Maharashtra at the time, but old Congress colleagues and friends from the state of Uttar Pradesh wrote asking me to leave my post and seek election to my brother's constituency.

When twenty or more such letters had been received, I phoned Lal Bahadur and told him about these requests. He asked me to send the letters to him as he would have to check with the Congress high command. It was the opinion of some, who felt my return to national politics might pose a threat to them, that I should not be allowed to contest this election. The argument they used was that, as I had been out of the country on foreign assignments for fifteen years, Indira would have a better chance of winning this election. Indira was then not a member of Parliament and would before long have to contest a seat to the Lok Sabha (House of the People) in order to remain in the Cabinet. Uma Shankar Dikshit, an old Congress leader and close friend of Indira, was asked by the Congress high command to go to Phulpur and find out what the chances were for Congress to retain the seat and who would be a likely winner. His report was that both Indira and I would be acceptable to the constituency. It was now left to the high command to decide to whom to give the ticket.

Just as I was leaving for the United Kingdom, where Oxford University was honouring me with the degree of Doctor of Civil Law, I received a phone call from Lal Bahadur. He said Indira and I should decide the matter of the Phulpur seat between us. Uma Shankar Dikshit was pressing Indira, but she seemed reluctant. No message had been received from Indira when I left Bombay. Harold Macmillan was then Chancellor of Oxford University, and the date for the conferment of the degree was fixed for the day after my arrival in the United Kingdom. I arrived in London to find a message from Lal Bahadur saying that Indira was en route to London and would meet me the next evening. Returning from Oxford I found Indira had arrived. She told me of the decision of the high command, that either of us could have the Phulpur ticket, but said she would like me to accept as she did not 'feel ready to face an election just then.' I told her it was my firm view that she should retain her father's parliamentary constituency, but she seemed genuinely reluctant, so I said I would gladly accept the offer. I left for Bombay immediately and on arrival offered my resignation as Governor of Maharashtra to the President.

I then proceeded to my constituency to file my papers. Decision-making had taken so long that the deadline had been reached. The election took place in November 1964. Lal Bahadur and Indira were among the top leaders who gave me their cooperation and canvassed for me, and I won with a big majority, only a little less than my brother had had.

My victory was welcomed by the party and I looked forward to working with Indira for the implementation of my brother's policies in which we both had faith. For some days I lived in her house until my own accommodation as a member of Parliament was allotted to me. According to custom, I called on all the ministers, mostly old friends and colleagues. I visited Lal Bahadur a couple of times to reassure him that I did not want any post but would be happy if he could use me at any time. This was necessary because, immediately after becoming Prime Minister, he had come to me and, in the usual Indian way, had asked for my blessings and cooperation as an 'elder sister'. I told him he had both, including my affection, and hoped he would always trust me. Sometime later I repeated this to Indira and she said with quiet sarcasm, 'I hope *you* will not trust *him* too much. He is about as reliable as a snake.'

During the period he was Prime Minister, Lal Bahadur sent me abroad as his special representative on several occasions, to discuss matters (Konrad) with Adenauer, and De Gaulle (Charles), to Algeria, and to represent India at Adenauer's funeral. But whenever I mentioned work at home he seemed embarrassed. Once he said he had been 'discussing the possibility with Indiraji.' It was easy to see he was not very close to her and did not wish to take issue with her about me.

I did not see much of Indira, but it became evident very soon that tales were being carried to and fro by persons interested in driving a wedge between us. A speech I made in the Lok Sabha did not ease matters. I felt that the government had been drifting for some time and many important decisions were hanging in the balance. In my speech I called the Cabinet 'prisoners of indecision'. This received a big cheer from both sides of the House and wide coverage in the press but naturally did not please the government benches. Matters were not improved when Krishna Menon's speech following mine supported me, ending with the *bon mot* that 'even drift had a direction which the government lacked.' However, the term 'prisoners of indecision' caught on and is even now a slogan often used and referred to in political talk.

Lal Bahadur's untimely death in Tashkent made Indira Prime Minister. I remained a backbencher but did a good deal of work in my constituency. What became very disturbing was a growing tendency by some people, obviously inspired from above, to eavesdrop on conversations of members of Parliament in the Central Hall and carry distorted versions to Indira. I was able to confirm this from some ministers and even from the Prime Minister's secretariat. Several times I tried to speak to Indira, but opportunities were denied on grounds of her being 'heavily occupied'. I felt a barrier growing up between us, deliberately erected by those who were always on the lookout to prove their personal loyalty to the Prime Minister by 'telling tales' in the hope of reward. Indira easily believes tales of anything said against her and does not take criticism well. Whenever I met her I was unable to have even an ordinary, friendly conversation because her most effective weapon has always been a stony silence.

There is an interesting incident of the time which I recall. Our relations with the United Kingdom were at a low ebb. Lord Mountbatten had broken journey in Delhi en route to another destination, carrying a letter or message from Harold Wilson with the suggestion that I should be sent to the United Kingdom again as High Commissioner. He met me, and said he and others were disturbed at the way relations were deteriorating between our two countries. I had received letters from other friends in Britain voicing the same concern. I had no particular desire to go back to the High Commission in London or to accept another diplomatic appointment. A week or so later, during a session of the Lok Sabha, I had a message to see the Prime Minister in her office. As I have said before, Indira cannot talk easily even to her closest friends. I sat opposite her and waited for her to say something. Finally she stopped her doodling and told me about the suggestion from the United Kingdom. Then there was silence. 'Well,' I asked, 'what do you think about it?' Silence...then in a very soft voice she said, 'Well, Puphi, I don't really trust you.' I had lived with pretence so long that what she said actually came as a relief. I walked round the table to where she sat and, kissing the top of her head, I said, 'Thank you, Indu, for telling me the truth!' She then asked if I would 'care to go to Paris for a year. De Gaulle likes you, you know.' This offer I refused. I was certain I did not want to resume a diplomatic career.

The personal gap between us kept widening. I was not invited to the Prime Minister's parties for members of Parliament or included in any committee at home or delegation going abroad. My long experience, success, and prestige with the United Nations was completely ignored. The break was so obvious that it made me unhappy. Morarji bhai had always been a friend and counsellor though we did not see eye to eye on all matters. I had several talks with him and said that under existing conditions I felt staying on in Parliament was useless. He was himself distressed by the growing flattery surrounding the Prime Minister. But he advised me to wait. I also spoke to P.N. Haksar, then principal private secretary to the Prime Minister. I have known him a long time—he is a good, upright man, but there was something already in the environment that prevented people from speaking freely. He spoke of 'loyalty to Panditji' and attempts 'to help his daughter' but did not answer my question which was simple and direct: Was it any use my staying on in Parliament when the Prime Minister did not trust me? It prevented my work as M.P. and damaged our personal relationship.

I decided to resign. The reason I gave to the press was

that I was increasingly out of tune with my party and with government policies. The manner in which my resignation was accepted was most extraordinary. The usual procedure is for resignations to be dealt with over a period of days. My letter went to the Speaker, Mr Sanjiva Reddy, now President of India, around noon. He had left his office for the airport en route to Hyderabad, and the letter was sent to him by special messenger and his acceptance taken at the airport. The news was announced on the radio the same evening!

After considerable thought, I decided to retire from public life. It was a hard decision to make but I felt compelled to do so. I had tried to raise my voice but had been misunderstood, my words distorted and motives attributed to me even by those who should have known better. There seemed to be no alternative. My sense of duty to the country and the discipline which had been so firmly ingrained under Mahatma Gandhi's leadership led me to the further decision to remain out of focus of the power structure and watch events from a distance.

In 1969 came the split in the Congress which now became two parties known by the names of Congress (R) and Congress (O). In spite of pressures by Congress friends to intervene in the situation, I remained aloof for the same reasons that had led me to resign from Parliament. A midterm general election to the Lok Sabha was called by Indira in 1971. Indira was almost at the zenith of her power. The election slogan of the Opposition was 'Indira Hatao' (Remove Indira) to which Congress (R) cleverly replied 'Garibi Hatao' (Remove Poverty)—magic for the masses, since it touched them directly. The Congress (R) won a sweeping victory at the polls.

The election had been fought with every available weapon, which included the use of large sums of money and wide publicity on a scale unknown before. The whole country was covered with large posters describing Indira as the protector of the underprivileged. In Delhi itself there was not an inch of wall space left bare, and a smiling Indira in various poses offered promises of a 'golden tomorrow'. One had imagined that the posters would gradually disappear after the election victory, but, to the growing amazement and concern of many, they increased, and billboards were covered with huge pictures of the Prime Minister and only the Prime Minister. The slogans were frightening, so close were they to Fascism. Little by little Indira was referred to neither by name nor as Prime Minister. It was now the 'Leader' and beside her picture on huge placards were exhortations for unity under 'The Leader'. At this time a sort of Führer principle began to operate in government, with only one person (herself) deciding issues. The opinion of others in the Cabinet counted only to the degree of their faithfulness to the Leader.

In contrast to this it is interesting to recall another event forty years ago. Indira's father was the undisputed hero of the national movement all over India, much loved by young and old alike and greeted by admiring crowds with joyful shouts of 'Jai!' (Victory!) wherever he went. Partly to amuse himself and also to create a reaction among the public he wrote an anonymous article about himself implying that the adored idol of the people might well turn into a dictator! In this article he said, in part, 'A little twist and Jawaharlal might turn a dictator, sweeping aside the paraphernalia of slow-moving democracy. He might still use the language and slogans of democracy and socialism, but we all know how Fascism has fattened on this language and then cast it away as useless lumber...His overmastering desire to get things done, to sweep away what he dislikes and build anew will hardly brook...the slow process of democracy. He may keep the husk but he will see to it that it bends to his will. In normal times he would be just an efficient and successful executive, but in this revolutionary epoch, caesarism is always at the door, and is it not possible that Jawaharlal might fancy himself as a Caesar?' It seems an irony of fate that words written in jest should have come true and that not he, but his daughter, should have made a travesty of democracy in India.

The word now in vogue was *commitment*, which meant the total abandonment of one's own political views to echo those of the 'Leader'. Everyone was judged by this—civil servants, lawyers, doctors, professors, journalists—whatever or whoever they might be had to be 'committed'. If not, they soon found themselves on the outside and, as things developed, often in personal danger of losing their jobs.

One of the side issues of the growing authoritarian trend was constant interference with the functioning of state ministries by the Prime Minister's secretariat. Those chief ministers who did not toe the line were dislodged by political manoeuvres. This attempt succeeded because the courage to face the Prime Minister was dwindling and chief ministers replaced one another so rapidly that it was difficult to remember their names. Not many were interested in economic affairs in their states and many state governments were in actual disarray. In Gujarat, public resentment against the Congress government in the state mounted until a students' agitation, joined by a citizens' movement, demanded its removal. When the intervention of the Central Government's special police force did not succeed in quelling the agitation, President's Rule was imposed on Gujarat, bringing the state directly under central control. According to the Constitution, this measure has to be followed by an election in the state, but no election was announced.

In Delhi, Morarji Desai, after visits to Gujarat and unsuccessful attempts to resolve the situation through talks with the Congress President and the Prime Minister, went on a fast unto death to focus attention on the situation in Gujarat and to persuade the government to act constitutionally. This caused great concern to people all over the country, and hundreds flocked to his residence to inquire after his health and pray for him. I had come from Dehra Dun as soon as the fast began and had stayed on in Delhi until Morarji bhai was able to drink the glass of orange juice that terminated the fast. It ended after the government's announcement of fresh elections in Gujarat. It was with this background and emotion-charged atmosphere that the Gujarat elections were held. They gave the opposition parties a sweeping victory.

This was the situation that ultimately led to the return of Jayaprakash Narayan to the national scene with his demand for a clean government and for a return to the moral values that had previously guided government policies. J.P.'s appeal made an instant impact on youth. He addressed gigantic meetings mainly in his home state, Bihar, where conditions were even worse than in other states. To those who were present at these meetings, it was an emotional experience to witness the start of a real mass movement led by a true Gandhian.

◆◆◆

2

Coming Home and Elections

On returning home we found conditions even worse than we had imagined. The first thing that one noticed was the silence. We Indians are a talkative people and there is constant chatter everywhere. Now this had changed. At parties one talked about the weather, about some item of foreign news, or a trivial happening at home. But for the most part there was deafening silence wherever one went. Thousands of people were in prison without trial.

Another aspect of the Emergency was the Twenty-Point Programme—a rehash of many of the economic and social tenets that we had adopted since the early years of the struggle for independence. These twenty points were announced daily on radio and T.V., and billboards everywhere gave them the greatest publicity.

I went straight to my home in Dehra Dun. My phone

was tapped, my letters censored, and a gentleman, who tried to merge with the foliage, watched my gate and took down the names of those who came to see me. In the months of June and July Dehra Dun is hot, and I asked my cook to tell the man to come in and sit in the veranda or under the shade of a tree in the garden. Budhilal, my cook, always exceeds my instructions and is a law unto himself. He told the silent watcher that 'we' were accustomed to be watched; 'we' had survived surveillance, jail, and other indignities; 'we' recognized him for what he was and had no objection but 'we' wanted to make him comfortable, so why not come and sit in the garden and have a drink of iced water and do his dirty work in greater ease! The man was withdrawn some weeks later. His removal coincided with the appearance of an item in one of the British papers to the effect that I was under surveillance. I could not say if the withdrawal was due to this or not.

During the Emergency and before, Mrs Gandhi had been keen to show the West that the government had taken all actions in a democratic way. Invitations were now sent to 'friends of India' in various countries to come and see conditions for themselves. Indians who had been living abroad were also invited, all expenses paid, red-carpet treatment given, to write favourable articles on the Indian situation, telling people that peace and order, security and progress, now existed, omitting of course that all this could have been achieved under the ordinary laws of the land. Since fear had reduced the intelligentsia to puppets there were plenty of people available to give fulsome praise to the Prime Minister for her wise leadership, and this impressed the foreigner. It is impossible to convey, without seeming to exaggerate, the despair I felt as I watched this stage-managed show. Indira had forgotten, among other things, that in 1962, after we had suffered reverses against China and nearly the whole country was against her father, he rejected the advice of Krishna Menon, then Defence Minister, and refused to impose an internal emergency on the ground that such an act would harm democratic traditions.

The Emergency was legitimized in a session of Parliament called for this purpose on July 21, 1975, with leaders of Opposition parties in jail and the press gagged. The resolution seeking the approval of Parliament for the proclamation of the Emergency was moved by Mr Jagjivan Ram and, in spite of strong protests from the Opposition, was passed because of the large Congress majority in both houses of Parliament. The Constitution Thirty-Eighth Amendment Bill was introduced, by which the President's reasons for proclaiming an Emergency could not be challenged in any court. The bill had to be ratified by special sessions of the Legislative Assemblies of the states. This was done in record time and the President's assent given on August 1. The government also introduced the Thirty-Ninth Constitutional Amendment Bill regarding election disputes relating to the President, the Vice-President, the Prime Minister, and the Speaker. This invalidated, with retrospective effect, the ruling of the Allahabad High Court and saved Mrs Gandhi from the consequences of her violation of the election law. The Allahabad High Court had indicted Mrs Gandhi on misuse of official help during the 1971 midterm elections, declared her election invalid, and debarred her from holding office for six years. On August 7 the then law minister introduced in Parliament another amendment to the Constitution Bill, providing that problems arising out of the election of the President, Vice-President, Speaker of the Lok Sabha, and the Prime Minister could not come under the scrutiny of any law court. So it was guaranteed that Mrs Gandhi would not have to answer to the law.

Although fundamental rights had been suspended as a result of the Emergency, the government announced the suspension of seven specific rights guaranteed by the Constitution—those of speech, assembly, the right to form associations and labour unions, to move freely out of the country, to live in any part of the country, to own property, and to pursue any profession, trade, or business (Article 19 of the Constitution). When I read of this ban in the newspapers, I was shaken and distressed beyond words. Why had we undergone a struggle for independence, where was our pledge to the people? My mind went back to the stirring words with which my brother, on the midnight of August 14, 1947, had ushered in the era of independence:

> Long years ago we made a tryst with destiny, and now the time comes when we shall redeem our pledge, not wholly or in full measure, but very substantially. At the stroke of the midnight hour, when the world sleeps, India will awake to life and freedom... We end today a period of ill fortune and India discovers herself again. The achievement we celebrate today is but a step, an opening of opportunity, to the greater triumphs and achievements that await us. Are we brave enough and wise enough to grasp this opportunity and accept the challenge of the future?

The morale of the people was sinking lower and lower and a pattern of fear was being relentlessly woven in our lives. Gandhiji had called fear the close companion of falsehood. How right he had been! Fear and the falsehood it generated were now the guidelines of government functioning.

Sitting alone on my veranda, watching the majesty of the Himalaya mountains facing me, I lived with pain almost physical in its intensity. How could we who had lived in the light, who had believed in truth and values, who had almost touched the stars in the joy of striving for what we believed in—how could we have become such little, mean people, full of fear and sycophancy? Night after night I went to bed only to lie awake, not willing to accept what was and yet not knowing what to do. It was not the fear of jail that held me back from speaking. I had had more than my share of the good life and was also familiar with jail. But nothing one said would reach the public, so why try to become a martyr? That has never been my way. I would have liked to go to Indu, to open my heart to her, to beg her to think of what she was doing, to remind her of the values we had shared, of the ideals we had fought to preserve in what now seemed a very distant past. But access to her was not possible. She was always 'too busy with important work.' People began to speak of her as the goddess Durga, and the President of the Congress party repeated *ad nauseam* that 'India was Indira and Indira, India.' Trying to approach those around her was equally futile. Even the men I had known all through my political life and with whom I had worked and gone to jail were afraid to be seen with me. I was on the wrong side and their chances of retaining the positions they occupied would be jeopardized. Often one thought of the time when Gandhiji's magic touch made giants out of pygmies—alas, today the case had been reversed. Swami Vivekananda used to say that a nation was not judged by the beauty of its buildings but by the quality of its men. Judged by this standard we had fallen low indeed.

One October morning I had a phone call from the representative of *The New York Times*. He was in Mussoorie on holiday and asked if he and his wife might call on me on their way back to Delhi. I invited them to lunch. I am nervous of foreign newspapermen as a rule and do not talk freely unless they happen to be personal friends, but I had been suffocated for so long that I had to speak. What did it matter if this young man distorted what I said? Were we not living with distortion? Had not all that was noble and part of our shining heritage already been distorted? So I let William Borders talk and I answered him without reserve. This conversation was published in a short interview in *The New York Times* of October 31, 1976. Apart from stating that I was profoundly disturbed at what had happened, I wondered where we were going and why the freedom and democracy we had fought for had been so ruthlessly suppressed. Conditions today, I felt, were in some ways worse than they had been under British power at its height.

The Emergency was lifted unexpectedly on January 18,

1977. One of Indira's political assets had been her sense of timing, which had been perfect in the past. But now she miscalculated badly in her own interest. One does not know by what process of reasoning she came to her decision. It may have been because the parasites around her believed that the common man, the voter, was as cowed as they, or perhaps her not too intelligent Intelligence advisors read the omens wrong, or perhaps her own wishes distorted her thinking. Whatever it may have been, the January 18 announcement set the stage for what turned out to be the greatest democratic electoral victory in world history. Morarji Desai and other leaders were released from prison immediately and others followed less swiftly.

I rushed to Delhi in a fever of excitement but just missed Morarji bhai, who had already left for his constituency in Surat, Gujarat. Gradually one met old friends and colleagues, eager to give news of what they and others had been through. We heard barbaric stories of torture to elicit confessions of the whereabouts of those who had managed to evade arrest and were working underground, and of treatment in many of the jails where human beings were considered expendable. There were feelings of horror, anger, and extreme resentment everywhere. Concern for missing persons added to the tenseness of the atmosphere.

The Opposition leaders, some of whom had been together in Tihar Jail before release, had been thinking deeply about the vital necessity of getting together as a united political opposition to the government. There was now little time and very little money, and the whole country had to be approached within a period of weeks. Leaders and women and men belonging to the various political groups met urgently and plans were discussed.

I had met Morarji bhai on one of his brief visits to Delhi and told him I wanted to help his party in any way I could. He asked me if I would like to stand for Parliament, but I told him that all I wanted was to help to the utmost of my ability and strength to restore real democracy to India, to see again free men and women functioning in a free society where there was no room for fear; to feel that I had, in however small a way, struck a blow for the ideals in which I believed and which had nourished India through the centuries. He accepted my offer of work and referred me to the Janata party[2] office.

Meanwhile, I had been talking to friends whose advice I trusted, and fortunately for me my daughters Lekha and Rita were at home and brought me much strength at a time when I had to make important decisions. My other daughter, Nayantara, had been offered a research scholarship at the Radcliffe Institute in Cambridge, and with great reluctance, but encouraged by me, had gone abroad for some months. As a journalist critical of government policies and outspoken against the Emergency, she faced the threat of arrest at home. In America she had written and spoken against the Emergency, along with others, who were doing splendid work in enlightening American opinion. She had also been sending back news through the underground of what was going on in India itself, since total censorship kept people within the country in the dark about events going on around them. To her too I owed a debt. She had wanted to stay home and share with her comrades whatever good or ill was coming. I had pressed her to get away. Now I felt I must discharge my debt by working with double energy for the new freedom we hoped would soon dawn. I also felt that all the young men and women who had suffered in jails, and some of whom had died, were my own. They belonged to me because we shared a common faith. To those who had suffered I owed a tribute of admiration, and, for those who had died for a cause, I should help to keep their memory fresh.

I was rejuvenated. All the dreary months of sitting and dreaming dreams that might never be fulfilled were,

2. This was a new party formed to contest the elections, a merger of Congress (O), Swatantra party, Jan Sangh, and Bharatiya Lok Dal. It was later joined by Congress for Democracy.

thankfully, over. India would come out of the dark tunnel and please God she would never be forced to look back. My little Farhana, the small great-granddaughter around whom my life had begun to revolve, would be able to live in the sunlight and grow into a happy, fearless woman. To her and her generation I, and those who were left of mine, also had a debt to discharge. I could not wait for the campaign to get started. I began drafting a statement to be released to the press. In the opening paragraph I spoke of my retirement from politics, which I have already referred to, and then went on:

> The essence of democracy is the right to dissent. This does not imply disloyalty to the country. Exchange of views and discussions are a democratic way towards a solid base on which the future progress and prosperity of the nation should be built. It is shocking to see all dissent muzzled and those who disagreed with government put into prison. I remember how disturbed Jawaharlal Nehru used to be time and again by objectionable writings in the press. But he was firm in the belief that freedom of the press was basic to democracy and expressed himself clearly on the subject... More than anything else the situation created by fear is one which should be of concern to all thinking people. Gandhiji worked long and hard to release Indians from the fear caused by years of foreign rule. He put courage in our hearts and gave us strength and stamina to face and break a mighty empire... People are afraid to speak and by their silence have acquiesced in the denial of the very freedoms for which an earlier generation fought and laid down their lives. I have remained a passive spectator for too long but I cannot live at peace with myself if, by my silence, I seem to agree with the destruction of all I have been taught to hold dear. I speak now with a full sense of responsibility for what I am doing. My first duty and loyalty is and must always be to my country.

I had been meeting as many people as I could and was waiting for Morarji bhai's reply to my inquiry about releasing the statement. I was returning from a medical check-up on February 5 and had stopped at a chemist's in Khan Market to fill a prescription when I noticed a newspaper boy yelling 'Special Edition'. I could not understand what he was saying and went out to buy a copy. It contained the announcement that Mr Jagjivan Ram, Finance Minister, had resigned from the Cabinet that morning. This was unbelievably good news. Just for a moment I wondered what in heaven's name he had been doing up to now, but for a minute only. The news was far too significant for criticism. I wanted to go to him right away but remembered he would be besieged by half the population of Delhi. I phoned him that night and went to see him the next day. He welcomed my joining the 'fight,' and I had several meetings with him and Hemvati Nandan Bahuguna, his trusted lieutenant in the new party he started, the Congress for Democracy. Bahuguna had been Chief Minister of Uttar Pradesh and been replaced on Mrs Gandhi's instructions. It was arranged that Babuji, as we called Mr Jagjivan Ram, would present me to the press on February 12. The Indian President had died suddenly following the announcement of the elections, and during the three days of official mourning my announcement had to be postponed. On the morning of February 12, the lawns of Babuji's house were crowded with the press and T.V. people. My statement had already been distributed and questions were showered on me. Naturally they referred mostly to my relationship with Indira. Some days earlier, she had mentioned in one of her election speeches that the Nehru family had contributed more than any other to the independence struggle. This had not been received well by the public, and several members of the family, too, had felt ashamed that such a statement had been made. The question now put to me reflected the feelings of the press. I was asked if I felt the same way as my niece. My answer was immediate. I replied, 'For what my family has done for India it has been amply rewarded.' There were approving cheers, and my relations with the media were cordial throughout the campaign.

About this time I received two letters that touched me deeply and which I cherish. The first was from a member of the Socialist party just released from prison who is at present one of the secretaries of the Janata party—Madhu Limaye. I had known him in Parliament over the years when he was a very vocal member of the Opposition. He is a man of integrity, and no matter which side he is on I cannot imagine his doing a mean or unworthy act. He would only act on a deep conviction and not for any personal benefit. I admire and am fond of him. This is his letter:

Delhi 19th Feb. 1977

Dear Vijayalaxmiji,
My congratulations on your perfectly timed intervention in defenceof freedom, democracy and the cherished values of our national struggle.

You used to call me an angry young man. I am no longer young, but I was angry at the time of my release on 7th Feb. 1977. I was bitter not because of what they did to me in the last 20 months—part of which was spent in solitary confinement and without the company of friends—but because they ill-treated my young friends. They did not receive proper medical attention. This is how young Hashmat Warsi (29 years old) lost his life. The greatest blow that has hurt me deeply is the death of Mrs Snehlata Reddy, actress, writer, socialist. She was a sensitive soul and my dearest friend. The conditions of her detention were inhuman. I cannot reconcile myself to her loss. The death of these friends call to my mind Coleridge's Ancient Mariner, and these lines haunt me:

The many men, so beautiful!
And they all dead did lie;
And a thousand thousand slimy things
Lived on; and so did I.

Your powerful and dignified utterance has been a balm, and I am sullen no longer.

I do not know anything about your programme. But Jagjivan babu told me that you have agreed to campaign for the Opposition. I cannot ask you to visit my constituency (Banka in Bihar) because I know that is impossible, but I shall be grateful if you will address a public meeting in Muzaffarpur from where my friend George Fernandes is the Janata Party candidate. They have not released *him* even on bail.

I regret I cannot see you personally. To me you have represented grace and excellence in our public life. I send you my regards and my deep love.

Yours sincerely,
Madhu Limaye

The other letter was from a young man whom I met under strange circumstances but who has become as close to me as a son. He is from one of the well-known families that went to Pakistan at the time of partition but left soon after to make their home in London. Momin Latif, of whom I speak, was educated abroad and is a widely read person with values and intellectual honesty. He was in India attending to some business when he was arrested. In jail he was kept in a cell in 'irons' along with others and was physically ill-treated. He was released and again arrested under MISA. His letter, smuggled out of jail, reached me during one of my halts in Delhi at the time of the election campaign. He wrote:

15-2-77

My Dear Mme Pandit,
What a grand person you are! I wish to pay homage to the courage with which you have expressed your convictions—your hard brave and historic decision not only redeems the good name of your family but is a clarion call to the free people of India to assume their liberty and rights. I remember reading in André Malraux's autobiography, where in an interview with Nehru he asked him what most he wanted for India, the reply was: 'Just government by just means.' This is also the essence of your message which I just heard on the BBC at midnight and then this morning my newspaper rightly headlines your press conference.

The Nehrus are truly tied to India and do not have to force themselves on the people—you have proved it. I wish I could send you all the roses in India! Bravo! Bravo! For myself I am most cruelly deprived of my liberty—but there are very positive points to my detention. My love for India has turned into a passion, and I think of my destiny in Indian terms—prison has given me roots! I have controlled my anarchic personality, have learnt Urdu and calligraphy and have laid the foundation of Persian studies thanks to a wonderful teacher who was a fellow detenu. My deepest regret has been the constant humiliations my mother has had to endure. She goes from pillar to post and comes against blank walls of fear. I hope one day I shall be able to thank her.

I always thought you were wonderful but today I am proud to know the magnificent person that you are.

Yours ever,
Momin Latif

I have an unshakable faith in the younger generation of our country, and I am deeply and humbly grateful that so many of them trust me and turn to me. This has always been a cause of happiness to me, and perhaps it is what keeps me young though the years creep up.

My first campaign speech was also with Babuji in his home state of Bihar. The meeting was held in Patna, and as far as the eye could see there was a cheering mass of humanity. After Babuji had presented me I said I had had many misgivings about joining the struggle in which those dear to me were involved. I had given the matter much thought, but finally the message Lord Krishna had given Arjun gave me the strength to come out regardless of relationships and fight for truth and the right. In the Bhagavad Gita Arjun is full of doubts at the thought of engaging in warfare against his kin. Lord Krishna gives him advice that justice must be upheld. An Indian audience may not always be literate but it knows the Gita and the lesson it teaches. The audience could not have been more appreciative and it was a special moment for me.

The election campaign was in every sense a whirlwind. I have been through several other campaigns but never before had I seen such a surge, such waves of emotion. The meetings the Janata supporters addressed were literally seas of humanity and each individual knew what he wanted, what he was going to do. After the first few days there was no doubt that Janata would have a victory, but the question was by what margin? Till the end there were people who believed that Congress would come in with a slim margin of seats.

The key state was the Prime Minister's own, Uttar Pradesh, where both she and her son Sanjay were contesting. Uttar Pradesh has eighty-five seats in the Lok Sabha, the largest block of any state. The party that captured it had an edge on others. I asked Bahuguna halfway through the campaign how many seats he thought the Congress would capture from Uttar Pradesh. 'Not more than half,' was his answer. Then a few days later, 'We shall give them about one-third.' Then three days or so before the polling he said half laughingly, 'What would you say if we refused to give Congress a single seat?' And that is what happened. For the first time in election history a Prime Minister lost her parliamentary seat, and every one of the eighty-five Uttar Pradesh seats went to the Janata party. Both Mrs Gandhi and Sanjay were defeated in a dramatic manner, but that has been recounted many times and much has happened since, so I shall not repeat it here.

I was especially anxious to campaign in the constituencies of the key men who had supported Indira during the Emergency and misadvised her. I did not go near her constituency, nor Sanjay's. Among those who had in the public mind become the arch-villains of the Emergency were the Law Minister, Mr Gokhale, no longer alive, the Defence Minister, Mr Bansi Lal, responsible for many brutal acts, the Information Minister, Mr S.C. Shukla, and some others.

The campaign kept each of us constantly on the move. There was no time for rest, that would come later. All day, late into the night, there were meetings on an unprecedented scale.

On one occasion I went from Delhi by plane to Chandigarh at four o'clock in the morning and from there by car through a part of the Punjab, speaking in villages and towns and at wayside stops. The wayside meetings were so gigantic and enthusiastic that we were compelled to stop at them at least for a few moments even though such stops meant delay in reaching the scheduled meetings where the crowd waited patiently for sometimes hours before the speakers could arrive. On this occasion my last meeting was after midnight and I took the train to Delhi and from the station went to the airport to catch a plane to take me to Guwahati in Assam on the eastern side of the country. After a press conference at the Calcutta airport I arrived at Guwahati and spoke at several meetings, then back to Delhi to change into another plane for Madras in the south. And so it went on. We were exhausted, most of us had lost our voices but the 'show had to go on'. There was no respite, no desire for respite, and the interesting thing was that each of the campaigners was alight with hope and expectation. No doubts of victory any more marred our calculations.

As election day approached the enthusiasm reached fever pitch. There was fear that violence might occur, also that the government might 'rig' the polls or tamper with the ballot boxes. This of course was a probability, but in the face of the stupendous urge to remove the government it would have been well-nigh impossible for any tampering to be attempted with success. Apart from those who were genuinely with the Janata, small officials and others who had not been able to declare themselves earlier now threw in their full weight against the Congress. Policemen on duty at meetings were always willing to help us out of difficulties and we moved on a wave of confidence.

The day the first results were announced was charged as with an electric current. As time for the results drew near, the excitement reached a peak. Crowds and more crowds gathered in all places where the results would be flashed. I was living in the Imperial Hotel in Delhi and sat out on the lawn with a group of friends. My secretary ran between the lobby and the lawn to bring me the latest news as it came in. There were many foreign visitors and others in the hotel. As each Congress defeat was announced the cheers were deafening. Presently came the report that Indira was trailing by ten thousand votes, then by thirty thousand, then by fifty thousand. Even then I could not believe that she would lose. A candidate can go on 'trailing' and then suddenly make up. It is not unusual. For a while there was no news of her—other names were flashed and there were many questions in people's minds. Finally came the announcement, late at night, that the Prime Minister's lawyer was demanding a recount. My secretary brought me the news that the Prime Minister had lost by well over fifty thousand votes. A few hours later it was clear that Janata had swept the polls. The scenes in Delhi that night and in the early hours of the morning, when Mrs Gandhi's defeat was at last announced, were amazing. It must have been something like what happened in Europe at the ending of World War II. It was like New Year's Eve except for one thing—the difference between the Eastern and the Western temperament. There were lights everywhere, people were congratulating and embracing one another on the streets, sweets vendors were offering sweets to every passerby. There were smiles and relaxation, but no loud rejoicing as might have been expected in London or New York. No one slept that night. The day dawned with a new hope in the minds of the people, and millions went to offer thanks for deliverance in temples and churches and mosques. Once again India had met a challenge—democracy was alive and would flourish.

Indira is to me another daughter—in fact, my eldest daughter, and even though she has always been withdrawn by nature and not really close to anyone, I am sure that for many of her earlier years she has given me her affection. I have memories of her going back through the years when she was the only grandchild in Father's home, beloved and spoiled by all. Later she was like an elder sister to my three girls, much admired by them and one who took a great interest in them. I remember a holiday in Kashmir which she shared with us and how much we all enjoyed the trip. I know how much she loved my husband, Ranjit, and how tender she was to me when he died. I remember the radiance on her face when she told me that Rajiv, her elder son, was expected, and she spoke of all those little things a young woman says to an older one if she knows her joy is shared. And many years later, I remember her telephoning me to ask if I was prepared for a mild shock. My reply was, 'Obviously, we are all immune to shocks by now.' She laughed and said, 'Sit down while I tell you. Rajiv writes he is engaged to an Italian girl.'

'I don't call that a shock, but I do think the news is going to shock a lot of our own pretty girls,' I answered.

One of the tests of belonging is the sharing of an idea or a joke. One has been struck by something and one's glance goes instinctively to seek that other glance across a room, when one knows someone has reacted in the same way. This I have shared with Indira and, in spite of herself, or perhaps because she has let herself go for an instant, we have come together for a precious moment even during the sad days of the Emergency when we were on opposite sides.

Having known her since she was born, I have obviously seen other sides of her personality. I am aware that she has always been a lonely person unable easily to confide, unable to have close friends when she was a little girl. She developed all the faults of an only child. In addition, the fact that she did not have a normal home, that her father was mostly absent and her mother ailing, bred in her a sense of insecurity. This in its turn led to a degree of obstinacy and insistence on having her own way and believing that she was always right. She was an imaginative child and grew to be a woman with a strong tendency to build images that were not always real. She was a clever girl but did not devote herself to her studies. An able young woman, though widely read, she did not put her best effort into her period at Oxford; nor was she a good mixer, for always there was in her mind a hint of suspicion against people. The long years alone gave her strength of character, but they took away from her some of the qualities a settled home helps to develop—tolerance and a kindred spirit. Instead of compassion she developed hardness—a feeling that life had not been fair, therefore she would have her revenge. She has tremendous ambition, determination, and a will which she has always been able to bend to further that ambition. But because of the strain of obstinacy in her, she is sometimes unable to see that too much ambition can defeat the end it seeks to achieve. One fault, to my mind, is her easy acceptance of tales brought to her about others. This trait may well be part of that early insecurity when, instead of being trained within the normal discipline of a settled home, she was surrounded by servants and others who were sorry for the lonely little girl and said things to please her and let her have her own way. I am no psychiatrist, and when one writes about those for whom one cares it is not always possible to be objective.

We now come nearer the present time when the so-called break between us has been publicized to Himalayan heights. What is this break and why? It is largely the result of the inability, deliberate or otherwise, of our countrymen, particularly politicians, to recognize the difference between a genuine divergence of opinion and disagreement to further one's own ends—in more simple language, opportunism. Against this there are two views—first, can one generation compete with another, and secondly, do people belonging to a family in the limelight like the Nehrus lower their self-esteem by such actions? We of the Nehru family were immensely proud of doing what we believed was right—and my father and brother had set a high standard in their personal and public lives. How could we give importance to people who live by climbing on bandwagons and join the 'winning' side regardless?

When Indira became Prime Minister I commented to the press that I hoped the task laid upon her 'would not prove too heavy for her frail hands.' This was misinterpreted quite deliberately to irritate and annoy her. I had no doubt of her ability and, speaking frankly, thought her superior to some who had thrown their hats into the ring. The 'frailty' of the hands was symbolic. However, this was only the beginning of what was to be further distorted. To get an entrée to the p.m.'s house one had only to spin a story that I was jealous of her—that I disapproved some action of hers—and the door opened. People of integrity do not use such methods, but in the course of the years integrity has become a casualty in India. Gradually Indira became a stranger to me, and a lot of people, whom I can only despise, surrounded her for reasons of personal gain. I, who do not believe in Fate, almost reached the conclusion that some force greater than Indira and myself, some force for evil, was manipulating events. And thus it came about that Indira, who had been brought up in a noble tradition, began to lend an ear to people who were not in any way competent to advise her but who, by dint of flattery and the whispered comment against those they wanted kept away, influenced her on all levels. That she turned away from me or my immediate family I can overlook, but that she should have lost sight of the fact that India was greater than the little men who surrounded her and at whose insistence she destroyed the foundation on which democracy was so labouriously built, is hard to forgive. The many excuses now offered by all those who were involved in the Emergency is, to put it mildly, cowardly. They lay the blame on her, and, like the proverbial rats on a sinking ship, many have left her to save their own miserable skins.

Indira and I belong by upbringing and education on the same side, that of human rights, the need to work for freedom from oppressions that continue to crush humanity in so many parts of the world. When she strayed from that concept it was my duty to oppose her. Love for an individual must be kept separate from one's deep convictions and beliefs, and this I did with all the strength and faith I possessed. When I went to meet her several weeks after the elections, I embraced her and wept. Why had my child erred so grievously when she had reached a pinnacle and could have left a mark of greatness on the world? I cried for an opportunity lost, the creation of a situation which had made nonsense of her pledge to serve the people of India and had belittled us all. Her greatest mistake was in trying to build up her younger son, Sanjay, in allowing him to imagine he was some kind of crown prince. In his arrogance and thoughtlessness he brought upon India a tragedy and on his mother the hostility of the masses.

◆◆◆

3

The First Beginning

A story should begin at the beginning, but when there have been several beginnings, one's entry into the world is the least significant. The day one is born has meaning for one's family but it is the beginnings one makes for oneself that are important and they come a long time after one's birth.

I was born in the ancient city of Prayag, now known as Allahabad, in the state of Uttar Pradesh, on the 18th of August, 1900. The code word to my father, then in Paris, announcing my arrival, was 'Tempest'. No one has ever told me why this word was chosen, but I am sure it played a part in influencing my character, which has all the qualities of the tempest!

The India of my childhood was a period of startling contradictions and contrasts and a transition from age-old traditions and prejudices to new ways to living and thinking; great wealth and grinding poverty, wisdom and ignorance, the capacity to sacrifice for freedom yet amazing subservience to the foreign ruler—all these made the pattern of life in the early days of the century. But a new design was gradually created and India once again has become the mistress of her destiny. The story of my life is, in some respects, the story of the weaving of this new design. Like the rest of my generation, of whom, alas, so few are now left, I am acquainted with two Indias—the young India of today and the ancient land of yesterday in which I was born.

The years between the coming of Gandhi and the attainment of independence were a series of beginnings for thousands of men and women who joined the freedom movement under his leadership. Homes suffered hardship, families were separated, careers abandoned, in pursuit of freedom. The things we had looked upon as permanent vanished into nothingness. On many levels—the material, the political, the spiritual—changes took place that forced people to look at life and India from a new angle.

It was on a November morning in 1920 that I first met my future husband. He had come to Allahabad to consult my father on a legal matter and was invited to stay with the family. The winter in Allahabad is crisp and pleasant. The sun shines, the skies are blue, and the gardens are ablaze with flowers. Breakfast was served on the veranda outside my father's rooms and I came out to find a strange young man seated at the table. He had evidently been misinformed about the time and was embarrassed at being early. He introduced himself as Ranjit Pandit and said he had arrived late the previous evening from Calcutta, where he practised at the Bar. I thought him attractive—there was a serenity in his face that seemed unusual for one of his age. Presently, the family assembled and he was tongue-tied and ill at ease in the midst of the talkative Nehrus. When the family dispersed I lingered on and the young man, who obviously did not know what to do with himself, seemed glad of my presence.

'Do you like Sanskrit poetry?' was one of his first questions.

I admitted that my knowledge of Sanskrit was of the school variety. Inwardly I vowed I would devote myself to the study of Sanskrit immediately. My answer did not seem to disturb him and he said, 'You have a lovely voice. Do you sing?'

Not only did I not sing, I belonged to a family singularly lacking in musical talent. I could have run away, but good manners and the young man's charm kept me in my seat. Later I was to discover that Ranjit had great musical talent and a fine, well-trained voice. Before I could think of an answer, he went on, 'You are very beautiful, and I have come here only to meet you. I suppose you have guessed that.'

This was very pleasing and now I could relax. We spent most of the day together wandering in the garden where Ranjit recited beautiful Sanskrit verses and told me about his home and family. We went out riding. I loved to ride and was proud of my horsemanship, but I saw that my companion was a crack rider himself.

Three days passed swiftly, and the evening before he was to leave, Ranjit asked if he could speak with me alone. There had been a family gathering to celebrate my niece Indira's third birthday. Relatives and friends were scattered through the house and there was no privacy anywhere. We had to wait until the last guest had departed.

'It is only two days since we met,' he said, 'but I have thought about you for a long time and feel as if I know you. It has taken some courage for me to come from far-off Kathiawar to the home of the Nehrus to meet a daughter of Kashmir. But I have travelled with hope. Could you trust me enough to travel hand in hand with me through life?' I looked up at his sensitive, handsome face. I had known him for so short a time but there was something reassuring about him. Marriage in those days was arranged, and, though nothing direct had been said to me, I knew that Ranjit was in our home to meet me and, with my parents' consent, to ask me to marry him. I hesitated only a few minutes, then I held out my hands to him with a perfect and immediate confidence that I cannot quite explain to this day and said, 'Let us always travel together.'

It is customary in India to consult the stars before a marriage is arranged, and unless a certain number of points tally in the two horoscopes, it cannot take place. My father frowned on this and other customary practices that he dubbed superstition, so Mother had to resort to all sorts of devious methods to consult the stars and appease her conscience. In this instance she went to Pandit Madan Mohan Malaviya, renowned Sanskrit scholar, national leader, and friend of the family. Together they obtained Ranjit's horoscope and sent it with mine to a learned astrologer of Varanasi. The reply came that the horoscopes were perfectly matched and tallied far beyond the number of points required for ordinary mortals—except for two hostile points we would have been in line with the gods! Mother was so thrilled by the astrologer's prophecy that she confessed to Father what she had done. In a letter written to Ranjit about that time Father tells this story and ends by saying, 'So we are both very happy. I for my ability to judge human beings and my wife for her faith in the stars.'

Ranjit and I began our married life at a time of national turmoil. We travelled a hard road with unexpected turnings and steep ascents. Our wavelengths did not always synchronize, and the period in which we lived demanded constant adaptations and adjustments that were not easy. The remarkable thing is that we came through the hazards which beset a rebel family with few scars and created for ourselves and for our children some semblance of a normal home life in which love and shared ideals helped to sustain us through the many sad events we all had to face.

◆◆◆

4

The Nehrus

The Nehrus are Saraswat Brahmans and came originally from the Kashmir valley. Kashmiris easily adapt themselves to new surroundings but they cling with a remarkable tenacity to their own customs even though they have long since forgotten their language and Urdu has taken its place.

My father's father, Pandit Gangadhar Nehru, had settled in Delhi and occupied the position of chief of police at the court of Bahadur Shah, the last Moghul Emperor of Delhi. He died at a young age.

My grandmother, Indrani, known as 'Jiyomaji', was a remarkable woman. At a time when life for a Hindu widow was full of every conceivable hardship, she reared a family according to the traditional pattern and was respected and admired in the Kashmiri community—and feared a little for her sarcasm and sharp tongue, which she did not hesitate to use when she thought they were needed! She was a woman of determination and taught herself to read and write Hindi, and, later, by sitting with her sons while they were having their Persian lessons, she learned some Persian and was able to quote from the Persian poets, giving the impression of greater knowledge than she actually possessed. I may have inherited this quality from her because sometimes my brother, with a twinkle in his eye, would say, when I had spoken well at a meeting or conference, 'My dear, you make a little learning go a long way!' And I would answer back, 'Be glad it is not the other way round!'

My grandparents' family consisted of three sons and two daughters. Of these my father was the youngest, born posthumously. His sisters had the extraordinary names of Patrani and Maharani. They married young and died early, each leaving behind a son, Maharaj Bahadur Takru and Ladli

Prasad Zutshi, both of whom at some point were members of the larger Anand Bhawan[3] family.

Of Father's two brothers the eldest, Pandit Nandlal Nehru, was an advocate. My father, Motilal Nehru, was brought up by him and showered with affection and spoiled badly.

Father's education was haphazard and his academic career was undistinguished. Beginning at a madarsa, in the manner of the times, he went on to a mission school and later Allahabad University, which he left without taking his bachelor's degree. He was a cricketer and he also played a good game of tennis. His interests were wide and varied and there was little supervision of his studies, so he did much as he pleased. His mother tongue was Urdu, and Persian was his second language. He was proficient in both. It was only after he started practising law that he began to take life seriously, partly because he became the head of a large joint family at an early age and also because he loved his profession, worked hard, and achieved success rapidly. His law practice was the source of the Nehru family wealth.

Pandit Nandlal had one daughter and five sons. The two elder sons were already on their own when he died but the others naturally came under my father's sheltering care and lived with and were educated by him. Of these sons Biharilal Nehru and Mohanlal Nehru were both advocates. Mohanlal was an exceptional man. He was, from his early years, a dedicated social worker and had great organizing ability and a fund of love and understanding for the underprivileged. His profession was merely a means of giving his family a home—it meant nothing more—his interest was in the various types of work in which he involved himself. He wore swadeshi long before Gandhiji's coming, and from then onward wore only the hand-spun, handwoven material known as khadi. Shyamlal, the third son, was the unsettled one among the brothers and followed a number of callings. He was a most

3. The name of our family home.

lovable person and a great optimist, always in good humour and, like 'Mr Micawber', always waiting for something better to turn up. He had a large circle of friends and was generous beyond his means. The two younger sons, Krishna Lal and Brijlal, went to Edinburgh and Oxford respectively. They were my father's favourites among his nephews.

Father's second brother, Bansidhar Nehru, was in the judiciary—a learned man with an eccentric mind that he passed on, along with his learning, to his sons. He was strikingly handsome with grey-blue eyes and a head of prematurely grey hair as well as a fine flowing beard. He had three sons, the second of whom, Kuar Bahadur, was his exact replica. Bansidhar Nehru, a Sanskrit scholar and an astrologer of some repute, retired from the judiciary early and settled in Solan, a Himalayan resort, to study comparative religions. His eldest son, Raj Bahadur, left home quite young, abandoning his wife and daughter to be looked after by the joint family. He wandered around Europe and America, and my father used to tell a story of how once, finding himself in London in straitened financial circumstances, he became acquainted with Queen Victoria's Munshi and got employment under him for a while. I tried to check on this during my years in London, but all I could find out was that young Indians did go to the Munshi from time to time, probably to help or be helped by him, but there were no names available. Anyway, it's a nice story.

The youngest son, Shridhar, went to Cambridge and then joined the Indian Civil Service. He was, in my view, a misfit, since his real love was not for administration, but for one of his several outside interests, among them his devotion to science and linguistics. He had been to the Sorbonne and to Heidelberg and had studied seven European languages, which he spoke fluently and in which he wrote poetry that the rest of us were not always able to appreciate!

We were all one family living together in the manner of those days. The joint family has ceased to exist, but it had its uses since it was a form of social security and insurance and no one was abandoned. Every boy was provided with an education and a job, a suitable husband was found for every girl, and widowed aunts, grandmothers, and others belonging to the family were integrated into it. They were wanted and respected. There was, as always, another side of this picture that was less pleasant. Many a young man who could have made good on his own was content to remain a parasite under the sheltering care of a more prosperous relative.

The children of the family belonged equally to every member of it, and it was usual to see one sister-in-law bringing up and even nursing the child of another along with her own. The grandmother had a special status, and respect and affection for her grew with age. There was no fear in the minds of the older men and women in the family that they would be denied the love and shelter of the home at any time or for any reason. And they, in their turn, gave the children and young people a sense of perspective. Obligations and responsibilities were as important as privileges—there had to be a balance. In some ways these elders were anchors that kept the domestic boat steady and on an even keel. They also kept the best traditions alive in the family, and it would be unfair to brush aside the contributions they made. Obviously there were some who did not give as much as they received, but this is the way of life.

Eastern stories are full of horrors committed by mothers-in-law on young daughters-in-law who are entirely unprotected. Part of this picture is true, but the average home, in which the older woman kept the balance between sons' wives and other dependent women in the family, should not be forgotten.

The plight of old people in Western countries is heartrending. They are unwanted, and society, by building lavishly furnished and well-run homes for the aged, closes its eyes to the fact that four walls and three meals a day do not mean 'home' to any but the least sensitive of individuals. The race against time creates a pattern of fear in the lives of both men and women, and growing old gracefully and accepting the inevitable is not very apparent. Every time I see a head of hair in any of the shades recognized by fashion, above a face battered and unhappy, I am full of sorrow for the poor woman who should be glorying in her age, full of happy memories of her earlier life and content to accept the challenge of the future.

The family house belonged to everybody, and relatives could come at any time and stay as long as they wished. It was their unquestioned right to do so. A tonga, piled high with luggage, would drive up to the porch and a number of relatives would settle down in whichever room happened to be vacant, and if there was no room it did not really matter because the Western concept of a room of one's own did not exist. Mattresses were put down on the floor in winter and string cots on the veranda in summer. Everybody was perfectly happy. The orthodox ate in the Indian kitchen and others joined Father for meals in the Western dining room. It did not seem strange to anyone. Nor was it strange for a whole family to travel to a distant town to attend the wedding of a relative or close friend. It was one of the few reasons to undertake the effort and expense of a long journey. The ladies stayed away several weeks, and it was at marriages that one's daughters were shown off and often betrothed. It was a sort of Easter parade, when girls of marriageable age were decked out in their best and able to meet eligible bachelors. This was possible among the Kashmiris for there was no purdah, and girls and boys met and mixed freely with one another.

The younger women of our family—my cousins' wives, or bhabis, as they were called—were forward-looking for those days. Most of them spoke English and were interested in various activities outside the home. My cousin Rameshwari Nehru[4] (Bijju bhabi) had started a woman's magazine called *Stree Darpan, The Woman's Mirror,* which was the equal

4. The wife of my cousin Brijlal Nehru.

in content of any modern woman's magazine published in America or the United Kingdom—probably better, since it dealt with subjects important to the Indian woman such as the need for better education, inheritance, abolition of child marriage, divorce, remarriage of widows, and the right to vote.

When the British government appointed a committee to fix the age of consent for girls, Rameshwari Nehru was the only woman invited to serve on it and did so with distinction. She was ahead of her time in many ways, knew Hindi and Urdu well and some Persian and Sanskrit. In English she was exceedingly well read. During the Independence movement Gandhiji asked her to work in the Harijan uplift programme, to which she completely dedicated herself. Much later she became involved with the peace movement and was awarded a Lenin Prize. She was one of the finest, most lovable women I have known, completely selfless and with a consuming energy to work for whatever she believed in. There was no trace of malice in her—no envy or jealousy—but a lively sense of humour and a charming humility. She had a long and fruitful life and left behind a memory that will always inspire others.

Uma bhabi[5] came from a Kashmiri family settled in south India. She had had a wider education than was available to the girls of the north at that time. She even played the piano, and of this my father was extremely proud! My childhood memory of Uma bhabi's playing seemed to be a constant repetition of 'Home Sweet Home', but I am sure I must be mistaken. My young cousins and I thought it a stupid song and felt quite ashamed for Uma bhabi when she sang it. Uma bhabi had other talents and later served on the Municipal Board and was elected chairman of the Education Committee, a position that I occupied many years later. After Independence she became a member of Parliament and did valuable work for women's higher education and equality of opportunity in getting jobs.

---

5. Uma Nehru, wife of my cousin Shyamlal Nehru.

There was Lado bhabi, the wife of my cousin Ladli Prasad Zutshi, and a renowned beauty of her day. I remember as a child not only admiring her looks but being terribly proud that she belonged to us and comparing her sparkle and her good looks with those of less fortunate women I met in other homes. She too gave herself to the freedom struggle and suffered several jail sentences in consequence. It was the children of these cousins that fell in my age group, with whom I grew up and who are today part of the wider family to which I cling.

My father's pride in his family was tremendous, a feeling he passed on to each of us. The Nehrus, he seemed to convey without actually saying so, were better than other people, they did certain things but others were just not done. We grew up guided by this unwritten code of behaviour. In our small community we stood out. We were different because the family was more progressive than others and our way of living was foreign-oriented. Besides this, the Nehrus were amply endowed with 'charisma'—a word not in use at the time—and quite a few Kashmiri families thought us arrogant. Not long ago, I asked my cousin Bijju (B.K. Nehru), recently our High Commissioner in London, if he would agree that the Nehrus as a family had been a trifle arrogant and perhaps still were. He looked at me with his lazy smile and a twinkle in his eye.

'But of course. And why the hell shouldn't we be?' was his reply!

Father's great satisfaction lay in the fact that he kept the family united. It was not easy because there were powerful forces that could have separated us. During the freedom movement, for instance, there were Nehrus with Gandhi and Nehrus in the government that Gandhi opposed. In spite of this the family tie remained strong and Anand Bhawan's welcoming doors remained open to every Nehru. It was their home no matter what their political affiliation. This was a measure of my father's genuine love for every member of his family, which he kept in a compartment separate from politics. It was also, in my view, a measure of his greatness.

A characteristic of the Nehrus was their quick but short-lived temper. In my own case I like to think this may be partly due to the code word 'Tempest' by which my arrival in the world was cabled to my father. I have the mercurial qualities of a tempest, and perhaps this quality has made me more interesting—I do not know—it is for others to say!

The family records contain an amusing story about this special characteristic. An ancestor, Pandit Mansa Ram Nehru, was married to a beautiful young woman whom he loved dearly and who was never allowed to visit her parents because he said he could not exist without her. One day business took him far from home and his wife thought this a suitable opportunity to pay the long delayed visit. Pandit Mansa Ram returned unexpectedly, found his wife absent, and was enraged. He sent her a message saying that unless she was back by a certain date, he would find himself another wife. The young woman did not take this threat seriously and delayed her return. But Pandit Mansa Ram was in dead earnest. His anger had been growing and he could not bear to think that one on whom his happiness and peace of mind depended should defy him. He decided to teach her a lesson. He set out for Kashmir, where he married the first willing young woman. On his return home he found his wife was back. At the sight of her all his plans were upset. There was a passionate reunion and the second wife was informed that she might stay on only if she cared to serve the elder lady but would not be required to fulfil any other function! The chronicle does not record her decision.

◆◆◆

5

My Parents

My father, Motilal Nehru, became a legend in his lifetime, and many stories are told about him—each more heavily embroidered than the last.

Strangely enough no one, as far as I know, has ever tried to present a clear picture of the man as he really was—his home life, his hobbies, or his early fight against reaction and superstition, which he opposed at a time when such opposition meant social ostracism. With him action followed swiftly when he believed in an issue. Speaking six decades and more ago at a provincial conference in Agra, he pleaded with the delegates not to confine themselves to passing resolutions and went on to state what, for those days, was an exceedingly daring sentiment. Declaring himself an Indian first and a Brahman afterward, he told the conference he would not follow any custom of the Brahmans, however sanctified by age and authority, if it came in the way of his duties as a true Indian. Sixty-four years later, in independent India, there continue to be few Indians but many members of the various caste groups—a sad commentary on our national life.

Father's personal valet for many years, Bhola Ram, belonged to the Harijan community, and Hari Lal, my brother's valet, also an 'untouchable', became well known in his own right as a member of the Uttar Pradesh Legislature. My own cook, Budhilal, who has been with the family for forty-three years, and his brother, Tulsi Ram, who served my brother until he died, both Harijans, are to us the equal of any Brahman of the highest group. It is a joy as well as a matter of pride to know that their children are educated, hold good positions, and have considerably raised their standard of living because of our encouragement and trust. In the Uttar Pradesh Assembly one of the able younger ministers is a lawyer and the grandson of one of the Anand Bhawan employees. He was a Harijan, known technically as a member of the scheduled class. There are others also, who, but for the fact that my father had the courage of his convictions, would not have been able to make good as they have done. Parliamentary debates and various demands asking for a better deal for Harijans seem hypocritical to me. If those who shouted loudest had done one fraction of what my father did more than half a century ago the problem, by now, would have been resolved and all Hindus emotionally and socially integrated.

Father was a rebel and an iconoclast from his earliest years. His great delight was to attack blindly accepted patterns. At a time when social life was circumscribed and lived according to a confining set of rules, our family, because of Father's courage, was able to break many artificial barriers erected by caste and community. He boldly opposed everything he considered harmful to development and social progress and which had no merit other than the sanction of time. A voyage to the West did not mean 'crossing the black water' to him, nor was he prepared to do penance for the 'sin' of having eaten 'forbidden' food. He put into his fight against reaction and prejudice all the drive he later put into the freedom struggle. There were no half measures with him. He hated all forms of humbug and hypocrisy and attacked them wherever they existed. The disapproval of conservative sections of society that predicted a sad future for him amused him greatly, and he made jokes about it in the family circle. Fear of being ostracized by his own community disturbed him not at all.

He was severely criticized for his preference for the Western way of life. When he sent his only son to Harrow there was a great deal of hostile comment, but when I was allowed the same freedom as if I were a boy, many heads were shaken in sorrow and in anger. I remember one incident when I had just returned from a ride and went into Father's study to greet him. I found him in a state of great amusement. It was impossible to resist those peals of warm, happy laughter. He had been talking to a wealthy landowner who was one of his clients. Father had just won a lawsuit for him that was a *cause célèbre* in the province, and the old gentleman looked upon Father as a personal friend as well as a legal adviser. He was very old-fashioned and did not believe in freedom for women. I was the subject of the conversation and he was asking what Father envisioned my future to be. 'Is it necessary,' he asked, 'to let an Indian girl behave in the uncouth manner of the English? Why is she being educated according to foreign standards and being given so much freedom? Do you intend to make her into a lawyer like yourself?' This last remark had been the reason for my father's amusement. As I entered the room Father asked me if I would like to read law.

Twenty-seven years later, when I was a minister in the Congress government of Uttar Pradesh, I often wished I had studied law. The old gentleman's son sat facing me on the Opposition benches of the State Legislature. He seemed no more reconciled to my position than his father had been to my upbringing, but India was moving forward.

There were many sides to Father's character—the tenderness he showed to his family and his interest in the smallest experience of the youngest member; his identification with all those little events that go to the making of a day when he himself was in the midst of absorbing and important work; his exquisite courtesy, his biting sarcasm, and his wrath (and there is no other word to describe it) when he was aroused. But more characteristic than any of these was his laughter, which was like no other laugh I have ever heard. It was a complete reflection of his successful personality. It echoed through the house giving it life and well-being, and we were all affected by it and responded to it. In the evenings before dinner when he sat surrounded by family and friends, this wonderful laugh was a vitalizing force for the entire household.

Father was particular about the way he dressed and

disliked equally sloppiness of attire and sloppiness of mind. He was always well groomed himself, and mentally alert, and expected the same of others. Like Indians of his class and generation, he mostly wore European clothes outside the home. In the house his dress was the traditional pajama and kurta of Uttar Pradesh—wide trousers and a knee-length shirt of fine muslin, and for ceremonial occasions a long black or white coat or achkan with white trousers that are close-fitting and look like leggings. A ridiculous story still circulating is that he sent his linen to Europe to be laundered. He may have bought this linen in Europe, though of this I am very doubtful, but it certainly did not go there to be washed. I do not know what laundries in Europe were like at the beginning of the century, but, having had experience of them in several Western capitals during the last three decades, I would not compare the existing ones with the work of Gangadin, the family dhobi, who was an artist and who, together with his ever-increasing brood of children, took care of the laundry problems of our large household. Often in my elegant embassies I have thought of him as one beautiful and costly piece of linen after another was ruined by the harsh treatment of laundries and disinterested maids.

Father was a *bon vivant* and a perfectionist in all things. He would not accept second best in anything. Everything around him had to be right. He entertained lavishly and gracefully. Dinner parties in our home, Anand Bhawan, were occasions to be remembered. The guests were carefully chosen, the dining table set with Sèvres, crystal, and silver, and with flowers to match the particular dinner set used that night. Father maintained that good food must be well served and choice wine must have the best crystal available to contain it. During his visits to Europe he would bring back any beautiful article that caught his fancy. On one occasion he came back with a set of lovely Bohemian glass. This, it seemed, was similar to a set just bought by King Edward VII. My mother did not approve. 'Who in Allahabad is going to appreciate these,' she asked, 'and why should we be like King Edward?' Father replied that he bought things for his own enjoyment and it made no difference to him how few shared his pleasure.

Among his hobbies were his knowledge of and interest in jewels. There were, at that time, two foreign jewelers' shops in Allahabad—Dill and Company and Betchler and Company, both Swiss, I think. Mr Dill and Mr Betchler were personal friends of Father's. He would often go and sit in their back rooms and examine any special jewels that the firms had received. Had he not had the heavy responsibility of a large family I am sure he would himself have become a collector of precious stones. Before my brother's wedding he made time from his many commitments to design some of the jewels for the bride and found great enjoyment in doing so.

An entirely different interest was homeopathy. He devoted a little time every morning to people who came for treatment. I was his 'compounder'—made notes of cases for him, read up information he needed, interviewed the patients, and distributed medicines. If a case was difficult and the person was not recovering, he would sit up late into the night studying it. The number of his patients grew beyond what he could deal with, and a young homeopathic practitioner was employed by him to attend to the daily work, but he continued to attend to special cases himself.

He was fond of riding and hunting when possible, and in his younger days he played a good game of tennis. We had a stable of riding horses and we learned to ride almost as soon as we could walk. Our riding master was our coachman, a retired subedar, Mohammed Hussain, who did not really approve of girls' being taught to ride. He was a hard teacher and very proud of my sister and me, though he would never have admitted this.

In those days of horses and carriages Father drove himself to court in what was then known as a 'dogcart'. He had a pure-blooded Arab mare called Queen of the Road of whom he was very fond. One of the highlights of my babyhood, when I could not have been more than three years old, was waiting with my ayah in the garden for Father to return from court. As soon as he pulled up I was lifted onto the seat by his side and he drove me round the drive. Afterward I fed lumps of sugar or a carrot to the Queen and trotted along by Father's side to his room where, after thanking him in flowery Urdu, I received a kiss and went back to the nursery. This was not a daily occurrence but quite frequent and always very exciting.

My mother came from a conservative Kashmiri Brahman family settled in the Punjab. She was fourteen when she was married and there had been no Western influence in her upbringing. She was like a little ivory figurine, with big almond-shaped hazel eyes and bright chestnut hair falling in thick waves below her waist. Her actions and behaviour were quiet and restrained in the manner of the well-bred Indian woman, and, in spite of many limiting factors, she was never out of place in any society. She understood but spoke no English, yet this did not prevent her from doing her duties as a hostess at Western-style parties, and she accompanied her husband when they were invited to English homes. She even wore the hideous blouses then in fashion in the West, blouses which did not go well with Indian dress, and she had a Western hairstyle, also most inappropriate but the 'done' thing in so-called modern homes of the day.

Mother's horizon did not extend beyond her family. Her philosophy of life was simple and her mind uncluttered by doubts. She accepted the background and traditions that she had inherited and was content to function unquestioningly within that framework. She was religious and in this too she followed a set traditional pattern. Devotion to husband and family, which is deeply rooted in Indian women, was strongly developed in her, and she gave my father unswerving loyalty in all things. Even when she herself could not accept or approve, she would offer no obstruction to his wishes. In spite of every outward appearance of fragility, she had a considerable reserve of inner strength which was obviously the sustaining force in the uncongenial atmosphere in which she was obliged to spend the greater part of her life.

Those early days of the century were full of contrasts on many levels and were nowhere so vividly expressed and so tolerantly accepted as in our home. My mother's rigid orthodoxy was confined to her side of the house and in no way affected the pattern of my father's life. In a carnivorous Kashmiri household she was a strict vegetarian, in surroundings where religion was scoffed at she continued, with quiet dignity, her prayers and her religious fasts and all the paraphernalia of Hindu worship. She fed Brahmans and bathed in the Ganga on appropriate occasions, and sometimes she went on pilgrimage to the holy places, Varanasi or Dwarka or Rameshwaram. Living in Allahabad, the ancient Prayag, we were on holy ground ourselves for Prayag ranks high in priority among the places of pilgrimage. Where the rivers Ganga and Jamuna join each other is called the Sangam, and it is specially meritorious to bathe there when the stars are propitious.

The scene at the Sangam at any bathing festival today is not so very different from what it must have been a thousand years ago except that now planes, trains, buses, and bicycles bring the pilgrims who, in an earlier age, walked long distances in their bare feet for the purifying dip in the sacred river.

Pilgrimage, in my father's view, was a waste of time, and he teased Mother by saying, 'Pilgrimages should lead to the West—to Europe, to America, in search of the key to progress so that we can open the door to a fuller, richer life for ourselves.' Then seeing her look unhappy, he would say, 'I do not have to go on pilgrimage because my relations with the Almighty are cordial. He understands me. I have a feeling that on my last journey He will not expect me to struggle unaided across the Vaitarini, but will probably provide a motor launch with a high-powered Rolls Royce engine to take me over.'

By this time Mother's distress would be so apparent that he would hasten to add, 'If this should happen I know it will be due to your good life and intercession. So, of course, you must go on your pilgrimage.'

No two people could have been more unlike each other than my parents. The only things they shared in common were their children, and even in this my mother did not get her fair share, for I was my father's child in all respects. He was the dominating influence in my life. I loved him deeply and he was my ideal of all that was great and good and honourable. Even his fits of anger, which shook the whole house, passed me by. He was a loving and too-indulgent parent and I never remember a harsh word from him even when my own conduct had distressed him. His outstanding quality was his love of life and of his fellowmen, and it is my good fortune to have inherited these. I have been in love with life since I was born. I get the most out of every experience, and living to me means involvement with the human race and its problems.

◆◆◆

6

Life in Anand Bhawan

Allahabad was a gracious town. There were long tree-lined avenues, well laid out public gardens, and large houses standing in the midst of smooth green lawns. It was known for its High Court, where many stars of the legal profession practised and made great names for themselves. The university with its sprawling campus held a prestigious position in the province. The town was divided into the English and the Indian quarters, and only comparatively few Indians could afford to live in the Civil Lines, as the English sector was called. The Civil Lines had an English shopping centre where British goods, particularly wearing apparel, were available. There was a beautiful park named for Prince Khusru, and Company Bagh, called after the East India Company, where a military band played Western music every Saturday, and people drove out in their smart carriages to take the air and listen to the music. The benches in this park were marked 'for Europeans Only', and for this reason were not used. The 'Europeans', or, rather, the wives of the British officials, sat in their carriages, and the few Indians who went to the park would not risk an insult so walked around the garden or sat on the grass.

Beyond the Civil Lines lay the Indian section with its narrow roads, winding lanes, open drains, and ill-ventilated houses. But behind these lanes were the palatial mansions of wealthy bankers and landowners, a different world in every respect from the well-planned and well-ordered life that existed in the Civil Lines.

The main bazaar was called Chowk, and on either side of the road were small shops raised above street level on wooden planks, where one could find silks and brocades, fine muslins, piece goods, and vast quantities of Western china, glass, and foreign groceries.

In the centre of Chowk was the big sprawling fruit and vegetable market where shopping was always difficult owing to the numbers of whining beggars and diseased dogs, and even several cows lying across the entrance. No one seemed to mind these and there were no complaints. The dogs, the beggars and the cows—especially the cows—had as much right to be there as anyone else—perhaps more so, since they had no other place to go!

Beyond Chowk lay lanes, each named for a trade where the special article of that calling could be obtained. There was the ironmongers' lane, the lane of the goldsmiths, the long narrow lane of coppersmiths, where shining pots and pans piled high on the stall were a constant attraction to passersby.

This was a popular shopping centre for women, who came in large numbers at all times but especially during the days before the festival of Diwali when, according to custom, every housewife purchases a new copper or brass utensil for luck. The merchant did a brisk trade, as well-to-do people sometimes bought the year's supply of kitchen requirements at this time. The air was full of noise—the harsh voices of women bargaining and the clang of dishes being weighed on a pair of gigantic scales precariously balanced on the edge of a narrow plank.

Sweets and the highly spiced savouries Indians enjoy were made in the street of the sweet vendors called Lokenath Mahadeo after the temple of Shiva in the vicinity. Rules of hygiene were noticeably absent but the products turned out were equally pleasing to the taste and to the eye—one did not hear of people falling ill.

Shopping in the modern sense was unknown in my childhood. Ladies of good family never visited the bazaars and seldom went even to the English shops in the Western section of the town. When Mother wanted new clothes the shops came to her. When jewels had to be purchased, jewellers came from Delhi or Bombay.

Our home, Anand Bhawan, was situated in the Western section of the town. It lived up to its name for it was a happy house, a place where all were welcome, and it was always bustling with activity. I do not remember any long peaceful periods such as I now enjoy in my own home. Everyone seemed to be involved, and happily so, in work and play or whatever the interest might be, and the sound of laughter was what guests always associated with Anand Bhawan. Father had bought the house the year before I was born. It was a large rambling house, having been added to from time to time, and gave the impression of being several storeys high, although this was not the case. It was the many terraces on different levels that gave this effect. Anand Bhawan stood in the midst of a spacious garden, which was Father's special joy.

It had tennis courts, a riding ring for the children, an orchard, and an indoor swimming pool.

In the middle of the building was a big, square, open courtyard with shallow steps leading up to a deep veranda running all the way round and onto which opened the bedrooms. A tiered fountain in the centre of the courtyard was used during the hot summer evenings and kept the temperature bearable. Sometimes, when there was a party in the courtyard, the tiers of the fountain were filled with chunks of ice and sweet-smelling flowers whose scent was wafted into the bedrooms. Parties in Anand Bhawan were popular whether they were informal ones in the courtyard or formal ones in the dining room. The reason was Father's meticulous attention to detail and his talent in getting the right people together.

Our home too was divided into Indian and Western sections. The reception and dining rooms and Father's offices were in the front of the house overlooking the garden. It was here that Western-style parties were held. Indian social life went on in another part of the house, which was run in the traditional manner with a Brahman cook and Hindu servants. Although this was Mother's domain it was her elder sister who really attended to all the details. She had been widowed in her teens and, as remarriage was forbidden, such women could only fulfil themselves through service to others. Our aunt, Bibima, was beautiful and intelligent, and in a more liberal society she could have expressed herself in many ways. In India she was condemned to a life of work for others. We adored her and she loved us all dearly, and this love was later passed on to our children.

It was the Indian custom to sit on the floor, and our rooms had carpets, big bolsters, low stools, and cushions strewn around. There were also low divans called takhts in the living rooms. These too had bolsters to lean against and were far more appropriate than the cheap Western-style tables and chairs which afterward came into fashion. Because one sat on the floor, shoes were removed before entering a room. It was also important for the feet to be absolutely clean at all times. Women always washed their feet before going to bed, and I remember, during the hot summer evenings, Mother sitting in the courtyard while her maid washed her tiny feet in a silver basin with cold water poured from a silver pitcher. It was a daily ritual because Mother insisted that the soles of one's feet should be as soft as the palms of one's hands. First the feet were soaked, then the heels were rubbed with pumice stone before soap was applied. The last item was a fragrant oil gently massaged into the feet. As this was something we had seen every day of our lives it gave me great sorrow during the freedom movement, when our way of life had changed drastically, to see these perfect little feet rough and uncared for and that gallant woman, always before surrounded by every kind of luxury, sharing without a murmur the difficulties that became our daily lot. It is not easy to put into words, but Mother's feet somehow became for me symbolic of the hardships we had to endure during that period.

An important person connected with our household was Munshi Mubarak Ali. He came from a highly esteemed Muslim family who were refugees in Allahabad from the Mutiny of 1857. I suppose one could best describe him as comptroller of the household. He was greatly beloved by us all and was a handsome and striking figure, with his upright carriage, fine greying beard, and courtly manners.

The Western side of our house was looked after by Miss Smith, the Anglo-Indian housekeeper, and the Christian, Muslim, or 'untouchable' servants. A special member of the staff was our ayah, Jessie. She resembled Aunt Jemima of pancake fame and was a Catholic who went regularly to Mass, told us Bible stories, sprinkled holy water, and lit candles for us when anyone was ill. But she had a habit of disappearing on every Hindu holiday. This infuriated Mother, especially when she discovered that Jessie was visiting some so-called holy man or taking active part in a Hindu festival.

One day Mother told Jessie she must make a firm decision about her religion as she would not allow her to have a holiday on every feast—whether Hindu or Christian—in the calendar. Jessie was indignant.

'I am a good Christian and the Bishop will vouch for me,' she said. 'I go to Mass and Confession, but I am not going to leave my religion to please you!' To the end of her days, and she lived to be eighty, she continued in this fashion giving her devotion to the Church as well as to the Hindu faith. Very much later I came across much this same attitude when I was Governor of Maharashtra. One of my butlers, a Catholic from Goa, was greatly disturbed because he could not get his young sister suitably married. I was surprised because the girl was pretty and reasonably well educated. The reason, it seemed, was that the family were converts from among the Saraswat Brahmans of Goa and could marry only into a family converted from the same caste. That day I decided in my mind that the caste system and India were inseparable!

As a child I believed that educated Indians spoke Urdu but those employed by them spoke English for, apart from Miss Smith, there was de Souza, the cook, and Mr Dickson, the Anglo-Indian electrician who looked after the generator and who later, when motor cars came, was in charge of the garage. And there was Miss Ingles, the Eurasian nurse, who spent most of the year with Mother. All these people could speak Hindustani but considered it a loss of prestige to do so!

When I think of the way we lived I am amazed at our utter disregard of time and consideration for others. There seemed to be no coordination about meals or anything else and ours was merely a reflection of the well-to-do Indian home. Except for Father, whose meals were regular, adjusted to his working hours, and eaten in the Western dining room, the other members of the large family ate wherever and whenever it suited them. All day long servants were running back and forth between the kitchen to wherever the meal was served, carrying hot phulkas and replacement of other dishes. Tea trays went to separate rooms at different times. Only dinner was eaten in a proper manner in the dining room because Father liked his family around him, and unless there was some very real reason for absence, all the members of the household were present round the big dining table for the evening meal.

On festival days and holidays or when Indian dinner parties took place we used the long marble dining room where we sat on the floor on gaily coloured pieces of carpet and ate with our fingers in silver thals—big round trays with raised edges. In each tray were small bowls, each containing different kinds of meat or fish or vegetables. Here the servants did not serve the food. They brought it from the kitchen and passed it through a hatch and the daughters and daughters-in-law of the family served it to the guests. Father often made the final decisions on the menu, Eastern or Western, and also gave instructions to the cook on how he wished a special dish to be presented. This was a source of irritation to all the women of the house.

The food of India is as varied as its people. Each region has its own cuisine and they are as different from one another as the Scandinavian from the Spanish. The term 'curry' stems from a concoction made by a Colonel Brown a century ago for those Anglo-Indian colonels and others who, having served in India for a period, found their palates unable to appreciate the blandness of the English diet. This curry powder must have considerably enriched Colonel Brown's heirs. No housewife in India would use a ready-made mixture. The delicacy and success of a meal depend largely on the care with which spices are selected and used. The coriander, cumin, ginger, turmeric, chilli, and others are bought whole, then ground, strained, and placed in airtight jars or tins to retain their flavour.

Kashmiri food, for which our community is renowned, is to the rest of India what the French cuisine is to Europe. It is rich and tasty and is served with imagination. Rice is the staple article of diet in Kashmir, and Kashmiris settled in other parts of India still eat a good deal of it. Our rice has nothing in common with the coarse article of the same name that one sees in Europe, and which often cooks up into a sticky ball. The grains are long and delicately shaped and have a faint aroma. When cooked they look like flakes of snow and each grain is separate from the other. Rice is cooked in various kinds of pilafs with meat, chicken, or vegetables. These dishes are a meal in themselves. There are also different kinds of 'sweet rice' that are eaten with curds or thick cream and are delicately flavoured with saffron and cooked with almonds, pistachios, and raisins. Sometimes pieces of pineapple or orange are also added. Sweets and sometimes even pilaf are covered with thin, real silver leaf, which is edible and which plays an important part in decoration. Kashmiris love cheese and use a form of cottage cheese in many ways, especially cooked with vegetables. A well-served meal is colourful, consisting of nine, ten, or more courses for parties, not counting the rice or the various pickles that are always served. The meal is planned with due respect to appearance and should not contain any two dishes of the same colour. A bowl of meat roasted brown with spices will have next to it mince cooked with spinach giving it the colour of emeralds, then a bowl of cottage cheese fried with rich, red tomatoes, then lentils delicately golden, and a series of vegetables and kababs—ground meat with spices—making the meal attractive to sight and taste alike. All the courses are served at the same time in small silver or metal bowls and placed in the thal, the round silver or metal tray. Various kinds of bread made of wheat and other grains are served hot as one eats, and the bowls of food are constantly replenished.

In spite of seeming disorganized, our little world was a place in which life moved to a steady rhythm and every detail of one's existence conformed to a plan. One was born, grew up, married, carried on family traditions. There was no change, and little desire for change. A large family involved constant work and organization, and the women were always busy with a hundred and one chores regardless of their social position or the amount of domestic help they had.

The first days of each month were full of great domestic activity for this was the time when stores were laid in, when large quantities of rice and lentils were cleaned, and whole wheat ground into flour for the kitchen. Stone hand mills were used, and grinding took hours of hard labour. The wheat was piled up in the kitchen veranda and the wives of the gardeners and grooms came to do the grinding. Each mill was worked by two girls at a time. Sitting on the ground opposite each other with veils thrown back, legs spread out, hands on the wooden handle, they moved their arms in graceful circular movements, their bodies swaying back and forth as they worked. Gradually as their speed increased, they burst into song, keeping time to the whirring of the mill. At the end of the day, a huge mountain of flour took the place of the stacked wheat and this was placed in big steel casks and stored away.

All festivals and birthdays were observed traditionally in our home. The Kashmiri New Year, Navroz, was our big day. It falls in March and is celebrated in all Kashmiri homes. The night before, the lady of the house arranged a tray with new wheat, flowers, a small bowl of yogurt, a mirror, a pen, a gold or silver coin, green almonds, and the vermillion powder that is used as a caste mark on the forehead. Early in the morning she carried this tray into every room, beginning with the head of the house. One looked into the mirror, kissed the coin, ate a couple of almonds, and had the vermillion put on one's forehead. It was a day for wearing new clothes and visiting other Kashmiri homes. On these visits the women carried a lump of salt and a sheaf of green gram—all symbolic of spring and life's foundations. Presents of money were given to the children and there was always a party in our home for the clan. Weeks before, the preparations would begin. Shopping in the modern sense was not known. The shops came to the house and various merchants with whom the family dealt brought the required merchandise from which the women of the family chose their clothes. Mother would sit on her takht in her own living room surrounded by cottons, silks, and brocades, and the girls and daughters-in-law of the family would choose what they wanted to wear at the various festivals. It was one of the exciting events of an otherwise unruffled existence.

Among other festivals observed in our home was Diwali, the feast of lights. On this day Lakshmi, the goddess of good fortune, walks abroad. In the evening all homes and buildings are lit with little earthen lamps in which a wick is floated in oil. Lakshmi is a capricious lady who does not like the dark and visits only those places brightly lit, which is why even the simplest homes have lights on this night. Lakshmi is also a gambler, and it is usual for the evening to be devoted to gambling on a large scale. In earlier times fortunes were won and lost on this day.

Holi is a festival marking the beginning of the summer and is mainly observed in north India. It is a time of abandon and revelry. Coloured powder and coloured water are squirted by people on one another, and, though it is not altogether a pretty sight, young people get a great deal of fun out of it. There are special dishes that go with each festival, and these were prepared days in advance, giving plenty of work to the staff as well as to the family.

Birthdays were semi-religious occasions as there was always a puja (family worship) in the morning. Other than this it was just a day of happiness. The equivalent of a birthday cake in Indian homes is kheer, an elegant rice pudding—though this is far too simple a description. Beyond the fact that it is composed of rice and milk there is no other comparison in looks or taste. Kheer is flavoured with rose water, almonds, and pistachios and served in small earthenware bowls covered with silver leaf. Like elsewhere there are a great number of sweets in India, some special to different regions and others known to the whole country.

They are all delicious but rather too sweet, and Indians as a people eat far too much sugar and sweets for their own good. In my part of India the day began in many homes with hot jalebis, deliciously crisp, hot sweets eaten with morning tea or milk. Those who belong to Allahabad swear that there are no jalebis to compare with those of Neta Halwai, a well-known confectioner of the town. Even now Allahabad is 'home' to us, and when any of us go there our first request is for hot jalebis at breakfast.

The life of the house had another side. Where there were so many young women there was also time and care spent on one's looks. Western beauty products were unknown and creams in jars or lotions in bottles not sold in the market. They were prepared at home. In our home one of the basic beauty products was a dough made of orange rind powdered and mixed with a pinch of plain flour and the top of the cream off the morning milk. This was kneaded together and with it the face, neck, arms, hands, and even the feet, if desired, were massaged, some time before one had one's morning bath. This treatment left a permanent glow on the face, with the fragrance of orange lingering on the skin. Henna leaves finely powdered were made into a paste and used on the palms of the hand in all sorts of intricate designs and also put on the nails. This is customary not only at weddings but also on special festive occasions. In the hot weather the henna is applied to the soles of the feet to keep them cool. Soap was considered bad for the skin, and powdered gram flour, besan, was largely used in its place. Many kinds of balms, lotions, and oils made from herbs and flowers were in use and were good for the health as well as very effective for beauty. In the West I now see beauty parlours and cosmetic shops using or selling the products used by us over the centuries and recommending them to their clients as better and more pure than those in fashion earlier. It is the same on many other levels—dress, food, and even politics. It needs time and patience, and if India has patience she may see her ideas and pattern of life introduced in the West as if they were their own special creation! The other side of the picture is a sad one, for we in India have become great imitators of the West. This makes us despise things until the mark of approval has been given by America or Europe. The 'slave mentality', as Mahatma Gandhi called it, is far more serious than political slavery because it is more difficult to dislodge. I hope that we are beginning to realize this and will not abandon our own ways but will delight in sharing with the world those things that are specially Indian, for our mutual benefit.

◆◆◆

7

Summers and Bhai's Return

I have been writing as if I were an only child and in a sense this was true, because the difference in age between my brother, my sister, and myself was so great that we were all brought up separately. My brother was eleven years older and my sister, Krishna, seven years younger than I. He was fourteen when he left for Harrow and at the time of his one brief visit home I was still a very small girl—there could be no question of companionship between us. To my baby sister I was a little mother from the beginning and more and more so as we grew up, for her adolescence came at a time when the foundations of our well-ordered life were being shaken. By the time she was in her teens I was married and Anand Bhawan was being remolded to the Gandhian design. She missed much of the fun I had had and was somewhat neglected because the new changes claimed everybody's attention. This left her with a feeling of insecurity which she was never wholly able to shake off even after she was married and had a family of her own. She was an attractive girl with beautiful hazel eyes, a bright vivacious person of many talents, a zest for life, and always surrounded by friends.

In India anyone older than oneself is never called by name but is referred to by the relationship, and, as we have different names for maternal and paternal relatives, it is easy to know who is being spoken of. As our brother was older than my sister and I we called him Bhai and my sister called me Didda, which is one of the words used for an older sister.

A brother occupies a very special position in India. He is the guardian and protector of his sister, whose attitude to him borders on adoration. Brother's day—Bhaiya Duj—which follows the festival of Diwali, is an important occasion all over the country. The sister and brother renew the pledge of affection to each other and the brother gives his sister a gift. In all religious ceremonies the brother's part is symbolic of this relationship. In a period where women had no rights, personal, civil, or political, where there was no divorce for Hindu women and they were recognized through their relationship to a father, husband, brother, or son, the role of the brother was one of the greatest importance in the life of the sister, and his home practically the only protection she had in case of marital or other troubles. My unreasoning love for my brother did me considerable harm in my political life. I have a mind of my own and have always been able to use it whether in small matters or larger decisions. But gradually I found myself accepting Bhai's views without any questioning. It is one thing to implement a policy or carry out instructions of one's party leader but quite another to shut one's own mind and abandon one's judgment in favour of that of someone else, however loved and able. This was also unfair to Bhai, who never tried to bring pressure on anyone. His way was to lead you to the threshold of your own mind and let you do the rest.

My parents took me with them to England when my brother went to Harrow. I have no special memories of this visit, but two incidents have been repeated so often that I sometimes feel I actually remembered them. The first was my fifth birthday party at Bad Ems where my parents were taking the cure and to which my father invited a whole school to tea to celebrate the occasion. The second incident simply shows me up as a very precocious infant. It seems we had all gone to the Earl's Court Exhibition and Father got separated from us. My mother, who as usual was wearing far too many pieces of jewellery—including a nose ornament, which always attracted attention—was alarmed. Her knowledge of English was limited and she had no money with her and did not know how we could get back to our hotel. The story goes that I told her if she could get a cab there would be no question of payment as the porter at the hotel would take care of this. We reached home safely just as Father was desperately seeking police aid. This incident led to Mother's wearing fewer jewels when she went out, so it was perhaps a good thing!

When we returned home to India an English governess, Miss Lillian Hooper, accompanied us. There could not have been a better choice for she was adaptable and learned our language and our ways very quickly and, being practical, she stood no nonsense from me. Having come for two years she stayed for sixteen and only left us to get married. Even after her marriage she and her husband, a government official, continued to live in India for some years. Miss Hooper, soon known as Toopie, had become so much a part of our family that Father gave her away at her wedding and had a reception for her in our garden. From this fine English woman I received more than I was ever able to repay. In a very short time she had changed my outward appearance into that of a little English girl of the period, including the hideous corkscrew curls. Discipline was imposed, food habits regulated, and, most annoying of all, early bed enforced in the evening. I had been called Nanhi in the family though my given name was Sarup Kumari. This is quite a usual custom, for Nanhi means 'little one'. Toopie soon changed this to Nan and Nan I have remained since then, especially to my Western friends. My sister was named Krishna Kumari and called Beti, meaning 'daughter'. Toopie promptly called her Betty. My sister did not like this and went back to her own name as soon as she grew up, but in the family we continued to call her Betty or Beti.

Winter does not last long on the plains of north India, and by early April severe dust storms descend without warning. These follow a pattern, always coming at the same time of the day. The heat continues to increase, and presently the dust storms give place to a scorching wind known as the loo. This is a difficult period to live through—the loo dries up the grass and flowers and only mangoes and melons thrive, and the jacaranda, and the flamboyant laburnum tree, which flaunts its gaudy blossoms defying the heat.

There was no electricity and living was adjusted to the climate. A new schedule of activity was followed and, looking back on it, I feel it was in many ways more healthful and not so austere as it may sound. Rooms were closed to the sun by nine o'clock in the morning and the heat was somewhat relieved by hand-pulled fans. A pole was suspended horizontally from the ceiling and a cloth frill attached to it. There was a thin rope by which a man or woman sitting outside the room pulled the fan. This process went on all day, the fan pullers, or punkha coolies, as they were called, being replaced every two hours. There were also large palm-leaf fans, which were waved by men when one sat outside in the evenings. Another method of old-fashioned air conditioning used curtains of a fragrant-smelling grass, khus, later made famous in a perfume by Guerlain. These curtains were fixed to all doors and windows leading outside the house and kept moist by sprinkling water on them. When the hot loo blew through the khus curtain the air inside was cool and scented lightly.

It was not possible to sleep in a bedroom in the hot weather so, as the sun went down and the heat diminished, life was lived on the lawn or some part of the garden or on the terrace. Indian beds are light wood frames with heavy tape crisscrossed and attached to the frame. When the tape gets loose it can be tightened. These are called niwar beds and are very comfortable. They can easily be taken in and out, and sleeping outside used to be the general custom. Sleeping in the open inevitably led to early rising and one's day began soon after sunrise.

India is full of sounds and all of them are memories of my childhood. During the hot summers when one slept on the lawn there was the call of the night watchmen shouting to one another that all was well in the compounds they guarded. They made their voices as bloodcurdling as possible and I used to pull the bedclothes over my ears to keep out the sound. There was the wailing of children and the barking of dogs—sometimes the terrifying howl of jackals searching for food in the distance. But as morning neared the sounds grew gentler. There was the noisy chirping of sparrows on the lawn, the cooing of pigeons in the eaves of the verandas, and, from the road outside the house, the soft strains of devotional songs sung by men on their way to the Ganga for their morning bath. But it was the bells that were most exciting. The little tinkle of Bibima's prayer bell, the gentle chimes of the bells at sunset from the temple of Bharadwaj, the joyous peal of the bells of the Holy Trinity on Sundays, and all the other bells outside—goats and cows returning from pasture, an elephant on his way to join a procession, and endless hawkers who sold their wares in ditty and verse to the accompaniment of brass bells. The world beyond our gates was full of adventure in which we could not participate.

We moved *en famille* to a hill station for three or four months of each year. Father could join us only during the High Court vacation, and most years we had a house party as well as the family. Moving to the hills was rather like a military exercise for, besides the mountains of luggage and an army of servants, several riding horses and grooms also had to be taken as there were shooting and riding during the holidays. The hills were full of game—birds and various varieties of deer—and many people went for the shooting season alone.

The popular summer resorts in our province were Nainital, the summer seat of the Uttar Pradesh government, and Mussoorie. The latter was an imitation of a European resort and was considered exciting. The 'jet set' of the day went there, though Indians were still subjected to a number of humiliating rules and regulations, but this did not deter those who could afford a holiday in the hills. Benches in the park and around the bandstand in the public square were marked in bold letters 'For Europeans only'. Membership in clubs and libraries was closed to Indians, but European wives of Indians could join and were especially welcome if they were married to a Maharaja from whose purse the library could benefit.

Nainital is built round a lake and the Yacht Club was a very popular place. Indians, however, could not become members. After some years of growing irritation at not being able to sail, Father took his motor launch from Allahabad one summer and used it on the lake, to the great inconvenience of those who wished to sail their yachts. This infuriated the British members and was exactly what Father wanted. Having achieved his object he was satisfied and had the launch sent back to the Jamuna where it belonged.

My father's relationship with the British, as I have indicated, was cordial, and he had many close friends among them in the official world and outside—even some of the governors of the province were on friendly terms with him. One, Sir Harcourt Butler, was very close to the whole family and I called him Uncle Harcourt. Father entertained and, what was more unusual, was entertained by them. He believed in British fair play and justice and met them as equals.

I saw a good deal of English children in my home and in theirs and I also went to their dancing class where I was the only Indian child. There was no sense of difference between us in my mind. I enjoyed my English friends as much as I enjoyed my Indian ones. I was too young to understand any political implications or to realize that our home was not typical of others of our social class. One reason for this was that, having put aside all caste restrictions, we ate with everyone—Muslim, British, or any other group. Because of this we grew up without any sort of rancour toward or dislike of white people.

But somehow even the most sheltered Indian child heard talk against the British and had moments of resentment over some action or saying of the Saheb log. Once when we were in Mussoorie, where the rules of the road did not permit riders to trot or canter their horses along the Mall, the main thoroughfare, I was returning from a ride one afternoon and discovered I was late. Without thinking I spurred my horse into a canter, intent only on getting home as quickly as possible. I observed the rule of keeping to the hillside but the passing rickshaws and the coloured clothes of the women walking on the Mall frightened my horse, which became restive. An elderly British colonel was walking with his wife, and her bright parasol irritated my horse. The lady was very timid and moved farther toward the hillside, and my horse's head grazed her hat. She screamed and the colonel hit my horse's flank with his walking stick saying, as he did so, 'Keep your damned horse in order.' Controlling my horse, now ready to bolt, I shouted back, 'Keep your damned wife to the right side of the road.' After this unseemly outburst I raced home scattering pedestrians right and left. Severe punishment followed and I was not allowed to ride for the rest of the season.

The years passed and Bhai was home for good. Some cousins had also returned from their studies abroad, and Anand Bhawan was full of young people and their laughter. The tennis and swimming parties were resumed, the horses were used again, and there was a great deal of activity about the house. For me it was, in a very real sense, an awakening, a dream come true. The adored brother was home. He had time to ride with me, read with me, and encourage me to discuss things with him. We read, among other things, Bernard Shaw and a great deal of poetry. We would play a game in which one person recited a line of verse and the other continued with the poem. A question we often asked each other was:

If there were dreams to sell
What would you buy?

from the poem by Thomas Lovell Beddoes. Not only were the 'dreams' material ones, but they also related to wishes for India—and what kind of India we wanted—and so on. I do not remember how it started but it was interesting and amusing. Sometimes we got others involved in it too. Bhai made me write essays and brought into my life topics that had not until then had much meaning for me. He also opened a door for me to Buddhism, in which he was at that time much engrossed. As I have already mentioned, a brother occupies a very special position in the Indian family and the brother–sister relationship is a cultivated and meaningful one. He is the 'protector' of his sisters and in many cases their hero. To me Bhai was a knight *sans peur et sans reproche*.

The major event in our life in 1916 was Bhai's wedding. There was not a family in the community who would not have been happy if their daughter had been chosen as the bride of Jawaharlal Nehru. The wedding was lavish to the point of ostentation—again one of those contradictions in Father's personality difficult to reconcile with the kind of man he really was. His love for my brother was deep—nothing in the world was too good for him, and his bride must have the best of everything. Many of the ornaments given to her were designed by Father, the precious stones chosen by him and mounted in the house where a regular little goldsmith's shop had been set up and where Father spent every minute he could spare from his professional work. My brother's training had been British, he was reticent and not disposed to express his feelings. This is contrary to Indian ways, where one is never ashamed to express one's feelings. Father was typically Indian in this respect. Those were still the days when one did not oppose elders and express an opinion with any vehemence in their presence. The result was that while all the preparations for the wedding were going on Bhai kept himself severely aloof. I do not recollect his taking part in any of the family gatherings in which wedding plans were discussed.

Kamala, my sister-in-law, was a beautiful girl. She came from a conservative family of Delhi and was sent to Allahabad to live with an aunt for a year before she was married so that she might get to know the man and family into which she was marrying. But it was hard for her to adapt herself to surroundings totally different from those in which she had grown up. Her whole approach to life prevented her being able to enjoy the situation in which she now had to live and make a home. The excessive lavishness by which she was surrounded as well as the Westernized way of living were foreign to her and she did not fall into the pattern easily. There must have been many conflicts in her mind in those early days in which she did not even have the opportunity of being alone and coming to grips with her problem because she was surrounded by the family and, to what any normal young woman must have seemed a madhouse, with streams of guests always coming and going. In many ways it was a cruel custom that forced a young couple to live with in-laws and make a life for themselves without privacy. The fact that a few years later the freedom struggle demanded long separations and hardships did not make life any easier for her. But it brought her the opportunity of emerging as a person in her own right, giving meaningful leadership. Even in the early years of her illness she continued her participation and inspired those with whom she worked.

The marriage took place on the first day of spring, the festival of Vasant Panchami of February 1916, and a Nehru Wedding Special took the guests and groom's party from Allahabad by train to Delhi for the occasion. The real celebrations began with the coming home of the bride, when evening after evening there were feasting and gaiety in which it seemed as if no one in the whole province had been left out.

In the summer of that year we went to Kashmir. It was my first visit. We had grown up with legends, folklore, and history of our ancient homeland, and each day brought thrills of new discoveries. Once we camped for a few days in Achabal, one of the pleasure gardens of the Moghul Emperors, our tents being pitched under the giant chinar trees whose magnificent beauty seems eternal. One afternoon I was lying on the grass, chin in hands, reading a book. Suddenly I heard Father's urgent whisper telling me to stay still. Before I realized what he meant there was a sharp swish in the grass and from under my raised arm glided a huge king cobra. I screamed and jumped up. Father, who had now recovered from his own shock, told me that the cobra had been coiled close to me and with open hood had been swaying back and forth behind my head as if ready to strike. My scream had brought Mother to the door of her tent. She was absolutely calm, and Father's account of this incident did not disturb her at all. She announced in tones of deep satisfaction that it was an omen of good fortune. As a cobra shields only royalty, the presumption was that I would be elevated to royal rank! Father was very satirical and short-tempered about this, but his satire, his logic, and his anger did not move Mother. In response to his remark that 'the girl might have been bitten,' she replied quietly, 'How could she be bitten when the Naga was protecting her?' Kashmir is the home of the Nagas and the whole country abounds in stories about these semi-divine snake people and the wonderful deeds they perform.

On this same visit Bhai had a fortunate escape while mountaineering with friends. He made light of it in his usual way but it was a near thing. Bhai and some friends had gone on a trek in Ladakh. Beyond the Zojila Pass, at a height of over eleven thousand feet, they were informed that the famous Amarnath Cave, an ancient place of pilgrimage and a breathtaking sight, was only a few miles away cross-country. Guided by a shepherd they decided to climb a snow-covered mountain to reach it. On the way they passed several glaciers, and in crossing one of these Bhai fell into a deep crevasse of fresh snow. Fortunately the members of the party were roped together and he was rescued. In spite of the accident the party continued but eventually had to turn back without reaching Amarnath.

Kamala's baby was born on November 19, 1917. Eagerly awaited by the expectant grandparents, it was presumed that it would be a boy. The baby was born in one of the rooms across the courtyard from Father's room, and several of us were standing in the veranda awaiting the announcement. Presently Mother came out of the room and said, '*Hua...*' Before the others realized the implication Father laughed and said, '*Baccha hua?*' Mother had not said a son is born but 'it' has been born. In the traditional way she could not bring herself to announce the birth of a daughter!

Father wanted the baby to be called after his mother, Indrani, but it was considered old-fashioned by some, and finally the name Indira, then much in vogue, was chosen. Because of his love of things Buddhist, Bhai added Priyadarshini, meaning 'pleasing to behold'. The Buddha, the Enlightened One, was also known as Priyadarshini. The two names together have suited Indu, as the family soon began to call her.

◆◆◆

8

Education

A paradox about my father was his championship of women's rights but his disregard for his daughters' education. He provided opportunities but there was no supervision and no plan. Studies were haphazard, and because there was no competition they were also rather dull. Beginning with a governess, lessons were later conducted by a series of tutors. As often happens in such cases, I knew more than the average school-going child of my age, but there were subjects with which I had only the slightest acquaintance. The mental discipline which a formal education imposes was lacking and I am always conscious of what I missed. I envied my girl cousins who went to school and college, won prizes, and took degrees.

A constant stream of distinguished men and women passed through our home. Women like Annie Besant and Sarojini Naidu filled me with the ambition to be like them. To be an orator, to be able to sway people with my words, this was my great ambition. Sarojini Naidu was not only poetess and politician, she was a close friend of the family. Our home was hers and she was beloved by every single member of it. I met her elder daughter, Padmaja, for the first time when we were both fifteen, and from that time until her sad death in 1975 she was the closest woman friend I ever had. She was a most vivid and colourful personality, charming and hospitable, and during the eleven years she later served as Governor of Bengal she rendered distinguished service to the state. To my children she was a second mother and she always referred to them as 'our children'.

I developed a complex about my lack of a formal education, and a university degree symbolized for me a passport to opportunity. After I was married this attitude annoyed my husband very much. 'Stop pitying yourself,' he would say if I ever harped on the subject. 'Unless you get your values straight, you will never succeed in anything.' My values were ultimately set straight by Gandhiji, but it took a national revolution to start a revolution in my mind.

For a girl, all roads led to marriage, and this is still mainly true in India. Suitably, I had been betrothed at thirteen and the custom was so usual that it made no impression on me nor did it change my life in any way. A few years later, the engagement was ended by mutual consent because of the widening political gap between our families.

I was now seriously involved in my Hindi studies, which were opening a door of real enjoyment for me. My master, Pandit Mahavir Prasad Malaviya, was a good teacher, and my love of the Ramayana really comes from him, though in India, especially in the Uttar Pradesh, every Hindu—literate or otherwise—knows much of this epic by heart, quotes it, and lives by it. Ramachandra is everyone's hero. In Uttar Pradesh the ordinary greeting is Ram-Ram, just as at the time of death it is this name that leads to salvation.

But apart from this, the *Ramcharit Manas,* Tulsi Das's Hindi version of the Ramayana, is not only good poetry, it is a book of philosophical concepts and moral values. I was now writing on literary subjects for Hindi magazines. This too I enjoyed, and Sanskrit became a part of my studies. My English reading covered a wide area—Dickens, Shakespeare, Scott, poetry, and biographies.

The First World War started but was not of any direct interest to me and my generation. What concerned us, or rather what concerned me, was the Irish rebellion of 1916 which we all followed with an emotional interest. The Lord Mayor of Cork, Terence MacSwiney, had been inspired by what was the beginning of the non-cooperation movement started by Mohandas Gandhi against racial discrimination in South Africa. He undertook a fast of protest against British action in Ireland and died in a London jail. At the time this caused a tremendous wave of indignation in India. I participated in an All India essay competition with an essay 'On the Meaning of Terence MacSwiney's Death' and won the first prize, a gold medal. Many decades later I was Ambassador to the Republic of Eire, and one of the most moving and memorable incidents of my life was the invitation to Cork, where I was honoured in a big way for the small moral support I had given as a girl to the movement and also to Terence MacSwiney's action against the British. The beautiful silver salver given to me on that occasion is a cherished possession, but more cherished are the warm words with which I was welcomed.

We have always been very close to the Irish people. There are so many basic and endearing, though possibly irritating, qualities we Indians share with them. I involved myself with Irish playwrights, novelists, and poets, and when I was in Dublin *en poste* my greatest enjoyment was a visit to the Abbey Theatre.

I had my first contact with a political issue in 1916. India was indignant over the question of the treatment of indentured labourers in South Africa. These men had gone to the Union in 1860 as the result of organized emigration mutually agreed upon between the British-controlled Government of India and the Government of Natal. The importation of such labour was subject to certain conditions, one of which was that after the expiration of five years they would work as free labourers. Once free from their indentures, these Indians were to be entitled to the protection and benefit of the ordinary laws of the colony. Following this indentured labour, Indian traders, shopkeepers, and others went to Natal to cater to Indian needs and, through their industry and enterprise, gradually established themselves as moderately prosperous farmers and traders. The settling of the Indian as a free man was not welcomed, and the white settlers began an anti-Indian agitation that sought to discriminate against the Indian in every way.

Mr Gopal Krishna Gokhale, the renowned social reformer, worked to consolidate public support in the country on this issue. I was deeply interested and wanted to help in some way. I had great affection for Mr Gokhale, as he was among the few important people who stayed in our home who always found time for a little girl.

'Do you wear Swadeshi cloth?' he once asked me.

'This frock has come from England,' I said, 'and it is very pretty.'

'Nothing can be as pretty as the things we make in our country,' Mr Gokhale replied with a smile. It was my first lesson in patriotism.

For the first time I attended a women's meeting organized by my cousin, Rameshwari Nehru, at the Mayo Hall of Allahabad University, to publicize the South African issue. The meeting itself was, I imagine, unique for the time. It took consistent and patient effort for many days to persuade women to leave their homes for one afternoon and go out to hear other women speak. Outings at that time were confined to specific social occasions when one dressed up in one's best and could look forward to a good meal, and this new idea was not appreciated. South Africa was very far away—it was a pity Indians were being discriminated against, but what good could result by some women getting together and talking about it in Allahabad? A packed hall finally rewarded the efforts of the organizers and the meeting was hailed by the newspapers next morning as a great step forward in arousing the social conscience of the women of the Uttar Pradesh! My own part had been confined mostly to serving water and in trying to keep crying babies quiet, but I had a feeling of participation in the cause and felt happy. It is an interesting coincidence that my first appearance on the international stage was in connection with the question of discrimination against the people of Indian origin in the Union of South Africa, brought to the United Nations forum by the Government of India in 1946.

I went to the 1916 Congress in Lucknow. This session had an added significance because the Muslim League also held its session at the same time, and a pact emerged on the question of self-government. Mohammed Ali Jinnah, elegant and arrogant, was hailed as Ambassador of Hindu–Muslim Unity.

Nearly all the great ones in politics seemed to be present, and for me it was a thrill to see and sometimes even to meet these men and women. Mrs Annie Besant and Sarojini Naidu were both present and their oratory mesmerized me. I was their devoted 'fan'. Mrs Besant, who had not been directly concerned with politics, had now become prominent and had founded the Home Rule League. It made an impact on the country. I eagerly read and was impressed by the articles in her paper which came to Anand Bhawan. 'Let India remember what she was and what she may be—then shall the sun rise once more in the East and fill the Western lands with light.' I wanted to join the League but, being only sixteen, I could not do so. However, I enrolled as a volunteer and did odd jobs such as addressing envelopes and taking messages in the Allahabad office. That year for Bhaiya Duj (Brother's Day) Bhai gave me a gold pin with HR in emerald and rubies, representing the Home Rule colours.

◆◆◆

9

Satyagraha

As the war ended there was discontent on many levels—among the peasantry, from whom soldiers had been recruited and who had helped to win the war; among the Muslims, resentment over the Allied treatment of Turkey; and everywhere among the educated middle class, expectations of widespread constitutional reform leading to greater political opportunity. Change came, indeed, but in the form of the Rowlatt Bills, which contained drastic provision for arrests and deportations without trial or any check of the law. Expectations were rudely shattered, and every shade of political opinion openly opposed what came to be known as the Black Bills.

Mahatma Gandhi, since his return from South Africa, had been involved with agrarian movements in Bihar and Gujarat. The Rowlatt Bills, and the manner in which they were passed by the Imperial Legislative Council despite strong public opposition, shocked him. The constitutional method had failed and he began to think of satyagraha. He started an organization called the Satyagraha Sabha and published a pledge. Those who joined the Sabha had to solemnly affirm 'to civilly disobey' the new laws and 'follow truth faithfully and refrain from violence...' Among the first to join the Sabha was Bhai. Father, as deeply stunned as any, would never allow himself to be guided by emotions alone. As he frequently told all of us when we were enthusing over some issue, 'The heart is a fool, the only safe guide is the head.' He could not see the connection between the civil disobedience of individuals and bringing pressure on the government to rescind unjust laws. The thoughts of father and son did not synchronize and both suffered.

I first met Mahatma Gandhi in November 1920, when he came at my father's invitation to discuss his policy of satyagraha with our family. Before this I had seen him in the distance at the Lucknow Congress in 1916. In that elegant gathering he had been an incongruous figure in his large Kathiawari turban and swathed in shawls against the north Indian winter. Since then I had read and heard a great deal about him, much of which I could not understand.

When he came to our home for the first time there was great excitement in the family. Our house was still geared to the old pattern. There were large numbers of servants in their wine and gold liveries, rooms decorated with glittering chandeliers and beautiful carpets, masses of flowers everywhere. This, obviously, was not the proper setting for a Mahatma, and yet what was one to do about it? It was impossible to dismantle a whole house for a visit that would last only a few days. Finally, Mother's sitting room, which was furnished with takhts in the Indian style, was prepared for him, and arrangements were made for sitting on the floor. About Gandhiji's entourage one did not have to bother as they were happy to live comfortably for a day or so and needed no special arrangements.

The world knows now what Gandhiji looked like, what he ate, and what he thought of many issues apart from politics. Various authors, from their imaginations, have added to his known fads, thereby losing sight of the humanity of the man and portraying him as some kind of a freak. To me, with his naked body and his big ears, by no means handsome, Gandhiji was, at that time, a strange new sight. He had by now shed his turban and his Gujarati clothes and begun wearing a loincloth to identify himself with the poorest Indian. His food was served in tin dishes—a plate, a bowl, and a mug—and these he carried everywhere with him. All the cloth he used for his personal clothing as well as for sheets and towels was hand-spun and hand-woven by him and was of the thickest khadi, very different from any material we had seen. In those days he spoke bad Hindi, but as far as I remember most of the talks on that occasion were in English. Then, as always, he was economical with words and able to express himself clearly without using involved sentences or ideas. This was one reason he could reach the heart even when the brain was rejecting some of his arguments. Naturally, I had no part in the conversations which took place or in anything else because Mother and Bhabi, my sister-in-law, Kamala, looked after his meals and served them personally. In spite of this, his was such an unusual personality that it made itself felt to all of us in the house. Even then he radiated a quiet serenity. When he spoke it was clear that he would not say anything that he did not firmly believe.

It was during his stay in Anand Bhawan that Gandhiji suggested that I should be sent to the Sabarmati Ashram near Ahmedabad, where he lived, for some weeks, to be subjected to a simpler way of life. As far as I recollect nobody asked me specifically whether I wanted to go, but the idea of the simple life was about to begin in India. Bhai had already adopted it and it was obvious that there would be many changes in our lifestyle before long. I was the pampered daughter of the house and needed discipline.

A couple of years earlier, while still in my teens, I had become attached to a young man, Syed Hossain, whom my father had appointed editor of a newspaper he had just started, *The Independent*. In an era that proclaimed Hindu–Muslim unity, and belonging to a family that had close Muslim friends, I must have thought it would be perfectly natural to marry outside my religion. But in matters such as marriage the times were deeply traditional, and I was persuaded that this would be wrong. My mother felt, in any case, that my Western-oriented upbringing encouraged me in unorthodox ways. So she welcomed Gandhiji's suggestion that I should spend a little time with him in his famous ashram.

My heart sank when I first saw the place. Everything was so utterly drab and so unpleasing to the eye. I wondered how long I could survive there. As a concession I was to share Gandhiji's hut. He was known as Bapu, which means father in Gujarati, and that is the name I used for him ever after. Life in the ashram was austere beyond belief. Rising at 4 a.m. for prayers, we went on to the chores of the day, which consisted of sweeping and cleaning our living quarters, washing our clothes in the river, cleaning the latrines—which is a task impossible to describe. In order to let me down gently I was not required to clean the latrines, for which I offered thanks to the Almighty! In later years, however, and on other occasions, I had to do this chore the same as others. Then there was time for study and helping in the office from which Gandhiji's weekly newspaper, *Young India,* was issued. There was work to be done in the dairy, and daily spinning. Two meals were prepared every day. In those early days in the ashram the idea was to kill one's desire for food, which was eaten only to exist. Several vegetables grown in the garden were thrown together into a steam cooker without salt, spice, or butter and eaten with home-ground chapatis (unleavened Indian bread) or unpolished rice. Certainly no one in the ashram was in danger of putting on weight. No tea or coffee was drunk. In course of time this changed, but gradually, and though the food remained very simple it became more acceptable to the palate and was not cooked together into a stew. There were prayers again at 6 p.m. Gandhiji's prayers included readings from the Gita and the Koran. To these were later added verses from the Bible and recitations from Parsi, Sikh, and Buddhist prayers, as well as the singing of hymns from various religions.

At that period there were only hurricane lanterns in the ashram, and it was not easy to read by their flickering wicks so one went to bed early. At night my bedding roll was placed in the veranda next to Gandhiji's and he would talk to me about Hindu culture of which I knew a great deal, or of other things connected with the changes that were due soon. From the very beginning Gandhiji appreciated the fact that I never said anything merely to please him, and he seemed surprised that in spite of some Western ways I was basically rooted in Indian tradition. The fact that I had had no formal religious training worried him a little, but soon he discovered that I knew my Ramayana well and was in the habit of reading the Gita, though I might not have understood its deeper meaning. By the time I had left the ashram I had lost my fear of him and had, to some extent, come to terms with ashram life, not accepting it but beginning to appreciate the underlying philosophy on which it was based.

Certain things I could not grasp, and it took a long time for me to understand some of Gandhiji's views. For instance, a very pretty young girl living in the ashram, but not belonging to it, fell in love with a young man there. They slept together and this reached Gandhiji's ears. It pained him greatly as he attached the highest importance to chastity. He sent for the young people. I do not remember how the boy was dealt with but the girl, whose great beauty was her long, silky hair, had it cut off and Gandhiji went on a fast for several days to atone for the 'sin' that had been committed. It was a time of strain and not a little fear for everyone. At the time the whole incident seemed bizarre and primeval, though later I understood better this way of satyagraha, of taking another's weakness on oneself and punishing oneself rather than the sinner. In one way Gandhiji was a paradox. He was kind and loving and yet he would be as hard as steel and would not compromise on what he considered a moral issue. A lie he would never forgive, and any sexual aberration was a heinous sin to him. At one time he used to advise young married couples not to have intercourse, and this led to many forms of frustration among his followers. I could never condone this though I came to love him beyond words.

In all the years I knew him we had many arguments, but, because I think he appreciated my frankness, he was not only gentle with me but whenever I was in sorrow or distress his love seemed to envelop me and give me strength. I never had the slightest problem in joking with him for he had a great sense of humour, and in many ways I treated him as I had treated my father—as a comrade and one who, even if he did not agree with my views, would never let this come between our close relationship and the happiness I derived from it.

The one person who was really able to help Gandhiji to relax and enjoy a joke was Sarojini Naidu. She was herself a unique human being with a fund of amusing stories and could say the most outrageous things without giving offence. It was she who nicknamed Gandhiji 'Mickey Mouse' when he was at the height of his fame, and he enjoyed this name as much as anyone and asked all sorts of questions about Mickey Mouse, whom he never had seen on the screen. Sarojini was the only one who, as far as I remember, could joke with him on his views of brahmacharya, chastity. Once when an article appeared in *Young India* suggesting several ways of avoiding the temptation of females, the writer advised, among other things, the wearing of dark glasses. As C.R. Rajagopalachari, popularly known as Rajaji and afterward our first Governor General, always wore very dark glasses, Sarojini would make all kinds of naughty remarks about him in which both Gandhiji and Rajaji himself would join. Rajaji's views on the subject were as staunch as Gandhiji's, but both put up with Sarojini's merciless teasing. One thing to be remembered and admired is that in those days our leaders could laugh at themselves and at each other, even on matters they considered of great importance. Today, alas, this has become impossible, and the ability to laugh at anything is fast vanishing.

In course of time Gandhiji moved from Sabarmati Ashram to Wardha, a village in the then Central Provinces, now Madhya Pradesh. This was quite a different setting, and though the utmost simplicity was continued there was no drabness. The new pattern was introduced by Miraben, Gandhiji's English disciple. She had read Romain Rolland's biography of Gandhiji and been attracted to his ideals. When she arrived in Sabarmati Ashram, I happened to be there. She was a tall, big-built woman whose really lovely hair fell in chestnut masses below her knees. This she cut off, and she wore thick homespun khadi clothes like the other inmates of the ashram. She changed her name from Madeleine to Mira and acted as a secretary to Gandhiji and also as a translator, since she spoke fluent French and German. It was she who made Gandhiji's mud hut in Wardha into a charming place with village paintings on the walls. The effect was pleasing, and the mud walls and floor acquired a dignity of their own.

Among those who had dedicated their lives to Gandhiji's service was Rajkumari Amrit Kaur, a princess from the House of Kapurthala. English-educated and a woman of many talents, she had great devotion to ideals. In her young days she had been something of a tennis star. To serve Gandhiji she gave up a life of ease and wealth and remained one of his secretaries and a constant companion until after Independence when she became the first woman to hold the position of minister in the Central Government at Delhi. For many years she held the portfolio of health. Another young woman who gave up a medical career to serve Gandhiji as his personal physician was Sushila Nayyar. She too remained with him until he died and in later years she too was Minister of Health.

On that first visit of Gandhiji to Allahabad there was tremendous interest in this little man and his message. Practically the whole town turned out to hear him speak at a public meeting. He spoke haltingly in Hindi but his message came over crystal clear. I had persuaded my cousin, Kishan Bhai,[6] to take me to the meeting and we sat at the edge of the crowd. At the end of his speech Gandhiji sent around volunteers to collect money for a fund to help the families of those who would be arrested by offering satyagraha. He made a special appeal to the women present, of whom there were few, to donate whatever jewellery they were wearing. Like others, I had been carried away by Gandhiji's talk, and as the volunteers came toward me I pulled off the gold bangles I was wearing and placed them in the bag. Next day Gandhiji left, but for the Nehrus nothing was ever the same again.

From Allahabad Gandhiji had sent a telegraphic appeal to the Viceroy 'respectfully' requesting him to refrain from passing the Rowlatt Bills. This appeal was ignored and Satyagraha Day was launched with fasting, prayer, and a nationwide hartal on April 6, 1919. A fast is an ordinary event among Hindus, Muslims, and Christians alike, but this fast was different because it was for a political purpose and not for personal salvation. Many of those who did not fully understand the political significance knew that any big task is only undertaken after a process of self-purification. Gandhiji always based his appeals to the people on what was traditionally known to them. This was why he easily carried the common man with him while the more sophisticated and politically complex mind of the educated held him aloof.

The demonstrations were nationwide. Bazaars were closed, public vehicles ceased plying for trade, huge processions marched through cities, and business was at a standstill. For the first time peasants from the villages participated in a political demonstration along with townspeople. There was

6. Dr Krishna Lal Nehru.

firing by police in many parts of the country and arrests of numbers of people. The government declared martial law in Punjab, and strict censorship cut off all news of what was happening there. On April 13 a peaceful meeting of several thousand men, women, and children was held in the walled garden of Jallianwala Bagh in Amritsar, and, under orders of General Dyer, troops fired on the people, who could not get out of the garden because it had only one small exit. Over a thousand were killed and wounded in this infamous massacre, and while General Dyer was applauded in the House of Lords, the poet Rabindranath Tagore returned the knighthood he had earlier accepted from the British. One of the consequences of the Jallianwala Bagh incident was the murder of a missionary lady by an incensed crowd, which led to the now almost forgotten crawling order in retaliation for this killing. The order was to the effect that anyone wishing to pass the lane where the missionary was killed must crawl on his belly. This was the ultimate humiliation, and, though the law was enforced by British bayonets, many Indians refused to obey it. Punjab was cut off completely from the rest of India, but what news seeped through the censorship was horrifying and national leaders who wanted to go there were prevented from doing so. Presently, with the lifting of martial law, well-known and trusted men proceeded to the Punjab and started arrangements for an unofficial inquiry.

This was a time of great domestic strain, and constant adjustments and compromises were called for. New thinking was necessary for new designs that would affect the national destiny that now began to take shape. Mother felt acutely miserable over all that was happening. The person she loved most, her son, was deeply disturbed and unhappy. He was obviously on the verge of some action that she would have appreciated in a mythological figure but not in one on whom her hopes of happiness on earth and her place in heaven depended. Then there was the serious situation developing between her husband and her son. What was going to happen?

How could she take sides or understand this new 'Mahatma', whose business, if anything, should have been to look after people's morals instead of meddling in family matters. It was a ridiculous idea to fight a powerful government by getting oneself locked up in jail. It was wrong to abandon one's family and perhaps die in the course of the struggle.

The easy camaraderie that had existed in the family vanished. Meals were eaten mostly in silence, there was no more happy chatter of past times. Quite without cause Father would shout at Asgar Ali, our old butler, and send complaints to the kitchen about one dish or another, then in his most sarcastic manner he would ask the room at large whether a man was entitled to eat as he wished in his own home or if that, too, would contribute to the continuation of British rule in India! He was suffering deeply and would have liked nothing better than to offer his son the comfort of sharing his faith. But he was unable to compromise and was not yet ready to accept new theories that seemed illogical to him.

Meanwhile, Bhai was working more and more in the villages, reducing his personal needs and cutting down strictly on his diet. His night meal had now become bread and milk and this looked incongruous served in a steel bowl (preparation for jail) in the midst of the silver and crystal out of which the rest of us were eating and drinking.

One day Bhai came into the drawing room when we were all assembled waiting for dinner to be announced. He had a thick piece of twine in his hands, obviously just taken off a parcel. He kept twisting it in his fingers this way and that and suddenly, with a twinkle in his eye, he put the string round his throat and said, 'I wonder what it feels like to have a noose round one's neck?' At any other time this might have been a joke, but in a household as charged with emotion as ours then was, this statement had the impact of a bomb. Mother nearly fainted. Father got up and walked out of the room, banging the door. Kamala, my sister-in-law, made feeble attempts to laugh and try to ease the tension, but all peace had left the room. When dinner was announced Bhai said with some amazement, 'Has this family no sense of humour left? Let's go and eat!' That night, for the first time, Father slept on the floor to try to experience one of the minor discomforts Bhai would have to undergo when the time came for going to jail.

◆◆◆

10

Marriage

It was in this tense national atmosphere, and strained domestic one, that I met Ranjit Pandit, whom I was to marry shortly afterward. An article published in 1920 in the *Modern Review* of Calcutta entitled 'At the Feet of the Guru' had created considerable interest, especially among younger people. The guru of the article was Jawaharlal Nehru, the writer, Ranjit Pandit. At a time when all eyes were focused on Gandhi, the man with a new technique for freedom and about whom there was controversy in all circles, this article asserted that a new star was rising on the political firmament—a guru the young could understand and to whom they would give their loyalty—Jawaharlal Nehru. The article was an expression of the admiration Ranjit had developed for Bhai and which he never lost. As time went on, to this was added great love, which Bhai reciprocated.

As I have mentioned before, we were engaged during Ranjit's visit to Allahabad. No formal announcement was made immediately because my parents wanted us to get better acquainted and also because of my father's growing uneasiness over coming events.

When he was leaving, Ranjit gave me a tiny silk-bound volume almost in tatters. He told me it was a copy of the Gita that his father had always read and carried with him. 'It is the most precious thing I possess,' he said. When I showed it to my mother she was horrified. It seemed quite mad to her that a young man, just engaged to be married, should give his fiancée the Gita with its message of renunciation. Where was the diamond ring he should have given me? However, the ring and other gifts of jewellery followed later and somewhat appeased her! The Gita has in a way been symbolic in my life. Years afterward Bhai gave me a small beautifully tooled Gita as his present on Bhaiya Duj, the brother's day. This gift is always with me. Dr S. Radhakrishnan, our former President, also gave me one.

It was thought better to get the wedding over before Congress had to take a stand over the impending visit of the Prince of Wales. The All India Congress Committee was due to meet for the momentous decision in Allahabad, and the date chosen for the wedding was May 9. This happened to be the anniversary of the 1857 Mutiny, and at this period the government was always a little anxious. In 1921, with most of India's political leaders assembled in conference, the atmosphere was charged with electricity, and none of us was in the mood for the normal festivities connected with a wedding. Everything was simplified but there was still much to be done.

The Kashmiri community as a whole had announced its decision to boycott the wedding because, according to them, I was marrying 'outside the community'. In actual fact Ranjit and I both came from the same Brahmanical stock, the Saraswats, the only difference being that though our ancestors came originally from Kashmir, his had settled in Maharashtra and mine in the Uttar Pradesh. The boycott was quite ridiculous but caused tremendous comment at the time. Since then the young men and women of our family have married into various communities and religions and have even gone as far away as Europe to find marriage partners without anyone giving the matter a thought.

Gandhiji had been a close friend of Ranjit's father, and

this wedding had his consent and approval. Suddenly one day he wrote to inquire what I would wear for the ceremony. In Kashmiri families it is usual for the bride to be married in a pink cotton sari. The religious ceremony is a long one and usually late at night. When she leaves for her husband's home the bride is dressed in a gold-embroidered sari and wears the jewellery given to her by her parents. This was conveyed to Gandhiji, and back came a letter saying he could not approve of this at all. I must wear khadi and there was no question of jewels being worn! Mother could not have been more angry. She had, so far, not accepted Gandhiji as a friend, could not understand his politics, and certainly did not think he had the right to advise the family on personal matters. His growing influence over Bhai disturbed her greatly. She felt intuitively that this man was the enemy of her home. There was a great deal of argument and some correspondence between Gandhiji and Anand Bhawan.

Khadi at that time was not only coarse, it was made in a narrow width not suitable for a sari; to join two pieces together would have made it bulky to wear and very ugly. So far as jewellery was concerned, a Hindu woman at that time could not inherit in her own right. The only things that were her own property and could not be taken away from her were the jewellery and household articles given to her at the time of marriage before the sacred fire. For a girl to be married in a coarse white cloth was most inauspicious, as white is the colour of mourning in India and is worn only by widows. The problem was solved by Gandhiji's wife, Ba, who sent me a piece of cloth spun and woven by her. It was the correct width and also fine enough to be dyed the traditional pink. It certainly was not a wedding sari in any sense but was reluctantly accepted. Instead of the jewellery I should have worn, flowers were woven into various attractive ornaments for my ears, neck, and wrists.

Judged by the standards of the day, the wedding was a simple affair. The list of guests read like a political convention.

All the leaders of India were present. The auspicious hour for the religious ceremony was after midnight, so Gandhiji had been persuaded to retire at his usual time. Ranjit and I went up to his room later to receive his blessing. Bapu, as we all called him, was curled up on his bed in the veranda, a ray of moonlight shining on him. He woke immediately he heard our footsteps, gave us his blessings, and spoke of love and responsibility. Then he looked very grave and began to talk of our duty to the country at this time—the strength required could only come from purity of the highest order. Chastity in married life was difficult, he knew, but so was the great struggle for freedom upon which we had entered and which demanded every sacrifice. I was filled with fear that if he went on talking much longer I would find myself falling under his spell and make any promise he demanded—frightened also that perhaps his words had already struck a responsive chord in Ranjit's mind. What a situation to be in, I thought to myself, a few minutes after being married. Suddenly the Nehru spirit asserted itself. I looked at Bapu and said haltingly, 'Why did you give your permission to our marriage if you thought it was wrong for us to live together as husband and wife? I love Ranjit and I want a normal married life.' I stopped because I was breathless, expecting a sharp rebuke, but none came. Instead, a gentle sigh, then a slap on my burning cheek, 'So you love Ranjit? See to it then that you do not distract him from his duty!' And we were dismissed with a loving smile!

Among Brahmans, it is customary to change the name of the bride after the wedding ceremony, when the girl has been accepted into her new family. The name chosen by the in-laws generally has some relation to the name of the husband. Ranjit means the Victor. The name given to me was Vijaya Lakshmi—the conquering goddess Lakshmi. Because I had never liked the name Sarup Kumari, I immediately took the new one and became for all public and official purposes Vijaya Lakshmi. Though I did not think of it as anything but a beautiful sounding name, I could not have had a better or more fortunate one. It has lent itself to all sorts of good interpretations during elections and is, in any case, considered auspicious.

Two days after the wedding we left for Calcutta. Bhai had an appointment in some village that day but had promised to be back in time to say goodbye. He had not, however, reached home when we were leaving for the railway station. I was unhappy. Friends and relations were waiting to see us off and our good friend, Mr Clark, the Anglo-Indian station master, came up to shake hands. The time for departure was due.

'Oh, please, can't we wait five minutes?' I begged Mr Clark. 'I know my brother will come.'

As we reached our flower-decorated reserved carriage I saw Bhai sauntering up the platform. He was aware that he was late but it was his studied custom not to hurry or show any anxiety on any occasion. I was standing in the door of the carriage and he swung himself up.

'Oh, you came,' I said. He took my face in his hands and, kissing me between the eyes, he said, 'Be happy, little sister.'

The whistle sounded and we were off—a new life, a new beginning, and an uncertain future.

◆◆◆

11

Rajkot and the Pandits

We began our married life in Calcutta. May is a bad month anywhere in India, and the Bengal climate, with its high humidity, is very bad indeed. Only those completely absorbed in their work or in each other can forget the weather and overcome its handicaps.

While our apartment was being decorated we lived in a suite of rooms at the Grand Hotel in a style quite inappropriate to the times or to a young couple beginning life. I had my ayah and Ranjit had his valet, a gentleman who tried my patience and wore out my nerves because of his addiction to liquor but who, in Ranjit's eyes, was a sort of Super Jeeves. We also had a chauffeur and an imposing gentleman in livery and a bright turban whose only job seemed to be to lend colour and prestige to our establishment.

Ranjit and I were absorbed in each other and could think of little else. In Calcutta we had been made much of by numerous friends of both our families and by Sir B.L. Mitter, afterward Law Minister in the Viceroy's Council, in whose law office Ranjit was a junior member at the time. He and his charming wife treated us like members of their family. Ranjit was a good mixer, an accomplished musician, and fluent in Bengali, so he was popular in all circles. Time passed quickly and the court vacations drew near. We had not really had a honeymoon, and it seemed right to go to Rajkot where we could have the quiet needed to look at ourselves and the developing political situation objectively, to come to some decision about the future. Gandhiji had now made an appeal to students to boycott colleges and to lawyers to boycott courts. My marriage had not entirely pleased Ranjit's family because they were afraid the association with the Nehrus would come in the way of his success at the Bar. Indirectly, in many ways, they tried to influence him. On the other side his own political convictions, his deep admiration for my father and brother, and his love for me pulled him toward the national movement. My own feelings were mixed. Coming from a home that had been suddenly uprooted and where new ways of living and thinking were being established, I was acutely aware that unless Ranjit conformed to this pattern he would not have a close place in the hearts of Father and Bhai. They were too deeply involved for good or ill, and there was no place in their lives for those who were on the other side or those who hesitated on the brink.

Ranjit had a complex and versatile personality. His early

studies had taken place in Bombay, but after graduating with distinction from the university he went abroad where the Sorbonne, the University of Heidelberg, and the Middle Temple claimed him. He was a good sportsman and crack shot and also a fine musician. He had studied both European and Indian music, played the violin with considerable talent, and had a well-trained singing voice. He was also a linguist of ability and had studied many European and Indian languages, which he spoke fluently. He was a barrister by profession but a historian and classicist by choice. His two great loves were music and Sanskrit.

Ranjit called himself a pagan, but this was not correct. There was a strong Spartan streak in his makeup and always had been since he was little more than a teenager. From time to time he used to withdraw into himself and observe strict mental and physical discipline. During this period he became another person altogether. It was as if he was compelled to extract the utmost out of whatever he did, whether fulfillment of desire or renunciation of it. There were no half measures. Coming out of these withdrawals from life, as it were, he would pick up the threads of normal living as if nothing had happened. He never gave any explanation for this. He was not an easy man to live with!

In August the High Court rose for the summer vacation and we left for Rajkot. Kathiawar or Saurashtra is the state on the west coast of India that juts out into the sea, forming a little peninsula of its own. It has been a land of song and chivalry, and the ballads still sung there tell of beautiful women, fine horses, and gallant deeds. There is colour and music and dancing everywhere, and the people are by nature cheerful and happy in spite of frequent famines and other hardships.

The women of Saurashtra are renowned for their beauty as the horses are for their speed. The Kathi has the same love for his horse as the Arab, and there are innumerable stories about them. Legend relates that Shri Krishna, when he left his home in Mathura in the Uttar Pradesh, came to Saurashtra and built himself a golden city called Dwarka. This remains a place of pilgrimage for all Hindus.

The Pandits belonged to Maharashtra and came from the Konkan, the strip of land running along the sea coast below Bombay. Family records claim that the original ancestor hailed from Kashmir, and, in the course of his travels, decided to settle down in the little village of Bambuli. But where he came from is of far less consequence than the qualities he brought with him and which he passed on to his descendants. These were responsible for the high record of service to the community that the family established first in their village and, as opportunity offered, farther afield. Ranjit's great-grandparents were a deeply religious couple and his great-grandmother became a sati on the death of her husband. A banyan tree was planted on the site of her immolation, and to this day the village people and the passing traveller bow reverently before it.

Ranjit's father was the seventh son in a family of thirteen. All the boys showed promise of a high order and all did well in their studies. My father-in-law, Sitaram Pandit, after a fine scholastic record at home, went as a government scholar to England, a rare thing in those days, where he qualified for the Bar. On his return he decided to begin practising in Kathiawar and he settled down in the capital town, Rajkot. He lived and worked when India was rich in talent, and a galaxy of great names was part of the history of the period in which he too played a noble part. Rising rapidly in his profession he became a respected figure in the state. He was both social reformer and philosopher. Money for him had little personal meaning and he gave generously to all good causes. Theosophical institutions and Christian missions, Hindu universities and Muslim schools, all received moral and financial support from him. No student was turned away from his door, and the amounts donated in scholarships were princely. In times of famine, which in Kathiawar was a recurring event, he poured money into the relief centres, thus substantially supplementing government assistance. For this he had been offered but had declined a knighthood.

The doors of the Pandit home were never closed to anyone. Like my father, my father-in-law loved people and was always surrounded by friends of all nationalities, but unlike my father, he was simple to the point of austerity in his personal life though he entertained lavishly. While he lived, his home in Rajkot was a centre for those who were interested in the wider issues, and brilliant discussions among the great ones of the period took place there. He was a close associate of Gandhiji, who valued his advice as well as his friendship.

One of Ranjit's uncles, Shankar Pandurang Pandit, was an eminent scholar and linguist, a man of high moral courage. In an age when government servants, regardless of position, could not question the foreign master, he dared to express his views in the national interest at all times. His talented daughter, Kshamabai Row, herself an eminent Sanskrit scholar, has written his biography in Sanskrit verse.

My mother-in-law had been born and brought up in a village in Maharashtra. It must have taken considerable courage for her to go to Rajkot, an unknown and distant part of the country, with her husband. She possessed the pioneering spirit in full measure and she joined in all her husband's activities, even learning to ride in order to accompany him when he had to go long distances to his cases. The women of Maharashtra have had a fine inheritance. They held a place of honour and dignity in society, which has given them an advantage that the women of the north have lacked. It is apparent in their bearing and their approach to life—they are free and fearless. My mother-in-law was an example of this type of woman.

The Pandits were a sporting family, and riding, hunting, fishing, and games of every kind were part of the pattern of their lives in Rajkot. The stables had been drastically reduced after my father-in-law's death because both sons had settled away from Kathiawar, but there were still some riding ponies, and my own beloved Bijli, my favourite Arab mare, had been sent from Allahabad. Ranjit and I spent the mornings in long cross-country rides and the afternoons in reading—the Sanskrit classics, and poetry, drama, and history. I went through all the winding paths of India's evolution, and, as Ranjit unveiled and interpreted the richness of our cultural heritage, for the first time I became aware of myself as an Indian. It was an exciting discovery. Now I understood better what Gandhiji was saying to us. The national movement, which had seemed remote up till that time, became a compelling force.

The vacation was nearing its end; it was not possible to remain passive spectators of the changing scene much longer. The problem was whether Ranjit should respond to Gandhiji's call and suspend his practice. Gandhiji's idea was non-cooperation with government institutions and agencies for one year, but not even the most optimistic imagined that a powerful government could be brought down in this limited period.

Practice at the Bar was not easy to suspend. It would be difficult to start where one left off and would also mean loss of prestige. To go back to the same courts which one had renounced as instruments of the foreign ruler would be tantamount to admitting that the step had been wrong. Then what did one do? Joining the national movement was, in the words of Gandhiji, 'the fullest protection of one's self-respect and honour'—but it also meant loss of possessions and properties. The family property was owned jointly by Ranjit and his brother Pratap, who was not interested in politics. Would Ranjit's participation involve Pratap? I think we both knew what the final decision would be. Our talks about material things were superficial; what really prevented Ranjit from making an immediate break was Gandhiji's insistence on nonviolence as a creed and its observance in thought and action. According to this creed, the adversary could be converted by the sheer force of one's character and suffering.

As Gandhiji said, 'I seek to blunt the edge of the tyrant's sword, not by putting it against a sharper-edged weapon but by disappointing its expectation that I would offer a physical resistance.' Ranjit was a son of Maharashtra and the fiery blood of many ancestors intolerant of the foreigner flowed in his veins. He was a man of action and could only fulfill himself through action. In theory, he accepted Gandhiji's reasoning, but could he live up to it? The conflict continued for some weeks, but finally the call of Gandhiji could not be denied.

◆◆◆

12

Changing Attitudes

The Congress had decided to boycott the Prince of Wales's approaching visit, which was due in November 1921. As the time approached satyagraha gathered force, and it was known that those who were protesting would be arrested. By this time Father had joined Gandhiji, but with some reservations regarding nonviolence. Earlier he had suggested that since he could not give his complete loyalty to Gandhiji's programme, would it not be better to continue his legal practice, still a princely one, and donate the money to the cause? Gandhiji's reply, as one might have expected, was almost in the words of Christ. 'But it is *you* I want,' he said, and in a very short time afterward Father threw in his lot with Gandhiji and never looked back or regretted his decision.

Of the leaders who were arrested for boycotting the Prince of Wales's visit in Allahabad, Father and Bhai were among the first, as was our friend Purushottam Das Tandon, a man of wisdom and great integrity who became an important figure in politics, and a host of Congress people who had already given up some or all of their possessions to follow Gandhiji.

Ranjit and I received the news of the arrests in Rajkot and immediately left for Allahabad. The long train journey seemed never-ending, and on reaching Allahabad we learned that all persons arrested had been taken to the Lucknow jail after being sentenced to six months' simple imprisonment. Mother, Kamala, and Betty were already in Lucknow and we followed. It had been understood between Father and Ranjit before we went to Rajkot that whatever political step Ranjit might decide to take, he would stay with Mother during this first political crisis in her life, for which her mind was wholly unprepared. So this was our immediate plan. After a week in Lucknow, where Mother and Kamala were allowed daily interviews, we accompanied them back to Allahabad.

Big changes were taking place at home. Our staff had been drastically reduced, a part of the house closed, and our style of living altered to fit in with the new conditions we had accepted. The political situation was deteriorating and there was suffering in many homes where the breadwinner was now in jail. One's personal discomforts ceased to have any meaning. Anand Bhawan was always full, for those who had joined Gandhiji were now one family and were gladly given shelter and help by Mother.

Besides the six-month sentences for Father and Bhai, fines were also imposed. The rules of the national movement forbade us to pay these, and we expected the police to come and take away whatever they wished in lieu of the money. Gandhiji's instructions on this point were clear. The police must not be obstructed in the performance of their duty and should be allowed to take whatever they wished. Mother could not reconcile herself to this invasion of her home and, by the time the police arrived a few days later, she was seething with anger. Kamala, on the contrary, was quite serene and kept trying to persuade Mother that we must let the men who were present in the house deal with the situation. I insisted on standing around watching all that happened, and it was a bitter experience to see the conduct of the police and their manner of handling the things we had loved and which had become part of our lives. The word 'police' was synonymous with terror. They were symbols of the foreign ruler and, in most cases, brutal men who behaved ruthlessly. Their conduct in Anand Bhawan followed the expected pattern. The inspector, who thought this an excellent opportunity to show his superiors his ability to carry out orders, was free with his language and walked around the house with an arrogance that Kanhaiyalal, an old retainer of the family, could not swallow. When the inspector was holding forth in objectionable language, describing the might of the British Raj as vested in him, Kanhaiyalal, who did not subscribe to the theory of nonviolence, loudly called on heaven and the gods to witness that, but for the interference of this new Mahatma, he could have dealt adequately with those who sought to insult his master.

In lieu of a small fine of Rs 1000, van loads of valuables were removed. Carpets, pieces of furniture, and ornaments were taken and later sold by public auction. This was intended to destroy the prestige of the family and to humiliate us. We later heard that the auctioneer used unpleasant language and tried to describe the position of each article in Anand Bhawan—though not very successfully, since he had never been inside the house. It would have been a triumph for the national cause if the public of Allahabad had had the strength to boycott the auction, but that was not the way it was. Many years later I saw a few of our beautiful Chippendale chairs in the home of an advocate. They were hardly recognizable as they had been painted and varnished several times, but the owner proudly reminded visitors how and where his father had obtained them—as if it were an event of historical importance. Another time, I saw an exquisite Japanese screen which had stood in a corner of our dining room as long as I could remember—it was in the home of an Indian official who had no appreciation of its beauty. As in the other case it was a souvenir of a special occasion.

The world we now lived in was unfamiliar and also much smaller. It required a continuous effort to adapt oneself to new situations. Many old friends and acquaintances disappeared from our lives and new ones came into them. There was a difference, however, for those who became comrades in the struggle were simple people—men and women who did not share our background or our earlier interests, to whom we seemed as strange as they seemed to us. The bond between us was simply that of association in a common cause. We all dressed in the coarse hand-spun, handwoven material called khadi. Everything in use in the way of linen and towels also had to be of this material. It was drab and ugly in those days, its beauty of course lay in the fact that each yard one bought gave money to help a poor villager, and this economic aspect was exactly what Gandhiji wished to emphasize. Khadi became the uniform of those participating in the national struggle, and the men wore on their heads a little cap that became known as the Gandhi cap. All members of the Congress were expected to spin a certain amount of yarn every day as a personal discipline.

An incident that took place illustrates what I mean about changing social circumstances. One evening a Congress volunteer arrived at Anand Bhawan. He had travelled rather a long distance and wanted food and rest. Mother was informed he came from Gandhiji's ashram and she went to meet him. She saw a hefty villager clad only in a loincloth, carrying a rough blanket. She did not recognize him or the name he gave. In those days it was no longer possible to place people from their talk, or the clothes they wore, because a common vocabulary and the khadi dhoti and kurta had become levelling factors. The man's face was vaguely familiar and Mother was afraid lest she should seem discourteous to a national worker. She ordered a meal for him and arranged for him to stay the night. Still bothered by the familiarity of his face, she asked if he had any other name besides the one he had given her. He mentioned another one, and she recognized him as a man who had been our night watchman for several years! He had now been to jail as a Congress volunteer and was the equal of anyone! Being a lady, she suppressed her surprise, but her later remarks to us were full of un-Gandhian sentiments and sharp disapproval of people not staying in their proper place! It took her some years to accept Gandhiji's egalitarian society.

Such incidents were continually happening while we were getting to know those with whom we were now associated. It was not easy at first to adopt a natural attitude toward people who were not of our own world. One was either too reserved or too effusive. Having to travel third class by train was an experience that tried one to the uttermost. Going from Allahabad to Lucknow on one occasion, I noticed a familiar face under a Gandhi cap. Instead of merely acknowledging his polite greeting, I began to talk to him. When I saw the bewildered look on his face I realized he was not expecting to be treated like a comrade! Childhood habits cling and I had been taught to greet people with a smile. Now I was constantly being reminded by the family that there was absolutely no need for me to smile at every man wearing a Gandhi cap and claim every woman in a khadi sari as a long-lost relative.

The 'boycott' movement was reaching its height—foreign cloth and liquor shops were being picketed. For this purpose Gandhiji enrolled women, considering them better able than men to persuade people. Kamala and Betty had joined the Congress volunteers and were engaged in active work of various kinds, including picketing. Great bonfires of British cloth had taken place in every town in India. This was a great shock to me. I did not understand the symbolism, and it seemed wicked that mountains of clothing should be publicly burned when all around one there was nakedness. Gandhiji of course wore a loincloth in order to identify himself with the lowliest in the land, and one understood this great gesture.

But why destroy garments that could be used? However, in this, as in most other things, our family took the lead, with only Mother protesting and I silently abetting her. Cupboards, closets, and storerooms were ransacked. Trucks full of clothes went from our house. I could not bear to see them being taken away, nor would I go to see the public burning. It seemed pure vandalism and the thought of it hurt me. Was it necessary for India's soul, I wondered? Today, looking back, I can see not only the significance but the vital importance of this and other gestures, like the wearing of khadi, which were a decisive way of breaking with the past. At the time I was secretly pleased when Ranjit, having thrown away a great many articles of clothing, refused to give up his Middle Temple blazer and his riding things!

Ranjit's schedule in the past had included a week's shooting in the Central Provinces and other jungles at Easter and at Christmas, and he looked forward to these holidays very much. Now the question arose as to whether it was appropriate for a member of the Congress pledged to nonviolence to go on a shooting trip and, furthermore, to go as the guest of an Indian prince, even though he was an old friend. After some thought we decided to give up such visits in case they were publicly misconstrued.

Another problem in our lives was food. Many people were experimenting with their diet—some merely for the sake of discipline necessary for jail, others because, at that time, it was the proper thing to do. It was all rather a strain on the digestion of those who were used to particular kinds of food eaten at regular hours. Vegetarianism was greatly favoured, and all of us, except for Father and Ranjit, now gave up eating meat. Bhai had long since given up the normal evening meal. Ranjit, torn in two between his admiration of Father's logic and Bhai's idealism, swayed sometimes one way, sometimes the other. He fell ill with severe digestive disorders, and, under doctor's orders, took a holiday and went to stay with friends. There he made a remarkably quick recovery, which he attributed to a diet of teal and quails, since it was the shooting season. This apparently was what his system had been craving for!

But there were more serious problems in our lives than food and dress. Ranjit had left the Bar but so far was not occupied in any way. For a man who had worked hard and been active in many fields, the present life was not only boring, it seriously threatened our domestic peace. Ranjit had joined the Congress and did some work at the Congress office, but there were hours of enforced leisure. One could not go for a ride—our stables had been sold as part of the retrenchment scheme. One could not get a game of tennis because the club was ruled out and the tennis-playing people who had come to Anand Bhawan earlier were no longer on visiting terms with us. In fact, it was a period of emptiness and frustration for Ranjit, and my own existence became increasingly difficult. The people of our own kind who had joined Gandhiji were all in a similar situation. For those who had been assigned an active role in the movement there was enough to do, but for others who did not have specific tasks it was not an easy time.

Gandhiji suggested that Ranjit and I should return to Rajkot and work on the constructive part of the national programme there. So we went to Rajkot, but life now was different from what it had been on my earlier visit. The regulated days of work and sport were over, and, without social relationships and outings, just sitting around was very difficult. At times one did not feel wholly dedicated to the new changes and there was often cause for irritability. Nor was the atmosphere conducive to reading or study of any kind. So we threw ourselves into the suggestion made by Gandhiji.

The programme Gandhiji wanted Ranjit to work on was one that could have been done better by a less intellectual person than Ranjit. It amounted to starting centres in the villages for spinning and weaving, providing the cotton for spinning to as many villagers as possible, and later arranging for the woven material to be bought for sale at the Khadi Bhandars—special shops opened for selling khadi to the public. There was also the task of breaking down the rigid rules of orthodoxy existing in our social structure and bringing about the removal of untouchability. This was one of the basic tenets of Gandhiji's teachings and work, and one on which he had strong feelings. It was to remove discrimination in South Africa that he had originally given up his law practice, and the practice of untouchability, which was discrimination of another kind, was abhorrent to him. 'I should be content,' he said, 'to be torn to pieces rather than let down the depressed classes.' He did not ever move from this stand. Instead, he identified himself in every possible way with the Harijans, as he called them. He adopted a little Harijan girl as his daughter and called her Lakshmi, the name of the goddess of good fortune and wealth.

The treatment given by Hindu society to the untouchables is a blot on the fair name of India, and though much has been changed since Gandhiji began his opposition campaign, the blot has not been entirely removed. Since the time of the Buddha, saints and Hindu reformers have spoken against the evil of caste and untouchability and the need to remove it, yet it has remained. There is a charming story in the Ramayana, the ancient epic poem sacred to Hindus. Rama had been banished from his kingdom for fourteen years' exile and wandered in the forests with his wife Sita and brother Lakshman. During his wanderings he came across a family of untouchables. The young daughter of the family desired greatly to see Rama and she went to him carrying a small basket of berries from her garden. Offering them with an abundance of love she said, 'I had nothing else to bring you, but these are very sweet for I have tasted each one to make sure.' Rama smiled and patted her head, and, taking the basket from her hand, he ate all the berries.

In Rajkot we not only organized spinning and weaving centres but, by working in the villages, we came to know our people and problems we had previously not spent much thought on. We also started schools for the illiterate and developed programmes of all kinds to arouse social conscience and open up opportunities for Harijans and other underprivileged persons in the area. It was very good discipline though often dull work. The fact that our family home became a centre of the Congress constructive programme lent prestige to the work and attracted many workers who may have hesitated to join. We stayed for a year in Kathiawar and gradually found interest and stimulation in the work.

It was customary for a first child to be born in the maternal grandparents' home, and my first confinement took place in Anand Bhawan. Father had a room painted and fitted like a hospital, and instruments to meet every possible contingency were ordered from Calcutta. It was an irony of fate that I should have developed septicaemia and nearly died. In towns like Allahabad the best doctor was usually the civil surgeon, but probably, on account of the growing political tension, he was not approached, and the woman doctor who confined me was not as good as her degrees seemed to indicate. It was a prolonged and very difficult labour, but the baby girl born on January 23, 1923, was a healthy and beautiful one. My parents were disappointed, but 'Nan's baby' was special and the usual celebrations took place. Ranjit and I were happy, and, as his mother had died only a few weeks earlier, Ranjit decided to give the baby a Maharashtrian name his mother had liked. We called her Vatsala, 'Beloved'.

To our lasting sorrow little Vatsala did not live. She died in October of the same year—hardly nine months old. Her death scene is indelibly stamped on my mind as if it had taken place yesterday. Ranjit and I were sitting on either side of her and we knew death was not far away. She had been lying very quiet. Suddenly she turned toward me and looked into my eyes—her own were meaningful and were conveying a message as clearly as if she had spoken. She was saying goodbye. She looked at Ranjit in the same way, and I saw two tears roll down his cheeks. Vatsala died a few minutes later. Little as she was, she was a rare spirit. By losing her we lost something of great value.

◆◆◆

13

Demand for Independence

By the end of 1921 the national movement was expanding and Congress volunteers were coming forward in large numbers to offer civil disobedience. Arrests were the order of the day. Boycott of educational institutions was taking place and some national schools were being started. Law courts were, to some extent, also being boycotted. However, one of the main planks of the noncooperation movement—nonviolence—was being forgotten by the masses. Occurrences of indiscipline and defiance were increasing in various parts of the country and early in 1922 an ugly incident upset Gandhiji very much. In Chauri Chaura, a village in Gorakhpur District of the Uttar Pradesh, a crowd of peasants attacked a police outpost, set fire to it, and killed some constables who were on duty there. Gandhiji's horror at this incident made him suspend the satyagraha movement all over the country. This news came as a blow to many—there were already thousands of people in prison at that time. Father and Bhai, also in jail in Lucknow, could not understand why the behaviour of some villagers, however wrong it had been, should put an end to a national movement. They managed to send Gandhiji, who was out of prison, a message indicating their distress at his action. Gandhiji's reply was sent to me, and during a jail interview I was able to read his letter to Father and Bhai. In this letter Gandhiji explained that if he had not ended the civil disobedience movement the struggle would have lost its character and become a violent one all over the country and that the national cause would prosper as a result of his action, however illogical it seemed.

Gandhiji was arrested in March 1922 on the pretext that he was preaching sedition through his paper *Young India*. He pleaded guilty to the charge and told the English judge who tried him that 'the only course open to you, Mr Judge, is... either to resign your post or inflict on me the severest penalty if you believe that the system and law you are assisting to administer are good for the people.' The judge, Mr Broomfield, said in his summing up, 'It would be impossible to ignore the fact that in the eyes of millions of your countrymen you are a great patriot and a great leader.' The trial was among the famous ones of history, and Gandhiji was sentenced to six years' imprisonment. This was a tremendous shock to the whole country, and Ranjit, who had attended the trial in Ahmedabad, gave us details of the proceedings.

A political controversy of the times was whether the noncooperation movement should continue or if there should now be a change. Should Congress contest the approaching elections to the Legislative Council in Delhi, under the Montagu–Chelmsford Reforms, which had been inaugurated in 1921, and continue the 'fight' from within the Legislature? This issue assumed great proportions and Congressmen were divided into No-Changers and Pro-Changers. Among those in favour of change were men like C.R. Das, the Bengal leader, and Father. On the other side were equally outstanding names—C.R. Rajagopalachari, later to be Governor General of free India, Vallabhbhai Patel, our future Home Minister, Rajendra Prasad, our first President, and many more, including Bhai.

While serving his term in Yeravda prison in Poona, Gandhiji had to have a serious appendectomy. He was moved to a hospital, and after the operation he was released from jail in February 1924, two years after his arrest. He had his convalescence in Juhu, then a small seaside resort near

Bombay. C.R. Das and Father went to see him there to seek his support for their idea of forming a party within the Congress in order to contest the elections. Gandhiji gave his consent to the new party functioning as a separate entity. He had great faith in Father and C.R. Das and regarded this as an experiment, though he felt that it was bound to fail. Thus the Swaraj party was born. Father had not been too well and took the opportunity to stay on in Juhu. My eldest daughter had been born in Bombay a month before. It had been the day sacred to Shiva—the Shivaratri—and we had named her Chandralekha, the Crescent Moon, which is one of the symbols of Shiva. She was all the more welcome because of the loss of our firstborn child. I went to Juhu and after a long time had a brief interval with Father where, after his long discussions with Gandhiji, he could relax in a home atmosphere. Mother and Betty came from Allahabad to be with Gandhiji, but Father soon had to leave to begin the work of forming the new party.

The Swaraj party, of which Father now became leader in the Central Legislative Assembly in Delhi, had unexpected success in the elections and in the Legislature. Father was a born party leader and an outstanding parliamentarian. This was work he understood and enjoyed and in which he found satisfaction. He set a high standard of parliamentary conduct, which was often referred to years later after India had achieved independence. He was admired and loved by his colleagues, especially by the younger members of the party whom he helped to train and many of whom made their mark in free India.

Communal violence broke out during the latter months of 1925 in several cities in the north, including Allahabad, and Gandhiji announced a twenty-one-day fast as penance for what had happened. Leaders of all religious communities rushed to him from all parts of the country, and peace was restored while a formula for better understanding and communal unity was drawn up. I was with Gandhiji when he broke his fast.

Noncooperation as such had, for the time being, been suspended to give a chance to the Swaraj party to function, and the emphasis was on the constructive programme. Congress work was thus transferred to the villages, the spinning wheel became a symbol of the national struggle, and there was a change in the fee necessary for Congress membership; instead of paying four annas (a quarter of the rupee), the applicant had to spin two thousand yards of yarn in order to become a member. The constructive programme consisted of spinning and weaving, working to remove untouchability, fostering Hindu–Muslim unity, and boycotting foreign cloth and other British goods including liquor. I am ashamed to say I hated to spin; I was the only member of my family who hated it. Perforce, because I wanted to remain a member of the Congress, I was obliged to do the necessary quota. Ranjit, on the contrary, liked to spin and said it gave him peace of mind. He produced much more yarn than was required for membership, and we were able to get it woven for various household articles. Bhai's yarn was superb and he too did much more than was needed, and improved as time went on. I still have a sari woven out of his yarn and another given to me by Dr Rajendra Prasad, or Rajen Babu, as we called him.

Ranjit and I had been wanting to go abroad for a short holiday and finally decided to take advantage of the withdrawal of the noncooperation movement to get away for six weeks. We booked our passage by Lloyd Triestino in March 1926. Kamala had not been well, and doctors advised that she should go to Switzerland for treatment. Bhai too was very tired and badly needed a change. Finally we all left India together. Indira, then aged nine, accompanied her parents, but I left two-year-old Lekha with my mother. Ranjit and I had a happy holiday visiting friends in England and going to as many theatres as we could. Then on to France and Germany, where Ranjit literally lived in a world of music. We decided to motor through Italy and take the boat home from there. This was a time when Fascism was on the rise, and everywhere in Rome we heard cries of 'Viva IL Duce,' and the strains of the *Jovineza.* On one occasion we heard Mussolini address a large rally of Black Shirts.

One morning we were in a museum, wandering around in leisurely fashion and absorbing the beauty of our surroundings, when suddenly there was a great deal of coming and going of officials and a hurried closing of all the doors. Everyone was locked in and the guards on duty could give us no explanation. Then one of the other visitors came up to us and said that he thought that Mussolini was to visit the building opposite the museum and perhaps our being locked in was a security measure. As it turned out, Mussolini had been shot at by an Irish woman as he was entering the building. He came out onto the balcony very shortly with a bandage on his nose and gave the assembled crowd the well-known Fascist salute. There was much hand clapping and cheering while we were still locked up. Presently we were released, our passports examined, and, to our amazement, Ranjit and I were put into a police car and taken to the police station. In vain Ranjit explained in good Italian that we were just tourists and not interested in attacking the Duce or anyone else. As the only non-Italians in the museum we were suspect and as such detained for several hours in the police station. In those days Indians carried British passports. Finally we swallowed our pride and telephoned the British Embassy to tell them of our predicament, after which we were released. It was humiliating to have to appeal to the British whom, in theory, we had ceased to recognize! It spoiled the Italian holiday for us.

Ranjit and I had now settled down in Allahabad. His mother had died and the home in Rajkot had been closed up. My second daughter, Nayantara, Star of the Eyes, had been born, and the two babies, though three years apart, kept me busy part of the time. I associated myself with the constructive programme in the town, and Ranjit completely involved himself in this and worked in a group of nearby villages for rural uplift. Our personal life was slightly more peaceful and orderly than it had been for some time.

On the political plane, however, there was neither peace nor order. The year 1928 was remembered with bitterness by hundreds of Indians as the year of the Simon Commission—a commission sent out from England to inquire into the need for constitutional reforms. Unanimously condemned by all political groups, it was met everywhere it went in India with hartals (total suspension of business), demonstrations, and cries of 'Go Back, Simon!' With the exception of a few professional 'loyalists', all sections of the public gave it a wide berth. In the cities it was to visit, processions were prohibited and strict military and police measures taken to 'preserve the peace'. Preparations for peaceful demonstrations had been made by the Congress and the temper of the people was calm. Bhai went to Lucknow where the Simon Commission was due to visit, to join in the demonstration. Large crowds of peacefully demonstrating Congress volunteers were halted by mounted police and beaten mercilessly with batons and truncheons. Many sustained severe injuries, and Bhai experienced for the first time the indignity and pain of a lathi charge. But he was more fortunate than some others. His companion, Pandit Govind Ballabh Pant, was disabled for life by the terrible injuries received then, and Lala Lajpat Rai, the Punjab leader, died as a result of a lathi charge in a protest against the Simon Commission.

The Simon Commission led to the convening of an All-Party Conference at which the drafting of a constitution, with full responsible government, and dominion status were agreed upon. A committee under Father's chairmanship was appointed to draft the principles of the constitution, which was to include a parliamentary form of government with joint electorates. The Nehru Report, as it was called, had to be ratified at the next session of the Congress. This was also held under Father's presidentship in Calcutta in the winter of 1928.

The Calcutta Congress is still fresh in my memory. There was always a good deal of pageantry at a Congress session in those days, including the President's procession, and many forms of entertainments for the delegates. But Calcutta outdid previous sessions both in the enthusiasm it generated and in the entertainment it provided. Subhas Chandra Bose, the hero of young Bengal, was captain of the volunteers. In a smart uniform and on a prancing white horse he led the President's procession. The people of Bengal are lovers of the arts—music and dancing are a part of their lives, just as another part consists of argumentation and a high political consciousness. Some of our great orators have been Bengalis, and they put into their oratory the same emotionalism that they express in their music.

Calcutta was then a city of wealth and sophistication and, to my provincial eyes, it was full of glamour. The whole family, including my new baby, Nayantara, had gone to the Congress session. The children of our family seem to have grown up in the midst of political conventions and meetings, accepting these as part of the normal pattern of life. This especially applied to Indira, because Anand Bhawan had now become the centre for all important meetings of leaders of the country.

Father and C.R. Das had been close personal friends but we had not met the members of the Das family. Now we did so and were drawn to one another. Basanti Devi, Mrs Das, was a lovely woman, and since that first meeting the link between our families has remained firm through the generations.

The main resolution before the Congress at that session was of course the recommendation of the Nehru Report. There had been much discussion and controversy over dominion status, and many of the younger group had wanted a demand for full independence. The report gave an ultimatum to the government to accept the draft resolution for independence in the form of dominion status. If this demand was rejected by the government, the Congress would start a campaign of nonviolent noncooperation with the government, including refusal to pay taxes.

Gandhiji had not, since the Council entry programme—entry by the Swaraj party to the Legislative Council in New Delhi—spoken at a Congress session. He was convinced that nothing would come either from the legislative entry—except a few spectacular victories that would ultimately be meaningless in the context of freedom—or from the present resolution before the Congress.

The period following the Calcutta Congress was one of tension. Severe repression had begun again, arrests were taking place in large numbers, and it was necessary to prepare the people for greater hardships by stepping up the constructive programme. In this Bhai was now wholly involved. He and Father had been in strong disagreement over the Nehru Report, and Bhai wrote later of the mental conflict between him and Father saying 'differences of opinion we had had before, vital differences which kept us in different political camps. But I do not think that at any previous or subsequent occasion the tension had been so great.'

The next session of the Congress was held in Lahore in 1929 under Bhai's presidentship. This year was a landmark in the national movement. The time limit of the ultimatum to the government expired and the Congress voiced the yearnings of the Indian people in the demand for complete independence. A new spirit was abroad, and the solemn pledge taken by the delegates at midnight of December 31, 1929, on the bank of the Ravi river was an unforgettable experience, almost spiritual in its content. Now there was no turning back; we were pledged to the forward march whatever it might cost us. For our family this was the beginning of a deeper involvement in terms of work and prison. Of course we were all very proud, for it was a unique occasion for a son to follow his father in the position of Congress President. Actually all the provinces had elected Gandhiji to be Congress President, but he did not wish to accept and the choice fell on Bhai. This Congress session was attended by the youngest member of the family, my two-month-old daughter Rita, meaning Truth, who alone of my children inherited her great-grandmother's Kashmiri features and hazel eyes, though the auburn hair she was born with turned dark later.

For the first time the Congress session was attended by a group of Pathan volunteers from the North-West Frontier Province, led by their leader, Khan Abdul Ghaffar Khan, or, as he was affectionately known, Badshah Khan. They were tall, stalwart men, fair-complexioned and striking in their baggy khadi trousers and shirts. They called themselves Khudai Khitmatgars, or servants of God, and so totally had this organization dedicated itself to Gandhiji that they had completely renounced violence and were among the outstanding group of those who lived strictly according to the letter as well as the spirit of Gandhiji's teaching. This group was full of high spirits and the enthusiasm of the moment. They were the centre of all eyes. After the midnight pledge these volunteers could not restrain themselves and suddenly began to dance. Soon the Punjab volunteers had joined them, and Ranjit, coming from a land of song and dance, could not be kept away. Even Bhai was dragged into the group and presently, though shy and not uninhibited like the others, he enjoyed himself. The dance was appropriate to the moment and the mood of the night.

January 26 was declared Independence Day, and on that morning every year after the historic Lahore Congress, we foregathered on the upstairs terrace of Anand Bhawan to read the pledge, hoist the Congress flag, and sing the national anthem. In this ceremony every member of the family at Anand Bhawan, which included our servants, was associated, and generally the youngest member hoisted the flag. Even when the elders were in jail the flag was unfurled and the pledge taken by those who remained out, and there was a time when Tara and Rita had to have a flag hoisting by themselves. The whole country observed this day in town and village, and it became customary for arrests to be made on January 26. Men and women gathered together for the public ceremony would be put into police vans and taken off to prison. That is how my own arrest took place later on.

The pledge we took read as follows:

> We believe that it is the inalienable right of the Indian people, as of any other people, to have freedom and to enjoy the fruits of their toil and have the necessities of life, so that they may have full opportunities of growth. We believe also that if any government deprives a people of these rights and oppresses them, the people have a further right to alter it or to abolish it. The British government in India has not only deprived the Indian people of their freedom but has based itself on the exploitation of the masses, and has ruined India economically, politically, culturally, and spiritually. We believe, therefore, that India must sever the British connection and attain Purna Swaraj or complete independence.

◆◆◆

14

Father's Death

The year 1930 was full of action. The Civil Disobedience campaign had been started by Gandhiji on April 6, the first day of National Week observed each year in memory of Jallianwala Bagh. He walked to Dandi, a small seaside village in Gujarat, where he broke the British salt law by making salt from seawater. The Dandi March, as it was called, sent a thrill through the entire country. Gandhiji had begun his march, staff in hand, with a handful of volunteers from his ashram at Sabarmati, but by the time he reached Dandi, some weeks later, hundreds of men and women had joined him. The Salt Satyagraha, as it was named, began all over the country, followed by arrests. Bhai was arrested on April

14 and sentenced to six months' imprisonment. Every day the papers announced names of prominent figures who were being arrested. There were hartals, and processions of protest were brutally attacked by the police. From Peshawar, in the North-West Frontier Province, came the news of firing on crowds at peaceful mass meetings. The fiery Pathan did not retaliate, and this was, by any standards, a miracle. Gandhiji's message of nonviolence not only had reached but had been accepted by him. This incident had a tremendous morale-raising effect on the country, and soon after came the news of a Garhwali regiment's refusal to obey a shooting order on unarmed people. There was pride in our hearts.

Father and Bhai had met Gandhiji during his salt march, and Father had decided to give Anand Bhawan as a gift to the nation. This was done in a simple and rather moving ceremony when Father handed over the old family home to Bhai in his capacity as Congress President. The house was renamed Swaraj Bhawan, meaning Freedom House. It was used for many years as a headquarters for Congress work and as a Congress hospital. During various noncooperation movements it was raided by the police and taken over by the government from time to time. During the Quit India movement in 1942 the Congress flag, which always flew over the house, was replaced by the Union Jack and it was occupied by British soldiers. After Independence it was turned into a hospital and home for abandoned children.

A new house, referred to by Father as 'the cottage', had been designed by him and built in a portion of the grounds. It turned out to be a beautiful residence, with no resemblance to a cottage at all, and was in turn called Anand Bhawan. This new Anand Bhawan became the family home for more than four decades until Indira donated it to the Nehru Memorial Committee in 1970, six years after her father's death.

Sitting at home, caring for my family and not taking part in any of these national activities, I was very restless. The little work I did in the city Congress office was not enough to give me a feeling of participation. It was mainly office work and preparing leaflets telling of national aims. As each item of news about activities in other parts of the country came to us, I felt more and more left out and frustrated.

Gandhiji was arrested in early May. Father's health had not been good, and he had been shouldering a heavy burden and working much harder than his strength would permit. He was arrested in June of that year, together with our friend Syed Mahmud, the day before he was to leave for Mussoorie under doctor's orders. The Working Committee, of which Father was a member and Syed Mahmud the secretary, had been declared an unlawful body. The Congress party organization had a democratic structure. In each area there was a District Congress Committee, and every province had representatives of various districts in the Provincial Congress Committee. The A.I.C.C.—All India Congress Committee—was an elected body with representatives from every province, and the Working Committee was the chief executive body of the party chosen by the Congress President, who was elected annually. Father and Syed Mahmud were sent to Naini Central Prison, across the river from Allahabad, where Bhai had already settled down.

Noncooperation was now in full swing, and both Kamala and Betty were picketing and doing other Congress work. Even Mother occasionally participated. Kamala was actively organizing women's civil disobedience, and the manner in which sheltered women had responded to Gandhiji's call to participate in the national struggle was dramatic. From this time on, more and more women came forward to take responsibility and they did a splendid job.

While these stirring events were taking place at home a Round Table Conference was being held in London. But except for a very small group of people who showed some interest in it, the major focus of attention remained on events in India. The members of the Round Table Conference were men in high places and those neither connected with Congress nor sympathetic with Gandhiji's leadership. They were mostly friends of an earlier era, and it was sad to see them now following this path. There was considerable concern among 'moderate' leaders about the way things were shaping. Two of these, well-known and respected men, Sir Tej Bahadur Sapru and Mr M.R. Jayakar, tried to ease the situation between Congress and the government. For a while these 'peace makers', as they were called by the press, held meetings and discussions suggesting that Congress should cease to noncooperate and government, on their part, agree to a number of conditions. For some time either one or other of these gentlemen went back and forth between the Viceroy and the inmates of Naini Central Prison, where Bhai was. He was still Congress President.

The story of these negotiations is well enough known to all those interested in the various aspects of the freedom movement. I mention it because their outcome was of great importance to our family. Father was really ill—jail was no place for him. Obviously, he would not accept conditional release, and the success or failure of the negotiations could make all the difference—one might say of life and death—to him. There is an incident of this time that is so typical of Father's approach to life that I am tempted to write of it. The negotiations finally led from Naini Prison to Yeravda in Poona where Gandhiji was incarcerated. It was of course not possible for any political decision to be arrived at without consultations with Gandhiji so Father, Bhai, and Syed Mahmud were taken by special train to Poona. The journey was tiring and had a bad effect on Father. The Yeravda jail authorities felt he should have special diet, and the superintendent, an Englishman, asked Father to give him a diet sheet for the duration of his stay in Yeravda so that he could arrange for suitable food. Father said his requirements were simple and he genuinely believed them to be so. However, when this 'simple' menu for the day was given to the superintendent, he was quite astounded. As he said afterward, possibly the Ritz or the Savoy could have supplied it but he really did not know of any place near enough to Yeravda that could provide such food! He was familiar with Gandhiji's diet of goat's milk and orange juice, but the new demand was beyond the poor man's imagination or capacity to deal with!

Father's condition deteriorated on the journey back to Naini, and after several medical examinations by his own and other doctors he was released two and half months after his arrest. Ranjit had already been arrested and was sharing the barrack at Naini with Bhai and Syed Mahmud. His arrest was the result of his association with the report on the firing on the peaceful meeting in Peshawar mentioned earlier. Congress had appointed an inquiry committee to look into the circumstances and results of this firing. Sardar Vallabhbhai Patel was chairman, and Ranjit, secretary, of the committee. Their report, of course, came under the heading of sedition and was the reason for Ranjit's arrest.

It was Gandhiji's custom to correspond with those men and women who had been to jail or done something special in connection with the movement. Soon after Ranjit's arrest, in October 1930, I received his first letter. Translated it reads as follows:

> Chiranjiv Sarup,
> Ranjit has gone to the House of Rest and I feel like writing to you. Ranjit's arrest could not possibly have caused you any uneasiness! When you meet him give him my blessings.
>
> If you are with Father write to me fully about his health.
>
> Blessings to Krishna and Indu.
>
> How is Mother?
>
> Bapu

From jail Ranjit wrote to me:

> October 24, 1930
>
> I have Bhai to initiate me into life here. It amounts to a privilege to be with Bhai and share his life. All this is a

> windfall for me. In fact I entered here quite prepared to fag as a fresher—I found the Master, in the sense in which Christ was one, in Bhai in this strange barrack. He discourses on all subjects, is ever ready to teach all manner of things to everyone with whom he comes in contact, forgetful of his own wants he is always anxiously thinking of the needs of others and yet has more time than anyone else or all of us put together to do the various jobs he does. If you had not known him and perceived so truly his greatness, you could hardly believe any man was capable of so much goodness, gentleness and cheerfulness as Bhai...
>
> I have just heard the sentence passed on Bhai! So that's that! Tell Papa[7] that the Americans look at such things in the light of the story of Jonah and the whale—he came out all right! When Bhai came back [from the trial] I asked him if the judgment in his case had been delivered. He answered casually, 'The date of release is 28th March, 1933'!

Later that year Ranjit wrote from prison:

> I am very happy to hear that Gandhiji has written to you. Please send him my Pranams and my love and tell him that I spin every day regularly and think while spinning over many problems which agitate the minds of men and women these days and try to find a solution in the light of his teachings—sometimes. Also that my spinning is fairly good since I had lessons from Mirabai on how to take care of the charkha and from Bhai on how to prepare the yarn to be placed in the hands of a weaver. I owe many things to Bapu, one of them is the set of letters I have from you during our engagement. It was through him I got the right to correspond with you.

Bhai was released suddenly, and he and Kamala came to Mussoorie to see Father. Mother, Betty, and I were with him. After spending a few days with Father, Bhai returned to

---

7. Motilal Nehru.

Allahabad, and on the return journey he was again arrested and taken back to Naini after a week's absence. This news did not help Father's health, and the shock of hearing some weeks later of Kamala's arrest brought about a distinct deterioration.

Father met death as he had life—gallantly and with a smile. Even when speech and breathing had become difficult and he was in great pain, he had a pleasant word for everyone. He knew he was dying; he also believed that freedom was round the corner. Gandhiji had been released and he had come to Allahabad immediately, as had many other Congress colleagues and old friends, who were with Father up to the time he left us. His lying in state was a spectacle. From far and near people came to pay homage. His funeral took place on the banks of the Ganga in the traditional Hindu way. He was cremated on a pyre of sandalwood, and Gandhiji gave a funeral oration as inspiring as it was beautiful. Women do not as a rule attend funerals, but Mother insisted on going. I do not know where her strength came from at that moment. Participation in the national struggle had aged her and she looked frail, but she was silent, dry-eyed, and the embodiment of all the faith, all the courage, of the Indian woman through the ages. She walked three times with folded hands and bowed head around the pyre, then went up to Gandhiji and took her place by his side. For myself, Father's death left a void that I have never been able to fill.

◆◆◆

15

My First Jail Experience

Nationalism was now a rising tide and the whole country was in its grip. I participated actively in Congress work and was for some time joint secretary, with Lal Bahadur

Shastri, of the City Congress Committee. Noncooperation at this time meant breaking any law and courting arrest. The most popular form was defying the order that prohibited processions. Large processions were organized every few days with flags, slogans, and national songs, led by the leaders of the committee. These processions grew larger and larger as they proceeded through the town to the prohibited area. Here we were faced with the police and military, halted, and asked to return. At this point we would sit down in orderly rows on the street, shouting slogans and singing national songs at the tops of our voices. This situation sometimes went on for hours. Finally, arrests of the leader with a couple of hundred others followed, and the procession dispersed for the day.

The District Magistrate of the time was an Englishman called Bomford. He was much more aggressive than many others of his kind, and the sight of a Congress flag nearly sent him mad. Quite often he used to accompany the police to the place where processions had to be halted. His idea was, and such were his instructions to his subordinates, that flags carried by the processionists should be snatched out of their hands. Every time this attempt was made by the police there was naturally a struggle, ending quite often in the flag being retained by the volunteer carrying it. Many flags were also captured by the police. It was Mr Bomford's proud boast that he had the largest number of captured flags of any official. These were arrayed in his office for all to see!

When Bhai was home between jail spells he used to organize processions in the garden with the children, carrying the national flag and singing the latest song with great gusto. Sometimes the servants joined in to enlarge the procession. Bhai had, from the time Indu was very little and my three even smaller, started a system to train the children to be fearless. He had coined a slogan which was 'A lion cub never cries'. This became a sort of magic sentence in the manner of the Coué system, then very much in vogue, which was a repetition of the sentence, 'Every day in every way I am getting better and better.' The family version was 'A lion cub never cries'—*sher ka baccha rota nahin.* Whenever any child was about to cry this magic formula held the tears back. It had another meaning: We, the freedom fighters, were lions; those who were not helping to turn the British out of India were jackals, and the jackal is a cowardly beast!

The Congress Committee had arranged a panel of names by which an arrested 'leader' was immediately replaced by the next name on the list. These were known as 'dictators' because, in those abnormal times, it was not possible to have proper meetings of the committee to elect a leader, nor was it even possible always to meet because the office was guarded by the police or closed up on government orders. A 'dictator' therefore had full powers to issue orders for noncooperation activities and all Congressmen and women obeyed such commands.

On January 26, 1932, I was the 'dictator' of the Allahabad City Congress Committee and was to preside at the meeting where the Independence pledge was to be taken. The Purshottamdas Park, where the meeting was held, was crowded to capacity with men and boys even sitting on the branches of trees. We knew there would be arrests immediately afterward and, indeed, the police were present in full force. The pledge was taken solemnly and the meeting dispersed. That night, Betty, a colleague, Purnima Banerji, and I, among others, were arrested and taken to the district jail.

The Allahabad District Jail was a collection of mud houses in a large yard enclosed by a dilapidated wall. It was used for under-trials or for those prisoners about to be released after completion of their term in other parts of the province. We were taken to the 'female' section and told to settle ourselves in a long room known as a barrack, with gratings in the wall at intervals of four feet. Through these gratings we looked onto a dreary yard with one gigantic banyan tree in the centre. Under the shade of this tree the matron relaxed and allowed her favourite wardress to massage her. The inmates of this jail were mostly prostitutes, with a sprinkling of those who were charged for petty thefts. Their habits, morals, and language were vivid and obscene. As political under-trials, we were not locked up during the day and were free to do as we pleased within the compound. But as the yard was small and occupied for most of the time by the matron and her satellites, it was preferable to stay inside the freezing cold barrack. Our day ended with lockup at six o'clock, and the long night stretched interminably ahead. The only light came from the flickering wick of a hurricane lantern suspended from the roof, and even if one had wished to sleep, it would have been impossible because of the snoring of the wardress locked in with us and the hourly count of prisoners, which was done in a singsong voice loud enough to get across to the matron's house to assure her that all was well. It was a continuing nightmare.

After three days of such confinement, there was a comic opera trial and we were each sentenced to one year's rigorous imprisonment. In addition, I was fined fifteen hundred rupees or six months' imprisonment in lieu of the fine. Congress policy forbade the payment of fines, so my sentence amounted to eighteen months' imprisonment.

The convicting magistrate recommended to government the classification to which a prisoner was entitled. Politicals were divided into A and B classes, and C Class was reserved for ordinary criminals until, at a later stage in the movement when the numbers of persons courting imprisonment had increased beyond the expectations of the authorities, they were herded indiscriminately with ordinary convicts. At the time of our arrest some attention was still paid to classification. This was done on grounds of one's social and financial status. Sometimes a university degree was considered. The magistrate who tried us was new to the town and extremely nervous. He had never before had to deal with women politicals, and my sister and I, because we had the Nehru name, were an embarrassment and a problem to the poor man. He wanted to give us every advantage. We had a social position and, he presumed, a suitable bank balance. He was not sure if we had university degrees. The clerk of the court was hurriedly sent round to ask, and when we declined to give any information, the magistrate entered his comment as follows: 'Recommend for privileges of Class A as, besides having a high social position, they are probably graduates of a foreign university'!

Our transfer to Lucknow, where our prison term was to be served, took place one bitterly cold midnight. No previous intimation was given and we had already gone to bed when the matron, accompanied by several wardresses, came hurrying into the barrack and told us we were to leave immediately for an unknown destination. In a few minutes we had changed and followed her into the main office. The superintendent of police was waiting to drive us to a wayside station from which we were to entrain for Lucknow. This was done to avoid a demonstration of sympathy at the central railway station. Mr Measures, the police superintendent, was an Irishman with many of the charming qualities of his countrymen, and these came to his rescue on occasions when, in the course of his duty, he overstepped the dictates of prudence or of common humanity, for he was equally likely to err on either side. On this particular evening he had obviously come straight from some festivity at the club and was in good spirits, which we found irritating. The drive in his open automobile was the fastest I have ever had. We raced at amazing speed through the deserted streets, reaching ahead of time the wayside station where we were to entrain. Political prisoners accepted the discipline imposed on them, so were not strictly guarded. It was cold and I walked up and down the footpath alongside the railroad track. Suddenly I saw a dim shape creeping up the embankment; the first figure was joined by a second and a third. By the time I reached the spot, the place was crowded and our guards were vainly trying to form a barrier between us and the townspeople who, having heard that we were being spirited away, had come to say goodbye. When the train arrived, the place was crowded and cries of Jai! rent the air. Garlands of flowers were piled into our hands or thrown at us over the heads of the guards and policemen who formed a ring round us. The passengers on the train put out their heads to see who the political prisoners were, and some joined in the shouts of greeting as we were recognized. It was a triumphant send-off.

The overnight journey passed without incident and in the early hours of a cold morning we found ourselves in the outer office of the Lucknow Central Prison. After considerable delay, while our clothes and books were examined and we were made to sign numerous papers, we were taken to the 'Female Ward', which was a few hundred feet down the road beyond the male prison. Later, this little walk became a welcome break and gave us a glimpse of the outside world, but on this first occasion we were too excited and engrossed in the new experience to recognize any possible advantages in the situation. This prison was reserved for juveniles—girls between the ages of fourteen and eighteen. Those above this age served their terms in other parts of the province. Part of the prison had now been allotted for the use of the politicals with A classification. The Bs were in a separate yard on the other side. The criminals, or Cs, were again separate. None of the groups were allowed to mix with one another in the beginning, but later rules were relaxed for A and B categories.

Our new home was already full when we arrived, and within a fortnight our number rose to forty. We were packed into a space meant for half that many. The small iron beds were placed in rows facing each other with a narrow passage in between. We each had a stool and a tin box containing the few articles of clothing allowed under the prison rules. At the far end of the barrack, opposite the entrance, was a raised platform with a hole in the centre. It served as a latrine after lockup. A curtain slung between two poles gave a semblance of privacy, but nothing could be done about the stench, which was often overpowering. No one wanted to sleep next to the toilet and there were bitter arguments over this. Finally, my cousin Uma Nehru, who was generally loved and respected, persuaded us that the disabilities like the privileges must be shared, and we adopted a system of rotation, sharing the good and bad part of the barrack. This was a far cry from our homes and I felt trapped and very miserable.

In order to retain some sense of proportion, I reminded the inmates of the barrack of a story Bhai often repeated. It concerned a good man who feared God, loved his neighbours, and tried to do his duty. He was very poor and lived in a one-room shack. His highest ambition was to build a house in which he and his family might live in comfort.

In the same village there lived a holy man, and each morning the poor villager went to perform small acts of service in the hope of getting a reward. But the seasons passed and nothing happened. Grown desperate, the villager could remain silent no longer. With folded hands he begged the sadhu to intercede with God so that his modest ambition might be realized. The holy man asked the villager how large his family was.

'We are seven,' came the reply, 'myself, my wife, and five children, and there are also six goats and a cow.'

'Where do the animals live?' asked the Sadhu.

'They are tied, out in the open.'

The Sadhu thought for a while and finally said: 'Look, my good man, tonight when you go home, take all your animals into the room with your wife and children and keep them there.'

The man was bewildered, but, believing in the holy man, he did as he was told.

Two days later he went to the Sadhu and said:

'I cannot tell you how we suffered by following your advice. The animals took up all the space and my wife and children could not sleep. Furthermore, the smell is so bad that we shall surely die if we are confined in this way.'

The Sadhu advised that the cow should, that night, be tied up outside as before.

Two days passed and the poor man came again.

'We are still very unhappy,' he complained. 'The goats stink and make a mess and take up space.'

'Put out the goats too,' said the Sadhu. The animals were returned to their old place. When the man next visited the Sadhu he said, 'You are indeed a wise man. My room is clean and bright and I am content!'

Unhappily, though the story made us laugh, we continued to be very discontented with our lot.

◆◆◆

16

Life in Prison

In his first letter from jail Bhai wrote: 'Prison is the best of universities if only one knows how to take its courses. Physically, of course, one has the chance of regular and simple living, mentally its effect is still more noteworthy. Our age is the age of indifference. People have no real beliefs left, nothing sacred, nothing worthwhile almost, and so we suffer from ennui and life itself becomes a burden. Well, jail gives that back to us to some extent and we begin to appreciate the little things which we hardly noticed before, and the enjoyment of life becomes keener. So three cheers for jail.'

Ranjit had been more practical in his approach, and as soon as he began his first jail term he wrote: 'If you are thinking of coming to jail you might plan beforehand what you propose to do to spend your time exactly as if you were planning to go to the Fjords and the Land of the Midnight Sun, or journeying to Europe by the overland route and the desert via Damascus! It will save you much time and you can start your physical and mental improvement immediately you are locked up!'

The jail-going programme was taken as an opportunity to adjust our minds and bodies and get the rest we needed to work more effectively after our release. Ranjit and I had decided that when our turn for arrest came we would make going to jail into a sort of game for the children. For them this must be a normal occurrence, to be taken in their stride. They were used to hearing about arrests, but 'Papu' was closer, and when the first warrant for arrest came and a police search began, the unpleasantness of the situation had to be minimized. It was nearly teatime on the day of Ranjit's first arrest in 1930, and we knew the search would take an hour or more, so Ranjit suggested a tea party for the children. Immediately preparations began. Fresh flowers from the garden were brought in to make the room look festive and favourite tea snacks were hurriedly prepared in the kitchen. A chocolate cake was sent for from our local confectioner, Barnetts, and all was bustle and activity. Tara and Rita worked with me while Lekha went to help her father pack the few personal articles that could be taken with him. There was no time to think or feel sad. We had a hilarious tea party—telling jokes, asking riddles, and, every now and then, Ranjit throwing in a word or two about the necessity for separations because these were part of the discipline all soldiers of freedom must observe. Because of the atmosphere in which they had lived the girls had no difficulty in accepting this idea. I was the only unhappy person in that small gathering, tense with the strain of keeping up appearances in front of the police and joining in the gaiety of the 'tea party'.

Our efforts paid big dividends because never in our home was there any fear of police searches or jail going. It was part of the way one lived. Many years later, when Tara wrote her first autobiographical book, the name *Prison and Chocolate Cake* was almost inevitable.

In spite of the advice I had had from Bhai and Ranjit I found that it takes a long time to get over the pinpricks of prison life and benefit from the doubtful advantages it offers.

We lived according to a set of rules and regulations that bore no relation to our actual needs. The endless dos and don'ts caused friction with the authorities and often led to open defiance on our part. Most of us were sentenced to rigorous imprisonment, which meant we could receive remission for work well done and also for good conduct. 'Labour' in the Lucknow jail was twisting long strands of jute into lengths of rope. It looked easy enough, but very few of us could continue with it because our hands became completely lacerated and, in any case, it was impossible to fulfill the day's quota. Soon the authorities let us give this up, and we were allowed to choose between weaving, helping the matron with her registers, or looking after the children of the convicts.

The day took care of itself and we learned to use our time to some purpose cooking our meals, reading, writing, and walking in the prison yard or trying to grow a few flowers in the stony soil. But with the coming of darkness our troubles began. From six in the evening until six the following morning we were locked inside the barrack. Each one had a small hurricane lantern, which did not permit of much reading, and the nights seemed interminable. Forty women belonging to different social groups with entirely different backgrounds were not suited to a community life in such restricted circumstances. I soon discovered that I was Indian only by fact of birth. My thoughts, my way of living, my eating and sleeping habits, were all different from those of my co-prisoners, and all these placed a barrier between us. What seemed important to me was negligible to them, and the things over which they wanted to create issues appeared trivial to me. Among our group were two ladies from one of our great families, the Malaviyas. They belonged to the period when caste and class had strict meaning and they continued to adhere rigidly to the letter of Hindu orthodoxy, fashioning their lives, even in jail, after the conservative pattern of their homes. They suffered endlessly in consequence and the rest of us suffered from the effects of their irritation. I do not know what urge led them to participate in a movement, the whole purpose of which was to break down caste barriers and create a new social and political order. We had also with us Prabhavati, the wife of Jayaprakash Narayan. I had known her for a long time. She was a sweet, unsophisticated young woman, and we became close to each other in jail.

Once a fortnight, A Class prisoners could receive and send a strictly censored letter. Here the personal whim of the jail censor was allowed full play, and sometimes whole sentences, completely innocent of political innuendo, were heavily scored out. During this first prison interlude such things were frustrating and made me very unhappy.

A Class political prisoners were also allowed to receive a visit from a near relative for thirty minutes in the jail office. A small article of food such as a loaf of bread, a cake, some fruit, or a pot of jam was allowed, according to the whim of the matron. These meetings were most unsatisfactory. One could not embrace or kiss or even sit close to those who came to visit and the presence of a jail official inhibited one from speaking of personal matters.

In a letter to a woman friend I wrote: 'Jail is a good experience but it has its drawbacks, the greatest perhaps is the lack of privacy. There are all the disadvantages of married life with none of its compensations, and nerves are apt to get frayed.'

A year is a long period of time, and the inner resources that came to our rescue in later imprisonments were still undeveloped. In my own case the personal problem outweighed those created by jail life. During the excitement of public meetings and arrests there had been no time for quiet thinking. I had not allowed myself a moment to consider whether my decision to take a more active part in the struggle would be harmful to my children's interest. One knew, of course, that prison was the inevitable result of political work and that prison terms could extend to two years or more, but the emotional wave which was sweeping the country had me in its grip. I was swept along with the tide, a willing victim. It was not possible to think logically. 'Sacrifice' was the key note of the moment, a dangerous word that dulled the mind more effectively than any drug. It was a long time before one realized that 'sacrifice' was often a cloak for many actions that did not always stem from the highest motives. Many wore it to hide what lay beneath. It was a period when mass feelings were artificially stimulated, and many people—I among them—imagined ourselves instruments of freedom in the hands of Gandhiji. I write frankly because I have never quite forgiven myself for that first jail term which broke up my home when my children most needed its security and comfort. To stay at home and look after them would have been dull. Perhaps I was envious of my friends who had broken away from their ties and placed the burden of their personal responsibility on others; perhaps I had a too-lenient husband who seldom, if ever, interfered with my decisions. Whatever the reason, I am now sure that I acted selfishly, thinking in vague terms of personal political achievements rather than the satisfaction I could have gained through domestic duty honestly performed. Any one of or all these reasons together may have driven me toward the final choice, but I had no argument to still my conscience in those long dark hours in prison when sleep would not come.

I shall not pretend that this state persisted. Gradually, the urgent need to adapt oneself to the new conditions, and my own temperament, which always demanded complete involvement with any situation in which I found myself, helped me to snap out of this self-pitying attitude. Prison was a challenge. The British were not going to crush our spirit, let them try their hardest. It would be fun to test oneself and come out of the ordeal strengthened. With this approach came the desire for a planned life with exercise for the body and mind alike. I had regularly practised yogic exercises and I now resumed them. I also found reading a few pages from the *Bhagavad Gita* a mental discipline, helping to keep things in perspective.

Popular jail reading among the educated were the French and Russian revolutions and Gibbon's *Decline and Fall of the Roman Empire.* The majority of the women did not know English, and their reading was limited to an occasional Hindi periodical or to daily recitations from the Ramayana. In order to create a common interest, we all participated in chanting the Ramayana every day. This helped to bring us closer together. My reading that year consisted of Vivekananda, Plato, Saint Augustine, Thompson's *Rise and Fulfilment of British Rule in India,* Dickens, Shakespeare, an anthology of Oxford verse, and a great deal of Chinese history.

Across the high wall that separated the 'female' section from the men's prison were our male colleagues. There could, of course, be no communication between us, but very soon the men found ways and means of letting us know who was on the other side. They always joined in a common prayer before lockup, followed by a hymn and a national song. As there were a great many of them, their voices came over to us very clearly. In the national song, words were substituted to indicate the presence or absence of a particular person and other hints were conveyed so we knew who had been transferred and who remained. This was only possible because the warders were extremely ignorant men. Our own evening prayer had to be conducted at some distance from the dividing wall, under the hawk's eye and ear of the matron, so nothing similar was possible. Later the men arranged to throw a newspaper over the wall every day. This was done during the afternoon when the matron had gone home and the wardresses were having their siesta under the tree on the far side of the yard. One of our number would be on the lookout and dart out to retrieve the paper before it was spotted by any authority. Very occasionally a special message was enclosed. It added spice to the otherwise monotonous routine. The wardresses in our prison were ignorant, vulgar, incompetent. They supplemented their meagre salaries by acting as procuresses. They were in close touch with every brothel in the town, and more than one girl in my time was sold at the jail gate on the day of her release if no relative came to claim her. Everybody knew about this all the way from the matron and superintendent to the District Magistrate, but no effort was made to stop it. The wardresses could be easily bribed and we did not hesitate to do so, once we became hardened to jail life. I had letters posted and received clippings and even newspapers from outside for very small sums of money. One was not allowed to keep money but arrangements with a friend outside were always possible. This was conduct unbecoming a true satyagrahi, but I am afraid I indulged in it with a clear conscience.

The two events that broke up the monotony of the month were the weekly inspection of the female ward by the superintendent, and the fortnightly recording of weights.

The inspection took place on Monday mornings. All through Sunday the yard was a hive of activity, and even the matron condescended to remain on duty most of the day. The girls were released from their normal labour and a great sweeping and cleaning went on. The yard was a sea of dust and smelt horribly of the tar put on the gratings. All articles not permitted by the rules were hurriedly removed to places of safety. The convicts' clothes were checked, their tin bowls and mugs polished, and their bedding arranged in neat rolls in front of the space allotted to them in their barrack. An extra set of prison clothing was placed on top for inspection. This consisted of a skirt of very thick rough handwoven material with a blue band running through and an ill-fitting jacket with a veil of the same thick material. This was the standard uniform, but what the girls actually wore on other days was a pair of shorts and an abbreviated bodice. These were made of condemned material given by the matron for favours rendered, and, whenever possible, brassieres were smuggled in and sometimes supplied by the political prisoners. The wearing of a brassiere was especially forbidden and when a girl was caught, her punishment was more severe than the offence merited. The girls longed to have brassieres and would give up their weekly ration of oil or soap in exchange for one.

Sunday evenings we went to bed exhausted—the convicts, because of the extra work, the beatings, and the abuse that had been their share; we, because the dust and noise had reduced our capacity for endurance.

Monday mornings dawned with a sense of excitement which, after a few weeks of confinement, communicated itself to us. We saw the great door in the yard open and had a glimpse of the road beyond. Even a postman on his bicycle seemed to be an exciting object. There was also the possibility that if the superintendent was in a good mood he might let fall a bit of news. This hope was, however, rarely fulfilled. The door clanged open. The head wardress announced in a high, piercing voice that His Honour the Superintendent approached and in he stepped, smartly turned out in uniform, followed by innumerable minions, also uniformed and spruce. The matron led the way to the convict barracks where the girls were lined up, decently clad, with downcast eyes. Who could possibly guess that within a few minutes of the superintendent's departure the air would be rent asunder with their shrill laughter and vile abuse hurled at authority, while they mimicked or caricatured with considerable skill the gentleman who had just left? The inspection was intended to give the girls an opportunity to make complaints, but I never heard of anyone speaking though the matron frequently used the occasion to demand that punishment beyond her own jurisdiction be inflicted on some unhappy offender. The political prisoners were inspected last and with little relish. The superintendent could never be sure of our mood and always stepped out of our barrack as quickly as possible.

A more important event was the recording of weights. Long before the appointed hour, the girls were in a state of excitement amounting almost to hysteria in anticipation of the impending approach of the two male convicts who carried the primitive prison scales and adjusted them in the yard. A handsome young doctor weighed the girls and filled in their charts. Male officialdom that came on Mondays was far removed from their lives, but here were men of their own kind whom they could understand and, even though no conversation was permitted, the thrill of proximity could not be denied. The girls were hungry for men and made no effort to disguise the fact.

Quick medical aid was impossible in jail. One morning I woke up with a toothache that grew steadily worse. Toward noon, some oil of cloves was produced by the matron but did no good. All night the pain continued to worsen and in the morning I insisted that I should be allowed to see a dentist. This simple request fell on the prison like a bomb. There was no dentist on the prison staff and the visit to a man from outside could not be allowed. My face by now was swollen beyond recognition and I demanded to see the superintendent. After some insistence on my part he promised to get government sanction for me to go to a dentist. But here we encountered another obstacle. The government had moved to Nainital for the summer and, since it was a Saturday afternoon, the offices were closed. Therefore nothing could be done until Monday. I was so angry I forgot my pledge of nonviolence and threatened the jail authorities with dire consequences as soon as the Congress came into power, which I announced firmly and with conviction would be sooner than our jailers realized. Finally, after being made to sign a document promising to pay the charges, a personal phone call was put through to the Governor's secretary. As a result, orders for a visit to a dentist were issued at once, and on Sunday morning the superintendent took the matron and me in his car, followed by four armed policemen in the jail van, to have the offending tooth attended to. The dentist was a man of imagination and prolonged the treatment as long as he dared. I had three outings before my tooth was declared cured.

I was released two months before my sentence ended because I had earned marks for 'good conduct', and one fine morning matron came to the barrack to tell me I must be ready to leave immediately as a car was waiting outside for me. Two of my colleagues had been released some days previously and my sister had also left. But Prabhavati was still there and I hated the idea of leaving her. However, there was nothing to be done, so I hurriedly packed my few belongings and went to the jail office where my release papers were signed.

In Allahabad I learned that Mother was in Poona. My three girls were there too in a small private school started by a young and dedicated nationalist couple, the Vakils. It was a school run mainly for children of national workers, and we had come to know of it when Indira had been sent there. So I proceeded to Poona.

It was good to see the children again. Rita, the youngest, had completely forgotten me in the sixteen months of our separation. Lekha, being older and having had more experience of the national movement, had adapted to life away from home. But Tara was a child who needed a home and parents, and she had been most unhappy and had fretted constantly for me. I was shocked to see how she must have suffered, and now I suffered because of what I had done to the children. To this day I cannot forgive myself. On the day we were to return home there was a dramatic scene at the railway station. Rita refused to leave Mrs Vakil and clung to her, screaming all the way down the platform to our coach. It was as if she were being kidnapped and it was most embarrassing for me. Once in our compartment Lekha wisely suggested exploring the lunch basket, and a chicken sandwich helped to stop the screaming. At three years food is an important factor in bringing solace!

◆◆◆

17
Family Affairs

Betty was married in October 1933 to Raja Hutheesing, barrister-at-law, who belonged to a well-known industrialist family of Ahmedabad. Mother had been ill for some time and the movement was on, with many colleagues in jail, so the wedding was very simple. The ceremony was a civil one, and Bhai injected a new note by having invitations printed in Hindustani written in the Roman script. There was quite a lot of adverse comment, as those were still days when any departure from tradition was unacceptable. After the wedding Betty and Raja made their home in Bombay.

Kamala had for some time been wholly involved in political work and was a recognized leader in her own right in the province. Her health, however, was not equal to the strain of such an active life. Early in 1934 Bhai was suddenly arrested again, this time on a Calcutta warrant, and he was imprisoned in the Alipore Jail in Calcutta. This event did not of course help Kamala's condition, which continued to cause anxiety. Under doctors' orders she was taken to a sanatorium in Bhowali in the Kumaon hills, and eventually Bhai was transferred to Almora Jail, where he was nearer to her. Later she was advised to seek treatment in Europe, and she went to a sanatorium in Badenweiler in the Black Forest. Indira, then a student at Shantiniketan, Rabindranath Tagore's university, accompanied her. By September 1935 Kamala's condition was so much worse that Bhai was released from Almora Jail and left immediately for Badenweiler. Except for brief visits to Indira, in school in Bex, or to London, he stayed with Kamala until she died in Lausanne in February 1936. Kamala was too young to die. Marriage had flung her into a bewildering lifestyle she could not understand. But the national movement provided her with opportunities to express and fulfill herself.

She was a brave woman and in her short life she made a valuable contribution to India's freedom.

In memory of Kamala, a maternity hospital was built in Allahabad. It was a beautiful modern building, and Gandhiji delivered the address at the official inauguration in 1940. We had been fortunate in getting a brilliant and dedicated young woman, Dr Vatsala Samant, as medical superintendent, and a fine band of young nurses and doctors. Treatment to the poor was free. In the beginning there was amazement that a free hospital should have so many comforts—electric fans in the wards, nourishing food, and the best equipment. The women who came were themselves a little frightened, expecting some snag. But when healthy babies were born and women who had suffered from a variety of ailments were cured, the Kamala Nehru Memorial Hospital began to be popular. Some paying beds were added, and in a few years it had acquired a reputation for service where there was also concern and tenderness for those who came. I was secretary of the hospital for the first year and on its board thereafter. And this was among the first hospitals in India where birth control advice and methods were available. Every woman who came for her delivery, who had had a son and was now expecting her third child, was asked if she would be willing to have a tubectomy performed. At first the answer was invariably no and frequently the husbands were very angry. But through the years this changed, partly because there was no publicity and also because women, and men too, realized the need for smaller families. There were of course a number of women who did not agree, but the attempt to convert them in their own interest continued. It was not possible to teach the village women who came to the hospital the use of contraceptives, nor were the contraceptives at that time cheap enough for villagers and the underprivileged to buy. The problem of planned parenthood is mainly a matter of education, and until it is viewed from this angle no number of pills or any other method is going to make a dent in the growth of the population. All these years later, when much work has been done by the government and private institutions alike, we are still faced with opposition because people who need it are not educated enough in the right way.

I had corresponded with Margaret Sanger since my days on the Municipal Board and now invited her to visit India. She had been thinking about it and her own association had some plans for her to tour various countries. She visited Allahabad, where she was our guest at Anand Bhawan, and a friendship developed between us which I valued. Gandhiji had been angry with me for asking Margaret Sanger to come to Allahabad to lecture. He was opposed strongly to artificial methods of birth control, believing only in self-control. In his view intercourse was only proper if children were desired. Knowing his antagonism to her thinking and her work, Margaret Sanger visited him. The interview was an interesting one but neither was able to convert the other!

Domestic problems were now catching up with me and could no longer be ignored. The children were growing fast and I did not want to leave them to the mercies of ayahs or Anglo-Indian nannies. The school problem also had to be decided before it was too late. The English medium schools at Allahabad at the time were the convent schools or those run by missionaries. The standard of the Indian-language schools was poor. The local convent did not prove satisfactory and all three girls hated it. Indira had been in school in Switzerland, and at one time Ranjit and I—mostly I—thought we might send the two older girls there. The disadvantage in this arrangement was that we had no idea when we might be able to see them, for, as the national movement developed, the chances of leaving India grew more and more remote. After long deliberation we decided against this. About this time we met Dr Allan Parker, the principal of an American Methodist school called Woodstock, in Mussoorie. He suggested the girls might go to Woodstock for a trial. The advantages were that the school was coeducational, and this is what we wanted, but the main point in its favour was that Indian children were the equal of any other child, and the American teachers were in sympathy with the freedom movement and respected our leaders. In other English schools, where all subjects were taught through the medium of the English language and which were of course subsidized by the government, there was constant conflict for the Indian children who refused to sing the British national anthem and salute the Union Jack. There were so many other irritants for which children were punished. We decided on Woodstock and were never sorry. Our children were happy and, far from being discriminated against for belonging to a nationalist family, they were welcomed and soon felt very much at home in their new surroundings.

During the period the girls were at Woodstock I had my first contact with American missionaries. I would like to pay a tribute to the fine men and women I came to know who, in a number of cases, are still my friends. When we think of a particular country we are apt to judge it by its politicians and its policies, forgetting that the real people, those who are true representatives of a nation's traditions and way of life, are among those whom one does not easily meet. Among the missionaries there were dedicated people serving in remote corners of the country, unmindful of difficulties and not seeking rewards or recognition. It is my good fortune to have met many such, whose selfless labour has enriched India.

Sometime later we felt the need of a responsible governess and were looking around for the kind of person we wanted. We discovered her in a Danish lady who had been working as secretary to the noted scientist, Sir Jagdish Chandra Bose, who had just died. Anna Ornsholt was devoted to India and did not want to leave the country. We met and liked her and the liking was reciprocated. She joined the family, became Tante Anna to the children, and looked after them until the girls left for college several years later. Even then she did not go back to her country but remained in our family, finally settling down in the Nilgiris in South India, our loved and valued friend until she died.

After Anna joined us the girls ceased to be boarders at Woodstock. We rented a cottage near the school, and for some years this was their home from March to December. They now were day scholars at Woodstock and the arrangement was satisfactory. Ranjit and I visited them as often as we could and they were able to have a home life. The family consisted of the three girls, Anna, Tangle, the beloved Cairn terrier, and Tulsi Ram, our cook. I mention him because he became the buffer between the girls, whom he adored, and Tante Anna, of whom he did not approve. Tante Anna was a vegetarian and according to Tulsi ate very extraordinary things like nasturtium leaves and 'vegetarian' fish and tried to convert the girls, who were accustomed to a meat diet. I was constantly receiving letters from him inspired by Rita, pointing out that they refused to eat a lunch of raw vegetables and cottage cheese and were starving! Even poor Tangle, I was told, was being made into a vegetarian! Tulsi's comments were always amusing, and he felt if the children wanted something they should have it. Their favourite dishes were smuggled to them and, like most Indian servants, he spoiled them thoroughly. Fortunately Tante Anna soon accepted the inevitable and let the girls have the diet they preferred though she herself remained a health faddist to the end.

While Bhai was in the Almora Jail, Ranjit was able to have an interview with him. From Almora he went to neighbouring Binsar, a little hill town famous for its view of the beautiful sunrises over the Nanda Devi range of the Himalayas. On the way to Binsar he saw an estate built by a former English commissioner in the last century. This English country house, surrounded by a fruit orchard, was in a sad state of neglect and the property was for sale. Ranjit was much struck by the extravagant beauty of the setting and the potential of this estate, called Khali. He decided to buy it and use it for family holidays as well as a recreation camp for Congress workers. He named it 'Ritusamhar'—the Pageant of the Seasons, after a lyric poem of the same name by Kalidasa, the classic Sanskrit poet of the AD fifth century after Christ. Ranjit loved Khali and spent whatever time he could spare from his political work in developing it into a working fruit orchard and a centre for neighbouring villagers to bring their hand-spun woolen yarn for sale. He experimented with hens, bees, and wheat, and when we went to Khali we ate our own produce. For the children, some of the happiest childhood memories are of times spent in Khali. For Bhai, too, this became a refuge in the very brief intervals he could get away from work or jail. He loved the mountains and the simple life of Khali, and his visits, infrequent though they were, gave him health and enjoyment.

It was near Khali that Uday Shankar, the well-known dancer, decided to build a dance academy. Up to that time dancing was still an unacceptable art for girls of good family. Uday Shankar wanted to break down this thinking, and received encouragement from Bhai who admired his dancing. The trouble arose when he tried to acquire a piece of land for his academy. The Chief Minister of Uttar Pradesh, Pantji, was a most conservative man and did not approve of a school of dance for girls of 'good family'. I was able to play a small part in persuading him to let Uday Shankar have the land and build on it. The Uday Shankar Culture Centre was not far from Khali, and Tara and Rita were among the first pupils enrolled in its summer course. The centre flourished and gave an opportunity to many boys and girls to break tradition and enjoy the varied cultural facilities offered.

◆◆◆

18

The Municipal Board

Congressmen and women were allowed to seek election to municipal and district boards and try to improve civic life. In the mid-thirties in Allahabad the candidates were Dr Kailash Nath Katju, an eminent lawyer and a personal friend of ours, K. D. Malaviya, also a friend and until recently Cabinet Minister in the government, Saligram Jaiswal, Lal Bahadur Shastri, Ranjit, myself, and others. We secured a handsome majority.

Work in the Municipal Board was both welcome and interesting. The board consisted of forty elected members and one woman nominated by government. The lady at this time was Pratibha Banerji, a prominent social worker whose husband was a professor at the Allahabad University.

The City Fathers sat round a large table at meetings. Some of them had been there for years and were rather rigid in their attitudes—fortunately Congress members were in the majority. The seat allotted to me was between two old gentlemen who, quite obviously, were women haters as well as being anti-Congress. It was an unpleasant experience, and after some manoeuvering I managed to arrange to sit between Ranjit and Lal Bahadur. I am afraid I did not feel like the emancipated young woman people imagined me to be and Dr Katju, the chairman of the Municipal Board, teased me unsparingly about this.

I was elected chairman of the Education Committee, a position held much earlier with great success by my cousin, Uma Nehru. This committee was controlled by the conservative elements who had a vested interest in it. I came to my first meeting full of enthusiasm and bright ideas, but soon discovered that wherever else my ideas might have been needed, it was not in the Education Committee. A more narrow-minded, backward group of men I had never met before. Hindu and Muslim alike, all belonged to a feudal age. Their ideas on education were vague, and one and all they disapproved of the education of girls though they could not, under the rules, abolish the few existing primary schools. Had it not been for the fact that Congress members were in the majority on the committee, one would not have been able to make any changes. The buildings of the municipal schools were almost dilapidated and ill ventilated. The teachers were so ill paid that they were barely able to keep alive. Their looks told the story of their life more vividly than any words could have done. It was not possible for them to be interested in their work as their main preoccupation was in trying to keep out of the moneylenders' clutches. The superintendent of schools wielded great power, and it was to him rather than to the committee that the teachers had to look. He could manoeuvre transfers and dismissals, keeping the committee in the dark about the real state of affairs. He could and did do a great deal more.

On my first visit of inspection, my surprise and concern at the appalling conditions were equalled only by the shock of seeing how subservient the teachers were to the superintendent and how he, in turn, grovelled before me.

The Congress coming to the Municipal Board had raised the people's expectations, and it was hoped that the party would implement the Election Manifesto at an early date, but speed is one of the intangibles in India. One speaks of doing things quickly, but when the time comes a nice comfortable pace is adopted. We did not wish to get caught up in this way, and when opportunities came we were eager to get as much done as possible before some political incident forced us out of office.

Immediately after assuming charge I insisted on visiting all the primary schools. The superintendent was distressed and said I was showing a lack of faith in him and the veracity of his reports. I remained firm and insisted on a schedule being planned and began my visits.

After a quick inspection of schools, I decided to meet the teachers. They had so many legitimate grievances that one could not expect cooperation from them unless they felt they were respected as individuals and that those at the top had some concern for their future. This idea was frowned upon by the committee and most vehemently opposed by the superintendent. Did I not understand, the argument went, that some of these men were frustrated people with no manners—they might be rude—they might create a situation I could not handle, and then where would my prestige as chairman be? I did not wish to waste time in arguments, and even while the committee was still using its powers of persuasion on me, I issued an invitation for small groups of teachers to come and meet me at Anand Bhawan, beginning on the following Sunday. The meeting was successful. Nobody was rude nor was there any misbehaviour. I received nothing but politeness and the people who came seemed pleased to have been asked. Problems were discussed quietly and frankly and I am sure the men went away with the same feeling they left with me, that the meeting had been worthwhile. Encouraged by this, I continued these meetings throughout the period I functioned as chairman of the committee. The poor municipal teacher was made to feel he was a person and the committee was interested in his problems. We could not do all that was required to improve conditions and bring security into their lives, but enough was achieved to prove that we understood and sympathized. I have retained a sense of gratitude toward these men for the friendship and cooperation they gave me so ungrudgingly.

Having established contact with the men teachers, I informed the superintendent that I wished to meet the women and that his presence would not be necessary at the interviews. This raised a storm. The superintendent said it was his duty to point out that the women teachers came from a very low social group and many of them were 'morally' not the sort of women I should mix with.

The die-hard members of the committee put their opposition in a different way. The poor women, child widows and persons from underprivileged homes, would not know what I was talking about; our backgrounds were wholly dissimilar; by inviting them to my home I was giving them the wrong ideas, and more of this. But I held my ground and the teachers came. These meetings were less easy than the ones I had had with the men. The women were suspicious of me—nobody had wanted to meet them as equals before, and it took some time before I could persuade them of my genuine interest in their work and in them as human beings. It required a great deal of patience. Many of the girls were victims of the warped social system, with nothing to look forward to. Mostly child widows, they had taken this job because it required little in the way of training and because it carried a certain prestige, though they were exploited by the men who controlled their working destiny. Little by little I did succeed in getting to know some of their difficulties and problems.

One of the municipal rules required the dismissal of a woman teacher if she became pregnant. One day I heard that one of our good teachers, a girl for whom I had come to have respect, was pregnant. She was more educated than many of the others, obviously from a better background, and was a pleasant young woman. The order for her dismissal was put up to me for signature. I refused to sign and told the superintendent I wanted to talk to the girl. There was consternation. I must not, I could not, do such a thing! Did I not realize that the girl was a widow and had got herself into this situation because she was a slut? However, I insisted on seeing the girl and she came to my house. She was in a fairly advanced stage of pregnancy, unhappy and frightened and not willing to speak freely. It was only when I told her that I wanted to help her have her baby that she was able to tell me her story. It was a usual tale, common in those days, of having been taken advantage of by a member of her husband's family soon after he died. She had been only sixteen at the time. She had had an abortion and been very ill. Finally she had been turned out of the family and forced to fend for herself. This was the second time she had become pregnant, and the father of the child was one of the Municipal Councillors. She had nowhere to go.

I fought a hard fight to try and let her keep her job but was unsuccessful. What I was able to do was to help her to have her baby and get it adopted by people she could trust. I was also able to send her to a friend, a social worker in another town, where she found work and ultimately married. This was the kind of tragic situation in which any woman who left her home could find herself. The hypocrisy and double standards of the time were responsible for great misery and many suicides.

The children who attended the municipal schools were underprivileged—they came in tattered clothes and with bloated bellies. These miserable mites were taught their lessons from torn primers with a picture of King George V on the cover and one book was shared by several children. The first lesson was about Nelson and ended with his famous words at the Battle of Trafalgar! A picture of Nelson in his admiral's uniform accompanied the text. The dress was unfamiliar to the children and England meant nothing to them. The poor babies never had been taught anything about duty to their own country.

There used to be a periodic medical checkup of a kind, and children who were considered 'sufficiently' undernourished were given a cup of diluted milk. As the municipal budget was too low to provide many cups, most of the children went without it.

One of my disagreements with my committee was over the question of milk for every child. Tuberculosis was common in the slum localities from which most of the children came, and endemic diseases regularly claimed their toll of victims. The first problem was money. The amount required was beyond the resources of the committee. How about raising the money through donations from the wealthy people in the city? The word 'city', as I use it, applies to the Indian section of the town as opposed to the Civil Lines and cantonments where the British lived. In the city we had many extremely wealthy bankers and businessmen who could easily have contributed to any scheme for the betterment of the children's health or education. Unfortunately, their money was spent either on erecting temples or, under pressure from the Collector, for some scheme in which a Governor's wife was interested. For this, if the amount contributed was large enough, the reward came in the shape of a title, which the Congress movement had already ridiculed and made worthless.

My milk scheme was discussed threadbare. It was interesting to find how many arguments there could be against such a very innocent idea. One old reactionary, who had protested most vehemently, made a final appeal to me. 'Sister, you must realize the consequences of this dangerous proposal. Giving these children milk today—perhaps better educational facilities tomorrow—simply means that the day after tomorrow they will demand to sit in our places. Then what?' 'You have summed this up correctly. That's exactly my idea,' I replied. A hostile silence descended on the meeting, but neither consent nor money was forthcoming. I discussed it with Ranjit and some of our colleagues, and issued an appeal ward-wide for one penny from each home every month to build up a milk fund. Our chairman, Dr Katju, Ranjit, my brother, and several friends gave me generous donations, and others came from sympathetic outsiders, but the pennies poured in and filled to overflowing the little wooden boxes we had put up in each mohalla and the milk scheme was inaugurated.

Sometime later, Lady Linlithgow, the Vicereine, then president of the Anti-Tuberculosis Drive, appealed for subscriptions for a milk scheme for undernourished children all over the country. There was no argument at all, and wealthy people fell over one another in their haste to respond to the appeal. Flowery tributes and substantial cheques poured into Lady Linlithgow's lap. A prominent banker of Allahabad, perhaps ashamed of his previous behaviour, now sent me a large cheque. One of the most satisfactory moments of my whole life was when I returned it to him. My own scheme did not suffer while I remained in office, and it continued for some years afterward, mostly on the penny donations.

The Municipal Board also ran night schools for adults. The classes were held irregularly in a shack or broken-down mud hut with a flickering hurricane lantern. No effort was made to attract the older men and women, and few came voluntarily. The Lowenbach method was then being tried in some missionary schools and we adopted it, but it was hard going and people were simply not interested. After experimenting in various ways, we had some success by turning the schools into clubs with community singing (there were hundreds of new national songs being written all the time), reading items of interest from newspapers, and the telling of stories from the Ramayana, which every Hindu, literate or otherwise, knows. Together with all this, reading and writing were also thrown in and accepted without fuss. The difficulty always was to convince the men and women of the *need* to be literate. Some years later, when Congress came into power in seven out of the then eleven British provinces, all illiterates in government service such as warders and wardresses in prisons, watchmen, and peons were given a period in which to become literate or lose their jobs. We were then faced with the problem of maintaining literacy and persuading the people to go on to a higher level. Libraries with elementary books were few and could not in any case be of use to any but town dwellers. I made an attempt to interest some well to do people in a mobile library, which could make a round of the city and also go to the nearby villages. This time I was successful, and we had first one such van and later, another.

The period during which Congress functioned in the Municipal Board was marked by a number of changes in the municipal law and in civic life. Unfortunately, the time was short. In 1935 the British Parliament passed the Government of India Act (1935), introducing provincial autonomy. This Act envisaged responsible government in provincial legislatures but reserved the right of the centre, the federal government, in New Delhi, to have charge of defence, foreign affairs, tribal areas, and some other subjects. It also retained representation on a communal basis, which had been introduced earlier by the Minto–Morley Reforms of 1909.

While Congress condemned the Act, which was forced on the people, it decided, after some debate, to contest the elections that were due to be held.

◆◆◆

19

The Elections

Once the decision to contest the elections was arrived at, the election manifesto was prepared. This manifesto rejected the Government of India Act but resolved to continue the national struggle and resist imperialism by entering the legislatures. It reaffirmed faith in the resolution passed at the Karachi Congress in August 1931. At this session the most important resolution had been the one on Congress economic policy and fundamental rights. This policy was to end exploitation of the masses, and toward this end to work for a constitution that would grant each citizen of India the right of free expression of opinion and association, freedom of conscience, the protection of cultural and minority rights, equality before the law irrespective of caste, creed, or sex, and many other rights that were later incorporated in the

Constitution of free India which came into being in 1950. A committee in each province selected the Congress candidates who would contest. Ranjit and I were both offered tickets and accepted them. Ranjit's constituency was in Allahabad district—Jamunapar—and mine in Kanpur, known as Kanpur Bilhaur. The problem before Congress was one of finances. The other side, meaning those who would oppose us, were mostly big landowners, princelings, and supporters of the status quo. They lacked neither money nor support from their British masters. In the balance, however, Congress had a large section of the country behind it, and we were hopeful of doing well. Ranjit's opponent was the Raja of Manda, a zamindar (landowner) of the district. Mine was more formidable for she was Lady Srivastava, the wife of the Education Member in the Viceroy's Council—a powerful and wealthy industrialist, Sir J.P. Srivastava.

As my campaigning had to be done in the Kanpur district I made my base in town in the home of our friend Dr Jawaharlal Rohatgi, whose large family was Congress-minded and forward-looking. My constituency was a rural one and very spread out. Campaigning meant being on the move for several days at a time in village areas, only going to the town of Kanpur for a few hours' rest or for a meeting scheduled there. I started the campaign with five Congress colleagues, Balkrishna Sharma, Beni Singh, Radheshyam Pathak, Saligram Jaiswal, and K.D. Malaviya. Two of them were candidates themselves but were helping me to get started with my campaigning. We had for our use a Ford car which had seen better days. The plan was to stop each night in a village, and I had no clear idea of what was involved. The idea of the election itself was new and exciting and sufficient for the time being. We started off in high spirits, the five young men and I. Canvassing was easy because the issue was clear-cut. We told the people to repudiate the foreign government and to give their votes to Congress. We asked them, 'Do you want things to remain as they are or do you want to have your own chosen people who will fight for your rights inside the councils?'

The first day all went well and at dusk we reached the village where we were to spend the night. The villagers, always hospitable, insisted on supplementing the evening meal we had brought with us. Later, when it was time to retire, I found that the little village schoolhouse had been swept and cleaned and all our bedding rolls laid out side by side. For some reason I had expected a place of my own to sleep in. Seeing consternation on my face, which I could not hide, one of my colleagues explained gently that this was how it was going to be throughout the campaign, but I must not mind, they would all take care of me. I thought of the pajama suit packed in my case, but obviously I could not undress. I had never been to bed in a heavy khadi sari, but there was no alternative. Fortunately the long day's campaigning had been so fatiguing that I fell deep asleep almost as soon as I put my head on the pillow. Next morning another problem presented itself. The toilet facilities were primitive, and for bathing there was only one pump in the open, which everyone used. It meant bathing with one's clothes on in the traditional open-air manner of the Indian peasant. As there were five yards of thick material draped around me, besides my underclothing, the water never seemed to get as far as my skin. I decided immediately that I must go home once a week to have a proper bath and get clean! The experience from this kind of living was something for which I have always been grateful. My young colleagues—two of them completely unsophisticated and the others friends of long standing, educated young men with whom I had worked, marched in processions, and gone to jail—looked after me with a courtesy and sensitivity as charming as they were touching. In a couple of days, I was not only adjusted to my new way of living, I was enjoying it.

Ranjit and I had agreed that we should phone each other whenever possible and give news of how our respective campaigns were progressing. I phoned the second evening.

'Everything is going very well,' I told him. 'Last night there was no separate place for me so I slept with the boys.' A roar of laughter met my statement and Ranjit replied, 'Good for you!' I heard him repeat this to Bhai, more laughter, and then some talk I could not quite hear. What had happened was that Pantji[8] was dining at Anand Bhawan and what I had said was passed on to him. Unfortunately for me, Pantji had every quality imaginable except a sense of humour. He was stunned and horrified! It took the entire evening for my husband, with Bhai supporting him, to explain that this was a joke. It was meant to be funny. We were a mad family and said strange things to each other, but our morals were above reproach! For some hours my fate hung in the balance while Pantji wondered sorrowfully whether his love for and trust in me had been misplaced!

We were now sharing Anand Bhawan with Bhai. On his return from Europe, after Kamala's sad death a few months earlier, he had called a family conference and said that he could not possibly go on living in Anand Bhawan. It must either be converted into some useful purpose or sold. Ranjit and I suggested we take the house over and he should stay on as our guest. This was not only his home it was now a symbol of all that we were fighting for. He must stay there. Others also urged him to do this, and it was decided that Bhai would remain in Anand Bhawan and we would move in and share expenses. This turned out to be a good arrangement because I ran the house and Bhai was free from at least one small worry. Also, Anand Bhawan remained the site of important meetings and discussions, and to people from all over the country it was a symbol and a place of pilgrimage. Hundreds came to see the home of Motilal, Bade Panditji, as he was called, and of Jawaharlal. For Ranjit and me it was a great joy being able to live with Bhai. Mother and Bibima were with us, and to

8. Pandit Govind Ballabh Pant, Congress leader and family friend, who was a member of the Cabinet after Independence.

my children Anand Bhawan became home. The fact that they grew up near their uncle was a powerful influence in their lives.

Coming home late one evening from my constituency for the weekly bath I had promised myself, I found Bhai and Ranjit glued to the radio. The voice coming through was renouncing the throne of England for the love of a Mrs Simpson. It moved me very much.

Polling day drew near, and since it was impossible for us to compete with those who were opposing us in the matter of money, Bhai and other top leaders who were not contesting the election travelled around explaining that Congress could not give the voter any of the facilities that would be offered by the opposition. Bhai's appeal was couched in terms any Indian could understand and it had dramatic results. He reminded them that when we go on a pilgrimage we walk, and until we have fulfilled our pledge we do not eat. 'So I ask you,' he said, 'to treat this day of polling as a pilgrimage. There will be no Congress cars or buses to take you to and from your homes to the polling area, there will be no food provided for you, you must bring your own. But the vote you cast for us will carry merit for it will be a vote for your future.' The slogan was 'On Foot to the Polling Booth'.

Polling Day, I speak especially of my own province, Uttar Pradesh, was a day not to be easily forgotten. One wanted to shout with joy and cry at the same time—one was so proud of one's people, so glad to be one of them, so convinced of victory—not the election victory, but that larger one toward which we were moving and of which this was but a small part. The villagers came out in thousands on foot, on cycles, and in bullock carts, with the odd group even in a tractor. All were dressed in their holiday best, the bullocks wearing bright garlands of marigolds, the festive flower, around their necks. Carts, jeeps, and bicycles were festooned with the Congress flag bravely fluttering in the breeze.

The opposition parties had made a big effort to seduce

the voter, and there were extra buses plying the roads to the polling booths. At intervals there were arrangements for snacks—iced sherbets and, later in the day, meals of puris and other things the village people eat on days of rejoicing. But the buses remained empty and nobody went to the places where the tempting food was available. Straight to the polling booths they went, singing, joking, happy. And the most moving sight of all was that, having cast their vote, they opened their meagre little bundles of parched rice or gram and ate under the shade of the trees. Even the smell of the delicacies from the opposition kitchens being wafted to their nostrils did not entice them. It came to a point where the agents of the opposition, seeing all the good food being wasted in such large quantities, begged our voters to go and have some even if they voted Congress. But so deep was the contempt for those who supported the foreign rulers that the invitations were refused with a joke. I went around the polling areas like other candidates, and many times I thought to myself, 'These are the people of India. They and they alone will give the final answer. I will never forget this day. How right Bapu is—we must never forget them…' But, alas for us and for India, we keep forgetting them, letting them down when personal opportunity beckons us, running to them when their aid can tip the political scales in our favour. In every crisis in India the faceless multitude has rallied to uphold the great ideals on which our civilization has been based, but in the continuing crises in *their* lives what have *we* done, the so-called leaders, the educated, the 'upper' classes?

◆◆◆

20

Provincial Autonomy

Congress won a striking victory in eight out of the eleven British provinces, and the leaders of Congress parties were invited by the governors to form ministries. India was then divided into British provinces and princely states. The provinces were under the direct rule of the Viceroy, whereas a vast territory, about two-fifths of the whole of India, was under the rule of princes who had accepted paramountcy of the British Crown. These rulers were autocratic monarchs with little actual authority as their support came from British power, and the administration of the Indian states was carried on under the 'advice' of British-appointed Residents. The 1935 Government of India Act, under which elections were held, applied only to the provinces. According to the new Government of India Act, executive powers and functions of the Governors were of three kinds: those to be exercised at the Governor's sole discretion, those in which he exercised his individual judgment after first consulting his ministers, and those in which he acted upon the advice of his ministers.

The Congress permitted acceptance of office in the provinces where they had a majority in the legislatures, but subject to the condition that the Governor would not use his special powers of interference or set aside the advice of ministers in regard to their constitutional activities. As the necessary assurances were not given by the Viceroy, Congress leaders expressed their inability to undertake the formation of ministries.

Acceptance of office, we felt, was but a phase in our freedom struggle. The main objective of Congress remained to end the present Constitution and to have a Constituent Assembly to frame a new one. There had been differing points of view on the question of acceptance of office even within the Congress. At the A.I.C.C. meeting held in Delhi earlier to consider the matter, I had been among those who opposed the official resolution on acceptance. The Socialist party of the Congress had recently been formed, and though I was not a member I often voted with it. On this occasion Achyut Patwardhan asked me to second the resolution opposing the official one. I believe, though I am not certain, that Jayaprakash Narayan was to move it. When my turn came I saw many eyebrows go up, but I was so intent on what I wanted to say that it made no impact. Bhai was presiding—he was again Congress President that year—and I felt he treated me rather unfairly, ringing the bell even before my time was over. But I stuck to my guns and said what I had to say. As I was walking down from the dais my palla, the part of the sari that comes over the shoulder, was pulled. Turning around I saw it was Rajaji.[9] He said, with one of his mischievous smiles, 'We shall make you eat your words!'

For a while there was a stalemate—ad interim ministries were appointed by governors of the provinces, but the only sanction they had behind them was that of the British government. They were very unpopular, and the legislatures could not be summoned. Provincial autonomy was becoming a farce, and the situation could not continue as, under the law, the legislatures had to convene within six months and pass the budget. A crisis was fast developing, and this led to a slight advance in the British attitude. The Congress Working Committee met in July 1937 and in a forceful resolution made it clear that the assurances given by the British fell far short of demands. However, permission was given by the Congress leaders for office acceptance and Cabinet responsibility. The Working Committee stated that 'office was to be accepted and utilized for the purpose of working in accordance with the lines laid down in the Congress election manifesto and to further in every way the Congress policy of combating the new Act on

---

9. C.R. Rajagopalachari, later Governor General of India.

the one hand and of prosecuting the constructive programme on the other.' Bhai, as Congress President, suggested that in order to explain to the masses the real purpose of forming Congress ministries it was important to go to the people and tell them clearly the implications of the Congress resolution. Meetings for this purpose were called all over India in towns and villages on a specific day.

A few days later leaders of Congress parties in six provinces were invited to form cabinets. In Uttar Pradesh, Pandit Govind Ballabh Pant, or Pantji, was leader of the Congress party and became the Chief Minister. He invited Dr Katju, Rafi Ahmed Kidwai, and myself to join his Cabinet. Others were added later. The day for the oath-taking came. The plan was for all the elected members of the Legislature to collect in front of the Assembly building in Lucknow, the capital of Uttar Pradesh, and take our pledge of loyalty to the country. Then the cabinet ministers would proceed to Government House, where the oath of office and secrecy would be administered. It was a cloudy day, and as we assembled the rain poured down in torrents, drenching the huge crowd that had come to watch. Nobody moved, and the ceremony went according to plan. The pledge was taken with solemnity by the members and greeted with cheers by the onlookers. It was rather a bedraggled group of people who reached Government House, all loath to take any 'loyalty' pledge to the 'King Emperor of India'. It is interesting—perhaps revealing—to note how each of us reacted to the oath. As Chief Minister, Pantji was the first. He was a big man in size and heart but phlegmatic and not easily moved. He spoke the necessary words quietly and firmly. Next came Rafi. He got stuck twice, and it was obvious that he was having difficulty with his conscience. Dr Katju was almost jovial as if it were a matter of no importance. I had made up my mind that I would keep my usually uncontrollable emotions strictly in check. No one had asked me to vow loyalty to a King we did not recognize anymore, I reminded myself. I was here of my own free will. But when my turn came I could hardly speak. It was a most difficult five minutes. Shaking hands hurriedly with the Governor, Sir Harry Haig, whom I had known since I was a young girl and he the Commissioner of Allahabad, I followed my colleagues to the next room where soft drinks were being passed. As I picked up a glass the aide-de-camp to the Governor asked if I was feeling well.

'Thank you, I'm well,' I answered. 'It's just that the King is stuck in my throat.'

'Well, you must wash him down, then,' said the Englishman with a smile.

The portfolios of Local Self-Government and Medical and Public Health were allotted to me. The former I was glad to have, but with the latter subjects I was less well acquainted. However, I made up my mind I would study hard. Since my acceptance of Pantji's offer I had frequently cried myself to sleep, wondering if I would be able to do credit to the family and the country. Bhai, who was travelling at that time, had sent me a telegram on my appointment, but there had been considerable delay in its reaching me because the telegraphic employees could not believe that their respected leader, Pandit Jawaharlal, would send his sister such a strange message when he should have been so proud of her becoming the first woman Cabinet Minister. Bhai's message was:

> Remember the Chinese philosopher with four sons. The first was clever and trained to be a poet. The second was brilliant and learned the arts. The third went into the army. The fourth was the despair of his famous father who consulted many friends. Their advice was that the boy's intellect was limited so he might do well as a cabinet minister. Love and good wishes,
>
> JAWAHAR

The girls were thrilled that 'Mummie' was a Cabinet Minister and, together with their uncle, saw to it that I did not suffer from a swollen head. A matter of great enjoyment to them was the fan mail I now began to receive in enormous quantities. During the holidays they read as many of these letters as they could, and made jokes on the absurdity of poor dear Mummie at thirty-seven years getting such admiring letters! As I look back to earlier days I am struck by the fact that no matter how our fortunes fluctuated our sense of humour remained, helping us to see things in perspective. This was an anchor that kept us, especially me, in safe harbour.

My first day in office is naturally remembered. My office was drab and uncomfortable. The first thing I did was to have the furniture moved around. Then I sent a message to the gardener for some roses which were blooming in the garden of the Assembly building, and got a vase from home to put them in. There could not have been greater consternation if I had asked for the moon. But I was determined to have a congenial setting for work, and from that day there was always a vase of fresh flowers on my desk.

The secretary of the Local Self-Government Department was an Englishman, a member of the Indian Civil Service, called Arthur Reed. He was immensely tall, and I have always had a complex about my lack of height. I felt somewhat nervous and not quite sure what to say to him. He turned out to be very nice and was patient in explaining the intricacies of the work, though some weeks later he confessed that he could not understand why a woman was taken into the ministry. There were also two parliamentary secretaries, one for each of my departments. A.G. Kher was for Local Self-Government, and Chandra Bhal, for the Medical portfolio. We were all new to the functioning of government, but Kher had both experience and knowledge of things pertaining to his charge.

The minister before me had been a Muslim zamindar of greater wealth than brains, Nawab Mohammed Yusuf, a charming gentleman, eager to be liked by the Governor. He had not devoted much time to his work and had left it to his departmental secretary, whom he rightly assumed to be more competent than he himself. There was a small mountain of files awaiting decision, and though no decision had been taken on these, they had actually been signed by the minister! The gallant Nawab, when faced with a file on which two alternatives were noted and his decision required, just signed. His signature was purely ornamental.

The salary of the new ministers was 500 rupees a month with a free house and car. This was the Congress ruling. We were not to use a private railway saloon when travelling, as had been the case formerly, but were to travel third class whenever possible. First-class travel was, however, permitted when it was in the interest of our work. This was a big change from the salaries and privileges of the earlier period.

A notice was sent from the secretariat asking the ministers to choose their houses, and a list of houses was attached. I decided I would go after work to look at them, but at lunchtime Pantji sent for me and said he wanted me to stay with him. 'It will be more proper,' he told me. 'You can live as you please without interference from me or my family.' I was surprised and tried to explain to him that, as a minister of the government, I was a responsible person and must live on my own. Besides, during the session of the Legislature Ranjit would be in Lucknow, and during their holidays my children would be with me. I wanted to make a home for them. After much discussion I had to agree, most reluctantly, to stay with Pantji for a month. Pantji was the kindest person imaginable. He was, in every sense of the word, my 'political guru', but in certain matters we were worlds apart. My colleagues Rafi Ahmed Kidwai and Dr Katju teased me mercilessly about having to be chaperoned, but both knew Pantji and agreed he should be converted to new ideas of women's freedom as gently as possible.

Rafi Ahmed Kidwai was a man of imagination and courage, and he brought these qualities to the many political tasks he was called upon to perform both in the provincial ministry and after Independence as Minister for Food and

Agriculture in the Central Government. He had deep roots in Uttar Pradesh, where he had been born and educated, and he could successfully deal with the complex problems of that province. He was a man of the highest honesty and integrity, a loyal friend and one who did not hesitate to share whatever he possessed with his political comrades. His home was open to all and so was his heart. He had a passion for fast driving and had more accidents and smashed more cars than anyone I have known. Once when Dr Katju and I were going to Delhi by train for a meeting, we saw a Buick lying upside down on the road. It was Rafi Saheb's car and Dr Katju observed cynically, 'Will Rafi be at the meeting or are we attending his funeral?' Rafi was at the meeting and showed very little the effects of the accident. He worked at a furious pace and his health was never good. He died at a moment when he was greatly needed in India.

My evening calls to Ranjit in Allahabad gave him much cause for amusement, but when I begged him to ask Pantji that he permit me to have a house of my own, he flatly refused to do so. 'You must do your own dirty work from now on—it's part of the game,' was his comment. The month seemed very long, but one day I was able to get a house. This was really the best of the ministerial houses but none of the other ministers had wanted it. It was on the banks of the Gomti river, with a lovely well-cared-for garden, and was situated in a park, part of which was a zoo. I soon became accustomed to waking up when the lions roared and it seemed as if my bed was being shaken.

I had hoped that moving into my own house would make life easy and that I would be able to do as I pleased, but this was not the case. In spite of his heavy duties Pantji kept a vigilant eye on my style of living. Every evening when he left his office, and it was always late, he would drop in to see me even though we might have met in the office during the day. He nearly always found a group of friends, often men, and much talk and laughter. This he did not like, and one day I was summoned to his office and asked who the 'men' were who visited me and whether Ranjit knew them! I explained that Lucknow was the centre of the Kashmiri community. The men who came to the house were people I had grown up with, and some were related to me. There was absolutely no problem between Ranjit and myself. I ended by assuring him on my word of honour that I would never do anything to betray his trust in me or to degrade the name of Indian women. This last, of course, was important, since our views on women differed. Instead of melting his heart my words had hardly any effect on him.

'Well,' he said grudgingly, 'we shall see, but you are too good-looking to be living alone.' To my response that I was nearly thirty-eight years old he merely replied, 'I do not think I shall be happy about letting you live alone even when you are sixty-eight!' Pantji lived to be very proud of me and paid me what, to him, was the highest tribute—that I had upheld the name of Hindu womanhood!

The state of affairs in the municipal and district boards in the province was deplorable. Few of the duties of the City Fathers were performed, and the bribery and corruption shocked me because they were part of the accepted pattern. Chairmen of boards were generally wealthy men who had bought their positions through promises that had to be kept and which came in the way of important public tasks being performed. According to the prevalent system, from time to time the Minister for Local Self-Government was invited to visit a municipality. Elabourate arrangements for entertainment were made and an expensive gift in silver presented with ceremony. The report read by the chairman was a cooked-up affair and the minister's reply, drafted by his secretary, full of clichés. When the Governor was invited, the programme was even more lavish. Meanwhile, roads lacked repair, drainage was bad, electricity inadequate, schools in a shocking state, teachers unpaid for months, and money for parks and other amenities diverted illegally for other purposes. I made up my mind that I would set my own pattern the first time I visited a Municipal Board. When the time came to do so, I received an effusive welcome and the speech in my honour could not have been more flowery or complimentary. The work of the board, I was told, was progressing wonderfully well, and they all awaited further guidance from me. I was presented with a beautiful silver tray decorated with Kashmiri engravings. In my reply I explained that the whole object of Congress was to bring clean and efficient administration to the towns, and that I was determined with their help, to do so. There was much to be done and a lot more to be undone and I was especially interested in the finances of the boards. In the end I said that I would auction the beautiful gift they had given me so that the proceeds could go to the local hospital, which was much in need of funds. This gesture was not appreciated, but I proceeded to auction the tray there and then and discovered in myself a very good auctioneer. The tray had cost 250 rupees. I auctioned it for 5,000 rupees because, in order to keep the minister from prying too much into things, the landed gentry went on outbidding themselves! Unhappily for them I could not even recommend any of them for a title from the King Emperor!

It was interesting work. I did a great deal of travelling, making speeches about the new order we were trying to usher in, looking into conditions of municipal employees, especially trying to make the existing schools and hospitals effective.

Work in the Public Health Department was equally slack. There were all manner of reports of work done, reports that were grossly exaggerated. Here, too, though the scope for patronage and corruption was not so great as in the Local Self-Government Department, plenty existed. My insistence on personal inspections was a sore point even with the top officials, but I was adamant and some changes were effected in my time in both departments under my care.

The Medical Department also had its troubles: hospitals uncared for, insufficiency of beds, lack of trained nurses, lack of funds. The poor, especially the women, were terrified at the idea of going to a hospital, and they had a point. Once admitted they were more or less left to fate. Certainly women's hospitals in Uttar Pradesh were not places that cured, and the general hospitals were much the same, except for one or two that had better standards. In the rural areas there were no medical facilities at all. Trying to get money allotted was a thankless task. The Health Ministry was a sort of 'untouchable' among the ministries, and though everyone needed its services, nobody wanted to do anything to help it. This had been, for some reason, an age-old attitude. The director of medical services sat in his office, and his personal visits to the field were few. When he did go on an inspection visit it was announced well in advance, and what he saw was the stage as it was set for his coming.

I started touring and, much to the director's annoyance, would not fix a day for my visit to any clinic or hospital. These visits revealed in many instances a pathetic disregard for human life. The poor were expendable in any case.

When the new Legislative Assemblies opened, the first resolution moved by the new ministries was a demand for a Constituent Assembly to draft a Constitution for India. This resolution should have been moved by the Chief Minister, but Pantji was indisposed and the privilege of acting in his place fell on me. It was the key resolution of the session. I felt honoured to move it.

In the early days of the Congress ministries there was constant tug of war between the ministry and the bureaucracy, neither having any confidence in the other. The things to which the ministries were pledged seemed unrealistic to the Governor and the bureaucrats, and all sorts of small technical impediments were put in our way. Another hurdle to smooth functioning was the relationship between the newly appointed parliamentary secretaries and the officials of the Indian Civil Service. Conflict on several levels from protocol onward was a feature of the early days. The parliamentary secretaries then appointed rose to occupy important positions in free India. Lal Bahadur became Prime Minister, K.D. Malaviya and Ajit Prasad Jain were ministers in the Union Government. A. G. Kher became Speaker of a later Uttar Pradesh Assembly and functioned in that position for many years. The Congress government in the provinces was rich in talent and did good work in the short time it remained in office. Both my parliamentary secretaries were most helpful, especially Kher, whose knowledge of civic laws and contact with the masses made him a very valuable guide and counsellor. They both gave me their unstinted personal loyalty and devotion, and but for their help I could not have had to my credit those few successes that I managed to achieve.

This was the first time a woman had been given the position of minister and had to work with men as her subordinates and colleagues. It is natural, I suppose, for a relationship tinged with chivalry to have developed. I can remember so many instances when Kher would work far into the night doing some research for a speech I had to make, or explaining matters he felt I must be acquainted with before facing some knotty problem with the Governor the next day. Early in our association I had to present my budget and I had no idea at all how this was done. The departmental secretary had put up the draft budget of the department and I found the figures perplexing. I wrote a note on the file to Kher: 'P.S. I find the Budget figures confusing. Would you have time to explain them to me.' The reply, unwisely noted on the file, was as follows: 'I do not believe figures can confuse H.M. who is moulding the destiny of the nation with her beautiful hands!' He came over to my office and we worked hard for some hours, after which I was able to face the Legislature with some degree of confidence and answer questions clearly and correctly. Pantji had suggested to me that if I ever felt unsure of any subject I should let the parliamentary secretary handle it, but my pride would not permit this. My parliamentary secretaries did deal with some matters in the House, but never because I was unable to do so myself. On this subject I had spoken to Ranjit and Rafi, whom I always consulted when in difficulty. Both were emphatic that what I did not know I must learn, and in any case I and not officials must be in charge of my departments. I have seldom worked so hard as I did in those days. There were many things I had to learn to understand, and this stood me in good stead later on. I had a husband who was always at my side when needed—critical and understanding. I had good colleagues whose sincere interest and help made most things possible for me. I was very fortunate.

I was fortunate, also, in another matter, and that was the support and admiration of women all over India. Many were my friends and comrades. Many more I did not know, but from all directions waves of affection and encouragement came to me. There was no jealousy at all, just shared pride, which I like to think was special to India and to my Indian sisters.

Large numbers of women used to bring me their problems, and one day, when I received an appeal signed by several women calling my attention to the action of the Lucknow Municipal Board in ejecting them from their homes, I was not surprised. The appeal was written in Urdu, which I cannot read. Neither Kher nor Chandra Bhal could read the Urdu script, so we had to have the letter read to us. I sent for Kher and said we must get in touch with Chaudhri Khaliquzzama, chairman of the board. He happened to be out of town and was not expected back for some time. So I decided to go personally and look at the place in question and speak to the lady who had written the letter. There was a cold silence in the room, and presently Kher said, 'This matter can be looked into by one of us, there's no need at all for you to go.' I said that as this was a matter pertaining to women and the appeal had been made to me as a woman, I should look into it myself. Kher's next argument was that Pantji would object.

'How does Pantji come into the picture?' I asked. No

reply but the atmosphere seemed to get icy. I announced that I would go the next morning.

But the following morning my chauffeur, very embarrassed, eyes on the ground, voice subdued, said, 'Madam, I regret I cannot drive you to the address given to me by the secretary.'

'Why not?' I inquired. There was no answer.

'Well, I must drive myself,' I said, and got into the driver's seat. Just then an angry Kher arrived and got in with me. The chauffeur got in the back. On the way Kher did what he should have done much earlier. He explained to me that the appeal I had received was from the red-light district, and the ladies of the locality were being moved elsewhere on orders of the Municipal Chairman. I could not understand why he had not told me this before, and he could not understand how, after reading the appeal, I was so innocent that I had not known! We reached the place and I was received by a woman with courtly manners and great poise who spoke beautiful Urdu. Iced drinks were produced and refused by Kher who told me afterward that they might have been poisoned! I was then taken round part of the area and told that by being moved from here the girls would lose many clients! I promised to speak to the chairman, knowing fully well that he, being an arch-conservative, would not speak to me about prostitution. Nor would he appreciate my involvement in the situation. As I was leaving, a doctor arrived and I was told one of the girls was very ill. The doctor wanted her in the hospital but, as her case was infectious, the municipal hospital would not admit her. I saw the girl, very pretty and young, and told the doctor and the madam that I would arrange for her treatment.

On the way home Kher nearly passed out in anguish. He had a strict moral standard—right and wrong were black and white. He told me I had no business to get involved. When I telephoned the doctor in charge of the medical college, a good man and a friend, he too was horrified. He told me the infectious diseases ward was not for the likes of this girl. Finally I had the girl admitted to the hospital by giving an order in writing. It turned out that, apart from having syphilis, the girl was pregnant. When I look back on my life there are a few incidents that give me satisfaction. This is one of them. The girl was cured, and, because of her, I was able to start, with stiff opposition from Pantji and officialdom, the first clinic for pregnant women suffering from venereal diseases. The story has a sequel. A year later, on my birthday, I received a charming letter of gratitude for my help. Enclosed was a Banaras handkerchief. Every birthday for several years thereafter, the handkerchief and good wishes came regularly, and then one day, much later I received the news that she was married, was going to Pakistan to live, and was very happy. I hope she is still happy, and I sometimes think of her. I hope she has not forgotten me.

During the time I was Minister of Health, Hardwar, one of the cities of pilgrimage for Hindus, was to have its Kumbh Mela. This festival falls every twelve years, and it is considered especially auspicious to bathe in the Ganga in Hardwar. Millions of pilgrims come, and nearly always some form of epidemic occurs. We were determined to take all precautions this time and I, together with the health authorities and the Collector of Hardwar, went to the town to explain to the people the necessity of cooperating with the local authorities and the provincial government to prevent any disaster. Hardwar is a city of paandas—hereditary priests of the Hindu families who go for worship and the performance of various religious rituals on the banks of the Ganga. The pandas are mostly enormously wealthy, and some are heads of big religious foundations. They are also, by and large, ignorant and bigoted but very influential with the pilgrims and worshippers. We met the pandas, and I was appalled to see the manner in which they practically fell on their faces in front of the British officials, flattering them, garlanding them, and walking a step behind them with folded hands. On my return to the Dak Bungalow, the rest house where I was staying, a deputation of pandas came with a written petition requesting the government to prevent cow slaughter in Hardwar. This was a perfectly legitimate request as Hardwar is a city holy to Hindus. In the ordinary course I would have accepted the petition and given an assurance that I would convey it to the Chief Minister. As it happened, I read the petition carefully and to my amazement found that the request was for cow slaughter to be banned in Jwalapur, one of the three areas that made up the municipality of Hardwar. It was also the area where Muslim butchers and vegetable sellers lived in large numbers. It was obvious that the pandas did not dare ask for the ban to be applied to the whole city because a number of English officials lived there and beef was a part of their diet. The Muslims, on the other hand, could do nothing to retaliate and were easy victims.

I was furious. I asked the deputation why the ban should not be applied to Hardwar as a whole, and the reply was that it would be easier to begin in one area at a time. I then asked them if it was not true that they were afraid to offend the foreign rulers but did not mind destroying the livelihood of a Muslim group. At this they lost their temper and started to shout abuse at me and at the Nehrus for being traitors to the Hindu creed. As the situation became more and more unpleasant my secretary asked them to leave. They did so, threatening to return with the whole town. After their departure the superintendent of police suggested placing a police guard around the rest house and my parliamentary secretary wanted me to agree to this, as he felt that the temper of these ignorant men could lead to an ugly situation. But I refused to have a guard. I told the superintendent of police that my husband would not approve of such an action. Also, I was a popularly elected minister and if those who had voted for me wished to demonstrate against me it was their privilege to do so. Within an hour the shouting of slogans gave us warning that a large crowd was approaching. I gave orders that all the doors and windows should be closed, and the crowd soon surrounded the house screaming vile abuse and threatening to break down the doors. They did shatter nearly all the window panes. After half an hour of this I suddenly decided to face the mob. In spite of the entreaties of my companions I flung open the door and surprised the shouting crowd. For a moment they were silent, shocked at seeing me, and I climbed onto a chair. Taking the watch off my wrist I held it out to them. I told them that if they could behave in a civilized manner I would speak to them and I gave them exactly ten minutes to calm down. If they wanted to harm me, I told them, it was their privilege to do so, but such an act would only hurt them. Here, on the banks of the holy Ganga, an assault on a Brahman woman would hardly be to their credit. For a moment it was doubtful whether or not the violence would continue, but as I remained standing on the chair holding my watch for all to see, the temper of the crowd suddenly changed and they became quiet. I then told them that I would pass their request on to the Chief Minister in an amended form to include the whole of Hardwar, and if they objected to this I would not intercede for them on this issue at all. There was silence and gradually they dispersed.

When I returned to Delhi the next day Pantji told me he had passed an anxious night on hearing the police report from Hardwar, and that in future I must have adequate protection. I pointed out with some pride that I was competent to look after myself. Some weeks later an apology was received from the leading pandas of Hardwar for this incident.

All possible arrangements were made in preparation of the Kumbh. One essential was that people should have inoculations against cholera. This was another uphill task, and even a man like the Speaker of the Uttar Pradesh Assembly, Babu Purushottam Das Tandon, refused on principle to be inoculated. The festival attracted a larger crowd than usual and caused a cholera epidemic that swept the province like a prairie fire. It was a terrifying thing, and in spite of every effort we simply did not have the means to control it. I appealed to medical interns and retired medical men to come to the villages to help where the situation was at its worst. I decided to tour the province with my Director General. It was a risk, and all the officials were against it, but my conscience would not let me rest. I toured with officers of the department trying to do everything possible to check and control this horrible disease. It was an experience that led me to the verge of a nervous breakdown. Our officers worked splendidly, as did those who had volunteered to help. The epidemic, which had taken its toll of thousands of lives, was finally controlled, but it had been a hard battle. It had also set an example that those at the top must involve themselves personally in disasters concerning the people even at personal risk.

◆◆◆

21

A Holiday in Europe and Back to Jail

My mother, who had been ailing most of her life, became almost normal in health when she was faced with the rigours of the freedom movement. She often took part in public meetings. On one such occasion there was a lack of discipline in the crowd, leading to a police lathi charge. People were scattered hither and thither, and Mother, being about four feet eleven inches in height, small-boned and slight of build, received several lathi blows and was knocked down. She lay semi-conscious until someone recognized her and she was taken home. When this news reached Bhai and Ranjit, then in prison, they were greatly distressed, and in protest they both gave up all privileges such as letters and interviews for three months. This was the way of satyagraha—one protested by inflicting suffering on oneself. Mother's bloodstained sari is still in the museum in Allahabad, I believe.

Once during a previous imprisonment Mother had gone

to interview Ranjit in Naini Jail. The jailor had treated her very rudely and Ranjit, incensed at this, had forgotten the rules of satyagraha and struck him. As punishment he was put in solitary confinement in a cell for one month. For those who cannot imagine the infinite mental torture of solitary confinement in a cell there is a rhyme:

As he went through Cold-Bath Fields he saw a solitary
cell,
And the Devil was pleased, for it gave him a hint
For improving the prisons in Hell!

Mother had gone on a visit to Betty and her family in Bombay and while there she suffered a mild stroke. But she recovered quickly, and on her return to Allahabad she seemed well. We were all in Anand Bhawan in January 1938 for some reason I cannot now recall—Bhai, Betty and Raja, Ranjit and myself, and all the children. I was to leave that night for Lucknow as the Legislature was in session and I had to present the medical budget next day. Mother referred to my departure several times during the day and seemed depressed at my having to leave and also at the thought that Bhai was to go on a long tour two days later. Seeing that she was really upset we suggested that she should come to me in Lucknow as soon as Bhai had left. This cheered her and she was quite bright during dinner. When it was time for me to leave I went up to her and bent down to kiss her. She put her arms up and as she did so she suddenly collapsed. She had had a stroke and was dead in a few hours. Bibima, her older sister by ten or more years, had so identified her own life with Mother and her family that this sudden shock was a great blow to her. After the funeral we tried to make her drink a cup of tea but she said she only wanted to sleep. She would not lie on her bed but lay down on the floor, wrapping her shawl around her. We thought it best to let her sleep, but, when she was not up four hours later, Bhai went to wake her and persuade her to take some nourishment. She was dead. Death had occurred almost as soon as she lay down. It was certainly a case of dying of a broken heart. It was a sad and very empty household after these two wonderful women left us.

Meanwhile the news from Europe was most disturbing, and India had been acutely aware of the steady growth of Nazism and Fascism. Year after year Congress resolutions had condemned these ideologies and disapproved in the clearest terms of their theory and practise. Bhai was among the few people in the world who, in the years preceding the Second World War, consistently raised his voice against the invasion of Manchuria and Abyssinia and the march of events in Europe and China. British policy, in spite of statements to the contrary, was one of appeasement, though this word came into popular use later on.

I had been unwell ever since the cholera epidemic, and now my doctor suggested a holiday. There was no provision for a minister to take a holiday abroad but Pantji, in consultation with the Governor, made it possible for me to go to Europe. Ranjit and I had planned to go together in the summer of 1938, but just then he was elected General Secretary of our Provincial Congress Committee and could not leave. I decided to go to one of our mountain resorts instead of to Europe, but Ranjit insisted that I should go abroad as planned and, in his typically generous fashion, he threw his London checkbook on my table and said, 'Have a good time and spend all the money you want!'

Bhai was also going to Europe to attend a conference organized by the International Peace Campaign in Paris and to see Indira, who was then at the Badminton School in Bristol. The health minister of Czechoslovakia, Mr Necas, had been in correspondence with me regarding some schemes in which the Uttar Pradesh government was interested at that time. When he heard I was visiting Europe he invited me to Prague as the guest of his government.

In Prague I stayed at the same hotel as the Runciman

Mission. It was a moment when the question of the Sudeten Germans was a vexing problem and there was much unrest—a most unfortunate time for a first visit to beautiful Prague. One thing I remember with pleasure was meeting Jan Masaryk and being able to spend an interesting hour with him, though he was under great strain. It was while I was still in Prague that the German army marched into Sudetenland and the war moved closer.

From there I went to Hungary. In Budapest Indira fell seriously ill with pneumonia, and Bhai and I had an anxious time. After her recovery she went to convalesce in Switzerland while Bhai and I proceeded to London. While we were there Mr Chamberlain was negotiating with Hitler and buying 'peace in our time'. The evening when he returned from his visit to Berchtesgaden and waved the infamous White Paper from his window in 10 Downing Street, we stood with the crowd and watched the rejoicing with which Mr Chamberlain's words were greeted. It was perfectly understandable but sad, for one could see that peace was farther away than ever before. For hours that night we wandered around London. The churches had been kept open and were full of people, mainly older women, on their knees thanking God for deliverance from war. I was near to tears and wanted to join the worshipping throng, to pray that in spite of all the signs to the contrary peace might still be possible. It is an unforgettable memory.

During this visit Mussolini expressed the wish to meet Bhai and invited him to Rome. The invitation was regretted. Later, as Bhai was about to return home, a second invitation was received and this, also, was regretted. It would have been impossible for Bhai to meet the Fascist leader at any time—more so now. Ever since the early beginnings of Fascism, Bhai's voice had been raised against the danger that threatened, and Congress resolutions had emphasized the shape of things to come as we envisaged them. Unfortunately the Western world at that time had turned a blind eye to the developments so soon to engulf the world in hideous tragedy.

After my return to India the news came of Germany's invasion of Poland, and the Second World War began. India was made a belligerent in the war without reference to the elected representatives of the people. For this purpose the Constitution was amended in great haste by the British Parliament and all powers in the event of war emergency were centred in the hands of the Viceroy and the Central Government. The provincial governments were made subject to the direction and control of the centre, and ministerial responsibility and provincial autonomy became a farce. In 1939 Indian troops were sent abroad without reference to the legislatures, and as a protest the Congress withdrew all its members from the Central Legislature in Delhi.

Since the middle twenties the Indian National Congress had, time and again, declared that the Indian people could not permit the exploitation of Indian resources for the furtherance of imperialist aims, and that they would not cooperate in any imperialist war. In September 1939 the Congress gave a long statement on the war. The Congress stand was that if the war was being fought for the purpose of defending the empire and all it stood for—colonies, vested interests, and so on, then Indians would have nothing to do with it. However, if it was indeed a war for democracy India would be behind the war effort. It was ridiculous for India to fight for liberties for others while these same liberties were denied to her. Therefore the Congress asked the British government to make a declaration for the independence of India and to recognize the right of the Indian people to frame their own Constitution. By doing so Britain would prove her *bona fides* and give the Indian people a stake in the war against Fascism. The government's answer was a rejection of this demand—it did not define British war aims at all. All it said was that when the war ended His Majesty's Government would be 'very willing to enter into consultation with representatives of several communities, parties and interests in India and with Indian Princes with a view to securing their aid and cooperation in framing such constitutional modifications as may be deemed desirable.' Indian opinion, not only Congress but other groups, was aghast. On such terms the Congress could not associate itself with the war and called upon the eight provincial assemblies to resign. In the Uttar Pradesh Assembly the resolution disassociating Congress and the Indian people from the war effort and expressing disapproval of India's having been declared a belligerent without our consent was moved by me. The next day the Cabinet handed in its resignation. The Constitution was suspended and the rule of governors took the place of popular elected governments.

Throughout, the period during which the Congress ministries were in office, the Muslim League had been encouraging communal unrest, particularly in Uttar Pradesh, by talking of the Congress being a Hindu organization wanting not Swaraj but Hindu Raj in India and by insisting that Congress ministries were suppressing minorities and that Muslims in the Congress were traitors to Islam. The purely Hindu political party in India was the Hindu Mahasabha, much less influential among Hindus than the Muslim League was among Muslims. During the 1937 elections the Mahasabha had not made any impact on the voters. It was an organization motivated by religion and not sympathetic to Congress ideals. Talks between Congress and League leadership had been going on to find a solution to the Hindu–Muslim problem, and at one stage there had been a daily exchange of letters between Bhai and Mohammed Ali Jinnah on the subject. Bhai, personally involved as he was in the grave world crisis and its implications for India, could not understand Mr Jinnah's insistence on the purely communal aspect. In one of his letters to Jinnah he wrote that 'my own mind moves on a different plane and most of my interests lie in other directions. And so, though I have given much thought to the problem and understand most of its implications I feel as if I was an outsider and an alien in spirit.' To Congress the matter that was urgent was to have the Muslim League's cooperation in getting rid of the foreign power, after which internal matters could be sorted out.

After the resignation of the Congress ministries Mr Jinnah fixed December 22, 1939, as a day of deliverance and thanksgiving as a mark of relief that Congress governments had at last ceased to function. The day fell rather flat, but Mr Jinnah's statement led to a sense of frustration and depression among those who sincerely wanted a solution to the problem. It created a psychological impasse, and the gulf between Congress and League seemed greater than ever because it seemed clear that there was no common ground for discussions. The Congress could not accept the League as the representative organization of Indian Muslims and the League would not endorse the Congress demand to the government for a definition of its war aims and independence. These basic demands were, as Bhai said, the very essence of Indian nationalism, and to give them up or to vary them was not possible.

In the months that followed Congress members were once more suspect. Private letters were censored, our telephones were tapped, and even bank accounts examined by the government. Gandhiji now announced that there would be symbolic civil disobedience. This was not to be the mass movement of earlier times but confined to individuals chosen by himself. Notice of the act of civil disobedience was to be given beforehand to the magistrate of the locality and everything done in a quiet and civilized manner. There would be no act of satyagraha on a Sunday because this was the British holiday and therefore the authorities should not be disturbed!

The first person chosen by Gandhiji to offer civil disobedience was Acharya Vinoba Bhave because he had fulfilled in his life all Gandhiji's ideas of purity. The second civil resister was Bhai. It had been planned for Bhai to give notice on November 7, 1940, in the Allahabad district and to make a speech explaining the policy of Congress in regard to the war. However, he was arrested before this date in Gorakhpur, where he had gone on work. His trial was attended by Ranjit and me and we, along with many others who heard him on that occasion, were deeply moved by Bhai's statement. It was a forceful one and ending it he said:

> I stand before you, sir, as an individual being tried for certain offences against the State. You are the symbol of that State. But I am something more than an individual also; I, too, am a symbol at the present moment, a symbol of Indian nationalism, resolved to break away from the British Empire and achieve the independence of India. It is not me that you are seeking to judge and condemn but rather the hundreds of millions of the people of India, and that is a large task even for a proud Empire. Perhaps, it may be that, though I am standing before you on my trial, it is the British Empire itself that is on its trial before the bar of the world. There are more powerful forces at work in the world today than courts of law; there are elemental urges for freedom and food and security which are moving vast masses of people, and history is being moulded by them... It is a small matter to me what happens to me in this trial or subsequently. Individuals count for little, they come and go, as I shall go when my time is up. Seven times I have been tried and convicted by British authority in India, and many years of my life lie buried within prison walls. An eighth or a ninth, and a few more years make little difference. But it is no small matter what happens to India and her millions of sons and daughters... If the British Government imagines it can continue to exploit them and play about with them against their will, as it has done for so long in the past, then it is grievously mistaken. It has misjudged their present temper and read history in vain.

Bhai was sentenced to three consecutive terms of imprisonment amounting to a total of four years and taken to the Dehra Dun jail.

The various town Congress committees now drew up

lists of those who were eligible for civil disobedience, and the plan was that those who had held office of any kind should be among the first to offer themselves for satyagraha. Since Ranjit was secretary of the Uttar Pradesh Congress, his name came high on the list, but he was not able to offer disobedience because, on receiving the notice from him giving the time and place of his proposed civil resistance, a warrant for his arrest was issued and he was taken to prison. The same happened in my case. Ranjit was taken to Dehra Dun Jail, where he joined Bhai and shared his cell. During his various terms in prison Ranjit had done valuable work in translating some of the Sanskrit classics into English. During this term he began to translate a play written in the fourth century by the playwright Visakadatta. It was entitled *Mudrarakshasa, The Signet Ring*. This play was probably produced at the court of Chandragupta II. The Gupta period is spoken of as the golden age of Indian history. It is a political drama of great importance concerning the foundation of the Mauryan Empire in the fourth century BC. Unlike much of Sanskrit drama, which deals with themes of mythology and love, this is a play about strategy and the struggle for power. Apart from his translation of the play, Ranjit's commentaries and notes are of great interest to the scholar and student of history.

I was taken after my arrest to the Naini Central Prison. This time there was no overcrowding in the barrack and there was less vigilance. The matron knew that political prisoners would not try to escape and spent time chatting with us and even gave, to those of us who wished it, permission to go into the criminal yard and talk to the women convicts. There were a number of tiny children in this ward who, not having a home where they could be left, had been brought to prison with their mothers. I offered as part of my 'labour' to care for these mites, and a small barrack in the political ward was cleaned and whitewashed for the use of the children. Every morning they were brought there and I looked after them until time for lockup. 'Looking after' meant bathing them, washing their clothes, giving them their meals, and keeping them amused. There were seven toddlers between the ages of one and three—after the age of three the rules did not permit a child to accompany the mother to jail. It sounds easy enough, but some days those babies nearly drove me out of my mind. Since their mothers had long sentences—two of them were 'lifers'—I had the care of these children during the entire period of my imprisonment.

There is a hierarchy in jail as elsewhere, and the murderess is at the top. She despises the woman who is in for theft and hardly acknowledges the prostitute. She is the queen, and many were the gory stories I heard of murder, told with great pride and with absolutely no remorse.

I had an interesting experience during this term in jail. A young woman sentenced to death for murder was brought into the political ward and kept in a solitary cell. The appeal for her case was pending before the High Court but, according to the jail authorities, it was bound to be rejected. The inhumane treatment of those under sentence of death includes feeding them with all sorts of good things. This girl—her most inappropriate name was Rajkumari, which means 'Princess'—was about twenty-two years old, pretty but in a state of terror. I used to hear her crying at night and I felt that I would go mad unless she was removed. Finally I asked for permission to see and talk to her, and was permitted to visit her for half an hour every day. There is not much one can say to a twenty-two-year-old who is soon going to be hanged, but I did what I could to calm her and she became attached to me and started to call me 'mama'. She had been a child widow and, after the death of her husband, had had an affair with a married man who persuaded her to part with her jewellery, which he gave to his wife. Thereupon she found a suitable opportunity to murder him. She told me with great relish that she cut him up in little pieces and put him into a sack!

Fate plays strange tricks. One afternoon I heard a tremendous noise in the yard and I could not make out if it was one of joy or sorrow. Presently the matron presented herself in my barrack and told me the High Court had accepted Rajkumari's appeal and that she was to be released but refused to leave. I was asked to explain that she could not remain in prison. I found Rajkumari sitting outside her cell howling and swearing that she would not leave me! Lockup time in jail is six o'clock, and already it was four. She had to be out of the prison in an hour but would not budge. It was a most awkward situation for me as well as for the prison authorities. Finally I asked the authorities to telephone a cousin of mine to come as quickly as she could and take the girl away, but I was told that this would not be possible as it was necessary for me to sign a document before a magistrate, assuming responsibility for the girl. The jailer eventually phoned the District Magistrate, who was on his way to the club for his usual game of tennis. This official arrived about the same time as my cousin, both very angry. I signed the necessary papers—foolishly, as it transpired—and assured my cousin that I would take over the girl after my release, which was due in six weeks' time. But in six days Rajkumari had run away from my cousin's home and settled herself in the red-light district of Allahabad, having first stolen whatever she could lay hands on!

On my release I went to see Gandhiji. The individual satyagraha was slowing down. People were tired and some were evading arrest. Gandhiji appointed exempting authorities in every province. If any man or woman whose name was on the list for arrest wished to be exempted, he or she had to go to the exempting authority for permission to withdraw from civil disobedience. I was appointed such an authority in Uttar Pradesh, and if necessary I forwarded the request of the person concerned to Gandhiji. It was the most difficult and fruitless task I have ever had to perform.

Meanwhile the war situation in Europe was getting worse and the Japanese were advancing in Asia. They were now close to India's borders. The British government suddenly decided to release all Congress prisoners in detention. The explanation given was that in view of the new dangers, leaders of Congress should be given a chance to revise their opinion about participation in the war effort. Ranjit and Bhai, among others, were released, but civil disobedience as such was not withdrawn by Gandhiji, who regarded the government's gesture with misgiving.

It was about this time that Subhas Chandra Bose, who had been ill for several months and more or less confined to his house, suddenly disappeared, causing much concern and surprise. No clue seemed to be available. We learned later that he had made a dramatic escape from Calcutta and gone through the Soviet Union to Germany from where, eventually, he flew to Japan and organized the Azad Hind Fauj (Indian National Army), composed mainly of some Indian officers who were serving in the British army. The story of the escape from Calcutta has now been published by a nephew who was the only person in Subhas's confidence.

◆◆◆

22

The Cripps Mission

In March 1942 Mr Churchill, the British Prime Minister, announced in the House of Commons that he was sending Sir Stafford Cripps to India with concrete proposals from the British War Cabinet for constitutional changes. He said, 'The crisis in Indian affairs arising out of the Japanese advance has made us wish to rally all the forces of Indian life to guard their land from the menace of the invader.'

The draft declaration issued by Sir Stafford Cripps proposed that after the ending of the war a Constituent Assembly would be elected that would frame a Constitution for India. There would be provision for the participation of Indian states. Any Constitution framed would be accepted and implemented. The right to opt out on the part of any province disagreeing with the Constitution would be conceded, and the same right would apply to the Indian princely states. A treaty would be concluded between His Majesty's Government and the Constitution-making body covering all matters connected with the transfer of power. The Indian Union would have the right to secede from the British Commonwealth. These proposals had to be accepted as a whole or not at all.

Maulana Abul Kalam Azad, then Congress President, and Gandhiji met and discussed these proposals with Sir Stafford Cripps for several weeks. The Working Committee of the Congress also met to consider them. The points of difference were vital. Congress wanted freedom as a condition precedent to cooperation in the war effort and was not prepared to wait for changes until after the war ended. Congress was not prepared to have nominated representatives of the princes on the Constituent Assembly because the princes were semi-feudal individuals and recognizing them meant ignoring the then ninety million people of the Indian states who were largely in sympathy with the national struggle for independence. The proposal giving an option to the provinces or the princes to leave the Union was also unacceptable as it went against the whole concept of Indian unity. The thought that any princely state or any province could decide to leave the Indian Union would create grave problems in the future. In the case of the states the people themselves had no vote, and all decisions would be made by the rulers. In the provinces, elections would be based on separate electorates for Hindus and Muslims, which had been long imposed by the British, and religious and backward forces could well sway the vote for secession. Under these circumstances it was difficult to visualize a strong and united India. A big hurdle between Congress and the Cripps Mission was the idea that there should be a British war minister controlling the defence policy of India. In effect this meant whittling down India's freedom and her right to defend herself without foreign advice. The Congress could not, under any circumstance, acquiesce to this. Sir Stafford Cripps was a member of the War Cabinet, but he was also considered a friend of India. Yet the proposals drafted in London were such that separatist elements would inevitably gain ground. These and many allied topics were discussed with Sir Stafford, but at no stage of the discussions did the British government agree to the formation of a national government. In fact, their attitude made it clear that they had no confidence in the Indian people. In the end the negotiations broke down because it was obvious to us that the British were as reluctant as ever to relinquish their power in India. The proposals were rejected by the Congress. The Cripps Mission failed. Sir Stafford Cripps and his wife, Isobel, were personal friends of ours and spent two days in Anand Bhawan during the talks. Sir Stafford lived mostly on fruits, and we sent for melons from Kabul and grapes from Quetta to supplement what little our local market could provide in that season.

Indira had now come back from Oxford. She had left in her final year before taking her degree because of illness that necessitated treatment and convalescence in Leysin, Switzerland. She eventually returned home via the Cape as the war had begun and the quicker route through Suez was not possible. On her return to India she became engaged to Feroze Gandhi, a young Parsi who belonged to our hometown and whom she had known for a number of years. He had been involved in the national movement since his student days and had studied at the London School of Economics. He had long been devoted to Indira. They were married at Anand Bhawan in March 1942 at a simple wedding ceremony because the approaching political crisis did not permit of anything else. Indira's wedding sari was of fine khadi yarn spun by her father.

At the time of the wedding Generalissimo and Madame Chiang Kaishek came to India. Their visit was for the specific purpose of meeting Gandhi and Nehru and persuading them not to launch another noncooperation movement. They had President Roosevelt's concurrence—unofficial, of course—and hoped to be able to influence Mr Churchill in the matter of Indian independence.

Our relations with China were very close because, at the time of the Japanese attack, Bhai had called for mass meetings all over the country in support of the Chinese people in their resistance to aggression. News dispatches of this sympathy reached war-torn China, and Bhai received a letter from Chu Teh, then commander-in-chief of the Eighth Route Army of China, thanking the Indian National Congress for its support and asking for money or other aid for the Chinese volunteers who had come together from various parts of Japanese-occupied areas, to band together and prepare for a prolonged war. They had neither winter clothing nor arms and very little food. Congress had responded immediately by sending a small medical mission headed by Dr Madan Atal to China. It was an infinitely small gesture, but it was made at the right time and won the hearts of the Chinese people. On the arrival in China of the Indian medical unit, Mao Tse-tung wrote to Bhai from Yenan saying that the members of the team had been warmly received by the Eighth Route Army and that their manner of living and functioning, sharing the difficulties of the Chinese, had made a great impression on all who met them. Even today this mission is remembered and spoken of with appreciation.

In 1939 Bhai had gone to Chungking and made contact with many eminent Chinese. At that time he had suggested various forms of cooperation between the two countries including an exchange of professors and students, translation of publications and other matters of interest to both countries. This idea was accepted and a plan drawn up that led to some scholars like Dr Tai Chi Tao and others coming to India.

The Chiangs' visit at this time moved Indians. Their sympathy for Indian aspirations for freedom was obvious and Indians supported this Asian leader fighting against odds. Madame Chiang's impact on the women was immense. We saw in her a symbol. The All-India Women's Conference in particular, composed as it was of educated women, found in Madame Chiang an Asian woman leader of whom they felt proud. I had gone to Delhi with Lekha to see the Chiangs, had several meetings with them and, like most others, admired what they were doing to defend their country. Madame Chiang told me that my young daughters should not be kept in the country at this period, and she suggested Wellesley College, of which she was an alumna, saying that she would make inquiries when she reached the United States and let me know if the girls could go there. She kept her promise, but by the time she could get in touch with me we were back in prison. However, there is no doubt that but for her interest my daughters could not have gained the easy admission to Wellesley that they subsequently achieved.

Gandhiji was now wholly preoccupied in thinking what form the next movement could take. Japan was almost at our door for Malaya, Singapore, and Burma had fallen. Indian refugees from these countries were pouring in, and the threat to us was a very real one. In July 1942 a meeting of the Working Committee, the Congress executive body, met at Wardha, Gandhiji's home and ashram. It was a long session lasting a week, and the whole war situation as it affected India was thoroughly discussed. The resolution passed was in the nature of an appeal for the British to leave India. It said, in part, 'If such withdrawal takes place with good-will, it would result in establishing a stable provisional government in India and cooperation between this government and the United Nations in resisting aggression and helping China.' Should the appeal fail, however, Congress felt it would be compelled to use all its nonviolent strength for the vindication of its political rights. Any forthcoming struggle would, of course, be under Gandhiji's leadership. No response was really expected from Britain, and none came.

An A.I.C.C.[10] meeting was called in Bombay to consider the resolution of the Working Committee. It was fully attended, and the atmosphere all over India was very tense. It needed but a spark to set it in flames. The A.I.C.C. resolved that it was 'no longer justified in holding the nation back from endeavouring to assert its will against an imperialist and authoritarian government which dominates over it and prevents it from functioning in its own interest and in the interest of humanity.' This Quit India resolution, as it came to be known, took the decision of starting a mass struggle and called on the people to face the future with courage and endurance. The resolution was passed late on the night of August 8. In the early hours of the next morning, Gandhiji and all the members of the Working Committee were arrested and taken in secret to an unknown destination.

◆◆◆

23

Quit India

Throughout Allahabad people remained glued to their radios, and in the city itself and on the university campus there was serious unrest. I heard of the A.I.C.C. resolution with fear in my heart. Jail-going was upon us and this time there were not going to be any concessions. The national slogan now was 'Quit India', and it was a fight to the finish.

I went to the Congress office in the city and found turmoil—papers were being burnt, cyclostyle machines and typewriters being hurriedly sent away to places of safety for fear of confiscation by the government, and arrangements being made to organize peaceful demonstrations. Tandonji

10. All India Congress Committee.

and other leaders, who had not gone to Bombay, came in one by one, and we had hurried talks about what to do in case of sudden government action. This was the morning of August 8, and that day I received word from Lucknow that Mehrtaj, the daughter of Khan Abdul Ghaffar Khan, the Frontier[11] leader, who was my ward and in college in Lucknow, was seriously ill. I rushed off to see her though I was gravely disturbed over the political situation and had been asked by the city Congress Committee to take charge of the students and make myself responsible for the way they organized their protests. I was in the hospital with Mehrtaj when the news of the arrests in Bombay came. My first thought was to return home immediately, and I sent a friend to the railway station to make sure that I obtained a berth for the night journey. When I reached the station that evening I was met by the stationmaster, who told me in great agitation that the police had been to his office to inquire if I had a reservation for that night. He had denied it and begged me to hurry to the compartment where he had deliberately had my bed made up, thinking it unlikely that the police would look there. He rushed me to my berth and I thanked him for his concern and kindness. The other occupants of the compartment begged me to lie down and cover myself up quickly in case there was any attempt by the police to look into compartments. It was remarkable how much sympathy there was for political workers at this time.

At five in the morning the train reached Prayag, one of the stations of Allahabad and only a short distance away from Anand Bhawan. I got off there instead of going to the main station and took a tonga, a horse vehicle used as a public conveyance, and was home in a few minutes. Everybody was up and excitement prevailed. The girls told me that huge processions of students were being organized, and the government had proclaimed a ban on them so most certainly

---

11. North-West Frontier Province.

there would be beatings and arrests. I sent a note across to the Vice-Chancellor, our friend Amarnath Jha, to check on the university situation. He wrote back that the procession of the day before had been small and peaceful and been unmolested by the police. 'Today's procession,' he wrote, 'threatens to be very large—the boys are in a state of uncontrollable anger at the Bombay arrests. I fear retaliation by the police. Please do what you can to calm the students. There will be no objection to your entering the University at any time.'

The university campus is a few minutes' walk from Anand Bhawan and I went there and met some of the student leaders, including Bahuguna, who is now a minister in the Central Government. I begged them to be absolutely controlled, warning them that they would injure the larger cause if there was any violent action on their part. They promised to march peacefully but told me there would be processions every day. I then went to the city Congress office. At the crossroads where the City joins the Civil Lines, I found the road barricaded. A large number of young people on the City side were making the barricades firm and putting up national flags and 'Quit India' notices that had been prepared during the night. This was the point beyond which processions had been prohibited and police were expected to be present in full force. The situation was disturbing. Tandonji and some others had been arrested the previous night, and there was no leader of stature in the city itself who would be able to influence people should emotions get out of hand. We had received instructions by a messenger from Bombay that each individual who participated in any action against the government must conform to Gandhiji's guidelines of nonviolence. Since it was taken for granted that all leaders would be arrested, each person must be responsible for his conduct and try to give the correct advice to those who needed help or were in doubt. We were told that some Congress workers had escaped arrest in Bombay and had gone underground. They would contact me soon. I must be fully prepared for directions from this group, to be carried out by a picked number of young people who could be trusted.

The students' procession that afternoon was a very big one. As expected, it was stopped at a certain point by the police, but no arrests were made. The participants were angry—they had wanted to provoke the police but, that day at least, the orders were obviously to avoid confrontation. I went to the university in the evening and praised the young people for their restraint but found them hostile and determined to create an incident. The next day's processions also passed without arrests, and by this time the tempers not only of the students but of the townspeople were rising high. There was no news at all of where Gandhiji and the Working Committee members had been taken after their arrest. Meanwhile, the messengers I had been expecting arrived under cover of the night. They turned out to be Lal Bahadur Shastri and a colleague. I hid them in our guest room upstairs, locked the door from the outside, and put the key into my pocket. A warrant of arrest was out for Lal Bahadur, and I arranged to take up food to them only at night so that not even the servants would know they were in the house. They immediately started typing and cyclostyling instructions to be sent to the villages. Everything had to be done swiftly and quietly.

On the third day after the Bombay arrests the Vice-Chancellor rang me up saying that he had heard there would be lathi charges and possibly shooting, and could I have the next scheduled procession called off? In any case, could I persuade Lekha not to participate? I replied that I was powerless to do either. I had said everything possible to the students and now it was up to them to show their wisdom. The procession was expected to be very large, divided into two sections, each going by a different route and converging to hold a meeting. When I heard of the possibility of firing I asked the Kamala Nehru Hospital, which is next to Anand Bhawan, to be ready for any eventuality. Some beds had to be kept vacant and a doctor and nurse available on duty in the out-patient's department. I asked Bhai's secretary, Upadhayaji, to pay frequent visits to the university and report what police arrangements were being made. I was under great strain. Lekha had gone off to join the procession and Tara, then only fourteen, had accompanied her. Nothing was normal anymore.

By noon there was no news of where the processions had reached. I sat at home in the veranda straining my ears to hear shouting or any noise indicating the approach of the procession. The two men locked in their room upstairs were equally tense, but no action was possible and we could only wait. About two o'clock in the afternoon I heard the tut-tut-tut of machine-gun firing. The servants rushed into the street to find out what was happening, but the shouts of 'Quit India' and other slogans had begun to reach us and I knew the confrontation had taken place. I was just running out of the gate when three lawyer friends stopped their car out on the street and said the procession that had taken another route had also been fired on and that Lekha was gravely injured. They had come to take me to her. My heart almost stopped beating. I felt giddy and sick, and at this moment Upadhayaji rushed up to say that the boy leading the procession in front of the university had been shot dead. I pulled myself together. Like a flash of lightning, Gandhiji's voice passed through my mind—do your duty, it said. I turned to my lawyer friends who were waiting and asked if they would take Upadhayaji to check what had happened to Lekha and the others. I ran like a wild thing to see what was going on on our side. I do not mention this incident in any spirit of self-righteousness—that is far from my nature. But it is important for those who did not know Gandhiji to realize how deep his influence was on the people who loved and trusted him.

In front of the university the spectacle was a frightening one. A barricade had been erected, and before it were police and military facing a vast crowd opposite. The air was full of slogans: 'Quit India', 'Release our Leaders', 'Murderers', and so on. After the shooting of the student who was leading the procession, all discipline had gone to the winds. Lathi charges provoked hand-to-hand encounters between police and students and this, in its turn, led to firing. Many were wounded. I asked the police to let me get to the other side, but they refused. Seeing me, the crowd doubled their shouts and demanded that I be allowed to join them. At last I was permitted to do so. I climbed onto the hood of a car standing nearby and addressed the students, begging them to disperse and let us all attend to the dead and injured. I gave the police superintendent my personal word that I would calm the crowd if he would withdraw his men. The dead boy turned out to be the son of a zemindar of our district. Many injured boys were taken to the Kamala Nehru Hospital. I remember one boy whose testicles had been shot and he screamed in agony; there were others too with serious injuries. It had not been a case of firing on legs and shooting to disperse the crowd. The baton assaults too had led to grave injuries. Meanwhile, news came that the other procession had managed to reach a city park and hold a meeting. Lekha and others were safe and there had been no firing. Knowing this was a tremendous relief, and I devoted myself to giving what help I could to those in need.

I also had another anxiety during these days. There was no news of Ranjit. He had attended the A.I.C.C. in Bombay and so far had not returned. Because of complete censorship names of those arrested were not published in the press, and I could only wait for news to come from some trusted friend.

Coming back to the night of the procession, we went weary and heartsore to bed. Indira had returned from Bombay late that night, very tired. Feroze, we learned, had gone underground with several others. About 2 a.m., Binda, our night watchman, roused me and said in a whisper that the house was completely surrounded by police. The gates being high and closed at night, no one could come in without climbing over the equally high garden walls. I jumped out of bed and ran upstairs to warn Lal Bahadur and Indira. We decided that the police should be let in and Lal Bahadur and his colleague should destroy any material considered 'dangerous' and lie low if possible to avoid arrest. We had that day received cyclostyled copies of a series of instructions issued by the Socialist party, which was underground, to be sent to the rural areas. This meant organizing groups of young people who could do an effective job of explaining and controlling and who were prepared for arrest if they were caught by the police. There had been no time to arrange anything yet, but Bahuguna and other students could command a sizable group and be trusted to carry on. Lekha was also among them. These instructions as well as a couple of cyclostyle machines had to be put somewhere immediately so that they would not be confiscated. The machines were wrapped in soiled sheets and, looking like a dhobi's normal bundle of laundry, they were sent across the garden to the Kamala Nehru Hospital. Hurriedly I woke Lekha and told her what had happened and explained briefly that we must spread the leaflets under her mattress. Then I went out into the porch and, putting on the light, I saw the City Magistrate, the Deputy Superintendent of Police, and half a dozen armed policemen standing in the darkness. The grounds were full of plainclothesmen. I immediately switched on the garden lights as a signal to the neighbourhood.

'Why is it necessary,' I asked the Magistrate, 'for so many armed men to come to arrest one unarmed woman at this amazing hour?' He told me a search was to take place.

I went in and woke the younger girls. They immediately grasped the situation and no useless questions were asked as they helped me to pack a bag. Even the youngest was familiar with police methods by now. She looked at me with her big eyes full of sleep and said, 'How wonderful to live in these days, Mummie; I wish I could go to jail too.' Tara told me, 'Let's say goodbye to you outside. I want the police to see how we take these partings.' After I had left, the girls went back to bed and lay on the hidden leaflets while the police search went on. I was very proud of my children that night.

24

Jail and Parole

Outside the gates of Anand Bhawan three police vans were lined up and more armed men appeared out of the shadows. I was asked to get into the first van, where the Deputy Superintendent of Police took the wheel and the City Magistrate and others got into the back. The city had been in the hands of the military from the previous evening, with martial law in everything but name, and a curfew order was in force. We drove in tense silence along the familiar road to Naini Central Prison. My mind was full of earlier events, and pictures of many journeys to this jail from 1921 onward flashed through my mind. We reached the Jamuna Bridge, heavily guarded, and were challenged by the sentries. The words 'Friend' and 'Police Car' were shouted in return and we proceeded.

As I got to Naini the jail authorities said that they had received no information about my arrival! After half an hour's wait, the gate of the Female Prison was opened by the matron, who came rushing up, panting and puffing and very annoyed at the disturbance of her night's rest. I was taken to the old familiar barrack. It was four-thirty in the morning. I spread my bedding on the ground, was locked up, and a new prison term began. My head ached and I could not sleep thinking of the events of the past few days. I was especially worried about Lekha, fearing that she would land in jail. The previous evening I had had a brief talk with her, wanting to know her reactions to what she had been through. She spoke with great bitterness. 'It will take a long time for me to forget what I have seen, Mummie, and it will be longer before I can root out the hatred that is growing in my heart. We can't think in terms of normal life anymore—there's no going back for us. We have to go on to the end, whatever the end may be.' Of course she was right. But Tara and Rita were still so young to be alone, and the future was uncertain.

In the morning I saw that there were a few familiar faces still around since my previous stay in Naini, but there were no sanitary arrangements, no water, in fact, nothing at all. There was no sign of any rations being issued to me and I longed for a cup of tea. Toward noon some rations arrived, but without fuel to cook them with, so it was not possible to make a meal. The matron very kindly sent me a cup of tea from her house. It was obvious that this term was going to be different from past ones. The fact that no food, cooked or otherwise, had been supplied to me for nearly twenty-four hours was one indication. My morale was low, but over the wall from the men's prison came shouts of 'Inqualab Zindabad'—'Long Live Revolution!' It was like a shot in the arm, and the slogan revived me more than food could have done. It seemed that a great many political prisoners were being brought in at short intervals, for again and again the exuberant shouts came to me. This was good news.

One settles in prison quite quickly when the mind is adjusted to doing so, and one even finds interest and amusement in the daily life. A few days after I was admitted to Naini the Commissioner of the Allahabad Division paid me a visit. No doubt he meant well, but his questions were not very tactful. 'Are you comfortable?' he asked. I gave no reply and he beat a hurried retreat! Soon after my arrest it happened to be my birthday, and I heard that the girls had sent me some books. My pleasure at the thought of receiving them was short-lived because the jail superintendent informed me that, owing to a recent change in prison regulations, other politicals and I would now be classed as 'Q' (for Quit India) prisoners and be given second-class treatment. For this reason we would not be entitled to any earlier privileges, including books. We would have to wear clothes provided by the jail, and our daily food allowance would be reduced from twelve annas a day to nine! Since both these amounts were grossly inadequate, the loss of three annas did not bother me. What did bother me was the noise. The common idea of prison seems to be that it is very quiet and lonely. In no other place have I so yearned for solitude as I have during my prison terms. Even the night used to be full of raucous sounds, not the little unexpected noises such as one hears outside, but harsh, monotonous ones that jar on the nerves. As Ernst Toller has written about prison, 'Day after day chains of sound are strangling you with dissonance.' Only those who have been prisoners can understand fully what this means.

I had not been well for some time past and was in need of surgery, but this was no time to think of one's health. I did not sleep well, could not cope with the necessary daily chores, and was in very low spirits. On August 30, I was feeling particularly tired and remained lying down. Suddenly my friend and recent barrack-mate, Purnima Banerji, rushed to the yard, and I heard excited chatter. Looking up I saw Lekha, laden with garlands and a broad grin on her face, striding into the barrack, a prisoner. For a dazed moment I thought she was visiting us but immediately remembered we were no longer entitled to visits. In any case, jail interviews were conducted in the superintendent's office. I heard Lekha telling Purnima how her arrest had taken place but I was so stunned I could not speak to her. Pictures of Lekha from her babyhood passed through my mind, one, more poignant than the others, of when she was seven years old and going to school in Poona with a friend of ours just before Ranjit and I were arrested in 1932. A small solemn person, blinking away tears and clutching a large national flag. 'Don't carry that flag, darling,' I had said to her. 'It is to frighten the police with,' came her swift reply. The flag had become a sort of charm against evil for our children. Now I thought unhappily of Tara and Rita more or less alone at home.

It seemed as if we were to have many surprises. On September 11 a bruised and battered Indu, with some of her clothes torn, arrived in the barrack. She had been at a meeting and there was a scuffle with the police. She brought us news that Feroze had also been arrested and was probably in the men's section next door to us. There was still no news of Bhai, which was disturbing. Ranjit had been ill in Bombay and was leaving to spend ten days in Khali in order to recoup before his inevitable arrest. I worried about him because, in the past few years, even at the best of times, he had not been robust.

More and more people were being arrested in Allahabad, and the men's section was now full. Largc numbers of students were brought to jail daily but most of them were flogged and released. Some were little more than children, thirteen and fourteen years old. The women's section was also getting full.

About two weeks after Indu's arrival the jail doctor informed me that she, Lekha, and I had been placed in A Class and would receive twelve annas a day. Further, some of the former privileges would be restored. He gave no reason for this, and we all decided we did not want to accept any special treatment.

Having Indu and Lekha in the barrack changed the atmosphere because they made light of difficulties and had great imagination. The never-changing daily menu was discussed with as much enthusiasm as if we were dining à la carte at a French restaurant, and they named their parts of the barrack—Indu's was Chimborazo and Lekha's, Bien Venue. I was obliged to call mine Wall View! Their ability to give names to everything amounted to a talent. A bottle with a broken top was known as Reckless Rupert the Headless Earl. Our evenings were seldom dull.

We looked forward to the visits of Miss Williams, the official jail visitor. She always brought an armful of flowers, which was of course against the rules, and gave us the latest war news and also some news of other political prisoners. She told us Calcutta was having air raids, and the war situation, judging from the papers, was serious. From her we also learned which of our friends on the other side of the wall were still there and which ones had been transferred elsewhere.

In September Ranjit was arrested the day after he had arrived in Allahabad and was now in Naini. I was informed that Lekha and I could have an interview with him. Indira was also able to have an interview with Feroze. Prison interviews are very unsatisfying, but we looked forward to them none the less.

After more than seven months in prison my physical condition was still unsatisfactory and I was let out on parole. I did not like the idea of leaving Indu and Lekha but felt that I should go home to see to my health, which must not be allowed to break down at this time. I also was eager to look into domestic affairs. I left Naini in a tonga, not wishing to ask the jail authorities to inform my home of my arrival. I did not want Khaliq, our chauffeur, to bring the car to fetch me.

The first sight that met my eyes as I entered the gates of Anand Bhawan was dozens of policemen and the District Magistrate. A search was in progress, and what a search! Cupboards had been forcibly opened, clothes thrown anyhow on the veranda and in the garden, books taken out of shelves, and furniture and carpets piled on the lawn. It was as if a tornado had hit the house. I asked the District Magistrate severely what he thought he was doing. He answered that he was looking for a letter that Pandit Jawaharlal Nehru had written to President Roosevelt just before his arrest! I told him I did not think much of his intelligence—are important political documents hidden among clothes or put for safety between the leaves of a book? 'Please take my assurance that I know where that letter is,' I informed him curtly. 'I also know you will not find it, because it is not in Anand Bhawan.' I demanded that the police replace the furniture, carpets, and books with the help of our servants, and wrote a letter of complaint to the Governor of the province, Sir Maurice Hallett, under whom I had worked as a minister for a short period. Some of the clothes thrown on the damp grass were damaged, and of course the flower beds had been heavily trampled on. The garden was in a shambles. It was a strange homecoming. As it happened, the copy of the letter Bhai had sent to President Roosevelt was in my safekeeping. It had been written in April 1942, after the failure of the Cripps Mission. In the letter Bhai had told the President how distressed the Indian people were at not being given the opportunity to 'organize a real national and popular resistance to the aggressor and invader. We are convinced that the right way to do this could have been to give freedom and independence to our people and ask them to defend it.'

A week later Lekha was released from prison as there was 'no incriminating evidence against her'. I took this opportunity to discuss the question of her going away from India and entering Wellesley College in the U.S.A. She did not want to leave India, but, finally, when I told her how much Ranjit and I wanted her to have wider opportunities than were possible in India at that time (she would not have been able to continue her studies without giving a guarantee to abstain from political activity), and how much better she could serve the country if she had a good education and came in contact with people who were doing things, she agreed to go. I decided to send Tara also. She was young but had the necessary credits.

With the permission of the District Magistrate I cabled Wellesley College and some friends in the United States. I told the college that Lekha had, before her arrest, passed the intermediate college examination and stood among the first ten students in the province, and that Tara had just secured a first division in her matriculation. Mildred McAfee, then president of Wellesley, cabled me, 'Wellesley College proud and pleased to welcome your daughters.' In those days little things meant so much, and the phrasing of the cable warmed my heart. I felt my girls would be among friends.

All arrangements were hurriedly made before my parole of a month expired. Dr Parker, who had been principal of Woodstock School, gave us sensible advice as none of us knew much about the United States. Fortunately, officialdom made no difficulties, and I was allowed to communicate with my bank to arrange finances. Lekha had been offered a scholarship under the fund started by Madame Chiang Kaishek for Asian students. The girls were to go to Bombay to stay with Betty, who would complete arrangements for their departure. What these would be in the middle of war we did not know. Before Lekha and Tara left for Bombay the three girls were given permission to have an interview with their father in prison. This was the last time that Lekha and Tara saw him.

I was back in jail at the expiration of my thirty-day parole. My only solace was being able to meet Ranjit at occasional interviews, but suddenly one day I learned that Ranjit, with some others, was being transferred to a jail in the town of Bareilly. This was in every way a worse place, for apart from other inconveniences there were no medical facilities. Ranjit had been there in 1933 and had fallen ill because the jail was full of smoke from a neighbouring factory. He was not in a fit state to live with jail hardships, but there was nothing to be done. I had never before in our many partings been so full of forebodings as when I said goodbye to him on our last interview in Naini.

A few days later Indu and I were informed that we were to be released next morning but an order would be served on us requiring us to leave Allahabad and go straight to Khali, our estate near Almora. We were to live there at our own expense but under the surveillance of the Deputy Commissioner of Almora. Naturally we refused to do so. Later we discovered that jail rules were being further tightened, and, as neither of us was in normal health—Indu had been running a temperature for some time—it had been decided to remove us. Two days later, on May 13, we were released, but I was back in Naini within a week under Section 127 of the Defence of India Rule. Indu was ill with high fever, and, fortunately, no warrant was served on her. Purnima was still in our old barrack and it was good to have her there. Within a few weeks I was ill again, and by July I had been released on grounds of health.

25
Famine in Bengal

After Ranjit's transfer to Bareilly Central Jail he was not allowed any interviews and I felt apprehensive. I was sure his health was deteriorating and that this was one reason he was not allowed to be interviewed. In three previous imprisonments Ranjit had devoted himself to making translations into English from the Sanskrit classics. One of his labours was the translation of the *Rajatarangini,* which he called *River of Kings*. This monumental work was by the poet Kalhana, who lived in the twelfth century A.D., and it is considered the only work written in ancient times by an Indian that can be called a history. It is of great importance to scholars and students of ancient culture as well as being an account of Kashmir's history, legends, and social conditions of the era. A previous translation of the *Rajatarangini* had been made in 1892 by Sir Aurel Stein. Ranjit conceived the idea of attempting this work of translation because Father, who did not know Sanskrit, mentioned his regret at not being able to read this authentic history of the old family homeland. Ranjit decided to translate it for him and began to do so when he was in Naini Prison in 1930 and shared a term in jail with Bhai. The work was arduous and long and had not been completed when Father died. This labour of love was finally published in 1934 and dedicated to Father. It was well received by scholars everywhere. Ranjit's translation of *Mudrarakshasa* was done in Dehra Dun Jail, again while sharing a cell with Bhai during the individual civil disobedience movement. In his last imprisonment at Naini he completed the translation of Kalidas's *Ritusamhar, The Pageant of the Seasons*. He had been inspired to undertake this work on the suggestion of Rabindranath Tagore, but had not found time to start until he was once again in prison. During our brief jail interviews he used to recite certain stanzas to Lekha and me and tell us the

English rendering he had made. Apart from the translations of the Sanskrit texts Ranjit's scholarly notes and appendixes in all three books were of great interest, particularly in view of the fact that these were written without benefit of sources he would have been able to consult had he written under normal conditions.

News of the girls' safe arrival in the United States finally reached me. They had secured a passage on a troop ship that went to Australia and across the Pacific to the West Coast of the United States. They were helped to reach New York where our friend Mrs Frances Gunther awaited them and gave them hospitality. I had not realized the strain under which I had been living with the uncertainty of their whereabouts, but with this news I suddenly collapsed. It is always my custom, when there has been something good in my life, to try to thank God for it. I have not had any formal religious training but, as I have grown up, I have been more and more conscious of that Higher Being who holds the world in the palm of his hand. My God is a compassionate God whose hand is always held out to help one over stony paths of life—to clasp or not to clasp depends on one's own ability. Nature to me is far more conducive to worship than a building, by whatever name it may be called. I feel the presence of God when I am in the mountains or beneath the stars or on the bank of a river flowing majestically to its destination. I see him in the beauty of trees and flowers. I have no reaction to chanting hymns or incense. So that night, when I at last knew that my daughters were safe, I went into the garden where the soft darkness enveloped me, and there was a sense of peace and healing. I had moved from Anand Bhawan to a small house not far away, as Indu and Feroze were now out of prison and it was right that they should be at Anand Bhawan. As I sat in the small garden I felt that my way of saying thank you would be through trying to do something useful. I decided that since my children were safe I would go to Bengal, where famine was raging and children dying, and work to save them.

Next morning I sent Ranjit a letter with a request to the jail authorities to be good enough to deliver it and let me have an answer as early as possible. When it came it was typical of Ranjit. 'Of course you must go,' he wrote. 'It is the right thing to do. There are risks involved but neither you nor I have ever been afraid of them—besides, what is life without risk. So go but look after yourself a little.' There was no mention of his health.

I left for Calcutta within a few days. I had been President of the All India Women's Conference since the previous year, and, on arrival, got in touch with the Bengal branch. The members were glad to join in whatever kind of work could be done. Renuka Ray, one of the stalwarts of the Congress and a person of much social and political experience, was a tower of strength. Urmila Mehta, Secretary General of the Women's Conference and a woman of great courage and capacity, came all the way from Gujarat to help. There were many others of whom I think fondly and gratefully.

The emergence of Indian women as an important flank of the national movement had been yet another example of the magic of Gandhiji. His call to women had been answered by thousands, crossing all traditional barriers of creed and caste and encompassing all social and economic levels. The patriotic fervour that had us in its grip was something more than political, and by leaving the age-old shelter of the home and taking part in the noncooperation movement side by side with men, Indian women had achieved a sense of equality denied by immemorial custom. The constructive programme of the Congress, in particular, gave great scope to women to involve themselves in the social and economic aspects of the movement. The first woman to rise to political prominence had been Sarojini Naidu, who, in 1925, was also the first woman to be elected Congress President. She came from a scholarly family and was educated at Cambridge at a time when this was a rare occurrence for women in India. Married to a doctor and mother of a talented family, she set an example to women to rise above the daily domestic round and take an active part in national affairs.

The nineteenth century had seen some reforms and there were demands for many more. Raja Ram Mohan Roy and others had championed the need to end the seclusion of women, to create opportunities for their higher education, and bring about other social changes. Now, in the wake of political consciousness, there were women's organizations, the most important of these being the All India Women's Conference. It was started by a group of educated women from all parts of the country and, under the leadership of women like Mrs Naidu, Maharani Chimnabai Gaekwad of Baroda, Rani Rajwade, Begum Hamid Ali, Mrs Muthulakshmi Reddy, Kamaladevi Chattopadhyaya, and others, it sought equality of rights, the ending of legal disabilities for Hindu women, adult franchise, education for girls, and other related matters. The A.I.W.C. did a great service by setting up nurseries, kindergartens, and residential hostels for working women, and by looking into the conditions of women in mines and plantations. It also started a now well-known Home Science College for girls in Delhi.

As a result of the work of the A.I.W.C., as well as the Congress attitude toward women's rights, many legal disabilities were removed after Independence. In 1956 the Hindu Code Bill, passed by Parliament, created a dramatic change in the legal status of Hindu women by giving them the rights to inheritance and divorce. Other religious groups in India already had these rights. Equal pay for equal work was another legal enactment, a right still denied to women in some 'advanced' countries. However, legislation has not transformed social realities except among the educated; for the masses, ignorance of their rights and financial inability to seek redress of wrongs remain a severe handicap to emancipation.

To return to Bengal, as the main problem was in the villages, we organized receiving camps where babies and small children, whose parents were dead or missing, could be brought before being sent to the city, where better medical facilities were available. In Calcutta, a shocking sight met my eyes—streams of peasants from villages, in varying degrees of illness and incapacity, most of whom had walked miles to escape from the starvation in their areas. Children sometimes got lost from families on the way, parents got separated from each other, old people died. The scene was one of horror, extreme suffering, and despair. Two million people died in that famine.

The famine in Bengal was man-made. The Famine Inquiry Commission, over which Sir John Woodhead presided, published its report in 1945 and had to admit that the tragedy in which millions starved to death was the result of official mistakes and errors. 'The Government of India failed to recognize at a sufficiently early date, the need for a system of planned movement of foodgrains... Society, together with its organs, failed to protect its weaker members. Indeed there was a moral and social breakdown as well as an administrative breakdown.' The fall of Burma had brought an end to the imports of grain to this rice-eating area, and the apathy of the Bengal government no less than the shortcomings of the Central Government were directly responsible for the colossal food shortage that affected millions who were, in any case, living on a subsistence level. The needs of the military personnel aggravated this problem. The famine was under way in 1943, and at that time the government was wholly preoccupied in suppressing Indian nationalism. Large numbers of Indians were already in prison and unable to raise their voices in protest against the lack of any food policy on the part of the government. The province of Bengal, which had been a most prosperous region of India at the time of the advent of the British, had become one of the first casualties of imperial rule. It had declined into an area of economic stress with poor health and nutritional standards, little industry, and an ever-increasing pressure on the tired land. The most shocking aspect of the famine was not the catastrophe in terms of human life, horrendous though this was, but the fact that starvation existed side by side with plenty. In Calcutta the rich—foreigners and Indians alike—continued to live in a state of affluence surrounded by every conceivable luxury while people outside their gates died of hunger and despair. The corruption was such that fortunes were made during this period, and every death was balanced by enormous gains for food speculators and others. The Governor of Bengal during this period was Sir Richard (later Lord) Casey. He was not the usual type of governor. He shed as much protocol as he could and, being a humanitarian rather than a bureaucrat, he tried always to meet the social workers and others who were working in the famine areas. Occasionally, the government communiqués were not wholly correct, and we had to bring this to the notice of the Governor and not allow his staff to persuade him that a little whitewashing of the situation would help ease the tension and fear in people's minds. I had several meetings with Sir Richard, and we spoke and argued freely. He was always a most courteous person and in later years he and Lady Casey were among those whose friendship I valued. When he became Governor-General in Australia in 1967 he invited me on behalf of the government to visit Australia, and I spent a very pleasant three weeks there, before going on to Fiji for a few days.

◆◆◆

26

Ranjit's Death and After

I had gone to Allahabad from Bengal for a brief rest. There had been no news from Ranjit and no reply to my official letters requesting news of him. I now telephoned my friend, the civil surgeon of Lucknow, Colonel Clyde, and begged him to find out how Ranjit was. Colonel Clyde had been a friend of ours while we lived in Lucknow, and our family physician as well. He was aware of Ranjit's health problem. A few days later a telegram from the superintendent of Bareilly Central Jail reached me saying, 'Your husband suffered mild heart attack.' The date given was a week earlier. I phoned the District Magistrate and asked permission for an immediate interview, but he expressed his inability to help me because of the new rules for political prisoners. I then wrote to the Governor, enclosing the telegram I had received, and the permission was granted.

I went to Bareilly. It was a tremendous shock to see Ranjit brought in to the superintendent's office on a stretcher. His head had been shaved and he was emaciated and almost unrecognizable. It cost me a tremendous effort to restrain my tears. He had been seriously ill for more than a month and was not receiving proper medical care, yet I had not been informed. I was shocked by his appearance, did not know what to talk about, and did not dare mention that I had asked the Governor's special permission for this interview, for even in extreme illness he would have reacted angrily to this. The office of the superintendent of any Indian jail is a sordid and often dirty place. Warders, jailers, and various others besides the superintendent are in and out, listening to every word exchanged. Knowing how Ranjit hated any show of emotion I just sat by the stretcher holding his hand and trying to give him news of Khali, the garden in Anand Bhawan, and the latest letter received from the girls. Interviews are short, but evidently on orders from above I was allowed to stay an hour. I asked for information regarding his treatment, but the prescriptions I wanted were not given to me. As I was leaving Ranjit said, 'I have been hearing rumours that I may be released on some ground. I have reason to believe it is so-called friends who are making this effort with the authorities. Nan, darling, remember that I am in the camp of lions—Gandhi and Nehru. I refuse to howl with the jackals.'

I promised him I would not encourage any move against his wishes. I did not know how I got to the car and reached the place where I was spending the night. I was frightened by his condition, and I was seething with anger. How dared they treat Ranjit in this barbarous manner!

Returning to Allahabad next day I found a reply to my request to Colonel Clyde in which he said he was not allowed to see or examine Ranjit, but, from what he had been able to learn, it seemed Ranjit had had a severe attack of pneumonia and was suffering from pleurisy. He should be in hospital. Immediately I phoned our close friend Dr Bidhan Roy in Calcutta, a Congress colleague and an eminent physician, and gave him all this information. I also had to tell him of Ranjit's request for no special favours. Bidhan confessed that he was greatly disturbed by this news but asked me to rely on his being able to help. He told me to try not to worry too much.

After a very great effort Bidhan did manage to examine Ranjit on grounds of being our family physician. Knowing how Ranjit felt about the question of release on special grounds, and not wanting to disturb him in his serious condition, Bidhan wrote an official letter to the Governor asking permission to take him to his own clinic in Calcutta as a parole prisoner for the urgently needed treatment. This request was refused, but a week later Ranjit was transferred to the Civil Hospital in Lucknow, as a prisoner, to be treated by Colonel Clyde. He was allowed a brief interview with me every day. There was a guard inside his room and armed police on duty outside his door. Fortunately, the hospital room was clean and comfortable, and Colonel Clyde was not only a good doctor but a close friend and he kept in touch with Dr Roy in Calcutta.

At first, Ranjit responded to treatment and began to look very much better, but in a month he began to slip again. He had now developed wet pleurisy. At that time we did not have the wonder drugs that later saved so many lives, and by the time he was finally released 'on grounds of health' the doctors knew he had not long to live. Even I could see that he was sinking. He was too weak to undertake the train journey home, and a friend in Lucknow kindly offered us the hospitality of his home. For three weeks, with night and day nurses and the best medical attention possible during that period, his condition continued to worsen. He had been neglected too long and his release had come too late.

Ranjit died at 5.10 a.m. on January 14, 1944. Death is always unexpected, and the shock of seeing him die, struggling for breath and not being able to breathe, was torture for me. The nurse and I were the only people with him at the end, and even after death for some minutes his hand continued to grip mine. After the agony of the previous days, he was suddenly still and his face was calm and young—he looked beautiful and might have been sleeping after a disturbed night.

I was absolutely alone and very bewildered. Bhai was incommunicado—in Ahmednagar Fort, as we later learned; the two older girls were in the U.S.A. The few relatives in Lucknow were in government service and could not be expected to help. But I phoned my cousin Captain Anand Nehru, who was cantonment officer. He came over immediately, and we decided to take Ranjit to Allahabad. Anand took charge of everything and, risking government displeasure, he got in touch with a few people who might be helpful. He also telephoned to Feroze and Indira in Allahabad and informed Budhilal, my cook, to expect us later that afternoon.

The first thing to be done was to tell Rita, who was still asleep, but I did not wake her. When the news was broken to her, she was naturally hysterical, for the shock had been severe. It was not possible to give her a sedative as we had to leave Lucknow as soon as arrangements were complete, but soon she realized that she must help me and she pulled herself together.

We left by car. P.D. Tandon, a journalist friend from Allahabad, happened to be in Lucknow and had hurried to help me as soon as he heard the news. He accompanied me and was of great assistance. Feroze and Indira met us at Phaphamau Bridge and we drove straight to my little house on Mukerjee Road where Anna Ornsholt, Budhi, Lala, and Sundar, our domestic staff, who had been with us for many years, were all waiting. It was a sad homecoming, and though I was in a state of shock there was so much to be done I had no time for personal grief.

The news had reached Allahabad, and groups of people from the city started to arrive. Soon our small garden was full. My cousin, Ladli Prasad Zutshi, who was always a tower of strength during the hard days of jail-going, was present and took charge of funeral arrangements. By 5 p.m. the funeral cortege had gone to the Ganga. In death Ranjit had looked incredibly young and serene and it was hard to believe him dead.

The days that followed were not easy. The servants had completely broken down and were, for the moment, useless. But for Anna, who took charge of Rita, and Indira and Feroze, who made me their special concern, I would not have been able to get through the various necessary formalities.

The Collector of Allahabad was requested to send the news of Ranjit's death to my brother for at that time no newspapers were supplied to the political prisoners. I knew Bhai would receive information through the jail grapevine later, but it was important for him to be informed through speedier channels.

Gandhiji was in Juhu after his release some time earlier, and had been informed by telephone. In his usual way he sent his reply by postcard: 'You are the daughter, sister, wife of great men. I will not condole with you. Come to me as soon as you can.'

My first task was to cable the girls at Wellesley College. We needed each other so much at this timc, but I knew they could not be sent for—nor could I, in the near future, go to them. This was an added unhappiness. The girls were truly wonderful. Their reply to the sad news was: 'We are with you in spirit. Do not grieve. Papu lives on in us.' It brought the solace I so much needed. My cousin Ladlibhai came every day, and Sir Tej Bahadur Sapru[12] and his family were a great support. My brother-in-law and his wife, Pratap Pandit and Saraswati bhabi, arrived and, all the way from distant Hyderabad, our dear friend Sarojini Naidu with her daughter Padmaja rushed to be with me. How I welcomed their coming! Sarojini stayed at Anand Bhawan but Padmaja shared my small home, and both were a gift from heaven at that harrowing time.

My troubles began on the third day after Ranjit died. The ashes had to be collected, and it was customary for a male member of the family to perform this rite. Allahabad can be very cold in January, and the days after the fourteenth, on which date the Sankranti festival falls, are especially bitter, with a high wind. The ashes are collected from the banks of the Ganga where cremations take place. Pratap was subject to colds and bronchitis, and his wife felt it would be a risk for him to go out on a chilly day. I was upset because he had not been present at the cremation and the last rites had been performed by a cousin of mine; this, according to traditional Hindu custom, was incorrect. I was in a quandary—women do not as a rule go to collect the ashes. I wanted very much for a member of the Pandit family to be there. At this time I got a phone call from Sir Tej, who was full of concern for me and very angry that Pratap was not going to the Ganga. He said he had asked his son P.N. Sapru, another dear friend of mine, to do the needful. In the end, Raja (P.N. Sapru), Ladlibhai, and Feroze went.

During Ranjit's illness I had been drawing what money I needed from my personal bank account. The money in this account was what I had received as a minister of the Uttar Pradesh government. As salaries were only Rs 500 in those

12. Leading constitutional lawyer and family friend; one-time member of the Viceroy's Executive Council.

days, I was able to save this because Ranjit gave me a cheque each month for the children's school and our domestic needs. Now, it was necessary to get a large amount because medical bills had to be settled. I wrote out a cheque on the joint account I had with Ranjit, and Anna went to the bank to cash it. She returned very distressed and said the bank would not honour the cheque. Pratap had left that morning for Bombay, so I phoned Ladlibhai to ask what could be the reason. He did not hesitate a minute. 'Are Ranjit and his brother a joint Hindu family?' he asked, and when I confirmed this he inquired where Ranjit's will had been deposited. I said I knew there was no will. Ranjit had spoken innumerable times about writing one but it had not been done. Ladlibhai was very grave. 'This might have very serious consequences for you,' he told me. He was proved right. What had happened was that all our accounts were frozen. Obviously, Pratap had given instructions which, under the existing Hindu law, were valid. As the widow of a man who died intestate and was a member of a joint Hindu family, and because I had no 'offspring', meaning son, I was not entitled to any part of the joint immovable property. It seemed that this also applied to money. There was doubt, too, regarding the shares and securities bought out of earned income by Ranjit. This was, very briefly, the position. I would have to write to Pratap to find out what he intended to do. The first thing was to cut down all expenses.

A letter drafted by Sir Tej was sent to Pratap and I set about reducing my household. I gave notice to my landlord and told Anna it would be impossible to retain her. With the exception of Budhi, my cook, I gave the other servants permission to look for other work. It was one of the moving moments of my life when one after another, each responded in his or her own way. Anna, gruff and practical, said, 'You want looking after now, I can't see any reason to be asked to leave.' The reason, I argued, was a very practical one, but she firmly refused to move and said she wanted no salary. The other servants, Lala and Sundar, were in tears. I was their malik, they had eaten my salt all these years, and now they were being insulted and treated as if their purpose in serving me was money. They would *not* go, and whatever little I had they would share. They would take no salary—only a few rupees for incidental expenses until better times. Budhi, who had been devoted to Ranjit, also gave up his salary and left his own home to move into the servants' quarters on Mukerjee Road. Presently the landlord came. I had insulted him, I had doubted his loyalty to the Nehrus. Did I think his relationship with us was based on the rent paid for the house? He would not permit me to leave, nor was there any question of rent for the time being. This same story was repeated by many people as well as by the shops where I bought things, and for nearly one year not a bill was sent to me in the town of Allahabad. From the rich bankers in their palatial city homes to the humble fruit seller in the marketplace, I was treated as if I were a very special member of their own families. The tears I had not been able to shed when Ranjit died flowed freely and often now, and my heart was full of gratitude for many kindnesses. Solace for his death came through these human gestures—this abundance of love that enveloped me and made me feel secure.

There was much to do in dealing with the huge correspondence from people at home and abroad and in meeting the many friends and acquaintances who came to Allahabad personally to convey their sympathy. Even the most tragic situation has a light moment, and several of these found their way into my life by the unconscious humour of insensitive people. One such incident was the remark of a professor at Allahabad University when he saw me sitting surrounded by mountain-high letters of condolence. 'I am so glad,' he said, 'that you have enough to do to keep your mind off yourself. It is the only thing that can help!'

Meanwhile, Pratap's reply had come enclosing a copy of my father-in-law's will. I had never heard any reference to this document, and was very surprised to find that a man who had provided financial security for his own daughters far beyond what was usual in those days should have made a will so rigidly in conformity with existing Hindu law. Quoting from this will, Pratap said he felt he could not go against his father's wishes but that I would be entitled to a Hindu widow's maintenance, which was Rs 150 a month for me and Rs 50 a month for each daughter until she married. All these years later I still cannot believe that this was the reaction to my predicament on the part of the brother Ranjit loved.

For the next week I spent most of my time with Sir Tej and other lawyers. I was told that there was no bar to Pratap's giving me a share in any monies for life if he wished, but the law was not in my favour beyond that. However, Sir Tej was thoroughly indignant and said he would file a suit on my behalf. 'You can't win,' he said, 'but I want to make this an example and will appear in court on your behalf myself.' The thought of this great constitutional lawyer and former Law Member of the Viceroy's Council appearing for me in the magistrate's court was not very pleasant. I suggested there should be further correspondence with Pratap, and Ladlibhai also urged this course.

I had written to Gandhiji in Juhu, and he sent word that Pratap should see him to discuss the matter. This meeting did not take place because we were still in the middle of the Quit India movement, and Pratap was not willing to speak to or be guided by Gandhiji. In a general way he rather blamed Gandhiji for spoiling Ranjit's career and even for his untimely death. After some correspondence back and forth, my case contesting the will was filed, and Sir Tej himself appeared in court. We could not win, but it made headline news and overnight became a *cause célèbre*. Newspaper editorials on the injustice of existing Hindu law appeared all over the country. Women's organizations, particularly the All India Women's Conference, of which I was still the President, passed resolutions demanding immediate codification of the

Hindu law giving Hindu women the right to inheritance and divorce. There was agitation of one sort or another on many levels, and street talk as well as discussion in clubs was with reference to this case. Prominent lawyers who had known my father or had been colleagues of my husband or friends of my brother wrote offering to take my case up to the High Court. There was indignation that Pratap should have refused to make over some share of the property he and Ranjit had jointly owned, as he was a wealthy man, and, apart from the anachronism of Hindu law, I had a just claim to a share. Finally, and after much painful dialogue, Pratap consented to release what he considered Ranjit's money earned without any investment from the joint income. This was a small amount, and Gandhiji insisted that it should end the unhappy episode.

Meanwhile, Bhai had heard of Ranjit's death, but no news of further developments had reached him. As he had not known of Ranjit's long illness in jail, the news of his death hit him especially hard. In his letter to me (to write which he had to seek special permission) he mentioned that he was sure I was financially secure as he knew the amount of movable and immovable property involved. Sitting in faraway Ahmednagar, he had forgotten about Hindu law. It was Pantji, who was interned with Bhai, who raised the doubt that unless something specific had been arranged between Ranjit and Pratap, and Ranjit had left a will, I might be in grave difficulties. This disturbed Bhai greatly, and one day when I had reached a moment of near despair, with an exceedingly small bank balance, I received a visit from the Collector who handed me a letter from Bhai enclosing a check for Rs 2,000. In his letter Bhai said he was sure I was not in need, but a doubt had been put into his mind and he had asked for permission to send me this 'small cheque'. Soon after this, as freer permission to write and receive letters was granted to the prisoners in Ahmednagar Fort, Bhai soon learned about the case and other matters. His immediate reaction was that I should not ask Pratap for anything. Later, when he heard of an agreement being possible, he took the same line as Gandhiji had and said I should accept whatever was offered. The unhappy episode had to be ended and forgotten; we had more important things to do. Finally, against Sir Tej's advice, I signed a document giving up my personal claims and that of any unborn grandsons I might have, and the chapter was brought to a close. I went to Juhu to spend a fortnight with Gandhiji, whose tender care of me was like balm to my wounded heart. With Gandhiji's guidance I was able to still my inner turmoil and to make peace with my brother-in-law. The deep love that Ranjit had had for his family helped me to do this, and, because of the reconciliation, our children did not suffer from a break in the affectionate relationship they had always enjoyed. From Juhu I went back to Bengal to continue my work in the famine area.

◆◆◆

27

Another Beginning

News of where members of the Working Committee[13] were lodged was kept a strict secret for the first months of the Quit India movement, and even afterward it was only through rumours that we had some idea of where they might be. Naturally it was not possible to send books to the prisoners as in previous imprisonments, but after my release from prison I thought I might take a chance and inquire if a parcel of books for Bhai could be forwarded to him wherever he was. I wrote to the District Magistrate and received an answer

13. The highest executive body of the Congress party. All the members had been arrested on August 9, 1942, and taken to an unknown destination.

in the affirmative. Immediately I sent a parcel, but months passed and I ceased to wonder whether it had been delivered. One night I was roused by Binda, our night watchman, who said there was a Saheb at the gate asking for me. In those days one was accustomed to receive messages late at night or in the early hours of the morning by personal messenger, so I was not surprised. I went to the gate, which was some distance from the house, and found, to my surprise, that an Englishman was lurking in the shadows.

'Mrs Pandit?'

'Yes. What can I do for you?' I asked.

'I have a note for you, but please be good enough to tear it up in my presence after you have read it.'

I opened an envelope and found a small square of thick, expensive paper on which was written: 'The books have been delivered. W.' The sender was Lord Wavell, the messenger, Simon Elwes. When I was High Commissioner in London ten years later I was 'sitting' for Simon, and he asked me if I remembered the incident and did I recognize him as the bearer of the message I had received that night. Of course I remembered the incident. I had forgotten the name, but even had I recalled it I would never have equated it with this distinguished and renowned artist! So many strange things used to happen in those far-off days of the freedom movement.

In England there was a group of men and women who stood solidly behind India's demand for independence. Individual Englishmen or women had long been part of the Indian national scene. C.F. Andrews, known the length and breadth of the country as Deshbandhu, friend of the poor, was a friend of Gandhiji. Miraben, one of his closest colleagues in the ashram, had been Madeleine Slade, the daughter of an admiral before she renounced her country and family ties to become a member of Gandhiji's growing family of national workers. One of the staunchest groups of our sympathizers were the Quakers, then led by Horace Alexander, and among them were women like Muriel Lester and our close family friend, Agatha Harrison—women of remarkable courage. Agatha was quite untiring in her efforts to bring Indian and British leaders together. She not only worked to place India's cause before the British public but later was very active in the United Nations, always seeking to build bridges wherever this could honourably be done. She played an important part, quietly, behind the scenes in many negotiations, and Gandhiji reposed much confidence in her.

Even in India there were Britishers who supported the freedom movement, who were drawn to Gandhiji's philosophy of nonviolence, and who disapproved of the continuation of the imperial system. I remember one incident which, though in itself did not prove anything, was certainly a little oasis in the desert that seemed to stretch before us at that time.

There was a Congress meeting to be held in Bombay and we were staying in Betty's home. Coming back one afternoon I was told that a Saheb was waiting to meet Panditji, as my brother was called. I went into the living room and saw an Englishman in a dhoti kurta sitting in a corner. Soon Bhai returned from his meeting and we heard the young man's story. He was John Napier, a captain in the army, who had been getting more and more discontented with his country's role in India and much drawn toward Gandhiji. His regiment was under orders of transfer, and he had taken the opportunity to come and meet my brother and Gandhiji to offer himself in any capacity he could be used. John Napier was a descendant of the famous general of that name, afterward Lord Napier who, having conquered Sind (now in Pakistan) for the British, had announced the news to his government in a message that said, merely. 'Peccavi!'

Bhai told John Napier that Gandhiji would not approve of what he had done. Among the most basic of Gandhiji's teachings was the fact that means must justify ends. No action however good and worthwhile in itself could be correct unless the manner in which it was performed was also truthful and right. From this point of view the young man's motives, though sincere, were cancelled by the way in which he had thrown up his previous commitments. If he was in earnest he must go back to his regiment and resign with a full understanding of what were the consequences of the step. Afterward he could join Gandhiji and be welcomed. It took some persuasion, but in the end he agreed to return. Suitable clothes had to be found for him, and he was sent off to rejoin his regiment. He resigned from the army, giving his reasons for doing so, and was court-martialled and imprisoned. Gandhiji pleaded his case with the Viceroy, then Lord Linlithgow, on grounds that the young man had acted honourably. There was correspondence between Gandhiji and the Viceroy on the subject for some time, and finally John Napier was released. The last I heard of him was that he was farming in Rhodesia. I wondered if the news was correct and if so why, with his record, he had chosen to settle in Rhodesia. Few leaders of a national movement would have acted as my brother and Gandhiji did in this case and refused to exploit a situation that would have made headline news and given much publicity to our cause.

Back in Calcutta after Ranjit's death, I joined forces with Dr Shyama Prasad Mukerji, who was working in famine areas, and our workers cooperated with one another in the district where, by now, severe cholera epidemics were sweeping the countryside in the wake of the famine. My band of workers were wonderful, dedicated young women from several parts of India. One of them, Dr Phulrenu Dutte, was a well-known social worker and leader in allied fields. She was a great support to me, and we toured together all over Bengal. It was at this point that I thought of starting a Save the Children Fund on a national basis. My committee was enthusiastic, and Sir Richard Casey, the Governor of Bengal, was helpful. I had a strange relationship with him. From time to time I had to contradict communiqués put out by the government regarding the famine—sometimes press conferences became necessary and I did not mince words. The situation was far too vital for half-truths or political prevarications. The government could not tell the truth about the famine as the actual things happening in the famine areas were shocking. The accounts given by both British and Indian officials to the press were incorrect and slurred over the grim situation and government's inefficiency in dealing with it. Those of us who were in contact with the suffering people realized that the truth had to be told, and we told it as loudly and clearly as we could. Sir Richard Casey occasionally sent for me to explain some particular incident or to tell me I must be more guarded in my statements. Always he was the perfect gentleman and experienced diplomat. He would listen to me, and even when there was any argument he kept an open mind, though in his official position he had to follow the government line.

Money for the Save the Children Fund was coming in, but it was nowhere near the amount needed. The famine and allied epidemics continued, but our children's homes multiplied and, even with the simplest arrangements, and mostly honourary doctors and workers, our expenses increased. I launched an appeal to the women of the world to help us. The response was swift and dramatic—the first check came from Madame Chiang Kaishek for $10,000, another for $5,000 from Mrs Roosevelt, yet another from the India League of America, of which Pearl Buck was chairman, for $10,000. Money poured in from many places, and our children's homes began to assume proper shape and give more adequate help to the ever-increasing number of little ones, mostly orphans, whom we still picked up in the worst-stricken areas.

I was due to go in August from Calcutta to Bombay where Indira was expecting her first child. Just before I was to leave, Rita fell ill and had to have an emergency appendectomy, so Rajiv was born without any assistance from me.

During this period I paid brief visits to Allahabad and learned from Sir Tej that Gandhiji was anxious for me to go to the U.S.A. to tell the American public what was happening in India. In that time one did not write letters—messages were sent, mostly through Congress volunteers, and it was one such message sent to me in Allahabad during my absence in Calcutta that had reached Sir Tej. He was equally keen that I should get away and speak about actual conditions in India. He said that if I was willing he would explore various channels. I expressed my willingness to do so.

Sir Tej was President of the Indian Council for World Affairs, and a Pacific Relations Conference was due to take place in Hot Springs, Virginia, for the Allies to discuss the future of the Asian countries after their liberation from Japan had been effected at the end of the war. India had been invited to this conference as an observer, and Sir Tej decided to send a small delegation in which I should be included. The other members were Pandit Hriday Nath Kunzru, Justice Fazli Hussain, Dr Lokanathan, and Mr B. Shiva Rao. The conference was some months away, and I was the only proposed member with a problem. The hurdle was that my passport had been confiscated and there was no likelihood of its being reissued to me at this time.

Among those who had befriended me in Calcutta were the Chinese Consul General and his American wife. Dr Pao was a scholar and had been a friend of my husband's. He was a mandarin, very wealthy, and a member of the diplomatic service. His wife, Edith, was from Boston, equally wealthy and well born, and a charming hostess. Whenever I was in Calcutta during my famine work they insisted on my dining with them or spending part of my free time in their beautiful home. It was a refuge for me where I could rest, have delicious Chinese food, and, above all, keep away from the press. One day I received a letter from Edith while I was in some remote corner of the famine area. She said she wanted me to come to Calcutta on a certain day to meet some interesting people at an informal buffet dinner. I sent word regretting and said I was not in a party mood. However, she wrote again, and in the end I went to Calcutta. I could not understand why I had been asked as the party was obviously for the American

Air Force then functioning in the Burma theatre of war. I did not know anyone. At dinner we sat at small round tables and I found myself next to a very interesting man in Air Force uniform. As I was not familiar with the various insignia, I did not know the rank of my dinner partner. He asked me if I knew anything about America, and I told him I had two daughters at Wellesley College but had never been to the U.S.A. myself. 'I would very much like to go,' I added, 'but this is a difficult time to go abroad.' He agreed, and it was only after I got home that I realized I did not know his name!

Some weeks passed, and I received a telegram passed through the censor but delivered nevertheless, which was unusual. The telegram read as follows: 'If you still wish to go to the U.S., meet me in Calcutta on...' signed 'Stratemeyer'. This was General Stratemeyer, Chief of the Allied Air Command in the Eastern theatre of war. Ten days later I had a message from the American Consul General in Calcutta informing me that a signal from Washington, from Mr Sumner Welles, Undersecretary of State, gave clearance for my visit to be expedited and all help to be extended. A few nights later I found myself in a wartime plane with bucket seats and two rosy-cheeked, very young pilots, ready to start out on a flight that would mark a new and very important beginning in my life.

◆◆◆

28

A Lecture Tour

I arrived in New York in the early hours of the morning. There were no problems at the airport. I was met by a smart young WAC who said she had everything under control, expressed surprise at my lack of luggage, and took me to a waiting military car. We drove to a hotel which I later discovered was the Waldorf Astoria. It was a bitterly cold December day and I was miserable for want of proper clothing, but once inside the hotel I began to feel more cheerful. The young WAC suggested I should go to bed and have a good rest before getting in touch with my friends. In any case it was too early in the morning to do anything else. She also told me that all my expenses in the hotel had been taken care of for a week and that I had nothing to worry about. She left a State Department phone number with me in case of need. I went to my room and got between soft sheets. I was asleep in a few minutes—two days in a military plane with bucket seats had been an exhausting experience.

I awoke a few hours later refreshed and very hungry. Realizing that I had few clothes, none suitable to the climate, and only a twenty-dollar bill that a friend in Calcutta had slipped into my handbag, the first thing to do was to establish contact with people I knew—first of all, Lekha and Tara. It was a joy to hear their voices and to know we were so near to one another and would meet soon. The next call was to Pearl Buck. I told her that my immediate need was clothes, shoes, and a warm coat. She promised to come soon to take me shopping. She also informed me that there had been a message from Bhai to her husband, Richard Walsh, of John Day and Company, who were Bhai's publishers, asking him to advance five hundred dollars to me from his royalties for my immediate expenses. I learned some time afterward that this message had been sent through the personal courtesy of Lord Wavell. Pearl Buck was widely known in India through her books. I had corresponded with her when she was the head of the India League of America and with her husband in connection with Bhai's *Autobiography*, which John Day and Company had published some years earlier. For these reasons I felt I knew them both. We became close friends, and Pearl advised me about many things, and her home was open to my daughters.

My first view of New York was when Pearl Buck took me shopping. I did not know exactly what my mental picture of New York was, but I was wholly unprepared for and overwhelmed by what I saw. Great tall buildings, glittering shop windows, cars, well-dressed men and women and signs of affluence everywhere. We went—I now wonder why—to Saks Fifth Avenue, and I was dazzled and bewildered. The stores were all decked for Christmas and I had never before seen such decorations nor been subject to such temptation. It was all an unreal world into which I strayed by accident. The past, with its jail-going, was more real, and so were the filth and stench of the famine-stricken area from where I had so recently come. Those little abandoned, diseased babies were real enough, as were the piled-up corpses of men and women who died for want of food, quicker than they could be cremated. What was I doing here? Surely I could serve no useful purpose. My thoughts ran along these lines for many days, and I wrote something to this effect to my brother.

My first priority was to change my hotel and find one less ostentatious. Dick and Pearl Walsh warned me that the Waldorf Astoria would be harmful to my image, besides being far too expensive. As my purpose in coming to the United States was to reach the American people and tell them about India's freedom struggle, plans should be made so I could do so without delay. I was in a delicate position, as 'officially' I was not recognized by the State Department even though it was through the help of President Roosevelt that I had been able to come. Mrs Roosevelt had been very kind to my daughters and had invited them to lunch in her New York apartment soon after they had arrived from India. A day or two after my arrival a warm welcoming letter came from her saying that she hoped to meet me soon. While President Roosevelt was at Yalta, Mrs Roosevelt invited me to lunch. I was surprised by the near austerity of the meal itself as well as the simple way it was served. That afternoon was the beginning for me of a friendship that I have valued and from which I gained a great deal in the understanding of human beings. This was one of Mrs Roosevelt's special talents. It was also a privilege to work with her for several sessions in the United Nations, with which I was later associated. It was a great disappointment to me not to have been able to meet President Roosevelt, who died shortly after his return from the Yalta Conference.

Within a week after I arrived in New York the Chinese Consul General gave a big reception for me. I did not know him personally, but had letters of introduction to him from my friend Dr Pao in Calcutta. The Consul General and his wife turned out to be a very charming couple, and at the glittering reception they seemed to have collected everyone who had a name—social or political. I was somewhat bewildered at the number of hands I had to shake and by the men and women whose world I had long ceased to live in. Everyone was more than kind. Presently I found myself standing a little apart, and near me was an elegant but rather ugly man. He must have felt sorry for me for he said—pointing to the drink I had in my hand—'You have chosen wisely, madame. There are only two kinds of people in the world—those who drink martinis and those who don't.' I told him I did not know what a martini was and had taken the glass nearest to me on the tray. This seemed to amuse him and he suggested I now taste it. Later in the evening I asked my hostess who the gentleman was, and she was horrified. 'How dreadful, I have not introduced you, but, madame, surely you know that is Somerset Maugham!'

Among those who wanted to befriend India and had the power to do so was Henry Luce, the owner of *Life, Time,* and *Fortune* magazines. He was interested in our freedom movement and sympathetic to our aspirations. There was only one hitch—a fairly big one—he hated Communism and was afraid that India might turn toward the Soviet Union. His wife, Clare Boothe Luce, was an author and dramatist as well as a member of the House of Representatives. She was one of the most beautiful women I have ever met. Even today, in her seventies, she seems unaging and is very lovely. Henry Luce was anxious to help India. He gave a dinner-reception for me at the Waldorf Astoria, to which he invited the governors of every state in the U.S., many of whom flew over in their private planes just for the dinner. Besides these, Henry collected the elite of New York and all to whom he thought the freedom of India mattered. It was a remarkable evening, with speeches from a number of people and of course one from me thanking the guests on behalf of my country and its imprisoned leaders. Unfortunately, after Independence, we fell from favour because Henry could not understand our nonaligned policy and believed that Nehru would 'go over' to the communists.

Lekha and Tara joined me for their Christmas vacation from Wellesley, and Rita arrived soon after with other delegates from India who were to attend the Pacific Relations Conference in Hot Springs, Virginia. The conference was a new experience for me. First of all, Hot Springs was a surprise. Getting out of the train I walked along the platform while the luggage was being removed. The notices 'For Whites' and 'For Coloured' on different doors took me back through the years to the time in my own country when benches marked 'For Europeans Only' had been a familiar sight. I could hardly believe my eyes. I insisted on using the 'Coloured' toilet because I was so angry, though I was assured that there was no need for me to do so.

The conference was held to discuss the future of nations in the Pacific Ocean area after the war. The delegates were men whose names were familiar to me through the press. It was interesting to meet and hear them talk. War in the Pacific was still raging. The world had passed through a holocaust. One could imagine the serious after-effects of global war, and yet, here around the conference table, men with big names and big deeds to their credit spoke in the language of imperialism and division of the world so that the 'backward, weaker sections' could be 'protected' and led in the right direction.

Especially interesting was the difference between the then colonial powers—England, France, the Netherlands—and the United States. The colonial powers used diplomatic language in which nearly everything had more than one meaning. They were sophisticated, experienced in ruling others, and very clever. The Americans of those days were simple, with hardly any understanding of Asia and completely lacking in the diplomatic sophistication that, to some extent, they have since acquired. The Indian Council of World Affairs in New Delhi was an invitee to this conference, with observer status only and no right to vote. The five delegates were sent merely to listen and record proceedings as the area to be discussed was important to India. We were all new to this kind of meeting, but I learned a great deal then that stood me in good stead in later years when I was associated with the United Nations.

At the end of the conference I had to decide how to go about my work in informing the American public about India and the conditions then prevailing in my country. Among my friends were many Americans who had sympathy for our freedom struggle and admiration for Gandhi and Nehru. Among these were John Haynes Holmes, Roger Baldwin, Louis Fischer, Paul Robeson, Vincent Sheean, Dorothy Norman, and Walter White. I was assured that I could best reach the public through a lecture tour, and Pearl Buck introduced me to the Clark Getts Lecture Bureau. Mr Getts was an amazing little man and seemed delighted to have me on his list of speakers. He mentioned a string of illustrious names he had sponsored and how much they had earned from their tours. Neither he nor I then knew that my lecture tour would give us both more money than his bureau or I had earned for a long time!

We sat down to discuss lecture topics and related matters. 'What kind of saris will you wear for your lectures?' asked Mr Getts. I said that I did not understand what he meant. He soon made it clear. The American public, he told me, would expect someone from India to look exotic and to wear bright clothes and fine jewels.

'I suppose you have your jewels with you?' he inquired anxiously. I began to feel desperate. How did one explain the stark reality of the situation in India to someone like this? How to tell him that it was years since I had worn any kind of jewel, and that my life had been unconnected with the social round that demanded fine clothes and ornaments? I could but try.

'Please understand,' I told him firmly, 'that my husband has recently died under tragic circumstances. My brother and the leaders of our freedom movement are all in jail. I have been able to come to this country almost as a refugee to tell people the truth about India. The story of what is happening must be told, and it is so dramatic that it needs no props. I do assure you I am a good speaker. I can reach my audience. They won't bother about my clothes or the absence of jewels. Please let me do this my way.' I made one condition. I would not speak in any place where Blacks were not admitted.

After considerable persuasion and some help from his wife, Osa Johnson, who was famous as the photographer of wildlife and who, I discovered, had met Ranjit on one of her tours, a rough tour schedule was prepared for me. On paper it appeared easy and interesting. It was to cover a whole year and extend from coast to coast. After a very few weeks at the job I began to wonder why I had hated being in jail. On an extended lecture programme one is literally a prisoner—a prisoner of the lecture bureau and a prisoner of the audiences, few of whom had much information about India. The 'untouchables' and the maharajas were of great interest, but, alas, I hardly mentioned them. My talk was obviously on another level, but soon I began to reach people, and demands for my lectures doubled and trebled. I spoke in big cities and in the smallest imaginable places. The names of some of the towns were a source of constant diversion to me—Waco, Muncie, Tulsa, Poughkeepsie, and so on. I expect American tourists find the names of our towns much more extraordinary!

I started my lecture programme with an appearance on the 'Town Hall of the Air' in New York, where I was presented to a very large audience that terrified me. Roger Baldwin of the Civil Liberties Union was the moderator, and the person chosen to oppose me was Robert Boothby, now Lord Boothby, member of Parliament and parliamentary secretary to Mr Churchill. The subject was 'Is India Ready for Independence?' In spite of my initial stage fright I was no newcomer to the lecture platform and soon got into my stride. Question hour is my favourite time, and I always try to put something into my speech that will provoke a question. Several pertinent questions were levelled at me and also at a rather disconcerted Mr Boothby. I was very satisfied with my performance and so were my American friends. It was a good beginning and I received many press notices. The most enjoyable part for me was the aftermath of the lecture. On my return to my hotel I received telephone calls from many parts of the United States. People who had listened to the programme on their radios called to congratulate me. One enthusiastic man said, 'Honey, I didn't listen much to what you were saying, but your voice is like moonbeams and honey and I love you and am on India's side!' It was most amusing and indicative of the warm enthusiasm I received from many Americans.

This tour covered schools, colleges, clubs, and universities. It was gratifying to see how much publicity the media gave me for I was unknown and generally referred to as 'the Woman from India', but in a remarkably short time the press was with me and India was the focus of attention in various small towns across the country. Audiences everywhere gave me generous applause and recognition, and I had gracious hospitality in many American homes of every class and kind. This is perhaps the reason that, even when I am most upset over the gap between official America's capacity to help and inability to understand the problems of others—for there is a considerable gap—I never forget that the people are wonderful, warm, and generous. Some of the friends I made then have remained close to me, and even when there has been misunderstanding on governmental levels between our respective countries, our friendship has not been affected by it. I am truly thankful for the experience and personal contacts I gained from that first lecture tour.

During the tour reports were sent by the press to England, where a reporter asked Lady Astor what she thought of my speeches. Her reply was vitriolic and characteristic. 'If the British had not been in India,' she said, 'that woman would have been burnt on her husband's funeral pyre!' I refused to comment when the remark was conveyed to me. Curiously enough, when, as High Commissioner, I met Lady Astor, she was kindness itself, and I am sure she liked me. She was beginning to lose her memory, but told me fabulous stories about the 'old days' when people could live graciously, which I understood her to mean with several country homes and two hundred servants. She also told interesting stories of her own 'fights' to achieve recognition and equality. I was sorry I had not met her when she was younger.

Bhai wrote a letter on May 3, 1945, to the girls at Wellesley from Bareilly Central Prison, where he had been transferred from Ahmednagar Fort. He said:

> I have been following with interest and excitement Mummie's wanderings in the U.S. The accounts we get are of course very brief in the papers. From her letters I add to them. Even so they are fragmentary and I have to imagine a lot. I am so happy that she is such a success wherever she goes and has developed into a forceful and moving speaker. Do you know I have never heard her speak in English at a public meeting? That is something I am looking forward to.

There was a fairly large group of Indians settled in California, fruit farming. Some were immigrants of the usual kind, whereas others were those who had come away from India as revolutionaries during the Ghadr revolt in the Punjab in

1909. They were nationalists who had been exiled by the British government and had chartered a ship, the *Kamagata Maru,* to take them to Canada, but the Canadian government would not accept them, and they were given permission to land in the United States. As most of them were farmers from the Punjab they continued their hereditary work in conditions not too different from those in their native land, and many became very prosperous and good citizens of the United States.

Besides these one-time revolutionaries there was a considerable Indian community, mainly on the East Coast. This consisted largely of men who had come as students and remained to work as scientists, professors, and writers. In the past few years they had also been giving publicity to the freedom movement and trying to arouse public opinion to work for India's independence. In New York an India League had been started. At this time the president of the League was J.J. Singh, and many distinguished American names figured on the list of members. Another organization, based in Washington, was the Committee for India's Freedom. Syed Hossain was its president, and this too was supported by a number of well-known Americans. This committee published a weekly called *The Voice of India.* Syed was teaching at the University of Southern California where he had spent many years, and after Independence he was to be appointed India's first Ambassador to Egypt. I was happy to meet him again and to have his cooperation for our common cause.

As the time approached for the meeting in San Francisco, where the Charter of the United Nations was to be framed, it was the desire of both these organizations as well as Indian residents in the United States that something should be done to show Americans and the world that the Indian delegation, hand-picked by the British government to attend the meeting, was in no sense representative of our country; that India's voice was stifled, and her leaders, who alone among Indians were competent to sit at the conference table to take part in reshaping the world, were in prison without trial. Some time earlier Mr Churchill had made his famous Atlantic Charter speech, but there was no mention of India in this. When he was asked to clarify the position he did so very clearly indeed by saying that the Atlantic Charter did not apply to India. This declaration had embittered even those Indians who were not actively participating in the freedom struggle. It had angered those who had been living abroad for many years. It was blatantly unfair, and a statement in the best imperialist tradition. The Four Freedoms, for which men and women were fighting and losing their lives every day, were to be applied only to the chosen.

The two Indian freedom organizations got together and decided that a small group of Indians must be present in San Francisco to talk outside the conference hall, and that I must spearhead the attack against the British-chosen Indian delegation. Others in the group were B. Shiva Rao, an eminent journalist who had attended the Pacific Relations Conference with me, J.J. Singh, Syed Hossain, and Anup Singh. The Indians settled in California were mainly around Stockton, Sikh farmers who had been away from India for many years. Some were the second generation born in Stockton, but the years had not lessened in any way their love for or pride in the country of their origin. They were delighted that I should represent India even though the doors of the conference hall would be closed against me, and they subscribed a sum of ten thousand dollars to make it possible for our unofficial delegation to live in San Francisco and function as representatives of the Indian people. It was a gesture of love, and even after this passage of time I am moved when I think of what those fellow countrymen did for us.

But in spite of the generous financial aid it was a problem to find a place to live in San Francisco at that time. Every hotel, boarding house, and room to let had already been booked far in advance for members of official delegations and those accompanying them, and the accommodation problem, already acute due to the war, was greatly aggravated. We had no credentials and little possibility of being able to stay in the kind of hotels where we would be likely to meet and speak with delegates of other countries. I spent one night in the lobby of the St Francis Hotel. It looked as if that would be my fate the next night also, but just as I was looking for a comfortable chair a lady in uniform, whom I had noticed the previous evening at a desk, came up and asked if I needed help. I told her I was from India and explained the purpose of my being in San Francisco. She introduced herself and told me that she knew about Gandhi and Nehru and had seen some publicity about me in the press. Very cordially and simply she said, 'My name is Mrs Ogden Mills. I am living alone in a large apartment, and I shall be happy if you will come and stay with me.'

I was very touched by her kindness but reminded her that she did not know me. 'I'm willing to take the risk,' she said, smiling, 'if you are willing to look after yourself. I have no servants.' So I found myself in a beautiful apartment with every sort of comfort. My hostess and I met at odd intervals as she was on duty with the conference, and I soon discovered that though she was obviously very wealthy she was also simple, and we remained friends until she died a few years ago.

Having a base made a great difference to me, and I was able to concentrate on my work. The technique of our group was to issue short statements and have articles printed in the newspapers, to buy time on radio, and to hold public meetings whenever possible. In all these activities we tried to explain that the real India was not represented in the conference chamber. The press was cooperative and gave us good write-ups, but, obviously, with a meeting of the importance of drafting a charter for a new world order, much of the attention of the public was focused on this work and also on the important world personalities then present in San Francisco. Very often, however, one of the delegates did attend our meetings. Among those who came were General Romulo of the Philippines, M. Schubert of the French delegation, several Americans, and, most important to us, Mr Molotov of the Soviet Union. Later he spoke in the conference hall and referred to me as the real voice of India, saying that the delegates of India at the conference were but an echo of the voice of Britain and should not be given any serious consideration. This remark was widely publicized. The press began to refer to me as 'the lady with the lamp'.

During my tour I sometimes spoke on the radio on time bought for me by American sympathizers of India's cause. On one such occasion my subject was 'The Challenge of Asia'. In this talk I spoke of the need for America to become aware of the aspirations of that continent. The philosophy behind India's desire for freedom was something more than the ending of alien rule for ourselves—our struggle extended to all those who expected a new deal from the Allied Powers after the war.

My lecture tour and my speeches at San Francisco were widely reported in India and appreciated. It was inevitable, in a non-governmental mission of the kind in which I was engaged, that there could be no brief or prearranged plan. In San Francisco my companions and I were a rebel group, and I had the double disability of not having a passport and of being in the States by the courtesy of the President and the generosity of my fellow countrymen settled there. An effort of this kind is, as it were, played by ear, seizing opportunities as and when they come. There is no doubt that on my return to India I was received as something of a heroine. It is also correct to say that my American experience paved the way for the later role I played on the international stage as leader of the Indian delegation to the United Nations and as an Ambassador of India abroad.

Not long after my stay in San Francisco, I had an invitation from President Truman's office saying that the President would like to see me when I was next in Washington. The lecture tour had ended for the moment, and before the next phase began I went to Washington. The visit was obviously a brief one and at a delicate time. President Truman received me cordially and referred to my broadcast on the challenge of Asia. I explained that we looked on America as a friend of freedom—witness my own presence in the States—and yet arms were given by America to its allies to be used to suppress freedom movements in Asia, though the United States gave its moral support to such movements. The President had recently returned from Potsdam and told me an interesting incident. It seemed he had posed the question I was asking him to Mr Attlee, regarding misuse of American aid, including arms, and Attlee had replied that unfortunately once aid is given in any form the use of it could not be controlled. I did not know when I was talking to the President that I would be back in that same office a few years later as India's Ambassador to Washington. Mr Truman, then, and as I found out later, was simple and direct—two very important qualities in anyone at the head of affairs in our age.

During my lecture tour Mayor La Guardia of New York expressed a desire to meet me. I had heard a great deal about him and was pleased to have this opportunity. The meeting was rather amusing. Mayor La Guardia said he was interested in India's freedom struggle. He had read and enjoyed Nehru's autobiography. He admired Nehru but found it difficult to understand Gandhi. What was a saint doing in politics, and why were the millions of India following him? For that matter, he said, why was Nehru following him? I tried to explain that our struggle was a unique experiment, and, placed in the situation we were, vis-a-vis the British, without arms and also because of the influence of our history and tradition, the common Indian easily identified himself with Gandhi's values and methods. 'It doesn't make sense to me,' said the mayor. 'You come here and ask the Americans for their moral support. How far will anybody's moral support take you toward your freedom? Now if you had asked me for arms I could have understood and I would have tried to help you; but I begin to doubt India's ability to become an independent nation if she fights with abstract weapons. Of course you have my sympathy but it's of little value.' When I thanked him for giving me the interview I said his sympathy would be greatly appreciated by both Gandhi and Nehru, which turned out to be true. He was a little man—I mean in stature—rare to see in America—very likeable and, I was told, had a fine record of service. I was happy to meet him.

◆◆◆

29

Interim Government

When the Second World War ended, members of the Congress Working Committee were released, as were many others who had spent time in jails, but hundreds were still kept in detention. Mr Churchill's national government made fresh proposals through Lord Wavell for a reconstitution of the Viceroy's Executive Council, which would now consist only of Indians, with the exception of the Viceroy and Commander-in-Chief. Hindus and Muslims would be equally represented, and accredited persons would be appointed to represent India abroad. Nothing in the proposals would prejudice the framing of India's future Constitution. It was hoped that popular ministries, which had earlier been replaced by Governors' rule, would be reinstated. This offer opened the door for negotiations, and Gandhiji sought clarification from the Viceroy on some points. First, he wanted it made clear that the government was not implying that Congress was a purely Hindu organization. Maulana Azad, a Muslim, was still the Congress President, and he must be invited to the Simla Conference, where talks were to be held. Maulana

Azad was a distinguished scholar and one of the leaders of political awakening among the Muslims. After Independence he was Minister of Education in the Union Government for many years. In his presidential address in 1940 he had said:

> I am a Mussalman and proud of that fact. Islam's splendid traditions of thirteen hundred years are my inheritance... I am proud of being an Indian. I am part of the indivisible unity that is Indian nationality. I am indispensable to this noble edifice and without me this splendid structure of India is incomplete... It was India's historic destiny that human races and cultures and religions should flow to her, finding a home in her hospitable soil, and that many a caravan should find rest here... One of the last of these caravans...was that of the followers of Islam... We gave our wealth to her [India] and she unlocked the doors of her own treasures to us. We gave her what she needed most, the most precious of gifts from Islam's treasury, the message of democracy and human equality.

The second clarification sought was that the communal parity in the Viceroy's Executive Council would be accepted only on a temporary basis, and that it must be understood that the nomination of Muslim members could not be the right of the Muslim League alone. The Congress had large numbers of Muslim followers, many of whom had held positions of responsibility in the Congress organization as well as the provincial governments. Mr Jinnah found this last point wholly unacceptable and refused to permit the Congress to nominate any Muslims in its quota. The Viceroy had already given his assurance on these points to Gandhiji, but Mr Jinnah's veto led to a stalemate. Had the Viceroy been firm at this time the Simla Conference might have been the beginning of a fruitful effort. As it was, he tried to placate Mr Jinnah by backing out of the assurances given to Congress, and the inevitable happened. The conference ended in failure.

In August 1945 the Government of India announced there

would be a general election the following year. Bhai had been in correspondence with me in New York since his release from prison, and now wrote that I should come home immediately to take part in the elections, which would be held in January 1946. Lekha had already graduated from Wellesley and was also due to return to India after breaking her journey in London. I flew back directly. It was a great joy to be with Bhai again. So much had happened since we had last seen each other—to us, to the country. I had been through great sorrow, but exhilarating experiences in a new country had enabled me to look ahead with confidence. The most heartwarming of feelings was to know Bhai was proud of me. There was also the friendly and warm welcome I received from all sections of the press, which was encouraging. I was eager to get to work. Compared with 1937, the elections of 1946 were very tame. Most of the Congress candidates were returned unopposed, and I was among them. The Congress went back to the ministries and to working on the programmes begun during their last tenure. I was once again in charge of my former portfolios. But there had been one big change. The Muslim League had secured 75 per cent of the Muslim vote, a larger majority than had been expected.

The Muslim League had been started in 1906 with the encouragement of the British and had consisted of upper-class Muslims. Many Muslims, including Mr Jinnah, had cooperated with the Congress in the period after the First World War when the question of Turkey and the Khilafat Movement had been of great importance to Indians. When Gandhiji's noncooperation movement entered the nineteen thirties, many of these drifted away from the Congress, though large numbers of Muslims took part in the national struggle. Mr Jinnah retired from the political scene and went to England, where he practised law for many years. Mr Jinnah's marriage to Ruttie Petit, daughter of a wealthy Parsi banker, Sir Dinshaw Petit, caused a nine-day stir in India. Ruttie was a friend of mine. We were the same age but brought up very differently. She was spoiled, very beautiful, and used to having her own way. She was much younger than Jinnah and it was certainly not a 'love match'. But Jinnah was a Muslim, and the Parsis were, in those days, a very conservative group. This in itself seemed reason enough to Ruttie to shock the community—'wake it up', as she was fond of saying. Besides, he had made a name for himself at the Bar, was very much in the news, and a coming political leader. All these things appealed to her. In spite of the opposition of her parents and the Parsi community, she married him. For a short period she enjoyed the notoriety she had wanted, but she was too restless, always in search of new experiences and sensations and never able to settle down. She died tragically on her thirtieth birthday. They had had one daughter.

For the elite of the Muslim League the matter of importance was not independence so much as demands for protection and special privileges for Muslims, under the British. There was fear also, because Hindus in those days were largely better educated and better trained for government services as well as in the professions, apart from being by far the bigger religious community. This fear was not rational, therefore, it could not be reasoned with. However, it gave the British an opportunity to shift the focus of attention from political problems to those of a religious and communal nature. British policy had always been to encourage disruptive tendencies, whereas the national movement's endeavour had been to unite Indians. The enforcement of the separate electorates[14] by the government was an example of the 'divide and rule' policy, and it gave a boost to those who exploited differences in religion for political purposes. The Muslims were but one, though the biggest, of India's 'minorities'. In India there are people of many religions—Buddhists, Sikhs, Christians, Jains, Parsis, and Jews, besides the Muslims. Largely they belong

14. Law by which Hindus had to vote for Hindu candidates and Muslims for Muslim candidates.

to the same racial stock and were originally converted from Hinduism. Some came seeking refuge hundreds of years ago—the Jews and the Parsis—and were made welcome, for India has had a tradition of tolerance and has absorbed people and ideas that have come from outside. Christianity came to India shortly after the crucifixion of Christ. Buddhism, Jainism, and Sikhism were offshoots of Hinduism. Islam was known in India through Arab traders long before the first Muslim conquerors came and established a dynasty in the north of the country. During the centuries when Muslim rulers held sway in large parts of India there was a synthesis of the Hindu and Islamic cultures that affected every facet of living—art and music, language and food, literature and philosophy. In several regions of the country, and particularly in my home province of Uttar Pradesh, the blend of these two ways had, over the centuries, created a very sophisticated way of life. Though differences existed, one was not aware of them, and the deliberate encouragement of discord and strife was something unheard of in the years I was growing up.

When Mr Jinnah returned to India and became the undisputed leader of the Muslim League, Gandhiji and Congress leaders met him and corresponded with him on many occasions in order to determine what exactly Muslim League demands were; but these were never clear, and, apart from wanting greater protection by the British from the Hindus, the League had no programme comparable to that of the Congress constructive (social and economic) programme or the national independence demand. In 1940 the Muslim League demanded a separate state—Pakistan—based on its theory that India was composed of two 'nations', Muslims and Hindus. At the time, this two-nation theory was not seriously considered by most Indians. The Muslim League had never been in conflict with the British government or suffered the consequences of the freedom struggle. As against Congress, which was a gigantic mass movement of people of differing faiths—peasants, workers, intellectuals, and others—the Muslim League remained an upper-class group of Muslims only, with a semi-feudal approach to the varied problems of the day. In this context it was impossible for Congress to accede to the League's demands to be the only spokesman of the Indian Muslim.

In Britain the general elections after the war brought to power the Labour party, and Mr Attlee, the Prime Minister, announced that after the elections in India a body should be constituted to frame a constitution. In March and April of 1946 a Cabinet Mission consisting of the Secretary of State for India, who was Lord Pethick Lawrence, Sir Stafford Cripps, and Mr (afterward Lord) Alexander came to India and had long talks with Congress and Muslim League leaders in Simla and elsewhere to find some basis for agreement for the transfer of power from Britain to India. The growing resentment against British rule was clear, and Britain, after the long war, was tired and confronted with many national problems. After months of discussions and debate the Congress decided to accept the proposal to participate in a Constituent Assembly for the purpose of framing a constitution, and it eventually also agreed to take part in an interim government in Delhi, with my brother as interim Prime Minister. Elections for the Constituent Assembly were held, and though the Muslim League secured the majority of the Muslim seats allotted, the bulk of the remaining seats went to the Congress and to those who supported it. The Muslim League, which had previously accepted the Cabinet Mission proposals, changed its mind and decided to have a Direct Action Day on August 16 to demand the formation of Pakistan.

During this period I was once again a minister of the Uttar Pradesh government and living in Lucknow, and as far as I remember August 16 that year coincided with Janamashtmi, the Hindu festival of the birth of Krishna—which is also my birthday according to the Hindu calendar. However, no thought of birthday celebration was in my mind as the day progressed and I sat listening to the radio broadcasts giving news of horrors perpetrated, mainly in Bengal. Thousands of lives were lost and blood flowed in the streets of Calcutta as well as in rural areas, as atrocities were committed and Hindus slaughtered by followers of the League. One particular area, Noakhali, was the worst affected by this ghastly communal bloodbath, and Gandhiji went immediately to Noakhali and toured the area on foot, bringing relief and sanity by his presence.

The day after the terrible Direct Action holocaust, Bhai, who was again Congress President, handed the Viceroy his list of nominees to the interim government. They included himself, Sardar Patel, C.R. Rajagopalachari, Asaf Ali, Rajendra Prasad, John Mathai, and Jagjivan Ram. Later Sarat Chandra Bose and Sardar Baldev Singh were added to the list. The members of the interim government took office on September 2. This day was denounced by Mr Jinnah as Black Day, and throughout the country further acts of violence took place and hatred and terror once more swept the country.

It was six o'clock on a hot steamy September morning. I had had a bad night and was still dozing when the telephone rang outside my room. I let it ring. Presently there was a knock on the door and Rajab, my peon, said there was a long distance call and that there was some very important person on the other end. Rajab was one of the three peons I was entitled to as a minister. From the moment he came to the house he appointed himself a sort of majordomo, though he was the youngest of the three. He looked after everything that concerned me and in the process antagonized Ahmad, the senior peon, known as a jamadar, and my cook, Budhilal. I never discovered what his working hours were, as he always seemed to be on duty. Struggling out of bed I went to the telephone. I spoke irritably, but someone far more irritable than I was at the other end.

'I have been trying to reach you for nearly half an hour.' I knew that voice very well. It was Sir Girija Shankar Bajpai from the Ministry of External Affairs. In a minute I was wide awake. Sir Girja was a member of the I.C.S. He had served on the Viceroy's Council and had been Agent General for India under the British in Washington when I was on my American tour. He was a man of the old school, correct in speech and deportment, a polished diplomat with a command of several languages. When the interim government was formed he was relieved of his post in Washington, and, in the face of much hostile public criticism, my brother made him advisor in the Ministry of External Affairs. Public suspicion of all who had served under the British was at its height but my brother, with Sardar Patel's concurrence, had decided to use the I.C.S., and Sir Girija was among the ablest of these. After Independence he was appointed Secretary General of the External Affairs Ministry.

'What can I do for you?' I asked.

'Haven't you received the Viceroy's telegram?' At that moment I noticed a closed telegram on the telephone table. I opened it hurriedly and told him, 'It has just arrived but I don't understand...'

'You must come to Delhi immediately. A plane is being sent to fetch you. The Prime Minister wishes to see you as soon as you arrive. Mahatma Gandhi will see you at 5 p.m., and you are having dinner with the Viceroy at 8.30 p.m.'

I explained to Sir Girija that I could not possibly come to Delhi for several days as my Gaon Panchayat Bill was before the Legislature and I was having difficulties with the Opposition. The bill was a major reform initiated by Congress to bring self-government to every village in Uttar Pradesh. Uttar Pradesh was the largest province in the country and had at that time a population of more than sixty million people. The Gaon Panchayat Bill was founded on the traditional Indian system of village democracy, which went back many hundreds of years, and the experiment we proposed to bring before the Legislature was of the greatest importance in a country composed mainly of villages. As Minister of Local Self-Government I had worked hard on the bill. But Sir

Girja insisted on my leaving as soon as the plane arrived and said he would meet me at the Delhi airport. The phone was disconnected and I was left wondering why I should be summoned to Delhi in this way and what would happen when I faced the Trinity.

I called up Pantji to explain the situation. As I had anticipated, he was very annoyed and seemed to think the whole thing had been my idea. I suggested he phone Bhai for a clarification, and I began to get ready for my departure.

In a beautiful official limousine Sir Girija met me at the airport and told me the reason for my being summoned. Lord Wavell and Gandhiji had decided to send a delegation to the first General Assembly of the United Nations, due to meet later in the month, and I was to be appointed the leader. I was horrified.

'I can't possibly go,' I told him. 'Apart from my bill, what qualifications have I got to lead a delegation to an international conference?'

Very quietly and in his most cynical manner he said, 'You managed pretty well on your unofficial tour—I personally witnessed that!' Then he gave me some advice. I was not to argue with any of the three men I was going to meet. A decision had been taken in the best interests of India, and nothing more was to be said. I was also to remember that Lord Wavell was very shy and was meeting me for the first time. It was up to me to put him at his ease. By the time I reached 17 York Road, where my brother, as Prime Minister of the interim government, was staying, I was reduced to pulp and would probably have agreed to any proposal.

Bhai's greeting was loving as always. 'Hello, darling. Forgive me for dragging you away from your work, but this is important. I expect Girija has explained everything.' I told him that Sir Girija had explained nothing but had bullied me all the way from the airport and frightened me by saying I had to dine with Lord Wavell. Bhai had a good laugh, and while I was having breakfast on a tray in his office he explained that the government had decided to send a strong delegation to the U.N. as this would be the first from an 'about-to-be-independent India.' Gandhiji particularly wanted me to lead the delegation. He would explain when I met him, and actually it was he and the Viceroy who had come to this decision.

That afternoon I went to the Bhangi Colony, where Gandhiji usually lived when in Delhi, to see him. We always touched his feet, and to people he loved he generally gave a slap on the cheek or tweaked an ear. But with it was his smile—a smile not easy to describe. It was radiant, loving, comforting, all at the same time. For me it was the most wonderful smile in the world. It had kept me alive in my darkest hour, it had given me hope and courage when I needed them most. I loved it and him more than I would ever have been able to say. Because he pampered me and forgave me many things I burst out, 'Bapu, I can't go to the United Nations—I don't have the qualifications.'

'*I* am doing the talking,' he said, 'and *you* are going to sit very still and listen.'

He explained that it was his wish that India should inscribe an item on the U.N. agenda protesting against discrimination against people of Indian origin in South Africa. He had chosen me to handle this item and knew that I could do it as he would wish. The U.N. was not a debating society where a good speech or a *bon mot* was all that was needed. He envisaged the U.N. as a place in which friendships between nations were cemented, where discussion and debate were kept on the highest level, and truth and ethics were the guidelines.

'Remember,' he told me, 'I want the delegation of my country to set an example. I shall be happy if we get votes, but I shall be most unhappy if these are gained in any manner that is divorced from our guidelines.' He went on to tell me that Field Marshal Jan Smuts, Prime Minister of South Africa, was his friend, even though he had opposed his policies in South Africa. He was a man of God. 'I would not like to lose his friendship and respect for the sake of gaining a majority vote.

This is another reason I have chosen you, because I know you understand what I am saying and will do what I ask.' He told me that Wavell was in full agreement with him.

That night I went to meet the Viceroy. It was the first time I had been in the Viceroy's House. I told Lord Wavell I was pleased to be able to thank him personally for his previous help. I also wanted to thank him for the privilege of sending me on such an important mission for India, and I asked him to tell me something about it. He said my name had come to mind as soon as Gandhiji suggested inscribing the South African item on the agenda. 'The Mahatma and I are fully in accord with this. I have also told the Prime Minister you will make a good Ambassador. I hope he will take my advice when the time comes.' He spoke a little about my recent tour in the United States and wanted to know if I had enjoyed it. I told him I had, but was much happier with my present work in the ministry. It was not at all the difficult evening I had anticipated.

Next day I sat with Bhai and Sir Girija while a list of delegates was drawn up. It was an all-star cast. The delegates were: Raja Maharaj Singh, ex-Chief Justice Chagla, Mr Frank Antony, the leader of the Anglo-Indian community, and Nawab Ali Yavar Jung. The alternates were: Mr V.K. Krishna Menon, Mr P.N. Sapru, Mr G.S. Pathak (later Vice-President), and Mr K.P.S. Menon. And once again I found myself with a group of men, nearly all specialists in their own line but friendly and courteous and ever helpful. Never did any one of them show the least resentment at being led by a woman. On the contrary, they were rather proud of me.

The journey to the United Nations was full of all manner of difficulties. It was too soon after the war for air travel to have been restored to normal, and we were divided into two groups, one of which, myself included, was stranded in Casablanca for a day and a night. We fretted over time being lost and were served omelets for every meal. Because of the delays en route we reached New York only a few hours before the General Assembly was due to open.

30

United Nations

The announcement of the Indian delegation's departure for the U.N. was welcomed by the whole country. We left with the good wishes of all sections, and our work was widely publicized by the press. There is a special kind of satisfaction in knowing that one's country approves of one—no laurels from a foreign country or government are quite the same. It has been my good fortune to have had both, and though foreign appreciation or awards bring their own satisfaction, nothing can compare with the sense of achievement that comes through the encouragement and approval of one's own people. So all of us were in high spirits on the flight to New York. None of us had any experience of big international conferences and everything was new and exciting.

Before we left my brother had given us a briefing, if such it can be called, but what he really said referred to our conduct rather than specific instructions about the work before us. He reminded us that we were inheritors of the high traditions of Mahatma Gandhi, and that this tradition was an ethical and moral one. Gandhiji had placed before us a technique of action unique in the world, combining political activity, political conflict, and a struggle for freedom based on certain principles. We now had to face practical problems, and it was not easy to apply that particular doctrine to the solution of such problems.

He reminded us of India's total acceptance of the U.N. Charter and her determination to work with other member nations to make it a reality. The preamble of the Charter was almost our personal pledge to the world: 'to promote social progress and better standards of life in larger freedom.' He told us that in order to function effectively we had to keep ourselves acquainted with what was going on in the world, to stay clear of rival power blocs, and try to ease the tensions that such blocs generated. This, then, was our brief on that first occasion.

The United Nations was then at Lake Success, and going and coming from New York took up much time. To my eyes the assembly hall, the lounge full of world personalities, and the complex translation facilities all seemed quite fascinating. It was a small United Nations, of fifty member states, and one was able to get to know many of the delegates personally. The wartime leaders, except President Roosevelt, were still alive, and the standard of oratory and of ethics was of a high level. The world was full of hope. The Charter of the United Nations was a challenge to the most cynical, and it was a moment in time when it seemed possible to remould the world to a design in which justice, equality, and opportunity would help to establish the peace for which exhausted humanity yearned. The grim tragedies and unmentionable sufferings of the war had finally ended, and human beings everywhere looked with hope to a future in which they would find security. So little to expect when so much had been given!

In those early days when colonialism was dying there were high expectations, in what is now known as the Third World, of better days to come. The U.N. was referred to as the 'conscience of humanity', and men and women everywhere believed this. Even though statesmen and politicians were aware of the dangers inherent in the world situation there was not, at that time, the brazen disregard for everything that nourishes and sustains a nation's soul. But neither people nor nations seem to have souls anymore.

Our main concern was of course the item India had inscribed on the agenda. It was also the most important item of that session. The immediate cause for bringing this question to the General Assembly in 1946 was the passing of the Asiatic Land Tenure and Indian Representation Act, otherwise known as the Ghetto Act, by the South African Parliament. My formidable adversary in the debate was the late Field Marshal Smuts, who raised the plea of domestic jurisdiction under Article 2(7) of the Charter. In reply to this I said, in part, 'For us this is not the mere assertion of certain rights and privileges. We look upon it primarily as a challenge to our dignity and self-respect. India has resisted every attempt to divert the debate to a consideration of the legal aspects of the issue... What the world needs is not more charters, not more committees to define and courts of justice to interpret, but a more willing implementation of the principles of the Charter by all governments.' The debate lasted in the First Committee for several days, and Field Marshal Smuts took part in the earlier stages. Whatever his arguments, he was always restrained, but when the Law Minister, Mr Heaton Nichols, took over from him, his aim seemed to be to humiliate India by accusations that were entirely irrelevant to the matter under discussion.

Treatment of our Harijans was of course emphasized, but he went on to tell the Committee that 'South Africa was upholding a Christian civilization in a dark continent inhabited by polygamous races.' This called for an intervention, and I said that I was not aware that polygamy, whether sanctioned by law or otherwise, was confined to the East. As for a Christian civilization, I continued, were Jesus Christ himself to visit South Africa, he would be treated as a 'prohibited immigrant'.

The last phase of the debate was exciting for the General Assembly as a whole. Our delegation was tense with expectation. Time was passing, and though it was already midnight the final intervention was yet to be made. India had the last approach to the delegates. It was to be an approach to conscience—neither aggressive nor humble, but an appeal to those who held the political fate of Asia, and indeed the world, in their grasp. I said,

> I ask no favours for India...no concession for the Indian population of South Africa. I ask for the verdict of this

> Assembly on a proven violation of the Charter, on an issue which has led to acute dispute between two member states; on an issue which is not confined to India or South Africa, and finally on an issue the decision of which must make or mar the loyalty and confidence which the common people of the world have placed on us. Mine is an appeal to a conscience, the conscience of the world, which this Assembly is.

The voting took place at 2 a.m. in a tense atmosphere. We had asked for a roll-call vote, and as each 'yes' came we could hardly restrain ourselves. The resolution was passed by a two-thirds majority, and as the President announced this, pandemonium broke out. Those who had voted for us rushed from their seats to shake our hands and congratulate us and themselves. It was an Asian victory and we were jubilant. It was some minutes before order was restored. I went into the lobby and the press surrounded me. 'What do you feel?' and similar questions were hurled at me. I was happy, excited, a little proud. Restraining myself I said to the press, 'We are grateful to our Asian and African friends through whose help this victory has been possible—it is shared by us all.' The next thing I did was to send a message to Gandhiji, glad that I had been able to fulfill his mission.

I had of course met Field Marshal Smuts when I first arrived in New York and had given him Gandhiji's warm regards. Now I felt I must see him again. He had gone out of New York for a few days on a speaking engagement but was now back. He had not been present in the assembly hall during my last speech and the voting. Hearing that he was in the lounge I went up to him and said, 'I have come to you to say that if, in the course of this unhappy debate, I have said anything which was not up to the high standard Gandhiji had imposed on me, I ask your pardon.' He took my hand in both of his. 'My child,' he said—he was eighty-plus to my forty-plus—'you have won a hollow victory. This vote will put me out of power in our next elections, but you will have gained nothing.' He was proved correct. He was soon out of power, and the Asiatic Land Tenure and Indian Representation Act became apartheid.

If on that first occasion there could have been a unanimous vote for the Indian resolution, or if the vote had been less sharply divided between the colonial powers and Asia, there is no doubt the binding force of the mandate would have been greater and South Africa may have not been able to flout the will of the U.N. year after year as it did. It was a decade later that South Africa left the Commonwealth in protest against the growing pressures being brought on her from all quarters, and to show its determination to adhere to its own policies. Another reason that racial discrimination grew and thrived was that we had not been able to shake world opinion out of its lethargy and thus force an implementation of the mandate given by the U.N. Since 1946 this evil has reached mighty proportions, and even the combined effort of the United Nations cannot now stem the tide that may engulf the vast continent of Africa. It has taken too many years to convince a part of the world that times are changing in favour of the underprivileged. Men grown desperate do not always discriminate in the manner of their protests.

One can argue that in the context of history a few years do not matter. But we live in an age in which every moment counts heavily and the price of delay is human lives. This is what has happened not only in South and southern Africa but in other parts of Africa as well, and that continent has suffered untold humiliations and retaliated with violence and sometimes brutality. Nor has the tale ended yet.

When the United Nations was born it was believed to be a positive instrument for peace. From this exalted position it became an organization in which nations would at least keep talking instead of shooting. Soon it was discovered, to the dismay of even those who were its most ardent champions, that words were as deadly as any weapon, and when these words had a number of interpretations they could and did lead to conflict. The views I am expressing here have developed after seeing the mistakes that led to them.

During the first U.N. session we met and came to know the leaders of all the delegations present. The Soviet delegation was led by Mr Molotov, and Vyshinksky and Gromyko were also present. Vyshinksky was the Permanent Representative at the U.N. The cold war, whose chilling shadow was soon to engulf and divide the world, was emerging, and America's fear of Communism was growing and sometimes showed itself in ridiculous ways. For instance, when Vyshinksky, who was a fine speaker and a brilliant lawyer, made a speech, people would say, 'Couldn't you see from his face what an evil man he is?' and comments to this effect. But the facts were that whatever his political record may have been, Vyshinksky had an open face, a twinkle in his eye, and a great sense of humour. His speeches, whether one agreed or disagreed with their content, were pieces of oratory. Molotov, on the other hand, was a dull speaker, as was Gromyko, who at that time was young and not the polished diplomat into which he has since developed.

The American Permanent Representative was Senator Warren Austin. President Truman had selected this retired Republican senator from Vermont as evidence of the desire of U.S. policy to place the U.N. above domestic politics. Senator Austin was a man of dignity. In his approach to the Russians, he made no attempt to seek the limelight and try to gain applause of the T.V. audiences. He was respected and admired for this. President Truman had also raised the status of the American Ambassador to the U.N. to that of a member of his Cabinet. This action, too, was symbolic of his recognition of the U.N. Personally I think this is an unwise thing for any government to do, as there is a tendency for the Ambassador to disassociate himself from the official delegation and consider himself responsible only to the President. This happened in the Indian delegation. It was not our Permanent Representative but Mr Krishna Menon who constantly flouted the united decision of his delegation by saying he was responsible only to the Prime Minister. This caused trouble with our Permanent Representative, Sir B.N. Rau, for some years. Many members of the Indian delegation also resented this attitude of Krishna Menon. Sir B.N. Rau was a man of great ability who was among those who drafted the Indian Constitution. He was gentle and had the reputation of being a bridge builder. He was very highly thought of by my brother and also by delegates at the U.N.

Another member of the U.S. delegation to the U.N. was Mrs Roosevelt who, from the beginning, was involved in human rights, and it was largely due to her continuous efforts that the Commission on Human Rights came into being. Delegates to the U.N. function in the different committees to which they have been assigned for their special knowledge of that committee's work. There are now seven such committees, and it is only after a full discussion in this forum that a resolution can go up to the General Assembly. One lives and moves, as it were, with one's colleagues in the committee, and there is little contact with other delegates except for a specific reason. As Mrs Roosevelt and I were on different committees—she in the Third Committee, dealing with social, cultural, and humanitarian matters and particularly involved with the problem of human rights, and I in the First or Political Committee—we did not meet very frequently. Being in the U.N. does not imply meeting all the delegates—there are some one never meets at all or knows very slightly.

Britain's chief delegate was Philip Noel-Baker, a man generally liked and one who seemed to understand Indians better than most as he was a friend and admirer of Gandhiji and a believer in nonviolence. His opposition to the atom bomb was firmly expressed, and his passionate efforts for disarmament later made him a Nobel Peace Prize winner. I was pleased and a little touched when, after my speech in the general debate, he was the first to come up and congratulate me even though my statement had been liberally sprinkled with the anti-imperialist jargon of the time. Another person was Molotov, who came on behalf of his delegation and later sent me an enormous bouquet of red roses.

Among the British delegates then and in following years were outstanding names. Some of them were already friends, others became friends during the session. Hartley Shawcross, Q.C., now Lord, was the legal advisor who argued in favour of the domestic jurisdiction clause in the South African debate. Later when I met him in London he said I always used the *mot juste*. Coming from a man whose profession demanded the right use of words, I appreciated it greatly. There were Hector McNeil and Sir Alexander Cadogan and, last but not least, Ernest Bevin, the British Foreign Minister, whose looks belied his brilliance and good humour.

Mr Paul Henri Spaak of Belgium, who looked and spoke like Churchill, was one of my favourites. One might have described him as an imperialist and of course that is what he was, but there was something very likeable about him. His language was almost poetry. Among other orators was Senor Belaunde of Peru. He was very conscious of his power to sway people and used every trick known to oratory. Spanish lends itself to poetic imagery as does Hindi, and, once he began, it was difficult to get him off the podium. Our present Foreign Minister, Atal Bihari Vajpayee, also an orator of no mean dimension, reminds me of Senor Belaunde. There were so many good speakers and able men in that hall. In later years, the number of women gradually increased. Our own delegation always had a woman member, though India has never, since my time, appointed another woman to lead the delegation.

With the Asian and African delegations we had a good relationship and understanding, but one special friend was the Permanent Representative of Mexico, Senor Padilla Nervo. He was helpful in many ways, and Mexico voted with India and the Asian group on many important issues.

For the whole of that session my presence in the U.N.

continued to surprise people who could not equate me and the position I held with their firmly established view of an Indian woman—a clinging vine subservient to all manner of caste restrictions. I would be untruthful if I did not admit that I enjoyed all this. At one U.N. dinner General Romulo of the Philippines, who later became a close friend, referred to me as 'the Pinup Girl of the U.N'. This was reported in the Indian press and caused a mild sensation in Parliament as members were not sure of the term, and some thought a formal protest should be made by India as they were under the impression that 'pinup girl' was an unsavory term! I do not think any ambassador was 'on the mat' as often as I during my diplomatic career for the simple reason that we were new to certain words, terms, and ideas generally used in the West and we misunderstood them. I am thankful that my career started after forty. Had I been younger life would have been very difficult, for it is hard to convince those who have already made up their minds.

Being new we were constantly faced with problems of protocol, publicity, and entertainment. In the matter of public relations we were mere children. While other delegations were 'selling' their viewpoint to the world, we of India were content to leave the winning of votes to our own 'moral' record or to the Almighty who, we were convinced, was on our side. It was next to impossible to convince our government that much of the success achieved at the U.N. was due to expert public relations. Even when the need for publicity was recognized, one of our own delegates was put in charge—never a professional man who was trained for the job. We lost out many times because of this obstinacy. It is strange how easily the average man and woman is influenced by the media in other countries, especially in America. In India we are just beginning to understand this, and, who knows, in time our people may judge an issue because they like a man's voice or a woman's face. There is always that danger but, if asked, I would take the risk!

The delegation of 1946 represented an interim national government, and there was no question of a national anthem. The next year, 1947, India was an independent country. Our government had been involved in matters of immediate importance and no attention had been given to the choosing of an anthem—nor had our delegation realized we might want one. The question came to a head when we were asked by the protocol department of the U.N. for the score of the national anthem to be played at our reception for the U.N. delegates. Here we were faced with a dilemma. India was too far away to discuss the matter and get an immediate reply. Of course we got in touch with our government, but meanwhile something had to be done quickly. One of the Indian students in New York had a record of Tagore's famous national song, 'Jana gana mana', which was beautiful and a sort of anthem. There was only one course open to us. We gave this record to the chef d'orchestra of the Waldorf Astoria, where our reception was to be held, and it was orchestrated and played. It was greatly appreciated. This occurrence was discussed in the Constituent Assembly then functioning in Delhi, and after considerable controversy between the merits of 'Jana gana mana' and 'Vande Mataram', another well-known national song, the former was adopted as the national anthem of India.

I neither knew nor cared very much about protocol. My ideas of entertainment did not conform to formal patterns and my view then, as now, was that whether a party is given for friends or for diplomats, one should, unless the occasion is very formal, select guests who mix well together and have a good time or with whom one can converse in an informal fashion and gain something from the talk. The stiff sitting round a table according to one's official position is generally a failure besides being a deadly bore. After our big reception I decided to have some informal parties where it was possible to forget for an hour or two which country one's guests came from, remembering only that basically human beings have much in common. On my guest list, for one party, among others, were Mr Ernest Bevin, General Romulo, Mr Vyshinksky, the Burmese and Mexican delegates, Mrs Roosevelt, and Mr Hector McNeil. The Count de Noue, Chief of Protocol of the U.N., threw up his hands in horror and said such a group would be disastrous. I said it was a private party and everyone had already accepted. It turned out to be a huge success. In no time at all everybody was chatting and exchanging jokes. The food, mainly Indian and ordered from outside, was eaten with obvious relish, and after dinner the guests sang songs from their own countries. The highlight of the evening was when Vyshinksky joined Tara in singing Russian songs. It was a delightful evening, and Mr Bevin, between his whiskey and joining in the singing, enjoyed it as much as any. We did not break up until far into the night. After that evening I was on much easier terms with my colleagues. Even diplomatic discussions were more relaxed, and political ideologies did not come in the way of the personal relations we had established. As I continued to be on the Indian delegation for five sessions and many of the other delegates remained the same, I was able to keep up the friendships. Among those I especially valued was Lester (Mike) Pearson of Canada, whom I succeeded as President of the General Assembly in 1953. Another person whom I met through the U.N. was Mrs Evelyn Emmet, now Baroness Emmet of Amberley. She was on the British delegation, and we became close friends and have remained so ever since.

Apart from the men and women I came to know through the U.N., I found friends all over the U.S.A., and because of my frequent visits I kept in contact with many of them. With some I have developed the close bond that is the outcome of shared ideas and deep affection. To them I owe happiness and a feeling of belonging. No matter what the political relationship may be between our two countries, to me these American friends represent the finest that is in America, and I shall always be thankful for the circumstances that brought us together.

I am especially thankful for the chance that brought Paul and Essie Robeson into my life. During a visit to the United Kingdom, Ranjit and I had gone to hear Paul Robeson sing in *Show Boat,* which was playing in the Drury Lane Theatre, Covent Garden. Afterward we went backstage to shake his hand and tell him how much we had enjoyed his singing.

When I was next in England with Bhai in 1938, Paul's reputation had soared to great heights and he was living in London in Highgate. Bhai and I were invited to dinner in his elegant house and served by a 'white' butler. For us both it was a memorable evening. Paul was, besides being a great artist, an even greater human being. We spoke about his coming to India some day, where he said he would like to study Indian folk songs. It was even suggested that he should stay at Khali, Ranjit's farm near Almora, and make it his base.

The last time I saw Paul he was in Harlem. He was not too well, and the emotional damage he had suffered from the way he had been treated in his own country had hurt him beyond measure. He was a great American and America had rejected and humiliated him, or tried to do so. No one can humiliate a man of the dignity, courage, and faith in values that Paul possessed. When my girls came to the U.S.A. in 1943, one of the warm welcoming homes open to them was the Robesons' beautiful home in Enfield, Connecticut. This was burned down by an angry mob when, several years later, Paul Jr married Marilyn, a white girl. Paul and his lovely wife Essie were like parents to Lekha and Tara when they went to Wellesley, and young Paul, about the same age, was a brother.

I have one personal memory that I have always cherished. The first year at Lake Success I had tried to reach Paul and learned that he was on tour for several months outside the U.S.A. When he got to Ottawa he arranged to fly to New York for a couple of hours to see me. He came to Lake Success while the South African debate was on, and I was waiting for him in the lounge when he came striding in. He gave me a hug, lifting me off my feet. 'Good to see you, little sister,' he said. 'I'm so proud of the wonderful job you are doing.' The delegates sitting around the lounge looked on disapprovingly. They were, in those days, much more stiff and formal than they are now and it was still a 'white' U.N. The sight of this black man, famous though he was, embracing me so affectionately, shocked them, or so I was informed afterward. As far as I was concerned, I was too pleased at seeing Paul to notice other people's looks!

With Essie I had an equally close friendship, and in the days when she attended the U.N. sessions as one of the non-government observers, we saw a great deal of each other. Toward the end of that period the Robesons had already been pushed into Harlem. One day I suggested that Essie should let me go home with her for dinner. 'You can't come to Harlem, honey,' she said. 'Your delegation and others might not like it.' It was 1953, the year I was President of the General Assembly. 'If Harlem is all right for you and Paul,' I said, 'it's all right for me. Anyway, I'm coming, and you will please take me with you.' Later I told Dag Hammarskjold I was going, and was surprised to see disapproval in his face, though he made no comment.

For many years Paul was not allowed to leave the U.S., and his passport had been impounded. I was High Commissioner in London when this restriction on travel was removed and he came to England on an engagement in 1959. It was a joy for me to give a reception in his honour in our Embassy. I invited friends from the entertainment world, the social world, and the diplomatic world, and all came.

◆◆◆

31

More Thoughts on the U.N.

Social life at the United Nations is not unlike that of an embassy—a whirl of festivity outside office hours. In the case of the U.N. there are innumerable cocktail parties and receptions, getting together at lunches in the delegates' dining room to discuss pending resolutions with other delegates or members of one's own delegation for purposes of canvassing support from others, drinks in the lounge to exchange views with other delegates. It involves a hectic round of sociability, very exhausting, and in the view of many people who have been through it, not sufficiently yielding of dividends.

The amount of money spent on entertaining seems especially absurd when one remembers that, after a debate on suffering or repression in some part of the world, delegates troop off to a reception where the choicest wines and most expensive delicacies are served to the already well fed. One cannot help thinking that money could be used to better purpose if the idealism that gave birth to the United Nations is to be maintained. The atmosphere, instead of being conducive to the implementation of one's pledge to mankind, has become artificial and appears to lack real purpose. What a tremendous psychological impact the U.N. could make if it changed its social pattern or if one day in the week (Hindu fashion!) every delegate would fast to identify himself with those who starve the world over. The emphasis on food and parties has become quite out of proportion to the objectives we are trying to reach through the U.N.

Public relations too are geared to Western methods, and, naturally, this is a one-way street. There is little understanding, for instance, of the way of thinking in the East, where example rather than competition pays. Gandhiji abandoned his lifestyle and conventional clothes because he knew he must identify himself with the lowliest in the land if they were to have trust in him. And this 'naked fakir', as Churchill called him, broke up an empire on which it was thought the sun would never set. He also changed the pattern of thinking of millions of people all over the world, and his influence continues to grow. The U.N., held as it is in a glittering setting and in a city that offers many diversions, especially for the rich, is not the appropriate place to concentrate on world issues. When the question of U.N. headquarters was under discussion an alternative suggestion had been San Francisco. There was a somewhat different atmosphere in that city, and it looked to the Pacific, seemingly closer to the East. But New York won the day partly because of the gift of land by the Rockefeller Foundation and partly through Wall Street pressures.

In India, during the early days of the national struggle, the annual session of the Congress was always held in a city, with a certain amount of pageantry and much social activity. When Gandhiji took the lead in national affairs, one of his suggestions was to transfer the location of these meetings from the city to the village. This move had two objectives: the simple, even rugged, life of the village would ensure all work being dispatched without unnecessary delay as there would be no attractions to tempt one to stay on; then also, rural problems most vital for India would surround the Congress delegates and keep them aware of their purpose. The experiment was a success and continued after Independence, but gradually more money was spent on the sessions and in recent times large amounts have been spent to make a village more like a town on the occasion of a political conference. Imagine a U.N. session in some part of Asia or Africa with the fewest possible modern amenities, where the *raison d'être* of the U.N. would be only too evident. Would any nation wish to prolong such a session? Would the polished diplomats who add elegance to the U.N. be able to exist in such a place? Would they know how to adapt, to express basic thoughts in simple language with a ring of sincerity? I wonder. I, too, have been a member of this sophisticated group and followed its ways for a while and I speak from personal experience.

The agenda of the United Nations is always a long one, and grows longer because some items are shelved but remain as matters still to be considered and settled. Each year, one issue more important than the rest dominates the proceedings. In 1946 it was discrimination in South Africa, then the situation in Korea continued through several sessions. The Kashmir 'problem' was an evergreen, and became famous for the number of hours it was discussed in succeeding sessions. Besides these there were, of the highest importance to the future of the world, the debates on the question of the freedom of Asia and Africa from colonial rule. India's independence had started the ball rolling, and India's forceful support for the freedom of others was a major effort of which we can well be proud. As one by one the nations of Asia and Africa have taken their place in the assembly hall of the U.N. we have rejoiced with them and extended our cooperation. This had always been the policy of the Congress. As far back as 1927, Bhai addressed the International League against Imperialism, held in Brussels, and in his message to the gathering he said:

> The Indian National Congress stands for the freedom of India; freedom for the poor and the oppressed from all exploitation... We realize that there is much in common in the struggle which various subject and semi-subject and oppressed peoples are carrying on today. Their opponents are often the same, although they sometimes appear in different guises. The means employed for their subjection are often similar... As our great leader Mahatma Gandhi has said, our nationalism is based on the most intense internationalism. The problem of Indian freedom is for us a vital and urgently essential one; but at the same time it is not merely a purely national problem. India is a world problem and, as in the past, so in the future, other countries and peoples will be vitally affected by the condition of India.

In December 1954, at a meeting of Prime Ministers from five Asian countries (Burma, Sri Lanka, Indonesia, Pakistan, and

India), it was decided to sponsor a conference of Asian and African countries to promote goodwill and cooperation and to review the position of Asians and Africans in present-day world conditions. Thirty nations attended the conference held in Bandung in April 1956 and were represented by their Prime Ministers, Foreign Ministers, or elder statesmen. President Sukarno as host made a speech that inspired us. Among the questions discussed at the conference was freedom for North Africa—Morocco, Tunisia, and Algeria. The nations at Bandung agreed that the Five Principles, Panchsheel[15] would govern their relations with one another to help in creating a better climate of world affairs. These Five Principles called for coexistence and non-interference, and the realization that nations may differ in outlook as well as development yet be striving toward the same goal of world peace and cooperation. At Bandung, the People's Republic of China was represented by Premier Chou En-lai, who announced that he was willing to enter into discussions with the United States regarding problems in which both these countries were concerned in the Far East. Bhai and Chou En-lai had several talks, and India was at that time actively involved in helping various Commonwealth and other countries to bridge the gulf that lay between China and the world community. It was from the basic principles agreed upon in Bandung that the nonaligned movement began. At first, nonalignment was considered by some nations as a bit of a joke, by others, as sitting on the fence. Yet Yugoslavia, Egypt, and India, led by Tito, Nasser, and Nehru, who gave direction and content to the nonaligned

15. The Five Principles of peaceful coexistence are:

1. Mutual respect for one another's territorial integrity and sovereignty.
2. Mutual non-aggression.
3. Mutual non-interference in one another's internal affairs.
4. Equality and mutual benefit.
5. Peaceful coexistence.

ideal, succeeded in getting it widely accepted. There were those who did not understand it, and others who deliberately misconstrued it, but nonalignment continued to project the need for understanding the problems and viewpoints of the Third World. Through the years the countries of the Third World have therefore been able to play a role of increasing significance in international deliberations.

In a sense Bandung was essential for the self-esteem and confidence of Asians and Africans, long subdued by foreign domination. The conference was not a lengthy one, but many practical agreements were arrived at in an atmosphere of give-and-take. For the first time countries whose voices had long been stilled—well over half the earth's population—were able to talk on their own terms, to declare their ideals and aspirations for international cooperation as envisaged by the United Nations, and to reaffirm their support for those still striving for freedom. As at the earlier Asian Conference held in Delhi in 1947, there was at Bandung an atmosphere of idealism and a sense of awakening for Asia and Africa, who were determined to fulfill their historic role. This feeling, that the peoples of Asia and Africa have a destiny of their own, must be understood by the Western world, for without this understanding there is no way to appreciate the political or economic stand taken by many countries that are outside the orbit of European culture.

The U.N. today is composed of one hundred and fifty members, and new ones may be added in the future. From China, with its population of over seven hundred million, to the little island of Malta, each member is, in theory, equal to the other. Yet the same problems do not beset them, and their needs, natures, and economic development are very dissimilar. The countries of Asia and Africa—now the largest bloc in the U.N.—are themselves faced with differing problems. The common bond is the colonial past, but each has present needs that are special and which arise from its own particular background. From a small mainly white U.N. we have today a vast organization of mostly non-white nations whose economic, social, and even emotional requirements differ from one another and from the ex-colonial and affluent powers, and whose political influence is not uniform. So the theory of equality cannot reflect the actual power position at the U.N. Yet the Afro-Asian group, varied though it is, could exert a greater influence than it does. If it were willing to unite and to give and take, it could, and still can, change the character of the U.N. The fears expressed in the West about one part or another of the Third World falling under communist influence would not be relevant because a Third World nation, with the help of others like itself willing to assist in its development, could not easily be taken advantage of by any power, communist or anti-communist, and a group of such nations could not become pawns in the game of power politics that controls the U.N.

A disturbing feature of politics is the competition between the two Great Powers to draw to themselves the weaker nations by promises of arms aid. On the one hand we have world leaders assembled year after year with much fanfare to disarm the world; at the same time these very nations—and not only the two great rivals—are busy providing instruments of destruction to those whom they would like to control. Noble sentiments sound hollow when one knows that actions are not in conformity with words. The shocking revelations that come to light about secret deals between various nations, quite contrary to their public professions, cannot but destroy the faith of the common man in those he looks upon as world leaders.

In my U.N. career my major efforts have been directed toward the elimination of discrimination in its various forms, and recently, returning to U.N. affairs after an absence of eleven years as the Government of India's representative to the Human Rights Commission, I was dismayed to find that the problem of racial discrimination is as current as ever and has reached disturbing proportions even in some developed and progressive countries. Even the educated seem to have forgotten that any action seeking to protect a particular culture and way of life through a denial of fundamental human rights to large numbers of people will ultimately lead to the undermining of that culture and of civilization as a whole. Through the years the Human Rights Commission also has become a debating society where members are content to score a point or two and then relax until the next session.

The building of a just and peaceful world order, *the* aim of the United Nations, is hampered not by a dearth of ideas, resources, and manpower but by the lack of will on the part of governments to take the required steps in pursuance of their accepted objectives. So our problems gradually become more complex, often taking on a rigidity that is frightening. I said in the Human Rights Commission that it now requires the skill of a tightrope walker to maintain the delicate balance between the sovereign rights of independent national states on one hand and their duty as members of the international community on the other. In today's world the most dangerous situation is not the one that divides the north and south, the rich from poor nations—which is real enough. It is the situation created by man's inability to adjust to the rapid scientific progress that his own mind has made possible. Bertrand Russell's view that, unless wisdom increases with knowledge, increase of knowledge by itself will be increase of sorrow, is apt. Great material advance has brought to those who have it neither contentment nor peace of mind; on the contrary, it has increased dilemmas and the distance between the 'developed' and the 'developing' nations, and affects peace and stability as a whole. At the U.N. year after year we see the unhappy spectacle of decisions vital to most of humanity being shelved for another year, because to decide remains the prerogative of the Western nations, and frequently their views are incompatible with the needs and aims of the Third World. Much as I hope for better days, I feel the facts available do not show that there is likely to be a change of heart in the statesmen who guide our destinies, and for some time to come the policies of power will continue to rule the world.

India has been too naive in her politics. She tried in the first years of her independence to carry through the Gandhian doctrine of using an ethical approach in political negotiations. She was right in doing so but lost out because this was not a doctrine appreciated or understood by the world of power politics, which did not need friends but welcomed satellites and had the means to charm them. But India is still the inheritor of a past that once illuminated the path of humanity. In speaking of the period of the Buddha René Grousset says, 'Every now and again humanity...achieves greatness and realizes its raison d'être in a brief period of outstanding success.' It may be that some of the ideals enshrined in Indian culture sound outmoded today. And when we speak the language of means and ends, the international community, geared to other thoughts from another background, may smile at our simplicity. But my experience, brief though it has been, has convinced me that if the objectives of the U.N. are ever to be achieved, it will be through the realization that means and ends must go together, and morality retained in politics. The question we must ask ourselves in all seriousness is whether we are willing to adopt this as a working ideal.

◆◆◆

32

Transfer of Power

I returned home from the first session of the General Assembly in December 1946 to find that Indira's second son, Sanjay, had been born. I resumed my duties as minister of the Uttar Pradesh government and also attended meetings of the Constituent Assembly. The Constituent Assembly had been inaugurated on December 9, and Dr Rajendra Prasad, later our first President, had been elected its permanent Chairman. Mr Jinnah had instructed members of the Muslim League elected to the Constituent Assembly not to take their seats, and the atmosphere in Delhi was tense and one of political suspicion. The functioning of the interim government was far from smooth, for although the Muslim League members had joined the government in October, the objectives of the League and Congress were so divergent that there was a constant tug of war between the two. The British government had proposed a meeting in London of Congress and League leaders, which Mr Jinnah and Mr Liaquat Ali had attended, along with Bhai and others. But it was obvious that no common ground could be found, and Bhai returned within a few days to attend the opening session of the Constituent Assembly. Gandhiji was not present on this occasion, as he was wholly involved in touring areas affected by communal passions. The members of the Constituent Assembly consisted of many well-known personalities, men and women elected to this body. They were specialists in their own fields and highly respected—legal celebrities, social workers, economists, educators, politicians. They included various religious and minority groups of the country. I felt privileged to be of their number. Unfortunately, the Muslim League continued its boycott and the Constituent Assembly formally regretted its absence and waited six weeks in vain for the League to change its mind and join the deliberations. The majority of those elected to frame the Constitution kept in mind the function of the Assembly, which was not to represent any one part but the people of India as a whole. Congress was the dominant party represented but, as Bhai said in his speech when he moved the Objectives Resolution, 'We are not here to act as one party or one group, but always to think of India as a whole and always to think of the welfare of the four hundred millions that comprise India.'

Meanwhile the state of tension and strife within the

country continued and grew as riots and communal clashes became the order of the day. Bengal had already suffered greatly from Hindu–Muslim clashes, and now Punjab became a victim of communal fury. Appeals by Gandhiji and Congress leaders seemed to fall on deaf ears. Lord Wavell had been replaced as Viceroy by Lord Mountbatten and a time limit set for the transfer of power from Britain to India. With growing chaos and the Muslim League's insistence on Pakistan, there seemed to be no way out of the situation now facing us. Lord Mountbatten prepared a draft plan for partitioning the country by dividing Bengal and Punjab into Hindu and Muslim majority areas and creating two sovereign states—India and Pakistan. To Gandhiji this was inconceivable. He was totally against the idea of partition on grounds of religion, as were many Indians. The demand for Pakistan was based on the 'two nation' theory of the Muslim League that Hindus and Muslims were so different they could not exist as citizens of the same State. The entire political and social philosophy of the Congress party, as I have already said, was wholly opposed to this concept. In any case it was a theory impossible to implement as, taken to its logical conclusion, it would mean the division of practically every town and village in the country. Hindus and Muslims did not live in separate pockets in special areas. They lived all over the length and breadth of India side by side with one another and also with Indians professing other faiths. Through the ages India had been one unit, and the lack of political unity had never come in the way of the actual, indefinable unity of the country and its people. During the hard years of the national struggle for freedom the intention was never to seek independence for any one group or class but for the masses of the people with their infinite variety of cultural backgrounds. The Congress had faced many conflicts with the Muslim League in the functioning of the interim government and had tried to influence its opposition through goodwill for the larger cause of Independence. But this point of view had been rejected, and in the absence of cooperation nothing remained but the League's increasing mistrust and a deliberately incited lawlessness. The alternative to acceptance of the Mountbatten Plan threatened to be a bloodbath, judging from the acts of violence that were daily becoming more common. After painful deliberations, the Congress agreed—Mr Jinnah had already consented—to Mountbatten's proposals, but Bhai and Sardar Patel insisted that the Constituent Assembly must be the successor of the British government, and, if Pakistan must be created, it would come about under the permission to secede given by previous British proposals. By the end of May 1947 Mountbatten had British approval of the plan and the Congress and the Muslim League had also agreed to it. The deadline for the transfer of power was fixed for August 15. In Lucknow I heard this decision on the radio, followed by messages broadcast by Mountbatten, Jinnah, and Bhai. It was a historic and sad moment. The joy of attaining freedom was dimmed by the prospect of the country's being divided for the first time in its long history.

Bhai as Prime Minister of the interim government also held the portfolio of Foreign Affairs and he had spoken to me several times about an ambassadorship. He had wanted to send me to Washington, but Maulana Azad was keen on the appointment of Mr Asaf Ali, and Asaf was anxious to go. Maulana himself mentioned this matter to me. I told him I was happy at home and deeply involved in my work in the Uttar Pradesh ministry and now also in the Constituent Assembly. I had no desire to be sent abroad.

'To this your brother will not agree,' he said. 'You have to go abroad, but I want you to know that I am pressing Jawaharlal to appoint Asaf to Washington.'

A few days afterward Bhai had another talk with me and said he had decided on Moscow for me, and in a day or two the government would ask the Soviet government for an *agrément*. I expressed my doubts about a diplomatic career. *Ad hoc* visits to conferences and the United Nations were one thing, but to take on a task that needed special training, and at a time when the eyes of the world were on newly independent India, might be a mistake. I knew nothing of embassies or of Moscow. He suggested I should speak to Sir Girja, and later we could discuss the matter again.

Accordingly, I spent an hour with Sir Girija Shankar Bajpai, who was Secretary General of the External Affairs Ministry. He explained that the government wanted to select public figures for their first ambassadors. He himself felt it would be good for me to be sent to Moscow because I had already met several of the top Soviet representatives at the U.N. and established contact with them. Secondly, the Soviet Union would be pleased to have a woman ambassador, and there would be no prejudice against me. The third and most important reason, he told me, was that I was neither a pro-communist nor an anti-communist. I would be able to function objectively, which is what the government wanted. As regards lack of training, he said I would have experienced officials on my staff and would grow into my job. He pointed out that obviously, if I was joining the Foreign Service, I would be going on to other posts, and so long as he was in a position to help, he would do whatever he could to assist me in any difficulties that might arise. He made one prophetic remark: 'Public figures will be under sharp attack from Parliament much of the time, and you more than most—you are the Prime Minister's sister and it will be the national assumption that you will get favours. I know,' he continued, 'that actually the reverse will be the case. Your brother will bend backward to do less for you than for his other ambassadors, but people will not believe this, so you must shed your sensitivity!' This proved correct and caused me many heartaches throughout my diplomatic career.

I was told by Bhai that I must take my briefing from Sardar Patel, and so I accompanied him on his 5 a.m. walks for three days. What I had wanted was instruction and information regarding government thinking on India's overall approach to world problems as well as her specific approach to Moscow, in terms of politics. As in the earlier case when Bhai 'briefed' us on the U.N., Sardar Patel spoke of truth, adherence to values, friendship with all nations, and avoidance of war.

'But,' I said, 'these are expressions of hope, Sardar, you are not outlining a policy. Surely we must have a positive and realistic policy.' With some trepidation I reminded him that in the *Artha Shastra,* an ancient Indian thesis on the art of politics, one of the things Kautilya, the author, lays down as rules for the conduct of diplomacy is that diplomacy is not concerned with ideals but only with achieving practical results for the State. He also says that a militarily weak country should not get involved in the quarrels and alliances of stronger States.

'There is no point in quoting Kautilya,' Sardar answered. 'He was a learned man, but quite definitely an opportunist! One unchangeable aspect of *our* foreign policy will always be ideals, from this base it will evolve gradually and honourably.' I was in a highly unsatisfied mood when I left him, and more unsure of myself than ever.

It is interesting to note that Sardar Patel told me that the strictest prohibition of alcoholic beverages must be enforced in the Embassy. In actual fact, this rule was not enforced in any embassy, because no actual directive was ever issued.

The arrival in India of Lord and Lady Mountbatten with their daughter, Lady Pamela, had caused much talk and speculation. Apart from the special mandate from their own government, they had given themselves a mandate to make as many Indian friends in as many circles as possible. It was not difficult for them to do so as both possessed in abundance a rare gift for friendship. They reduced the distance which had existed for nearly a century between the Viceroy and the public, and no one in India to whom they held out their hand thought of them as the famous and glamourous Mountbattens. People saw instead two warmhearted human beings who were making a tremendous effort to give themselves to India.

During the ghastly aftermath of Independence, when millions crossed borders between India and Pakistan and untold lives were lost in the barbaric fury let loose, the Mountbattens persevered no less than our own leaders to still the madness and, by their good faith, to calm passions and bring a sense of security to the threatened and displaced persons. Edwina, Lady Mountbatten, particularly was greatly loved as people came to know her. The manner in which she behaved during the bloody riots was the act of not only a brave woman but one who involved herself with humanity. To me she was a close and dear friend. I admired her for several reasons, and I know she did all she could to help many people in India. The poor and underprivileged were her special concern—not as Lady Bountiful, which she might easily have become, but as an ordinary woman with a heart responsive to the troubles and sorrows of others. Even after her official connection with India had ended she continued to visit as the head of the St John Ambulance and keep up her contacts with Indians. Her sudden death in 1960 was untimely.

Lord Louis Mountbatten was, of course, on another level. His official position could not be ignored and the role he had to play was a most delicate one. Politically he was disliked by some and blamed by many for the breakup of India into two countries. People often speak of his 'conceit'. There are few people in the world as entitled as he to be a little conceited. Dazzlingly handsome, a member of the royal family, successful in his chosen career, gifted with great ability, his charismatic personality was something many must have envied. To our family he was Dickie, a dear and loyal friend. He spent fifteen months in India, some of them as Governor General, invited to remain in that capacity by the Indian government after the transfer of power. This choice must have baffled many in the world in view of our national struggle for freedom, but it is better understood in the context of Gandhiji's teaching that it was always the system, and never the individual Britisher, that we were against. After the Mountbattens left India, Rajaji—

C. Rajagopalachari—became the first Indian Governor General, a role he fulfilled with distinction.

Rajaji would have achieved greatness in any country. A profound scholar, a shrewd politician, a wise statesman, and, above all, a humanitarian—how many can claim to combine these qualities? In his white khadi dhoti and kurta he was a commanding figure, and in the short period he served as Governor General of India after Lord Mountbatten, he lent grace and prestige to that high office. An outstanding quality in Rajaji was that he was not afraid to change his mind—a sign of strength in politics. It is only weak men who exaggerate the importance of not changing their minds, and there are innumerable instances of the harm this can do. Rajaji's ability to interest himself in any and every subject was a sign of his vitality. He could be a good companion to young and old alike. Of his learning and his leadership he has left ample proof behind. I was close to him throughout my political career and often sought his advice.

I was not in India when the day of freedom came. Despite all my protests I had been obliged to leave for Moscow early in August 1947. On the midnight of August 14 power was transferred from the British Parliament to the Constituent Assembly of India. It was a moment of jubilation all over the country and of mammoth crowds in Delhi cheering our national leaders as well as the Mountbattens. At that historic midnight session of the Constituent Assembly, where Bhai made a most moving speech, all members present took the following pledge:

> At this solemn moment when the people of India, through suffering and sacrifice, have secured freedom, I,..., a member of the Constituent Assembly of India, do dedicate myself in all humility to the service of India and her people to the end that this ancient land attain her rightful place in the world and make her full and willing contribution to the promotion of world peace and the welfare of mankind.

August 15 was Indian Independence Day, and in a broadcast Bhai reminded the nation of the role of Gandhiji, the Father of the Nation, of those of our comrades who had not lived to see this day, and of India, 'our much-loved Motherland, the ancient, the eternal, and the ever-new,' to whom he asked us to pay homage and renew our pledge of service.

But before this, the atmosphere of suspicion and tension that had been growing had led to a desperate fear of insecurity among people living in the border areas that were to divide India and Pakistan. A movement of Muslims leaving for Pakistan and Hindus and Sikhs for India began to take place. In the weeks following partition this exodus grew to formidable proportions, and it is believed that about ten million people crossed borders at this time. The announcement of the partition had increased the fears of minorities in both Hindu and Muslim regions, and now it unleashed the most brutal passions in otherwise sane human beings. Freedom had certainly come, but with a river of blood flowing over countless corpses, and fratricide the like of which the world had not known. Though this lasted a few weeks, the holocaust is a never-to-be-forgotten horror. The intolerance and bigotry of both Hindus and Muslims was responsible for this calamity, and terrible deeds were enacted by both groups. During the worst of the riots and killings our leaders, led by Gandhiji, showed great courage and a grim determination to end the madness. Bhai and Indira went into Muslim localities in Delhi, at considerable personal risk, to save lives endangered by bigots.

Apart from the loss of life the loss of property was tremendous. The poor lost all they possessed, the rich left behind their lands and ancestral homes. An immediate result of the partition was the acquiring of great numbers of refugees by both India and Pakistan. In Delhi a new ministry was added to the government to care for displaced persons and help in their rehabilitation. These refugees, uprooted from their homes and belongings, dispossessed of all they owned, were bitter and proud. They did not want charity, and in their state of shock they could hardly understand how this catastrophe had happened. Our government's handling of this gigantic human problem deserves great praise. The refugees of this period who came to Delhi, mainly fleeing from West Punjab, made new and meaningful lives for themselves. Thousands who settled in Punjab and Uttar Pradesh have prospered and made a great contribution to the agriculture and industry of their new home states.

The leadership of Pakistan had come mainly from the landed gentry of Uttar Pradesh, but this area remained in India. Over thirty-five million Muslims also remained in India, as did the main centres of Islamic culture, which are around Delhi and in Uttar Pradesh. This was a bitter disappointment to Mr Jinnah and the Muslim League, and led to many frustrations that corroded their relations with India. Despite the wounds of partition, India emerged strong and confident to face the myriad problems and responsibilities of a free nation.

I have been in Pakistan twice at the invitation of the Pakistan government. On both occasions it was a joy to meet old friends—men and women I was devoted to, with whom I had shared the period of my growing up; who spoke the same language, and who, until the deadly poison of suspicion born of political intrigue infected the atmosphere, shared the same bright dreams for the future.

We are physically separated and emotionally hurt, and it requires courage and abundant goodwill to weave a new design of mutual understanding and benefit. But the generation now growing up in Pakistan and India has no firsthand memories of the past. They have the future to look forward to, and, in spite of everything, I dare to hope that they will some day come close to each other and link their countries in bonds of lasting friendship.

Among high priority problems at the time of Independence was the question of the Indian states. When power was transferred from Britain to India the position of the feudal princes, formerly upheld by the British, lapsed. Each princely state was free to become a part of either India or Pakistan.

Among the Maharajas there were bad rulers and good ones; some whose people lived in feudal conditions, whose states were islands of darkness, and who, unmindful of the welfare of their states, spent lavish sums of money to satisfy their slightest whims. But there were others, educated and enlightened men, who had a long and honourable tradition of Indian monarchy and whose ancestors had ruled over the same state for over a thousand years and more. They had good administrations, more advanced in some cases than administration in parts of British India. The system was, however, already an anachronism even before Independence, dependent as it was on the powerful support of the British government, whose authority had been accepted without reservation from the beginning. The states' peoples had been aroused to awareness during the national movement, and a 'unification of the mind' with the people of British India had begun to take place.

Some larger states, Travancore and Mysore among them, hesitated to give up their 'independence', but the nationalist surge among the people of these states forced the rulers' hands. Thoughts of independence were encouraged by Mr Jinnah, and, in the case of Jodhpur, he promised the ruler the right to use Karachi as a seaport if Jodhpur State remained independent. However, a more realistic approach prevailed. Thus, with the exception of two large states, Hyderabad and Kashmir, most of the others united with India.

Through the great tact and wisdom of Sardar Patel, together with the willing cooperation of most of the rulers, who recognized the inevitability of change, this remarkable event was made possible. It was as historic in its own way as the freedom of India itself. It is to the credit of a large number of princes that they placed themselves at the disposal of the new government, and some served India with distinction as governors and ambassadors. The world is not generally aware that there are no more Maharajas in India. As in so many other instances, the species is extinct. The rubies as big as pigeon eggs, the flashing emeralds, the sparkling diamonds, are now in the possession of India's new industrial elite. The stately palaces have been converted into five-star hotels and their Highnesses are just citizens of India, with no special rights or privileges.

In 1971 an act of Parliament ended the privy purses and privileges of the princes, which were part of the agreement made in 1947 between princes and the Indian government. This created considerable bitterness, which was not unnatural. Such acts were perhaps necessary in the context of the new world order and developing conditions in India, but the change could have been made with more grace and less speed. The princes were sensitive, especially to small pinpricks like having to give up using titles they had borne with pride for centuries and the retention of which could have harmed no one. The feeling engendered in their minds, and in the minds of those who believed in the sanctity of the pledged word, was that India had behaved contrary to her own accepted principles. At a moment when the coöperation of every man and woman was needed for the innumerable and gigantic tasks facing us, a group that could have given help was antagonized.

I hold no brief for the princes. If, after their 'derecognition', I had seen a new social pattern emerge in which earlier misdeeds were replaced by the actions of dedicated men who understood and accepted the grave responsibilities they had undertaken, I would have considered the sacrifice and even the indignities inherent in the situation as the price the princes had to pay for the centuries in which they enjoyed every kind of right and privilege but did not remember to discharge the responsibilities these entailed. Unhappily, this is not the picture that has emerged. The princes have been replaced in many instances by men in high office who, while talking about simple living and high thinking, are only too happy, under cover of this copybook maxim, to satisfy their ambitions in ways far removed from the ideas of the Father of the Nation whose name they so loudly invoke from time to time. A double standard of living and thinking has grown up; its disastrous effects can already be seen and in the next generation this standard will have become a settled fact.

We have seen in the West how well-established patterns were rejected and trampled underfoot by the young, who could not equate the talk of elders with the way they acted. In the ten or more years since the revolt of youth, serious damage has been done and a generation has suffered in consequence. In our own country, young men and women are no longer content with being told they must follow their elders. They find double standards and hypocrisy spreading tentacles in the social and political systems; they grow desperate and show this sometimes in unfortunate ways, through violence of thought and action. Leadership, to be effective, must provide example. It must be shorn of platitudes, must express itself in language fitting into the new urges, which are in part the result of that same need for change that led to the 'derecognition' of a whole class. So, after putting aside a class that had ceased to fit into the new socialist pattern, the very least we can do is to prevent the creation of a group with another name that gradually assumes the same attributes without having the redeeming qualities that existed in the princely class. Let us be simple, by all means. Let us also be honest with ourselves and the nation.

◆◆◆

33

Moscow

For some still unknown reason I was to leave for Moscow before the day on which the transfer of power was to take place. I pleaded to be allowed to remain in India until then, but was told that Moscow was important and that August 15 must be celebrated there. If Bhai and others had realized how little importance the Soviet Union attached to this day we might have been permitted to celebrate it at home, as we had longed to do.

We left Delhi on August 3, 1947. An Air India plane had been chartered for us, and it stood on the field like a great silver bird flying the Indian flag. We were full of excitement and a sense of pride, for India's first mission abroad was to be opened. Our relationship with the world was about to begin. In London we already had a mission from British days, but the first Indian High Commissioner to Britain, Krishna Menon, was appointed after August 15. The Washington Embassy also was established after that date.

We had a tremendous send-off. It was a full plane containing all our diplomatic staff, the Indian domestic servants we were taking with us, Lekha, and myself. Since coming home from Wellesley, Lekha had been working on the *National Herald,* a Congress newspaper started in the late nineteen thirties, and she was now accompanying me as an honourary attaché.

There was to be a stop of two days in Tehran at the Shah's invitation. This was too brief for us to see much of the city, but it was interesting because we met the Parsi community of Iran, which had remained in that country, unlike a section of it that had fled to India to escape religious persecution. The Shah's lavish hospitality was overwhelming. In Iran we were met by a Soviet plane, which escorted us to Moscow, stopping en route in Baku and Stalingrad. The reason for this escort was that no foreign plane was allowed to enter Moscow. Our government had insisted on my flying in our own plane, and finally a compromise had been reached and a Soviet plane sent from Moscow to accompany us. In Baku, where the smell of oil dominated everything else, we were given a grand banquet at breakfast time with the table loaded with caviar, cold meats, salads, sweet dishes, Georgian champagne, vodka, and Russian tea. Unaccustomed to hearty eating at that hour, most of us could not take advantage of the meal, and when we arrived, hungry, at Stalingrad, at lunch time, there were naturally no refreshments! We saw something, however, of the utter devastation of war in Stalingrad. Arrival in Moscow had been eagerly anticipated, and our welcome was warm—red carpet, red roses, and assurances of friendship and esteem.

I had been allotted a house, not usual in those days of housing shortages after the war. Some ambassadors who had been waiting several months for accommodation were not at all pleased with what they termed favouritism. The house allotted to the Indian Mission had belonged to the famous Russian conductor Koussevitzky, then in charge of the Boston Symphony Orchestra. I had met him during my visit to Boston in 1945, and he had placed a box at my disposal. The house was not quite ready for occupation, and we stayed in the Metropole Hotel for a fortnight. I attached no special significance to this, but my colleague, the American Ambassador, General Walter Bedell Smith, warned me that the delay was only for the purpose of 'bugging' the rooms. Just before my arrival a high-level meeting had taken place in the American Embassy, a huge palace called Spaso House. It had been checked very thoroughly for 'bugs'. However, when the meeting was over it was discovered that a microphone had been cleverly put next to the telephone on which the American Secretary of State had a direct line to Washington! Coming straight from Sardar Patel's briefing I replied, much to the wry amusement of General Smith, that we in India were followers of Mahatma Gandhi and what we said was the same in private or public. We did not believe the Russians would treat us with suspicion as there was no reason for them to do so. We were friends. Bedell Smith told me he did not believe in Santa Claus!

We began life in Moscow in a large but shabby suite in the Metropole Hotel, and our chief concern was to arrange the presentation of credentials and the Independence Day reception. My first shock came when the Foreign Office rang up to say there was a small mistake in my credentials. These had been signed by King George VI, which our government should have realized was a mark against us, but I did not think this could be called a mistake. My First Secretary went to the Foreign Office and discovered the credentials had been addressed to Stalin and not, as they should have been, to (Nikolay) Shvernik, who was Chairman of the Presidium of the Supreme Soviet of the U.S.S.R! Our government had given some thought to these credentials, and it had been decided that they must be presented in Hindi. The translation of the English text was made by Purushottam Das Tandon, who had done a beautiful job. No one had remembered or bothered to inquire to whom the letter of credentials should be addressed! I had a shock not because there might be mistakes in the text but at the thought that there were Hindi experts in the Soviet Foreign Office who could pick them out.

Each country has a somewhat different way regarding the presentation of credentials by envoys. Normally in Moscow it was a simple affair, but mine was a special case. It was India's first Embassy and a woman was at the head of it. There was also the hope then that we would completely side with the Soviet Union. My United Nations speeches against imperialism, and the fight we had put up against discrimination, on both of which the Soviets had given us their full support, had led to this conclusion. So the presentation ceremony was somewhat formal, and received, for Moscow, considerable publicity. I had another mild shock in store when Shvernik spoke to me in his den after the ceremony was over. His first question related to my Gaon Panchayat Bill, still before the Uttar Pradesh Assembly, and he asked if the Muslim League attitude had softened toward the clause regarding joint electorates! Other questions on India were equally well informed.

On the matter of arrangements for our Independence Day reception we kept coming up against innumerable hurdles. We wanted a pole to hang our flag from the window of our hotel suite. The directress of the hotel, a stout blonde with an excessive sense of humour but very unobliging, could not understand why we wanted a flag. It was explained to her that we were having a reception to celebrate our independence and must hoist our national flag. What independence, she asked? Through our translator, Dr Ghoshal, I explained once more, and told her about the transfer of power. She burst into hysterical laughter. 'How can you be independent,' she positively roared, 'while the British army is in control of your country and a British Viceroy and other British officials remain there? That isn't what we call independence!' Finally we managed to get a flag staff, put up our flag, and even have a reception.

The fifteenth of August was not wholly a day of rejoicing for Lekha and me. Our thoughts inevitably were in Delhi, and the radio was kept turned on all day. We listened to Bhai speaking in the Constituent Assembly on the midnight of the fourteenth. The 'tryst with destiny' speech is now a part of Indian history. '...Before the birth of freedom we have endured all the pains of labour and our hearts are heavy with the memory of this sorrow...' It was this memory that made us, Lekha and me, shed tears on a day of fulfillment. So much had happened to India, so much not only to those whose lives were known to us and those we had lost in the struggle, but to the thousands of men and women who had shared our faith, joined our fight, faced difficulties with courage, whose names would forever remain unknown. Theirs was the achievement we celebrated on that day. It was ironic that in our small

Indian group in Moscow only the servants, besides Lekha and myself, had been involved actively in the independence struggle. All the officers, with the exception of Dr Ghoshal, were members of the I.C.S.!

Our embassy residence was a jewel of a house and, because it had belonged to a musician, it had a most delightful studio on the top floor. Moscow was still, in 1947, suffering heavily in many ways from the grim aftermath of the war. Food, consumer goods, and accommodation were very difficult to obtain. Our house was too small for Embassy requirements, and officers and staff were obliged to live in the Metropole, where our Chancery was also located. Another problem was that the house had been fully furnished for us with heavy, dark, Victorian-type furniture and there were several telephones in every room. The rent charged for all this was calculated in a very strange manner. An arbitrary price, which bore no relation to the real cost of the article, was marked against each piece of furniture, and we had to pay 15 per cent of the price of everything by way of rent. The furniture, carpets, chandeliers, and telephones came to an astronomical figure and gave us little comfort. From the beginning we began trying to ascertain how and where we could get furniture more suited to our needs and taste and to rid ourselves of the useless telephones, which rang night and day.

My arrival had caused a flutter in diplomatic circles. Our doyen was General Georges Catroux, Ambassador of France and friend and colleague of General de Gaulle. Madame Catroux was a powerful lady and a sort of Queen of the Corps. My coming created problems for her of a sort she had not till then encountered in diplomatic life.

'What are we to do with Mrs Pandit?' she asked the Foreign Office. 'Is she to sit with the men after dinner? Do we include her in women's parties, and does she speak any language we can understand?'

The answer from the Soviet Foreign Office was clear. Mrs

Pandit is the Indian Ambassador and will be treated as such. This did not enlighten Madame Catroux greatly, but there was nothing more to be said. I was there! Yet, in spite of her early dismayed response we became good friends from our first meeting, and she extended every kind of assistance to me. During the first weeks of settling down I leaned on her heavily for advice, and she literally adopted me as her own. Among other colleagues was Dr Fu, the Chinese Ambassador, who was a historian and a good friend. His Embassy was a treasure house of rare editions and valuable books. The Yugoslav Ambassador used to be a great favourite at the Kremlin, and he told us many interesting stories about people whom we knew only by name. There was great informality among members of the diplomatic corps, which is unusual and was created by our dependence on one another. Among the Commonwealth group, Frank Roberts, chargé d'affaires of the British Embassy, and his charming wife became my close friends, as did John Holmes, the Canadian chargé. But actually we were on good terms with all our diplomatic colleagues.

Housekeeping was a headache, and hours had to be spent in trying to get food. What was known as the 'open market' was too expensive, and the one shop from which diplomats could buy at somewhat reduced rates did not have enough to serve the entire Corps. It was a question of first come first served. The Western European embassies supplemented their diets from canned goods, but here again we were in trouble because this was an expensive way of eating and far beyond our allowances. Stores had to be ordered from Sweden in those days, and the orders placed months in advance. All through the winter there were no vegetables, and potatoes, cabbages, and beetroots had to be stored by September or even these would not be available. Settling down was a trying business, and the members of our staff were naturally unsettled and unhappy in the early months. Several of them, especially the vegetarians, had sent for vitamin pills to supplement their diets, and one day I discovered that these young men were consuming vitamins especially prepared for pregnant women and nursing mothers! The wrong make had been supplied by mistake and they had not noticed!

During this early period the fact that everything is relative was forcibly brought home to us. While we were distressed at the suffering that the Soviet people had endured during the war and the hardships they still had to face, we found Moscow a gloomy place and grumbled at difficulties and shortages. Therefore it came as a surprise to me when our Indian servants, my cook Budhilal and the two butlers, Rafiullah and Afzal Khan, were full of praise for the standard of living, the equality between the sexes, and various other facets of life in Moscow.

'What do you mean by standard of living?' I asked them. 'Have you not seen the queues in front of the soup kitchens in the streets, or the women who are doing such hard work shovelling snow with their legs wrapped with rags instead of having boots, and so many families having to share one room?' With one voice they answered that I had missed the point. There were no naked people in Moscow. No one starved or went without some shelter. All children went to school. One other incident is worth mentioning: Rafi and Afzal were staunch Muslims from Uttar Pradesh, and they wanted to know if there was a mosque in Moscow. We made inquiries and were told there was one, and that Friday prayers were held. Rafi and Afzal attended the next Friday and came home full of happy talk. They had been received as friends, and the mullah had welcomed them in his address and presented them to the congregation. After the prayers he had taken them to his home and given them tea. This simple gesture made these men friends of the Soviet Union for life. As for Budhilal, who was a Harijan, his admiration for the Soviets is still as strong as ever. He learned to speak fluent though inaccurate Russian and made many friends in Moscow. When I left my post he gave some interviews to the Hindi press in Allahabad expressing his views on the Soviet system. The result was that when I was transferred to Washington, the United States Ambassador, Mr Loy Henderson, refused him a visa on the ground that he was a communist. I was put to great inconvenience without him, though Lekha and her husband benefited by having Budhi with them for the next few years!

The Russians treated me with great respect and I was given no special consideration on grounds of sex, which pleased me. It was not a period of friendship, but one of the 'uncementing' of the relationship of the latter period of the war. There was a feeling of suspicion in the air, which was not directed at any one individual but to all who came from outside. This was a great disappointment to us, to me in particular, as I had wanted to establish personal relationships as I had done elsewhere. Lekha, and later, Tara, who joined us in Moscow, were a little better off. They went to theatres and the Park of Culture and Rest where they met students and young people of their age, and, knowing Russian, they were able to talk to them. But none of these contacts could lead to real friendship, because young Russians were not able to visit us at the Embassy.

Some of my diplomatic colleagues were amused at my distress. They had been predicting the end of the 'honeymoon', and none could resist saying, 'I told you so!' But I went on hoping we would make some contacts and be invited to Russian homes. The one exception was in the case of Alexandra Kollontai, a former minister of the Soviet Union in Norway and Sweden. She had been considered a brilliant woman in her day, and now, in her seventies, she was still alert and beautiful. She was partially paralyzed and confined to her home, but was an advisor in the Ministry of Foreign Affairs. I asked permission to call on her, and she was the one person who opened her home to me. She tried to explain her country's problems and to dismiss prejudices from my mind. Her son, who was studying for his foreign service examination, was introduced to us. Madame Kollontai had not been an ambassador, but this was a small technical difference. She was the first woman in the world to hold a diplomatic post. The only other had been Señora Isabella de Palencia of Spain, another brilliant and handsome woman and a revolutionary. She was exiled ultimately and lived in Mexico for many years. Several years later, when I was Ambassador to Mexico, I met her there.

Because of the closed society in which we lived, whatever social activity existed revolved around the embassies and was excessively monotonous. The same denunciation of Soviet policies, the same complaints of what was lacking, the same lavish imported food. I attended these gatherings less and less often.

I had wanted very much to tour the Soviet Union and, especially, the Asian republics. My interest in the land and the people was genuine, and although diplomats were not allowed to go anywhere except to Leningrad at that time, I hoped that perhaps, because of the welcome given to me, an exception might be made in my favour. Accordingly, soon after my arrival, I applied for permission to travel. Replies were never immediate, and I was not unduly impatient when no answer came. But as time passed I was greatly disappointed. We went to Leningrad, however, and spent an interesting week there. It was summer, and we had our first experience of the long day without darkness that is usual in those latitudes. We visited the Summer Palace and the famous Hermitage, drove around the countryside, and had a new impression of the country, since Moscow and Leningrad are very different. I was invited to the university and was presented with a copy of the first Russian translation of the Ramayana. Meeting professors was also an experience, because for the first time since our arrival in the Soviet Union we were able to speak informally with a group of interesting Russians outside the Foreign Office.

The year we arrived in Russia was the eighth centenary of the city of Moscow, and I have never forgotten the celebrations that marked the occasion, or the manner of rejoicing. There was a big meeting in the ornate Bolshoi Theatre, where all the members of the government were present on the stage. It was whispered that Stalin was ill of a serious complaint and that it was his double who took his place and received the tremendous applause. The new Indian Ambassador was given a standing and, as far as we could judge, enthusiastic welcome. I felt very happy. At all the main street corners platforms had been erected, and leading artists and ballerinas sang and danced for the people. These entertainments lasted far into the night, with dancing in the streets and much merriment. From the rural areas big trucks of grain and other foods, including fruits and vegetables, had been sent to Moscow as gifts—eight hundred trucks to mark the eight hundredth anniversary, and each region sent the special produce of its area. Sitting on top of these laden trucks were young men and girls in bright-coloured clothes, with bandanas round their heads, playing concertinas, singing, laughing, and waving to the people along the road—happy and obviously enjoying themselves.

Cultural life in Moscow consisted of a variety of entertainments. There were ballet and opera in the world-famous Bolshoi where Ulanova, the great ballerina, was at her height. I enjoyed seeing her in many memorable performances. There was also folk dancing from the different Soviet republics, concerts, theatre with many translations of classics, including the plays of Bernard Shaw and Oscar Wilde. The puppet theatre was remarkable of its kind, as was the circus. I encouraged my office staff to visit as many of these as possible, and sent my domestic servants to the ballet, which they greatly enjoyed.

We had not been able to find accommodations for all our staff and the Chancery. This was not satisfactory, and finally we were offered a very large mansion that could be used not only as embassy and Chancery but accommodate many of the members of the staff as well. Our government agreed to our taking this, but we had to furnish it before we could move in. The nearest and most inexpensive place to make the necessary purchases was Stockholm, and, with the permission of the External Affairs Ministry, I went there, accompanied by Lekha and Mr T.N. Kaul, the First Secretary, to buy what we required from the large store, Nordiska Kompaniet, which catered to Moscow embassies. I selected articles of furniture in all good faith and, I believe, some judgment of what was suitable and lasting. I also took the opportunity to call on members of the Swedish government and was honoured at a luncheon by the Prime Minister, Mr Undén. Some foreign journalists in Sweden, trying to give us publicity, flashed a small item of news about Swedish furniture being purchased for the Indian Embassy in Moscow. This was completely misunderstood by our parliamentarians, many of whom knew nothing of embassies or their needs. Few had ever been abroad, and they raised a hornet's nest around the External Affairs Ministry. My brother, as Foreign Minister, had to reply to these questions, which were in the form of a *cut motion*[16] by Mr Kamath. Bhai made a statement that included the following remarks:

> A great deal of criticism has been made about our Ambassador in Moscow getting furniture from Stockholm. Well, how a house has to be furnished in Moscow, of course, Honourable Members do not realize. It is just not possible to furnish easily in Moscow. You get an empty house. We thought of sending things from India, but it was almost a physical impossibility unless you spent vast sums of money on aeroplanes to carry chairs and tables from here. Of course, it could have been furnished alternatively with Russian furniture. The Russian people, all credit to them for this, ever since the war, are so intent on doing what they consider to be the fundamental things, that

16. A parliamentary term used when a member moves a motion in Parliament to attack an item of budget presented by the minister in charge.

> they refuse to waste their time on the accessories of life. They have to rebuild their country after the most horrible suffering and damage suffered in the war and they are concentrating on major undertakings. They go about in patched-up clothes and broken-down shoes. It does not matter, but they are building dams, reservoirs and factories and the rest which they consider more important... The only things you get in Russia are antique pieces of Czarist days which are frightfully expensive. The result is that our Embassy in Moscow had to go to Stockholm and get its chairs and tables, and these are urgently required office equipment... But of course the visit to Stockholm was not merely, Members of the House should realize, to buy furniture. When an Ambassador goes somewhere, that Ambassador does other work too, and any kind of shopping that might be done is incidental.

The furniture arrived in time and was installed, and we moved into our new home. Our government was new to Embassy problems, and sometimes the most ridiculous instructions came from Delhi, such as what type of furniture was allowed for a First Secretary. The list we received was a classic, and not only did it have no relation to life in Moscow, the items were written in the Anglo-Indian jargon of East India Company days, which probably even a British store would not understand, yet it remained in the book of rules of the Ministry. This list, for instance, entitled a First Secretary of the Indian Embassy to a limited number of wooden chairs and tables, two cotton durries (floor mats), a cot, and, lastly, a commode. This did not imply an elegant piece of French furniture—something to be bought in a Christie auction—but an old-fashioned toilet apparatus used in India consisting of a bulky wooden chair fitted with a 'potty'!

Ambassadors get a representation allowance, which is referred to as *frais de représentation.* As my obligations to entertain in Moscow were less numerous than we had anticipated, because of the difficulty of meeting Russians, some of the allowance would be left over. This amount I returned to the government. When Dr Radhakrishnan succeeded me as Ambassador to the Soviet Union we had a long talk about Moscow, and I told him what I had done. He said he was glad to know this, and in his period as Ambassador he did the same.

While Ambassador in Moscow I was appointed to lead the Indian delegation to the United Nations again, and attended the General Assembly session in September 1947. The agenda had several items in which we were interested, but during the session the attack on Kashmir by Pakistani raiders took place, and the horror and misery of the situation, so far away, cast its shadow on the U.N. even before the matter had been referred formally to the Security Council. From that time onward for several years, Kashmir was a major issue in the Security Council and the General Assembly—a cause of heated debate and division of opinion among member states. The Soviet Union's sympathy and vote were with India, as was its veto in the Security Council. Politics are not based on humanitarianism. Countries vote for or against an issue to further their own interests, but the manner and timing of a vote is important because help given at a psychological moment cements a relationship. This was so in the case of India and the Soviet Union.

As India was still evolving her political policies there were, at this time, no special problems between the Soviet Union and us. No particular brief was given to me, and my work was limited. Had Soviet policies allowed, all of us connected with the Embassy could have made valuable contacts for India, but this phase was to come at a later stage. At the time of which I write the Stalin era was at its height and foreign envoys, except those from the eastern European countries, were not favoured people. We could not travel beyond a radius of thirty-six miles without permission; we could not go to the ballet or opera or any entertainment by buying our own tickets in the usual way, but had to go through the government agency called Burobin. Even for parties, if extra food was required, the number of people invited had to be submitted and Burobin would give a permit and cross out certain articles considered 'unnecessary'. It was not customary for any of the important Russians to attend either small dinner parties at embassies or big official receptions. A relatively junior member of the Foreign Office would represent the Foreign Minister, who was Molotov at that time, and, later, Vyshinksky. When the latter was Permanent Representative at the United Nations, I had the opportunity of becoming friendly with him and his family.

Not being able to meet Stalin was a disappointment and led to much criticism of me in Parliament. Freedom to criticize had risen to great heights in India and amounted to libel in some cases. A Delhi newspaper had reported that on leaving for my assignment in Moscow I had accepted a present of Rs. 20,000 and two hundred saris from the Uttar Pradesh government! The matter had come up in Parliament and had to be dismissed as nonsense by my brother. In the case of Stalin the facts were that, for whatever reason, he was not meeting anyone at that time. One reason given out was his ill health. During my time in Moscow an Indian couple, well-known communists sponsored by Voks, visited Moscow and were given a special plane to tour the country. They were also received by Stalin. In a speech at a dinner in his honour the gentleman said, 'We have seen many flowers in the garden of the U.S.S.R. Indeed we have seen the Gardener himself!' Stalin's first interview with a foreign representative during my stay in Moscow was given to the American Ambassador at the time of the Berlin airlift, when I was preparing to leave the Soviet Union. Recently, the public relations officer of the Soviet Embassy in Delhi came to interview me in my home in Dehra Dun in connection with a history he was writing of Indo-Soviet friendship on the completion of thirty years of contact between the countries. He confirmed that the criticisms in Parliament against me were incorrect, and that

Stalin had been seriously ill for most of the period of my stay in Moscow. But I have no way of knowing the truth.

We had been in Moscow barely five months when the news of Gandhiji's death was broken to me by Dr Fu, the Chinese Ambassador. Knowing what a terrible shock it would be to me, he had come over personally to say that he had just heard the news on a B.B.C. broadcast. We immediately turned on the radio, and the chant of *Raghupati Raghava Raja Ram*, Gandhiji's favourite hymn, made us realize that this incredible news was correct. Every little while the chanting was stopped and the senseless manner of his killing was announced. We were stunned and incredulous. How could such a thing have happened, and why? At the moment of Independence I had felt myself discriminated against by having to be abroad, but now, in the time of this national tragedy, I was overwhelmed by bitterness at not being at home. It was a disastrous moment for India and for all who loved Gandhiji. My heart was with Bhai, knowing the anguish he must be passing through. Lekha and I spent a wakeful night and a day of fasting to try, in spirit, to involve ourselves with what was going on at home. Later we heard on the radio Bhai's now well-known speech, 'The light has gone out of our lives,' in which he broke the news of Gandhiji's death to the nation.

The next day *Pravda* announced the death in a very curt manner, saying only that Gandhi had been assassinated by a Hindu reactionary. Today, changing events have altered the Soviet Union's attitude toward Gandhiji, and he is now accepted by them as a great Indian leader. This is an illustration of the way politics turns somersaults.

Gandhiji was shot as he came to his evening prayer meeting on January 30, 1948. As he ascended the terrace where the prayers were to be held, supported by his two granddaughters, a young man pushed himself forward and fired three shots in succession at close range. Gandhiji collapsed with the name of Rama on his lips. To the eternal shame of India it was the hand of a Hindu that brought about his martyrdom.

The partition of India had deeply grieved Gandhiji, but even more than the actual formation of two separate states, the price of freedom, he had been full of sorrow at the communal strife that followed, the surge of suffering humanity that crossed borders in terror and despair. Day after day people came to see him with tales of horror and he wanted to go where the suffering was greatest, and to newly formed Pakistan to give the support of his presence to people there. The last fast he undertook was a result of the anguish he felt. He decided on January 12 to fast for an indefinite period and announced next day at his prayer meeting that the fast was for 'a reunion of hearts of all communities brought about without pressure but from an awakened sense of duty.' This fast had an instant response among huge masses of Indians and Pakistanis and the governments of both countries. In Delhi, shortly after the fast began, the Indian Cabinet met in Birla House where Gandhiji was staying to consider the matter of Pakistan's share of cash balances—all property held by the undivided Government of India had to be apportioned between the two states, and the issue of cash balances had been a delicate one. Now the Indian government released 550 million rupees to Pakistan. Thousands of citizens signed a peace pledge to work for and restore communal harmony. On January 18 Gandhiji broke his fast.

But the bitterness that had prevailed before partition and after had poisoned the atmosphere. The frenzy of fanaticism reached a climax when Nathuram Godse, an orthodox Hindu from Maharashtra, took the life of Gandhiji. Earlier, the group of which he was a member had thrown a bomb into Birla House, and, hearing of a conspiracy to attack Gandhiji, the government had wanted to protect him from the public, especially during his prayer meetings, which were attended by mammoth crowds. But that was not Gandhiji's way and he refused to allow security officers to guard him. Godse was caught and stood trial for the murder. He was sentenced to life imprisonment and, having completed the required minimum number of years, was released a short while ago.

Tributes to Gandhiji poured in from all over the world, among them spontaneous messages from Pakistan. In the years since his death Gandhiji's lifework and his philosophy have come to have a special meaning in many parts of the world where human dignity and rights continue to be violated. The assassination of Gandhiji was not only the act of one madman but the failure of many to realize that anger and violence can never take the place of reason and compassion.

◆◆◆

34

Assignment in Washington

Shortly before he died I had met Gandhiji when I had gone to Delhi to report after the General Assembly and before returning to Moscow. He mentioned that I was to be sent to Washington soon. I told him I had heard a rumour but that nothing had been said to me formally, and one reason I had come to see him was to plead to be allowed to stay on in Moscow. I explained that there were difficulties all the time, and little cooperation from the Russian officials, but it was a challenge and I liked being there in spite of everything. I knew something of the U.S.A. and felt that I would grow 'soft' there. In Moscow one had to be tough mentally and physically and it was good training for me. Gandhiji smiled and said he was pleased to hear this but he felt there would be plenty of problems for me to face in Washington, though of a different kind. I would need discipline and toughness and the will to resist the temptations of an easy life. As I touched his feet he said, 'I would like to talk more but I am very tired.' Those were his last words to me.

I returned to India once more during my Moscow assignment because Tara was engaged to be married and I took leave in order to make all the necessary arrangements. Tara was married to Gautam Sahgal at Anand Bhawan in January 1949, and it was an occasion for the larger family to be together in the old home after having been scattered for a long time. I returned to Moscow after the wedding. I had told Bhai I wanted more time there, and he had agreed that this would be the right thing to do. But three months later I left and came to Delhi for Lekha's wedding, before taking up my new post in Washington.

Both the girls had simple weddings. In each case a civil marriage was followed by a brief religious ceremony. Bhai would not allow any wedding gifts to be accepted except those from relatives and very close friends. Because he was Prime Minister and Foreign Minister, many people who might, in ordinary circumstances, not send presents would feel compelled to give expensive ones to the Prime Minister's nieces, specially as Lekha was marrying a young Foreign Service officer, Ashok Mehta, and the wedding took place in the Prime Minister's House. Very soon after the wedding, in the summer of 1949, I left for Washington with Rita. Our Embassy there was a beautiful house bought and furnished by Sir Girija Shankar Bajpai when he was Agent General before Independence.

Moscow and Washington were planets apart, and though this may sound odd, the fact was that I had adapted myself to conditions of life in Moscow far more easily than I settled down in Washington. In Moscow I was *Gaspaja Pasol,* Madame Ambassador, and treated as such—no favours because I was a woman and no surprise that I was Ambassador. This made up partially for other problems. In Washington, however, I was Madame Pandit, Nehru's sister, and my being India's Ambassador was not taken seriously. It was an uphill struggle during the first few weeks to insist on this recognition, but I succeeded in obtaining it.

In Moscow my simple clothes (I usually wore subdued colours or black) and restrained style of living and entertaining had been appreciated and remarked upon. In Washington the newspapers were constantly commenting on my sari and my hairstyle. The general expectation was for me to 'live up to my position'. This was explained to me by one of my early callers, Perle Mesta (of *Call Me Madam* fame!), who was a most friendly person. But the world in which she lived was so different from mine, and her only knowledge of India had come from a Maharaja she had once known. Our wavelengths could not synchronize. I have always loved beautiful clothes and have enjoyed doing all the things that make a house into a home—decorating the rooms, arranging flowers, cooking and evolving new dishes, entertaining my friends, these give me joy. But public life in India immediately after Independence imposed many restrictions on one's way of living, and those who had been through long periods of jail and the rigours of the freedom struggle itself had moulded themselves on another and simpler pattern. In my case, even if I had wished to change it would not have been easy because I did not have the means to do so and it was best to keep to the old design and create an image of new India, which I tried to do. Besides this, I did not want to be a target for members of Parliament. I was still the only woman ambassador, and it was difficult enough to persuade Parliament that I did my work as efficiently as a man without having debates about my clothes or my parties. Fortunately I had the help of many American friends, men and women, whose advice I valued. They were always ready to guide me along the proper social path, and I was soon able to strike a happy medium between diplomatic ostentation and Indian austerity!

Among those who held out friendly hands on my arrival in Washington and helped me to understand the various aspects of Washington's bewildering political scene were Walter Lippmann, and Justices Felix Frankfurter and William Douglas of the Supreme Court. I think of them with feelings of gratitude for having translated their friendship for me and for India into practical terms. They were all men on whom I could rely for advice and support at any time.

In later years Hubert Humphrey joined the group that believed in India and her future. I loved him and his wife, Muriel, for more than one reason. He was a gentleman, and ambition did not dim his vision of the values and realities of life.

I had met President Truman briefly during my lecture tour and my relationship with him remained a good one. There were no diplomatic frills about him. Both he and Mrs Truman were what I call real people, with no pretentions, and I liked and admired them very much.

Dean Acheson, the Secretary of State, was a different type. One could not imagine him and President Truman as colleagues. He was a brilliant man, more British than the British in the heyday of Empire both in his dress, which was always immaculate, and his mind, which was ultraconservative. His knowledge of Asia was limited, probably because he was not deeply interested in that area, and of India he knew very little, past or present. The policy of nonalignment which was just being evolved meant nothing to him. The word was peculiar and the concept still more so. In this he was not unlike Mr John Foster Dulles who, under President Truman's bipartisan policy, was handling the Japanese peace treaty. Dulles's *bête noire* was nonalignment, and both he and Dean Acheson divided the world into two categories—friends and foes. They both had tidy minds in which everything was either black or white and the arch-enemy was Communism. To discuss any policy with either required great skill, which I did not possess. Wherever the discussion began, it ended up with Communism. There was no getting away from it.

Dean Acheson, outside Asian politics, was a charming and polished individual and an interesting companion on the social level. But he found it difficult to accept me as my country's official representative.

'Why do pretty women want to be like men?' he once asked me.

'They don't,' I replied, 'they only want equal rights and

privileges, Mr Secretary of State, and I insist on having mine!' Some of these 'privileges' related to protocol. The Chief of Protocol, Mr Stanley Woodward, was harassed and worried by problems such as whether I was to be treated like a man or a woman at formal dinners. Meaning, thereby, would I join the men for cognac and cigars and political talk after the dinner or go with the women for coffee and gossip? As firmly as I could, I said that I would go with the men, and I stuck to this. A few ambassadors felt uncomfortable in the beginning but they soon got used to my presence and, I might say, liked it!

Though my contacts with him were relatively few, one of the men I admired and with whom I could exchange views was, strangely enough, General George C. Marshall. Before I met him I thought of him as a great soldier, but I discovered that he was a great humanitarian also, and, contrary to his profession, was a man who sought to preserve life rather than to destroy it. So many people who have been associated with war and acquainted with its horrors at firsthand have dedicated themselves to the service of humanity. In some cases this is a sort of atonement. One such person is my friend Leonard Cheshire, the English air ace, who instituted the Cheshire homes for incurables in England and other countries, including India.

Bhai's official visit to the United States was being planned by the State Department when I arrived in Washington, and Bhai was looking forward to it. It was to be his first trip to America and he was to visit Canada after the United States. I was nervous. The setting I was now in and the plans I heard discussed would not, I felt, conform to Bhai's ideal of America. I wrote to Sir Girija and he spoke to the American Ambassador in Delhi about keeping the programme simple. I accentuated this point as much as I could in Washington because I wanted Bhai to see some of the things and meet the people he would like. Through knowing them he might be able to accept with patience the official attitude toward

India. I knew so well that the concentration on Communism would irk him and interfere with fruitful talks in our mutual interest. There was much our countries had in common, and the development of Indian democracy was in fact almost as vital to the U.S. as the preservation of her own. It was important that American political leaders did not take India for granted or talk down to us and tell us what to do. They must not bargain with us, for much of our past record was similar to their own. Our integrity as a nation had been proved, and they must realize that each country sees the world from its own position on the map, and its policies must be for its own advantage primarily. This did not mean antagonism against other nations with a somewhat different approach. As Indians, given our geographical and historical background, our conditioning, our philosophy, we were not able to divide the world into two different colours and put them into separate compartments. Since human beings of many shades inhabit the earth and there are as many shades of opinion, all these facts must be taken into consideration when formulating policies. These thoughts were in my mind, but I was still new to Washington and I had arrived at a bad moment. The friendships and unity of the war years had given place to the prejudices that preceded the cold war, and India was judged by her votes in the United Nations. A much more experienced diplomat might have been able to influence the State Department, though I doubt it. The time was not yet ripe.

During Bhai's visit in October 1949, the programme was a heavy one and he spent three weeks visiting several cities and speaking on a great many occasions. During this hectic programme he found time to write to the girls after a visit to Wellesley, which he enjoyed and where he spoke briefly to the students. He also went to Harvard and M.I.T. and made an important speech at Columbia University, where General Eisenhower was then the president. Everywhere the warmth of the welcome accorded to him was astonishing and touched him very much. There were many things he enjoyed and people whom he was pleased to meet and through whom he gained glimpses of the America of his dreams. In one of his speeches he referred to being on 'a discovery of the heart and mind of America.'

There were two functions, however, which could not have been more wrong had they been carefully planned to upset him. One was a luncheon of well-known bankers. It was considered by those who arranged it to be a great opportunity for Nehru to talk about India's poverty and problems and ask for financial assistance. The guests sat at a round table with a beautiful flower arrangement, gleaming silver, and good food. Everything seemed right. But after the meal the guests were introduced all over again in terms of the millions each possessed. I saw Bhai literally shrinking into himself and my heart sank. It is important to remember that though we all need money, our approach to it differs. The Americans are always talking about it—it is a most popular subject of conversation. So it is in India. We have no inhibitions on this subject. But Bhai, in this respect, was un-Indian. He had the Britisher's reticence toward talking about money, and when it was necessary to do so the subject had to be approached with subtlety and finesse. His embarrassment and annoyance were acute, and in his reply to the toast he made no mention of the need for financial assistance. Some of the gentlemen present, whom I knew, could not understand this and were hurt. They told me they had come prepared to help India but no help was asked for—why was this? I turned them over to Sir Girija but, though many were his personal friends, he was not able to do anything to clarify the situation for them.

The other function was a banquet for one hundred persons at the Greenbrier, in White Sulphur Springs, given by Colonel Louis Johnson, who had been President Roosevelt's personal representative in India toward the end of the war and was very sympathetic to India. However, he obviously did not really know the kind of man Bhai was. He took tremendous pains and produced a lavish and ostentatious banquet of which Bhai heartily disapproved. I felt sorry for him. Any one of our Maharajas would have enjoyed the evening and been pleased at being so entertained, but alas, Nehru was not a Maharaja! The banqueting hall was most elegantly decorated, the waiters were dressed in costumes of Civil War days, the menu was long and exotic, and afterward we were entertained by some of the leading artists of the Metropolitan Opera in New York, who were flown down for the occasion. The *pièce de résistance* was the presentation by Colonel Johnson of a gold cigarette lighter with two clasped hands on one side and an inscription on the other! Colonel Johnson was very pleased with all his arrangements. As for Bhai, the gift came as a surprise and a shock, but he carried it off well and said all that was appropriate for the occasion.

The official talks were left mainly to Sir Girija. Nothing particularly significant emerged except, and this was important, a better understanding of our stand in the U.N. Bhai's pronouncement on our foreign policy also was clear. In his Washington speech to the House of Representatives and the Senate, he referred to the manifesto issued by distinguished American citizens for the release of Indian leaders arrested during the Quit India movement and to the way President Roosevelt had endeavoured to influence events in India. In an address to the Foreign Policy Association and allied organizations that honoured him in New York, he said:

> Many of us have grown up in admiration of the ideals and objectives which have made this country [U.S.A.] great. Yet though we may know the history and something of the culture of our respective countries, what is required is a true understanding and appreciation of each other even when we differ... We realize that self-help is the first condition of success for a nation, no less than [for] an individual. We are conscious that ours must be the primary effort and we shall seek succour from none to escape from any part of our responsibility. But though our economic potential is

> great, its conversion into finished wealth will need much mechanical and technological aid. We shall therefore gladly welcome such aid and cooperation on terms that are of mutual benefit. The objectives of our foreign policy are the preservation of world peace and enlargement of human freedom. We are neither blind to reality nor do we propose to acquiesce in any challenge to man's freedom from whatever quarter it may come. Where freedom is menaced or justice threatened or where aggression takes place, we cannot be and shall not be neutral. What we plead for and endeavour to practise in our own imperfect way is a binding faith in peace and an unfailing endeavour of thought and action to ensure it.

India's foreign policy as it emerged after freedom was a result of our having gained independence at a particularly difficult moment in history. The world's economic and political structure had been upset, and moral values shattered, by the long years of Fascist power and the war. Indian leaders were very conscious of the fact that building up a country of 360 millions, as India then was, with its legacy of poverty and all that stems from it, was a herculean task. Only the world's sympathetic understanding could help us, and we on our part had to buy time to raise our country's standards and adjust ourselves to the new responsibilities crowding in on us. Therefore we began by proclaiming friendship toward all nations, and were resolved to stay clear of military blocs. On all world issues we considered it our right to judge each one on its merits and to stay free from entanglements. This had a profound meaning not only for us but for other countries then emerging into freedom. We earned the respect of Asian countries that achieved independence after us, and they, and newly emerging African states, made nonalignment an important plank in their foreign policies for reasons similar to ours. Nonalignment brought many headaches. To us it seemed simple—the logical follow-up of past tradition and present needs. But to the West, and more specially to America, it seemed the betrayal of freedom. On many occasions when I appeared on a public platform I was asked how many times India had voted with America and how many times with the Soviet Union in the United Nations. The very word nonalignment became synonymous in America with sitting on the fence. Sometimes it was very difficult for me to get our views across.

When the Japanese peace treaty was being drafted, day after day telegrams went back and forth between Washington and Delhi. It was my job to discuss these with Mr Dulles and to try to soften for him the blows that our messages seemed to deal him on the matter of reparations. India was not in favour of the reparations that the United States wanted to impose on Japan. Often these meetings took place in Mr Dulles's home at breakfast time and were a sore trial to me. I am not at my best early in the morning, and Mr Dulles used to pace back and forth as he talked, a habit that I found annoying. On the morning when I had to tell him that India refused to sign the treaty as it had been drafted by the United States, tempers were frayed and it was a difficult moment. I handed over my message with regrets that my country could not go along with the United States. Mr Dulles had been hoping against hope for a change of heart or a miracle that would make India side with America, and he was genuinely staggered by the final response. He was a religious man and believed in the power of prayer. He walked up and down the room with bent head and his hands behind his back while I waited to leave. Then he swung around and said, 'I cannot accept this. Does your Prime Minister realize that I have prayed at every stage of this treaty?' I could think of no appropriate response. I could hardly tell him that my Prime Minister's views disagreed with those of the Almighty. India was not present at San Francisco where the Japanese peace treaty was signed, but had a separate treaty with Japan.

A famine in India in the early fifties had made it necessary to ask for wheat loans from abroad, and Washington had been approached by me. There was a sympathetic response, but of course the matter had to go before Congress and the Senate. The debates went on and on. There was so much ignorance of India, and some of the reasons against granting the loan were due to fear that would have been ridiculous had the developing food situation not been desperate. While people were in grave need, legislators pondered on whether grain sent from the United States would be fed to the 'sacred monkeys' and the 'sacred peacocks' and much other irrelevance. But there are always two sides to every picture, and people all over the United States were sending us small donations to buy grain. Children were coming to the Chancery clutching a few cents and asking us to buy food for Indian children. Farmers were bringing truckloads of wheat to our door. CARE and other societies were active in their efforts to hasten collection of an amount of wheat that could be dispatched immediately. The goodness and sympathy that poured out were heartwarming and kept the links in the chain of friendship from getting rusty. The official sanction came at last, but long before that a ship carrying grain from the Soviet Union had reached Bombay and been received with rejoicing by the people and by Parliament. The amount that came was considerably less than the American loan, but it came at the right time and earned the gratitude of those who needed it. I was questioned many times about why the consignment from the United States had not been welcomed in the same way as had the Russian grain.

It was during my stay in Washington that Senator McCarthy raised the communist bogey and that he and the Committee on un-American Activities held sway. It is past history now, but in the terrible months during which men and women of integrity and high standing in politics and in public life were humiliated and labelled disloyal and untruthful, McCarthy's conduct was in itself un-American. By their actions Senator McCarthy and his associates denigrated the good traditions of their country and showed themselves up as little men with big egos while they tried to destroy those better than themselves for imaginary 'crimes'. I went to the trial of Judge Dorothy Kenyon, and the manner in which the inquiry was conducted was shocking and frightening. This period caused severe damage not only to many lives but to the very image that McCarthy thought he was trying to rescue. There were so many people I had called my friends among those accused during the time of McCarthyism—Owen Lattimore, the renowned scholar and China expert, Joseph E. Davies, a senior member of the Foreign Service and also a China expert of the State Department, Lillian Heilman, the author, Robert Oppenheimer, America's great physicist, and so many others. Oppenheimer's great preoccupation outside his scientific work was with Hindu philosophy. An admirer of Gandhi and the doctrine of ahimsa or nonviolence, which he referred to as non-hurt, he studied Sanskrit to be able to read the Mahabharata and the Bhagavad Gita and became involved in the underlying philosophy of the Gita. His admiration for my brother amounted almost to reverence, and, in the days when he was searching for spiritual comfort, he had some correspondence with him. He had been through a period of great anguish when I met him, but there were things of mutual concern we could share. I judged him to be as rare a human being as he was a great scientist. On one occasion I went to Princeton to lunch with him and his wife. It was the day General MacArthur was recalled to Washington by President Truman, and we saw the procession and subsequently heard on T.V. his famous speech to the Senate.

During my term in Washington a grave crisis that faced the world was the outbreak of the Korean War. The incursion of North Korea into the South was termed an aggression by the Security Council. India's stand was that this aggression must be condemned, and we supported the Security Council's resolution. From the beginning of the crisis India was greatly disturbed, and, because our government was among the few represented at that time in China, we felt that we were in some sort of position to offer help to nations that had no contact with Peking. There was also the feeling in India that some countries did not have an understanding of Asia and that colonial attitudes toward Asian peoples still prevailed in policy-making in the West. In this thinking we were not alone. Several Asian and African states felt as we did and supported India's stand in the U.N. on various occasions during the years of the Korean debate. To me, personally, the Korean War was brought home in a tragic way by the loss of a member of my staff, Unni Nair, a brilliant journalist and a lovable man who was killed in the early months of the fighting, leaving behind a young wife and baby daughter.

When the U.N. forces pushed the aggression back to the 38th parallel India did not consider that this point should be crossed but pleaded for negotiations to be started in order to prevent a worsening of the situation. From our mission in Peking we knew that the Chinese felt the crossing of the 38th parallel would be a threat to their security and that they would retaliate. The U.N. forces under the command of General MacArthur did cross the 38th parallel, and China came out in strong support of North Korea. Whether they were right or wrong in doing so was not the issue so much as the fact that they pushed back MacArthur's army and created a very critical situation. India believed that the world could be on the verge of war, for mounting tensions in the U.N. and in Asia made this a real danger. We did not therefore support the U.N. demand to term China an aggressor. To India it was unrealistic to so accuse a state not bound by the United Nations Charter. The People's Republic of China was not a member of the United Nations, and while it was being condemned it was, on its part, condemning the U.N. for its military action in Korea. In this context India felt strongly that at all costs name-calling should be avoided, a door kept open for an ultimate settlement, and efforts made to bring about a ceasefire. We believed that the hostilities, geographically much closer to us than to many of those participating in deliberations in New York, must be ended and sincere attempts made to curb bitterness that would hamper eventual negotiations. We also believed that no final solution would be possible without the voice of China, which was very much a reality in our region. For this reason Nehru had written to the Soviet Union and the United States in July 1950 advocating that China should take its place in the United Nations. The Soviet Union was boycotting the Security Council at that time, and India felt that unless all major powers were represented at talks no solution was possible. Dean Acheson's attitude, apart from 'containment' of Communism, was that a number of member states were opposed to the seating of China. This line of thinking was difficult for us to understand because large masses of people in Asia and Africa, for instance, were opposed to apartheid, yet South Africa continued to be a member of the U.N. One did not expect all members of this body to have identical views and policies. The Afro-Asian group within the U.N. sought to establish a commission to determine the basis of a ceasefire. This consisted of Sir B.N. Rau (India), Mr Entezam (Iran), and Mr Lester Pearson (Canada), but its efforts were not successful. Long and difficult months passed before negotiations were started at Panmunjon, and many more months before the armistice. In the unsettled question of the exchange of prisoners of war India played a part.

Korea marked one of the worst phases in Indo-American relations. One cartoon, captioned 'Nehru's Face Is Red', was indicative of this trend. Nor did we have the approval of the Soviet Union or of China.

The impression in the United States was that we were wooing China and maintaining a 'holier than thou' attitude. In view of America's disapproval of our Korean policy and consistently hostile attitude toward communism, it was ironic to see, two decades later, the secretive methods employed by Mr Nixon to meet communist Chinese leaders and finally to put his seal of approval on the People's Republic of China when he hoped that this diplomatic coup would lead to his re-election!

One of the great disappointments of our time has been that the United States, a beacon of hope during the freedom struggles of the Asian peoples, succumbed to the views and greater colonial experience of nations grown to power in an earlier period. In Asia, it has seemed to us that the United States has always backed 'the wrong horse', ignoring the legitimate aspirations of the peoples of the countries concerned and their desire to be rid of political and economic domination. Where India was concerned, the United States accepted the thesis that our refusal to join the so-called 'free world'—Dulles termed nonalignment 'immoral'—could be balanced only by a closer relationship of the United States with Pakistan. The results of this policy have been all too obvious. Starting with the first 'tilt' in the matter of taking sides over Kashmir in 1948 onward, to Nixon's famous 'tilt' at the time of the Bangladesh war, the United States stepped into imperial shoes and played one side against the other as in former 'divide and rule' days. This game had particularly tragic consequences for India and Pakistan. India had a political base that Pakistan lacked, but the manner of partition, with its attendant bloodshed and misery, created grave problems for both new states. In the time during which we should have been concentrating our energies on the economic and social development of our people, we were pulled into the stream of power politics.

Pakistan was given military aid and became the eastern hinge of CENTO—Central Treaty Organization. It received nearly two billion dollars in direct military assistance, and the United States constructed a base for Pakistan's armoured division barely thirty-six miles from India's western frontier. When Nehru protested to President Eisenhower on this instigation of an armament race on the subcontinent, Eisenhower replied with his famous letter that if Pakistan were to use any of the armaments supplied under CENTO against India, he would take every step within his constitutional powers to restrain her. A side effect of arming Pakistan was three conflicts between the countries, three coups in Pakistan, and, ultimately, thirty years after it came into being, the breakup of that country by the birth of Bangladesh after a terrible war.

Another grave problem has been caused by the creation of the State of Israel in the Middle East. This has led to tensions, terrorism, and conflict, and the problem still remains unsolved. For many years Britain was the predominant power in the Middle East, an area necessary for her lines of communication to the Indian Empire. Palestine was therefore a region of strategic importance for Britain. After the Second World War, Britain, with its diminished material and manpower resources, passed on many of its responsibilities to America. It was President Truman who, in 1946, authorized the immigration of one hundred thousand Jews to Palestine from Europe. Secretary of State Dean Acheson had had grave doubts of this action at the time, and he confirms this in his book when he says that this would be the beginning of American responsibilities for the region for which the United States would have to pay a terrible price at some time.

The Jews of this region had lived in harmony with the Arabs for centuries. Both had regarded Palestine as home and uprooting from their homeland was, for the Arabs, a wrong that remains to be righted. We must remember that the sufferings the Jews have faced throughout history, and the terrible mass killings under the Nazi regime, were confined to Europe. Asia had no share in this approach or treatment of the Jews and there seems no reason that a section of Asia should have to bear the brunt of a situation not of its making. There have been Jews in India for well over a thousand years. According to Indian Jewish tradition a fairly large community of Jews has existed in Malabar, on our west coast, since the first century A.D. Historical records of Cochin reveal that in the tenth century grants of land and other privileges were given to a Joseph Rabban, who was perhaps a leader of his community in that area. Jews in India evolved into two groups—those who married with the local Indians and came to be known as the Black Jews, and those who maintained their racial purity by marrying among themselves; these were called the White Jews. At no period of our history was there persecution of Jews on racial or religious grounds, nor indeed was there antagonism toward any alien faith until political considerations promoted such disunity.

In the United Nations in 1948 India proposed a confederation of Arabs and Jews in Palestine. Dominated as the United Nations then was by America and its allies, this plan was rejected. Unfortunately the principal Arab countries, including Egypt, did not see the merits of such a confederation. They rejected the idea. This helped to bring the State of Israel, which is based on Zionism and religious considerations, into existence.

We have accepted the State of Israel. We cannot, however, accept the Zionist basis of its creation, which has clear religious connotations, nor have we been able to support Israel's attempts to acquire territories. The Palestinians have an absolute right to a state of their own, and the displaced persons to return to their homes. Our stand is also backed by the fact that there are strong economic, political, and cultural links between India and the Arab countries—links that go far back in history.

I did not meet or come to know all the Ambassadors of the United States accredited to India because I was mostly in other countries myself. The first American Ambassador to India after our Independence was Henry Grady. He came from the business world and was not a member of the Foreign Service, but perhaps for this very reason he and his lovable wife, Lucretia, were able to get acquainted with Indians in a natural and informal manner. It was good for both our countries that they were not bound by protocol or prejudice. They were elderly people, and there was a gentleness in both that one does not always associate with ambassadors. Lucretia had a most disturbing habit of referring to her friends without mentioning their names. When I was in Moscow she once introduced Tara to a guest in her home as 'the daughter of our beloved across the seas', much to the bewilderment of the person being addressed, who was left in the dark about who Tara was! Lucretia became very much a part of our family.

The two American envoys to Delhi whom I think of with special affection and who have always remained my friends were Chester Bowles and John Kenneth Galbraith—two such different men, but both left friendship for themselves and their country behind when they returned to the States. Both have visited India regularly, and their homes in the United States have offered gracious hospitality to many Indians.

Chet and Steb Bowles had made up their minds to give themselves to India, and this was done in a manner that was typical of them. From their first day in Delhi they set the pattern of their future life there. Steb and the children adopted Indian dress and ate Indian food. The girls went on their bicycles to Indian schools and visited Indians in their homes. In fact, at one moment, so great was the family's involvement with India that in the Prime Minister's House there was a feeling that at any moment the American Ambassador would come to call on the Prime Minister in a sherwani, the long coat that Indians wear with tight trousers on formal occasions! The Bowleses patronized Indian dance and music and encouraged our younger artists by inviting them to perform at their residence. This was all rather different from the usual way ambassadors functioned socially, and it surprised us in the beginning. Personally I thought the habit of serving Indian food to Indians was unnecessary. Most people who attend an embassy dinner look forward to the food of that country and prefer not to be served an Indian meal which, however good, cannot be as authentic as the food they eat in their own homes. I remember once going to dine with the Bowleses. For some reason that I cannot now remember, I had expected to have Virginia ham, which is one of my favourite American dishes. I was disappointed when 'curry and rice' was served instead. Steb and Chet are such warm people, so outgoing and genuinely eager to establish contacts and make friends, that they have become 'honourary Indians' and are greatly loved. Chet Bowles's books are testimony to his understanding of India and Asia as a whole and to his closeness to the people. He is fondly remembered.

When Ken Galbraith arrived in Delhi there were some who shook their heads. This 'professor' would not be a success. But contrary to their expectations the professor became a closer friend to the Prime Minister than anyone expected. He and his wife, Kitty, both made a big impact on diplomatic and social Delhi—Ken by his deliberate disregard of whatever he considered unnecessary and Kitty by the quiet manner in which she involved herself in many aspects of Indian life. Ken is intellectually arrogant—he has reason to be—but this in no way reduces his capacity to make friends or to do an objective job. My brother was always able to talk to him with enjoyment on matters outside his diplomatic work, and he and Kitty were welcome visitors to the Prime Minister's House.

It was during Ken's term in India that Jackie Kennedy, as she then was, visited us. The President, unfortunately, could not accompany her, and very shortly afterward he met his tragic and untimely end. I had been sent as leader of the Indian delegation to the United Nations after an absence of ten years and President Kennedy had come to address the General Assembly. Afterward he met leaders of delegations, and I had a brief but pleasant talk with him. At that time there was considerable concern all over the States about the advisability of his going to Texas. Adlai Stevenson, a good friend of mine and then the United States Permanent Representative at the U.N., had spoken to me about this, and in fact the day previous to my meeting with President Kennedy he had expressed his deep disapproval of the forthcoming visit. I mentioned to President Kennedy the general feeling of anxiety which so many people shared, and he replied, 'I *have* to go.' I could not help thinking that I had made a meaningless remark because of course he had to go. Bhai would have done the same thing in similar circumstances.

The day of the tragedy we received the news while the delegates were at lunch. By chance the U.S. delegation was entertaining and so was I. In the middle of the meal a member of our delegation came up and whispered to me the news received that the President had been assassinated. I told him it could not be correct and we must not spread rumours. In fifteen minutes the sad news was confirmed. Later, when I was going back to my hotel, the chauffeur asked what India would think of this. He was choking back his tears and was most upset. I told him that India, and indeed the world, would share America's grief. 'But Madame,' he said, 'even if some did not like him there was no need for this—we have a vote.' How often I have thought of those words. Together with our Ambassador in Washington I represented India at the funeral. It is a poignant memory.

With Mrs Roosevelt I had a close friendship because we shared a number of ideals; but because both of us were busy women it was not often that we were able to meet. I was very happy when my government sent me to participate in the celebration held in Chicago for her eightieth birthday. She richly deserved the tributes paid to her, for she was a woman who had ideas and imagination as well as the courage to implement them. She was one of the most natural women I have known. On Bhai's first visit to the United States he, together with Indira and me, paid a visit to Mrs Roosevelt in Hyde Park and laid a wreath on the late President's grave. On that occasion, during a meal, something was said about maple syrup, and Bhai told Mrs Roosevelt that he liked it. Each year after that, at Christmas, she sent him a tin of maple syrup made at Hyde Park. It was appreciated, but the amusing thing was that the duty on it was higher than the cost of the syrup. Mrs Roosevelt probably sent an extra large tin under the impression that a Prime Minister would not have to pay duty on it. She did not know—how could she?—that Nehru never accepted any privileges, however minor. As Christmas came around we used to wait eagerly for the syrup which we enjoyed, and the inevitable jokes that followed!

Some years after his first visit to the United States my brother invited Mrs Roosevelt to India, and her itinerary included a visit to Allahabad where she was to stay in Anand Bhawan and, among other things, to address the Students' Union of the Allahabad University. The union was, at this time, communist-dominated and, though the invitation for the speech had come through them, it seemed that the decision had not been taken unanimously. For some days before Mrs Roosevelt's arrival there were street-corner meetings by students, and anti-American placards. I was alarmed at this show of animosity and suggested to my brother that the Allahabad programme should be cancelled. He said it would be unwise to do so and he was sure there would not be any untoward incident.

On arrival in Allahabad, without consulting Mrs Roosevelt, I sent word to the Vice-Chancellor of the university that I would like to know what he thought of the situation. He advised cancelling the lecture, and, accordingly, I sent a letter to the president of the Students' Union saying that, as Mrs Roosevelt was India's honoured guest, I could allow her to fulfill her engagement only if I received the assurance that she would be treated with the respect due her. No reply came, and I presumed that the lecture had been cancelled. Mrs Roosevelt went her round of various places and just before the talk was due I told her that it had been cancelled. She had herself seen some of the posters in the city, and the black flags, and she told me that she could have taken care of herself.

While we were having this talk noises from the street indicated that a large crowd was approaching, and word came that a few hundred students were marching to Anand

Bhawan, shouting hostile slogans. I went and waited at the gate and in a very short time the procession arrived. I tried to talk to the leaders but was shouted down. Then I ordered the big wrought-iron gates to be closed, and, climbing up them to be seen, I again tried to speak to the students. The crowd insisted that Mrs Roosevelt should attend the meeting and refused to give any assurance of their respectful conduct. They were in a belligerent mood. Finally the Vice-Chancellor arrived and between us we promised to take Mrs Roosevelt to the university, but we appealed to the students' sense of hospitality not to hold her responsible for the policies of the United States government. In India, if a crowd is allowed to relieve its feelings by shouting it quite often calms down. The students had been shouting for well over an hour and were tired and also anxious to meet Mrs Roosevelt. She went to the Union Hall and made her speech, handling with great skill all the questions asked. All went well, but a result of the commotion was that Bhai resigned from his honourary membership in the Union.

On the personal level Washington was a happy time for me. Several members of the family were able to visit me there. Rita, who had gone to study at the University of Geneva, used to spend her holidays with me and both Lekha and Tara came to me while they were expecting their first babies. I had the happiness of becoming a grandmother and of having Arjun and Nonika under my care during their first months. Betty and Raja also came from Bombay with their teenage sons, Harsha and Ajit. Many friends from India came with visiting delegations, and of course there were visits from American friends. The Embassy was full of laughter and many delightful times. My staff were a part of the 'family', and there were numerous occasions when we would all meet to celebrate an Indian festival or some special occasion. When one of my young officers got married in Washington, I had the wedding ceremony in my home and gave away the bride.

As Ambassador to Washington I was concurrently

appointed to Mexico. We did not have an Embassy there, and I opened our first mission in the Hotel Del Prado. I found the people friendly, the food similar to our own, and the culture and architectural beauty of the country filled me with the desire to learn and understand more of its history. Apart from Mexican colleagues in the U.N. with whom I had had a good relationship, I knew the famous artist Miguel Covarrubias and his charming wife, Rosa, who had befriended my daughters when they were students in the United States. I travelled a good deal in Mexico and met many interesting people, but inevitably the work in Washington did not leave time for frequent visits. I did not know that, years later, my son-in-law would be our Ambassador in Mexico and that I would have the chance of renewing my acquaintance with that fascinating country.

◆◆◆

35

Goodwill Mission to China

On returning from my assignment in the United States, I contested the first general elections held after Independence, in 1952. India became independent in 1947, and the Constituent Assembly elected to frame the Constitution functioned as a legislative body until its deliberations were concluded. On January 26, 1950, India became a republic. Elections had to take place under the Constitution, and preparations for these were a mammoth task. Electoral rolls had to be prepared, and, since our electorate was largely illiterate, special emblems and ballot boxes had to be arranged. The total number of constituencies all over the country was 3,293, including those for the central legislatures and those for each state. In all 4,412 representatives had to be elected by the people by adult franchise, and the number of voters was approximately 176,600,000. Our first elections after Independence caused much excitement in India and much conjecture abroad.

This time my constituency was Lucknow City. Lucknow had been the centre of my work as minister of the Uttar Pradesh government, and, earlier, it had been a second home to me during my childhood, when a great deal of my time had been spent there on visits. I was looking forward to representing it in Parliament. Lucknow was not only the capital of the state of Uttar Pradesh but a city of gardens and ancient monuments, with remnants of its past glory when it had held the court of the Nawabs of Oudh. It was the heart of the Urdu-speaking world and possessed a style and elegance all its own. Unhappily this is a thing of the past now, and Lucknow has become a shabby provincial town. The election of 1952 was a walkover for Congress, which gained a large majority, and I took my place in Parliament.

In the fall of 1952 the government decided to send a goodwill delegation to the People's Republic of China, and the delegates were carefully chosen representatives of all sections of Indian life—artists, authors, politicians belonging to all parties, academicians, scientists, communists and anti-communists, women and men. There were thirty-six of us, and I was appointed to lead the delegation.

We had recognized the People's Republic of China at a time when few nations had done so. India's stand was quite clear. It was based on the recognition of the government in actual control of a vast area and millions of people. The history of China in more recent times had been one of turmoil, with interference from European nations, with civil unrest, domination by warlords, and then a long involvement in war. The start of the Japanese invasion in east Asia was ignored by the powerful states of the West, and not until Britain and the colonial powers were themselves threatened did they realize the danger that had been steadily growing since the Manchurian 'incident'. The United States was a passive spectator until Pearl Harbor. When the communist leadership took control of China, greatly helped by the corruption that had become rampant in the forces of Generalissimo Chiang Kaishek, the Nationalist Government was forced to flee to the island of Taiwan and set up a government there. China had been a founder member of the United Nations, and Chinese was one of the four official languages used in that body. The question in our minds was not of the 'admission' of China to the U.N. but the recognition of the real representatives of that country—those who governed it and not those who had had to escape from it.

China had taken a new shape, but many countries of the world had not yet recognized the new government. We in India, with more than two thousand years of contact with China, felt that it was not possible to ignore the claims of the Chinese millions or the revolutionary changes that had taken place there. We had an exchange of diplomats between our countries, and India was for some time the only country outside the communist group of nations to do so. Through our Ambassador in Peking we were in a position to inform some friendly countries, including Britain and the United States, of developments in China. Year after year India strongly advocated the admission of the People's Republic of China to the United Nations.

When the goodwill mission was announced I received a personal request from Mrs Roosevelt, and the government had a similar one from the United States State Department, asking me to try, if possible, to find out what was happening about some missionaries who had been put under arrest without a trial. There was also concern for the whereabouts of a Fulbright scholar, a girl who had been at Wellesley with Lekha and Tara.

We spent a month in China, travelled widely, and met all the leaders from Chairman Mao and Premier Chou En-lai downward. This was the period of the three antis—anti-corruption, anti-waste, and anti-bureaucracy, and there was a government drive to get rid of the three evils. Each city we visited was scrupulously clean, and the people were all busy with some kind of occupation. We were taken to factories and rural areas, and to our questions about conditions the answer invariably was that under Chairman Mao's guidance everyone was happy and contented. It struck me with force that what is called *publicity* if done by the West is *brainwashing* when done in communist countries. I certainly do not mean to imply that publicity and brainwashing are exactly similar, but the end result is the same. The modern media use sophisticated techniques that literally mesmerize the public into accepting an idea; certainly in the field of advertising this is true. In China what we saw was a crude version of the same thing. Let me give an example of what I mean. We were to visit the Yangtze river dam then being constructed. For several days before we actually went there, all officials accompanying our party spoke of nothing else. They told us what a wonderful thing Chairman Mao was doing. The river that had done so much damage through the centuries was being held back, and people would be able to carry out their agricultural pursuits without danger. We were told that the dam was being built voluntarily by the people, who had offered themselves to the beloved leader Chairman Mao, and many more such things. When we finally reached the construction site we were taken first to see a museum, to give us a better understanding of the project and what it involved. In this museum there were photographs of young girls and men, middle aged and even very old people, contributing in some way to the work of building. Little anecdotes were pasted up on the walls telling of schoolgirls who came after lessons to add a few hours of their time to the labour, simply because of their love of Chairman Mao. Heroes and Heroines of Socialist Labour were given medals and great publicity. Across the dam, which was then in its initial stages, was a huge arch with Chairman Mao's slogan: 'Let the Yangtze be stopped'.

By the time we arrived at the dam itself our expectations

were sky high, but all we saw was a small sluice gate in process of construction. It was an anticlimax. There had been reference during the days of our briefing to the number of lives lost even at that stage of building, and I could not help asking the engineer in charge how many lives had been sacrificed. He mentioned a large figure, and I must have shuddered or expressed my feelings in some way because he looked at me in surprise and said, 'But, Excellency, do you realize how many millions of lives will be saved?' Of course that was one way of looking at the question, but difficult to appreciate without misgiving unless one was educated to accept the sacrifice of the individual for the common good.

I went to a court of law where only divorce cases were dealt with, and I sat through two cases. It was a different system of legal procedure from any I had seen elsewhere. The judge, in most cases a woman, sat on a chair and the court was held in the open air under an awning. On a wood bench at one side sat a few men who, it was explained, were lawyers and could be hired by participants in the cases. In both the cases I heard, the reason given for wanting a divorce was the same—the mother-in-law. In both cases the daughters-in-law alleged that they did not get enough to eat and were beaten by their husbands, who were completely under their mothers' influence. When both sides had been heard in each case, the judge appointed a counsellor whose task was to try for one month to effect a reconciliation between the couple. If this effort failed then the question of granting divorce would arise. The judge was a bright young woman. She explained through the interpreter that I had just seen a legacy of the past. Such cases were becoming fewer and fewer and even village women were now more independent, could earn their own livings, and defy mothers-in-law.

Among those who travelled with us was the Deputy Chief of Protocol, a young man with charming manners who never seemed to get ruffled. I asked him if he was married. He said he had recently married and had a year-old baby daughter.

They did not live together as a family but hoped to be allowed to have a room of their own before long. Meanwhile, he lived in a men's dormitory, his wife in one for women, and the baby was looked after in one of the crèches.

So far we had not asked for any alteration to our itinerary, though once or twice some members of the delegation had been indisposed and unable to accompany the rest of the party. I had seen some literature about the People's University and spoken about it to those who travelled with us. It seemed this was a university meant for those who had participated in the Long March and therefore missed out on their education. The men enrolled in the university were all above thirty years of age. I wanted very much to visit it. I thought of the large numbers of young people who had given up their educational careers in order to join the freedom movement in India, and after Independence had not had the necessary qualifications to earn a decent living. How good it would be if we could start a college on this Chinese pattern. I made a request that my programme might be altered to include the People's University. I do not know exactly what I expected to see, but the university certainly did not come up to my expectations. There seemed to be nothing going on—perhaps it was a holiday. Students were out doing some sort of 'labour' for the nation. Talking to some of the professors one learned that the education was confined to the things that would produce good citizens. The curriculum did not include the humanities or the social sciences—nothing about the past. It seemed to consist more or less of a set of rules by which new China must live in order to become great.

In two schools I visited I went into the classrooms. There was always a question written either on the blackboard or on the wall, 'Why do we learn…?' I saw an English class in progress, and here the answer to the question was 'So that we may know our enemies.' The enemies, it was explained, were the Americans. I asked the teacher if this would not teach the children to hate a whole country and was told, 'That is what we want.'

The nurseries and schools for small children were very well run and the babies were tenderly looked after. The Chinese children were adorable, and we all fell in love with them. Communism lavishes care on its most precious commodity. I had seen the same concern in Moscow. Thinking back to the situation at home, where our social conscience in this respect was still dormant and the government had far too many other pressing problems to cope with, I felt envious of all that was being done for the young in China.

We had a very crowded programme of sight-seeing and banquets, and visits to different parts of the country in a special train equipped with every comfort, but, in spite of being well looked after, it was very tiring. For me, with my appreciation of Chinese food, the meals made up for much else. Most of the members of the delegation, however, were vegetarian, and no matter how much one tried to explain this fact, our hosts could not understand that vegetarians would not eat any kind of meat in any form. Their concept of a vegetarian was that, though he may not eat big pieces of meat, if it was cut up fine and mixed with vegetables it would be acceptable! Even the vegetables themselves were often cooked in pork fat. It took several days to explain what was wanted, and I am afraid the poor vegetarians had a thin time. While some of us were eating ten or more delectable courses, they had to be content with several kinds of mushrooms and boiled rice.

Each city we visited had its own fascination. We saw Mukden, Tientsin, Yenchow, Shanghai, and other places, including the Great Wall. But Peking was a dream city out of some fairy tale of long ago. One could not think of it as a real place. The lovely gates in different parts of the city, lacquered red and green and gold, looked as exquisite as they must have done centuries ago. I have always hoped to return.

All of us wanted to buy something of the old China—a piece of brocade or porcelain or jade—something we had been taught to associate with the ancient civilization of the country. But the articles available in the shops we were taken to were modern. I decided that there was nothing I would want to take home. One gift, from the artist himself to me, was a scroll—a beautiful piece of art by a painter who was then ninety-two years old. He said he was a friend of India and hoped it would hang in my home and remind me of his friendship. 'And,' he said, 'when I am dead it will fetch you a big price if you do not wish to keep it.' I told him I was happy to have such a lovely gift by a distinguished artist and that there was no question of making money out of it. I have it today in the dining room of my small home in Dehra Dun. Curiously enough, it does not remind me of the China I visited but of that ancient culture that we had learned to admire even though, like our own, it had many flaws, which people are trying to remove today.

I had been looking forward to meeting Madame Sun Yat-sen. Off and on for some years she had corresponded with Bhai, had read his books, and admired him. From what we had heard of her earlier life, and from her letters, she seemed quite a different person from her sister Madame Chiang. Madame Sun had identified herself with Chairman Mao's party. She was, at that time, one of the Vice-Chairmen of the party.

An interview was arranged for me, and I went to meet her with excited anticipation. She welcomed me warmly but, to my surprise and disappointment, spoke through an interpreter, which put many restraints on me as the talk was superficial. I could not get close to her as I had hoped, or learn something of the situation from her. However, I was able to have one more meeting with her without the official interpreter, though a young woman who knew English was present in the room. Madame Sun told me it was the rule to speak only Chinese, and she had asked for special permission for the second interview when she could speak to me in English. She was a beautiful and cultured woman. What I could not understand was why a woman so high in the party still had to get permission to speak to me without an interpreter.

We met Chairman Mao on two occasions. His poetry and the book of his 'thoughts', which became so famous, do not give a picture of the man we met. The world is familiar with his looks, but they too do not indicate the jovial side of him that he revealed to us. Ours was a goodwill mission, and the talks dealt with cultural matters mostly. China and India have had a history of friendly contact that goes back to antiquity, and until the border problems in our time cast their shadow on these relations, we had enjoyed a record of unbroken friendship through the centuries. Indians considered Sun Yat-sen a father of Asian freedom at a time when we were still struggling for our own independence. Chairman Mao was informal and cordial with us. He talked slowly and with a knowledge of India. I told him I knew Edgar Snow and Agnes Smedley, and that I had heard much about China's leaders from them and others—of the famous Long March and the difficulties endured by those who participated in it, and that the story had impressed me. He smiled and said, 'Difficulties are made to be overcome and are good for people. You had your freedom struggle, too.' I replied, 'We too paid a price.'

Among the gifts given to the delegation the most imaginative and useful was the one Chairman Mao gave me. Immediately after arrival in Peking I was asked if Mao might send me a 'personal gift'. With the person who brought the message was a tailor carrying rolls of material. The gift was to be a Foreign Office uniform. I was measured for it, and within twenty-four hours the most perfectly cut grey gabardine coat and pants as worn by Chinese Foreign Office officials was delivered to me. I bought some blouses and wore this costume all through the visit. It was comfortable and smart, and had it not been a gift from Chairman Mao I would never have dared to wear trousers on an official visit. My using the uniform pleased Chairman Mao very much, and I was glad I had decided to do so because, apart from this, it was far more practical for traveling than is a sari.

Bhai had warned me that my inquiries regarding the

missionaries must be very tactfully handled and the subject approached only if the time seemed suitable and our hosts receptive. Toward the end of our tour, which had been successful from every angle, we talked among ourselves about looking into this matter. I wanted Acharya Narendra Deo, our socialist leader, a scholar of great merit besides being a very tactful man, to handle this problem. But he felt it would be better for me to do so as I had recently been in the United States and was a personal friend of Mrs Roosevelt. Accordingly, I asked for an interview with Premier Chou. He was a polished and sophisticated man possessing great charm. Even through an interpreter one enjoyed talking with him. He spoke good French and some English but of course would use neither. I began by saying that, as a friend and admirer of China as well as an Asian, I had been disturbed by rumours that the Americans arrested by the Chinese government had not been given a fair trial. They did not know why they were under arrest and their friends and parents were very anxious about them, as the Prime Minister could imagine. Would he be good enough to explain the situation to me? Premier Chou said that the only foreigners arrested in China were those who had tried to spy and send out false messages. It was essential that they should be kept in detention. As for democratic processes, he assured me that China was mindful of this, and, if I wished, he would let me see a film showing how his government dealt with miscreants and traitors after they were given the opportunity of proving their innocence. This was not a documentary meant for foreigners, he told me, but we, the Indian delegation, were friends and could see it. We did see the film and were very disturbed by it, for concepts of democracy can be so different.

The documentary we saw depicted how 'corruption' was dealt with. It was a true story of a merchant whose shops were well known in London, Paris, New York, and San Francisco. His brocades, jades, quartz, and other articles were world-famous and he was a moneyed man. When the film opens, he had not been allowed to leave China for some years. He is asked to submit accounts for his firms abroad, but is unable to give accurate accounts as he is not allowed any contacts outside. He is questioned by what the democratic world would call third-degree methods to extract a confession. The merchant is an old gentleman, and he finally 'confesses' that he has submitted 'false accounts'. Thereupon a rope, in token of his guilt, is hung around his neck, and he is marched through the streets of his hometown, jeered at by the crowds while insulting epithets are hurled at him. By this time the old gentleman is completely broken in spirit and is hardly recognizable as the person seen at the opening of the film.

The next step shows arrangements being made for a 'trial of traitors'. It is winter in Peking—bitter cold with an icy blast blowing. People are huddled up in padded cotton uniforms with masks over their noses and mouths against the icy particles that the winds from Siberia bring. The 'trial' is to take place in the open under a very large marquee. On one side sit the judges and, on the other, lawyers from among whom the 'guilty' can choose a counsel for defence. From their nonchalant attitude as they loll on the bench, the lawyers do not inspire any confidence in either their learning or their interest in what is about to happen. Before the 'trial' telephones have been installed at set distances all over Peking, notices plastered on walls, and news has been broadcast over the radio informing all citizens of the names of those to be tried and the charges against them. Citizens are told to telephone their vote for or against the prisoners.

The trial begins in a tense atmosphere with thousands of people present. The men charged with treason come onto the dais with ropes hanging around their necks. I do not think any of the prisoners has sought legal assistance; they look thoroughly broken and dazed. Some sort of charge is made against them and one by one they are convicted. There is, of course, no appeal, and the temper of the public is frightening in its fury.

I did not quite follow the details of the next few minutes except that the men on trial were condemned and removed. Since we had been told more than once that China had no jails these wretched men were, presumably, sent to the gallows. A report of a few months ago by a well-known Canadian journalist, Ross Munroe, quotes from the *People's Daily* of Peking as follows: 'The Chinese courts are an instrument of oppression, designed to strengthen the dictatorship of the proletariat.' I suppose this means that the Chinese believe that enemies must be 'oppressed' and that to do so is just.

The conversation regarding missionaries was taken up once again, and Chou En-lai said he would see what was possible in the case. No action was forthcoming while we were in China, but our next Ambassador, Mr K.M. Panikkar, made another effort, and, later, some persons were released. The story has a sequel.

Some years later I was appointed Ambassador to the Republic of Eire concurrently with my post as High Commissioner to the Court of St James's. In Catholic countries the Papal Nuncio is usually the dean of the diplomatic corps. It was so in Ireland. He happened to die *en poste,* and for quite a long time was not replaced. When a new papal delegate arrived I was on one of my visits to Dublin and was one of the first ambassadors to call on him. As I got out of my car I was surprised to see the door of the Embassy already open and the Nuncio standing waiting for me in the hall. This was most unusual, and while we were shaking hands I thanked him for this courtesy. Retaining my hand in both of his he said, 'This is no empty gesture. You may not know it but you saved my life.'

It turned out that he was one of those released by China after our intervention. He was a man of learning with the gentleness and humility often characteristic of such people.

I visited Mao's China in the days when the slogan was 'Hindi-Chini Bhai-Bhai'—Indians and Chinese are brothers. Since then there have been several changes. Our relationship had a very special meaning for many Indians who saw in it Asian resurgence and a new dimension in an age-old friendship, in spite of the different paths taken by each country. The problems between India and China started with border disputes and Chinese encroachment into the territory of India. Endless talks and discussions in which our government displayed a naive approach did not produce a solution, and the two countries had a confrontation in the high Himalayas in 1962, when the Chinese launched an offensive. The attack was planned in advance and there should have been an adequate defence by the Indian army, which has a history of distinguished action on many fronts. That there was not is attributed largely to the Defence Minister, Krishna Menon, who played politics with army affairs and selected, as commander of the forces against the Chinese, an officer who had had no experience in command. Whatever the reasons, the fact remains that India came out of the conflict very badly, with loss of confidence as well as 'face'. For Bhai, the Chinese attack and our performance were tremendous blows—from which he never recovered. It was a shock to him to realize that his sensitive historian's approach, and his loyal support of those he considered friends and advisors in his government, had not stood the test of the stern reality of international politics.

The Sino-Indian conflict created further problems in our relations with Pakistan, and these were exploited by the United States. When Henry Kissinger came to India in 1971, supposedly for an appraisal of the situation created by the influx of ten million refugees from then East Pakistan into India, it was soon evident that the actual reason for his visit to the subcontinent was for the purpose of going via Islamabad to Peking in order to arrange Nixon's pilgrimage to Mao.

Recently an American scientific delegation visited China to offer high-level technology, principally aimed to improve China's military establishment. No doubt the purpose is to help China to become a military counterpoise to the

Soviet Union, in the hope that in such a situation the United States could have greater freedom of political and economic movement. It is obvious that every country takes measures in its national interest, yet national interest is not served in the long run by shortsighted policies. Has the United States thought of the reactions in India of the evolution of such a policy toward China? There are many similarities between this move toward China by the United States and its earlier policy of containing the Soviet Union by setting up bases in the Middle East and creating military groupings like CENTO, the Central Treaty Organization, and SEATO, the Southeast Asia Treaty Organization.

◆◆◆

36

United Nations Presidency and a Diplomatic Tour

Home again, I was kept busy with work in my constituency, Parliament, and family life. After many years I had a home in India, and Rita, who had returned from Geneva, was with me. I was pleased that she had decided to work with the Red Cross, and when I learned she was doing a really good job, I was very happy. Tara and her two babies often visited me, and Lekha and Ashok returned from a posting abroad, also with two children, and shared my house while they awaited government allotment of a flat of their own. I was happy to have the young people and the grandchildren around me. During the summer of 1953 I was able to have a holiday in Kashmir with Padmaja Naidu and some of the family. Rita had become engaged to marry Avtar Krishna Dar, a young Foreign Service officer, and we planned the wedding in early September before I left for New York and the General Assembly session.

Bhai had told me that India would seek election to the presidentship of the eighth session of the General Assembly, and, if elected, I would assume that office. Lester Pearson of Canada, Nobel Peace Prize winner for his efforts in Korea, was then President of the General Assembly, and I succeeded him. It was a memorable moment for me because I was the first woman to hold the office of President. At a press conference in the U.N. building following the election, some of the questions asked by reporters seemed almost unintelligent and it was not easy to reply politely.

'When do you think there will be another woman President?'

'Not for a decade, and she will come from Asia or Africa.' I was being prophetic but did not realize it. Thc next woman President of the General Assembly was Angie Brooks of Liberia.

'How do you feel about being President?'

'Well,' I said, 'I was only elected a few minutes ago; there has not been time to analyze my feelings.'

'How would you describe the sari you are wearing?'

'Did you ask my predecessor to describe his suit?' I was very put out that in this age of women's emancipation, and after all the years I had been in public life, such inane queries should be put to me simply because I was a woman. No man would have been asked these meaningless questions by the world press.

My election was acclaimed by the world. Warm congratulatory messages began pouring in from women's organizations, from Asian and African countries, from remote corners of the world, from men and women whose names I did not know and from friends everywhere. These messages were not for me personally, but for the Asian woman to whom this honour had been given. I would be a hypocrite if I did not admit that this made me happy. It was a great moment and a great challenge for me.

Actually the role of President was less demanding than that of leader of an important delegation, but it had its responsibilities and opportunities. I was familiar with the rules of procedure and the various regulations of U.N. work, and had many friends in the Secretariat as well as among the delegates who had been coming to succeeding sessions. As President of the General Assembly I had to preside over the Steering Committee to consider the agenda and to decide on the items to be discussed by the various committees. In 1953 the items on the provisional agenda numbered more than seventy. Some of these involved much discussion and, indeed, a basic conflict in the views of member states, and I tried whenever possible to appeal for an objective view in the debates.

Of course the President can expand his role somewhat, as in the case of Lester Pearson, who involved himself in the Korean issue behind the scenes. He was a very able man, well liked and trusted by all, and succeeded in easing many tensions, which brought him the Nobel Peace Prize the next year. Naturally such activity presupposes the existence of an issue grave enough to demand involvement. The year of my presidentship, 1953–54, was a relatively quiet year, the fury on the Korean issue having been already spent. But, as in every sphere of life, personality counts enormously, and a part of one's success, at least, depends on it.

There were matters of procedure or making a rule when I needed help, and this I always got from Dr Andrew Cordier of the U.N. Secretariat, and, of course, from the Secretary General. Dag Hammarskjold was Secretary General, and in this I was fortunate. Dag was a man of many qualities and one who believed that ethics and politics can go together. He was diplomat and philosopher combined but also exceedingly practical in his manner of getting work done efficiently. He raised the falling standards of the U.N. Secretariat in a very short time. Dag could look at every angle of a problem calmly and would take infinite pains to get his view across. The respect and friendship he enjoyed were well deserved and his untimely death was the U.N.'s biggest tragedy. I happened to be in Cairo when we received the news of the plane accident in which he lost his life, and I received instructions from my government to proceed to Stockholm for Dag's funeral. When the Dag Hammarskjold Memorial Committee was formed I was invited to serve on it and did so for three years.

One of the satisfying results of that session was that UNICEF, which had been organized in 1946 as an emergency fund, was made a permanent part of the U.N.; another accomplishment was the expansion of technical assistance for the underdeveloped areas of the world.

Each year V.I.P.s from many lands and from America itself visited the U.N., and as President I had to entertain some of them. In my year King Paul and Queen Frederika of the Hellenes, President Auriol of France, and the young Crown Prince of Japan, then in his late teens, were among the distinguished visitors. I had to give a formal dinner at the U.N. for the King and Queen. As senior Vice Chairman, Mr Vyshinksky sat at the Queen's right hand at the dinner. He always had plenty of small talk, but Queen Frederika was not at ease with him and had asked earlier if it was necessary for her to sit next to him. At some point the talk between them turned to the Russian Crown jewels, and Vyshinksky smilingly pointed to the very lovely emerald necklace and tiara the Queen was wearing and said he recognized them as Russian pieces! They probably were originally Russian, but the Queen did not appreciate Vyshinksky's remark or his insinuation.

On U.N. Day, October 24, the American Association for the U.N. arranged a celebration held on the ramp at one side of the U.N. building. It was a well organized and impressive function, and Mrs Roosevelt presented me with a gavel with an inscription engraved on a silver band. It read: 'We the people of the United Nations'. She made a gracious speech in which she said, 'The President has lighted a lamp of understanding and goodwill in our hearts.' This gavel has been for me a symbol of the highest aspirations of the U.N. It also reminds me of those far-off days when our hopes for the U.N. were combined with a determination to make them come true.

The seventh anniversary of the establishment of UNICEF fell on November 14, which was also my brother's birthday. Seven New York schools each sent seven children to present me with a huge seven-tiered birthday cake. I received them in my office, and one of the little boys made a delightful speech. We all enjoyed the cake, and then I told the children that it was also my brother's birthday and, being far from him, I was feeling rather lonely. I asked if they would like to cheer me up by giving me a kiss each. They were very willing, and I had forty-nine wet kisses all over my face! The little boy who had made the speech asked solemnly, 'Do you feel better now?'

During the session President Eisenhower also paid us a visit and addressed the General Assembly. He spoke of the gravity of the times and the necessity to explore every avenue of peace, however dimly discernible. What was interesting in his speech was his reference to the use of atomic energy for peaceful purposes, an idea that India had sponsored from the time atomic energy and its uses were first brought up in the U.N. He referred to this as no idle dream of a distant future but a reality of the present.

Among the people I worked with was Ralph Bunche, who afterward received the Nobel Peace Prize for his work in the Middle East. I had already had the pleasure of presenting him with the Spingarn Medal in the Hollywood Rose Bowl before an overflowing audience. Ralph and his wife became my friends, and he often dropped into the President's office to have an informal chat with me about U.N. affairs.

Several member states of the U.N. had invited me to visit them in my capacity as U.N. President. There was not enough time to undertake a lengthy tour, which I would have liked, because my government had decided to send me as High Commissioner to London at the end of the year, but an attempt was made to fit in as many countries as possible where, besides the goodwill visit, I might be able to do some official work as well. The first visit was to Sri Lanka. I had never been there and was charmed with the emerald island and the warmhearted people. In the week of my visit I was able to travel to most parts of the country, meeting people and addressing various organizations. Lekha and Tara accompanied me. The Prime Minister at the time was Sir John Kotalawala, an amazing man whom the cares of state did not seem to worry as he was always ready to join in any fun. He was a genial and very kind host and made our visit enjoyable. Other countries I visited were Burma, Singapore, Indonesia, Yugoslavia, the United Kingdom, and Switzerland, where I had been invited even though this country was not in the U.N.

Burma was celebrating the twenty-five-hundredth birthday of the Buddha, and a world gathering of Buddhists sponsored by the Government of Burma was held in Rangoon. I was India's representative. I had been in Rangoon once before in British days. On this visit, the beautiful capital had still not recovered from the war's ravages, and even the Shwedagon Pagoda, the temple of the Buddha, looked shabby. The scores of flower sellers at the bottom of the big flight of steps to the pagoda allowed dead flowers and rotting leaves to lie around so that this sacred place looked unkempt and sad.

The big celebration took place a day after I arrived, and, unknown to me, my coming in an official capacity had made trouble for the government and the Bhikus, the Buddhist monks. Seating arrangements were on the floor, Eastern fashion, and people were to sit in allotted places. The delegates, all men, were in one enclosure; the visitors, also men, in another; and the monks and nuns in separate areas. The problem was, where was I to be seated, since men and women were not allowed to sit together? The evening before the function, Malcolm MacDonald, then Commissioner General in Malaya, who was representing his government, called me up and explained the dilemma the organizers were in. I told him I would gladly stay away from the function and that our government's message could be read by someone else. However, it was finally Malcolm who offered a solution acceptable to everyone. As I was President of the General Assembly of the U.N. it was decided that there was no question of sex, and so it made no difference where I sat. I was placed among the men delegates and I read my government's message to the Assembly.

Indonesia was a completely new experience to me, and I made my first acquaintance with this country with which India has many cultural ties going back through past centuries. Indeed, in India there was great feeling for the Indonesian struggle for freedom, and we had followed the trials of the people with much sympathy. The British example in relinquishing power in India after the war was not followed by the Dutch or the French. Liberation from Japanese occupation meant to the Indonesians and Indo-Chinese the return of their former colonial rulers, and the popular agitations in these countries had India's full support. It was a very exciting moment when Biju Patnaik, then an adventurous young pilot, now our Minister of Steel, flew the Indonesian patriot Shahriar from under the nose of Dutch authority and brought him to Delhi for the Asian Conference in March 1947. The British, still in India, were disconcerted by this act. Bhai had convened a conference of Asian countries in Delhi. For him it was a dream come true to have such a gathering of nations whose past was intricately connected with our own—the Arab world, Iran, and Turkey in the West; Southeast Asia, China, and Korea; in the north, the Asian Soviet Republics and Afghanistan. There were also observers from Australia and New Zealand. Many of these countries had had the closest relations for centuries, contacts that had been lost after foreign rule and the growth of Western influence in Asia. The Asian Conference was a historic occasion, and we were all aware of the significance of the moment. Several of the countries that had sent delegates were not yet independent, but the European domination of Asia was on its way out and there was a feeling of exhilaration, with a new future ahead for us all in spite of the tribulations still facing many. The Asian Conference had attracted considerable attention abroad, and there were even murmurs that such a get-together would lead to a sort of anti-West movement by Asia.

In 1949, when Indonesia was still struggling against the Dutch and not receiving much help from the U.N., a conference on Indonesia was held in Delhi. Represented on this occasion were Egypt and Ethiopia and many Asian countries, some newly independent. The purpose of the conference was vital to us all—to forbid reimposition of colonial rule, and to insist that Indonesians, still fighting against Dutch 'police actions', be free. After the forming of the United States of Indonesia, President Soekarno attended the Republic Day celebration in Delhi in January 1950, and Bhai returned the visit by making an official trip to Indonesia with Indira and his two grandsons.

As President Soekarno's guest, I stayed in the Merdeca Palace, where meals were elabourate and interminable though tasty. I remember the number of little bottles around Soekarno's plate, containing pills of every colour in the rainbow. I could not understand why it was necessary to swallow so many pills after each meal! The Indonesians are a people who love music and dance, and during my stay, as we drove through one village after another, we sometimes found a group of people dancing and singing. Immediately our car was stopped and Soekarno would jump out and join in the dance. As a rule we would proceed after a few minutes, but on one occasion he could not be dragged away. He was obviously enjoying himself so much that I felt it would not be proper to insist on proceeding though we were much behind schedule. I noticed that none of the village people were awed or surprised by the President's action. He joined in as would any ordinary person. Nobody interrupted the dance—some did not even seem to take notice of their President, though I was told that everyone recognized him.

With Soekarno I visited Bali, which was an enchanting place. We had lunch one day with the well-known Belgian painter, Le Meyeur, who had come on a visit years ago but settled down and married a Balinese girl. She was a well-known danseuse in her youth and must have been exquisitely lovely then. Even in middle age she was most attractive. Le Meyeur used her as his model, and however many women there were in any of his paintings she was the model for them all. Each panel in their dining room consisted of a picture of her. The women of Bali, in the past, wore only a sarong leaving their breasts bare, and this is how Le Meyeur had painted his wife, but they now wore shapeless blouses on top. I commented on this and told Soekarno that the native custom was so much more appropriate to the climate and the beauty of the women. My comments amused him very much. On leaving Bali, Le Meyeur presented me with one of the panels I had admired in his dining room, and it hangs now in my house in Dehra Dun.

The one thing that nearly spoiled the visit for me was the quarrel between Soekarno and Fathima Padmavati, his first wife. He had already married another wife and had children by her, and during my visit the resentment of Fathima was brought to my notice. Fathima was petite, elegant, and very pretty, and had five children. When Soekarno had visited India in 1950 for our Republic Day celebrations, she had come with him and had endeared herself to everybody who met her. Unfortunately, both she and her husband tried to involve me in their quarrel, which was very embarrassing, especially as all my sympathy was with Fathima. Soekarno was a charming man, and well known for his fondness for women. As a Muslim he was legitimately entitled to four wives. Perhaps it was the way he behaved to his wives on this and later occasions that made for his domestic troubles.

I had told President Soekarno one day, partly in jest,

that my stars that year were unfavourable and my horoscope predicted some personal disaster before my next birthday. It seemed he believed in the stars and was quite alarmed. As my birthday was due in a few days and was near his own, he insisted I celebrate it in Jakarta before leaving.

I flew into Belgrade in the middle of a frightening electric storm. We learned later that President Tito had tried to divert the plane but this had not been possible, and both the young Foreign Service officer who accompanied me on the tour and I were shaken on our arrival in Yugoslavia. I had met President Tito before but looked forward to knowing him and Madame Broz better. Yugoslavia and India had a very special relationship partly because of the high regard that President Tito and my brother had for each other. Tito's leadership during the war and the great sacrifices made by the Yugoslavs in their fight against the Nazis had won the admiration of India. On my visit I found the atmosphere in Brijoni congenial to relaxation and friendship and I enjoyed myself. I also had the opportunity to visit many parts of the country including the ancient and lovely city of Dubrovnik. Parts of Yugoslavia might have been India. In Macedonia the dress was similar to that of the hill areas of Uttar Pradesh, food very like what is eaten in parts of that state, and the hand-embroidered work looked very much like our own. We had admired Tito's stand when he was trying to break away from the domination of the Soviet Union and the manner in which he had fitted the communist creed to the needs of his country. He later became a powerful member of the nonaligned group in the U.N. and a close friend of both my brother and my niece. Whenever I met Tito after that first visit he treated me like an old friend, and I was touched when, after my brother died, knowing how devoted I had been to him, he invited me to come and rest in Belgrade as his guest.

A little later he came to India at Prime Minister Indira Gandhi's invitation. He missed me at the banquet given by the President, and was told I was unwell. When he heard I was in bed with a slipped disc he immediately told the Prime Minister he suffered from this trouble himself and knew how painful it was. His specialist travelled with him, and Tito insisted that he should examine me. The first severe attack had passed and I was gradually getting better. When I heard Tito was sending his doctor I was alarmed as my own medical advisor, Dr Shankaran, was one of India's best, and I really did not want a new doctor, however good. I rang up Dr Shankaran and told him about Tito's message and begged him to be present when the other doctor came. Dr Shankaran hesitated but finally agreed to come. Next morning Tito's doctor arrived, took one look at me, asked me to get up and walk up and down the room, and said, 'There's nothing wrong with you. You walk like an athlete.' I told him I had done a lot of riding and other forms of exercise in my young days. I was then put on a table and my back pummelled until I nearly screamed in pain. Meanwhile Dr Shankaran stood absolutely dumb. When the specialist left I asked him, 'What were you supposed to be doing while I was being crippled?'

'How could I tell the distinguished doctor of a man of Tito's eminence that he was ruining all my treatment of the past weeks? I might have caused an international incident.' I was in pain and my temper was hardly under control. 'Well,' I said, 'if I am crippled for life *that* will cause a national incident.' I had to have further treatment for another fortnight!

My invitation to visit the United Kingdom had come from Prime Minister Churchill, but before I reached there he had had a stroke and was living in his country home, Chartwell. He was recovering gradually and the nature of his illness had not been made public. The name of Churchill had been heartily disliked in India. To us he was the arch-imperialist, the man who, after telling the world about an Atlantic Charter, blatantly informed Asia it did not apply to us. He was the man who predicted that if India got her independence there would be a bloodbath. He was also the man who had announced that he had 'not become His Majesty's first minister to preside over the liquidation of His Majesty's empire'! It was not surprising that we did not love him. What was surprising was that when he finally met my brother after the formation of the interim government, they liked each other and were able to talk freely. When they parted, Sir Winston paid Bhai a handsome tribute: 'I want to say that you have conquered two of man's greatest enemies—hate and fear.'

I was not expecting to meet Churchill because of his recent illness and was therefore surprised to receive a message that I was invited to Chartwell at three o'clock on a Saturday afternoon. Presently Lady Churchill called me personally and explained that the Prime Minister had wanted to invite me for the weekend but his doctors thought he still needed rest. I had already arranged to spend that weekend with my friend Evelyn Emmet in her home at Amberley Castle in Sussex. As a Conservative member of Parliament she naturally knew the Prime Minister well, and an invitation was also extended to her. On Saturday afternoon we drove to Chartwell after lunch. Lady Churchill was waiting for us and told me that Sir Winston was far from well and very difficult with his doctors. Would I cooperate and not let him talk too much and, she emphasized, he was not allowed to walk and would surely want to take me around the garden and show me his favourite carp. Could I persuade him to sit down somewhere? Perhaps if I showed no interest in fish he might not take me to the pond. I did not feel equal to the responsibility as I was meeting Sir Winston for the first time, but I promised to cooperate in every possible way. Lady Churchill was a woman of great dignity and grace. She was also very good-looking, but at that moment she was an anxious and rather harassed wife. One had heard so many stories about Sir Winston's temper that one could imagine how difficult he would be in an illness. We talked for a little while before he came in. He greeted me as if I had been a queen. His manners belonged to a world that was rapidly vanishing and I was flattered. Tea was announced by an ancient butler, and from then on poor Lady Churchill fought a losing battle. The butler gave the Prime Minister a cup of tea.

'I don't want this,' he said. 'Take it away. I'd like some brandy.' In order to distract him I said, 'You know, sir, I had news from Tokyo today that I have had a grandson—my third.' He glared at his wife and demanded, 'Then why are we not having champagne?' Poor Lady Churchill! Before I could say I did not want champagne she told him very quietly, 'I think Mrs Pandit prefers tea at this hour.' I hastily concurred, but Sir Winston was not to be diverted. 'Nonsense, of course you like champagne,' he said, turning to me. 'Everybody does.' Fortunately a message came at that moment from the nursing home where his daughter Mary was in the process of having a baby, and this took his mind off the champagne. He spoke about one or two things, and while we were still drinking our tea he said he wanted to show me his garden and his carp. I looked helplessly at Evelyn and Lady Churchill, got no assistance from either, and could think of no adequate excuse not to go. So off we went into the garden. It was obvious that walking was not easy for the Prime Minister but he was determined to go on. Presently he saw his secret service man following in the distance, and he flared into a temper that was so like my father, the similarity could not be ignored and I had difficulty in restraining a smile. It seemed Churchill had given orders that 'these damned men' should not worry him in his own home. The real reason for their presence was that there had to be someone on hand in case he stumbled or fell. By dint of all the tact I possessed I managed to lead Sir Winston to a bench overlooking the Downs. Immediately he began speaking of various places of historical interest of the distant past and also those of the last war. Quite unexpectedly he turned to me and said in an accusing voice, 'How much English history do you know?' For a second I was taken aback, but my reply was swift. 'A great deal—you never let me learn anything else.' Sir Winston was a man after my own heart. He was temperamental but his hates and his loves were clear-cut. He said what he wanted, when he wanted, but with all this he had the redeeming quality of humour. He glared at me and suddenly laughed. I joined in. 'How do you make that out?' he asked. 'Well, the British taught us out of their own textbooks and just as much as they wanted us to know. For instance, I knew at a very early age that Nelson expected every Englishman to do his duty, but it was only after I was eighteen that I learned from Gandhi what India expected of me.' Sir Winston chuckled. Putting his hand on my arm he said, 'I hope you don't hold it against us for putting you in prison.' 'Not at all,' I replied, and meant it. This led us to talk of India, and he said things I did not expect. For instance, that one of the big mistakes the British made in India was not mixing socially with Indians. He felt this had led to difficulties and resentments that need not have arisen! He also told me he did not care for women in politics. 'I have accepted you,' he said, 'but don't start trying to incite anyone here.' I pointed out that England had many women far more qualified than I to hold high positions of responsibility; how did he propose to keep them out forever? As long as he could, he answered quite seriously! Then he again remembered his carp, and we walked to the pond before returning to the house. He insisted on showing me his beautiful landscapes and paintings of Morocco, which I admired. He asked if I painted, and I had to admit that I had no talent. 'Nonsense, I had no talent but I went on,' he told me. 'I shall make a bargain with you. If you buy yourself some paints and a brush and do a picture for me I will give you one of mine.' I cannot bear to think what an opportunity I missed by being too timid to try! As I said goodbye to him in the hall he insisted on coming out to the car. 'Did anyone ever tell you what I said to your brother?' he asked. I told him I had heard, and he went on, 'I would like to say the same to you.' He remained standing until my car moved on. I have never forgotten his words or his charming gesture.

In 1954 I had been to Japan, stopping at Pearl Harbor en route. This was my first visit to Japan, and it was a private one. I had gone to visit my daughter and son-in-law, who were with our Embassy in Tokyo, and to meet my newborn grandson. But in spite of the visit's being unofficial, I had been received by the Emperor and Empress as well as by the Prime Minister. At that time the scars left by the war were seen in many forms and Japan was a sad country. For the first time since the ending of the war the Emperor was going to be seen at a garden party. It was an experience for me to be at this function. The Palace grounds in Tokyo, perfect in every detail, were like a landscape painted by a master's hand. Large numbers of guests waited in orderly rows for the Emperor's appearance, heads bowed, and when he came into the garden shouts of *banzai* filled the air. For the people of Japan this was a big moment, and it must have been one full of unhappy memories.

Everywhere there was an outward subservience to Americans—the Occupation Force was still in the country. There was also a constant reiteration of faith in 'democracy'. I was invited to speak at a women's meeting. It was a gathering of interested persons, and most of the women wore Western dress. After my talk one of the questions asked was, 'You say India is a democratic country, but why do you wear your native costume?' I found it difficult to see the connection or to explain that dress and democracy were not synonymous.

On a later visit to Japan in 1967, on the anniversary of Hiroshima, I was invited to speak on cooperation and peace at a very large meeting held under the auspices of several organizations. The occasion seemed haunted by the memory of the ghastly fate that befell the innocent of Hiroshima and Nagasaki.

◆◆◆

37

London, Eire, Spain

I had known from the beginning that London would present me with many difficulties. Our first High Commissioner there had been Krishna Menon, whose appointment was supported by the Mountbattens but had caused discontent among a part of the large Indian community. There were a number of Indian nationalists settled in Britain who had risen to eminence as doctors and barristers, and among them were some who felt they were entitled to this prize. Though things settled down on the surface after a while, the feeling of having been bypassed remained with them, and a rift was created. Krishna had made England his home since he was sent there by Mrs Annie Besant as one of her scholars, and was meant later to become a pillar of the Theosophist movement in India. This idea did not materialize for, soon after arrival in England, Krishna left the college to which he had been admitted and joined the London School of Economics, came under Harold Laski's influence, and moved away from his early political background. A barrister by profession, he did not settle down seriously to practise but was more interested in left-wing causes. He worked for India through his Indian League, which was established in the early thirties. A brilliant and versatile man, he had overpowering ambition, which he sometimes tried to hide under a cloak of pseudohumility. He was like a Victorian woman, a person of moods and periods of depression. Although I had known him well for years before Independence, and we had been fond of each other, Krishna was uneasy about my political entry into international circles. From the first U.N. delegation when we were together, he had reservations about my capacity, and on later occasions in the U.N. he did his best to exclude me, as he did others in the delegation, from what he was thinking and from the talks he was having with other delegations on important issues. He had the capacity of investing even the simplest matter with an aura of mystery. With all this was his constant reiteration about being the Prime Minister's personal representative. While I was in London there was a definite movement by Krishna and various groups close to him to discredit me. I had written something of this to Bhai and in his reply he said:

> I have known Krishna now for a long time and have a fairly good appreciation of his abilities, virtues, and failings. All these are considerable. I do not know if it is possible by straight approach to lessen these failings. I have tried to do so and I shall continue to try. This is a psychological problem of some difficulty and has to be dealt with, if at all successfully, by rather indirect methods. I propose to deal with it both directly and indirectly.
>
> I hope I have the capacity to judge people and events more or less objectively. I am not swept away by Krishna; nor would I like my affection for you to influence my judgment to any large extent, though to some extent, of course, affection does make a difference and indeed should. Krishna has often embarrassed me and put me in considerable difficulties. If I speak to him, he has an emotional breakdown. He is always on the verge of some such nervous collapse. The only thing that keeps him going is hard work. There is hardly a person of any importance against whom he has not complained to me at some time or other. Later, he has found out that his opinion was wrong and he has changed it.
>
> So far as you are concerned, you should know that apart from my deep affection for you, I have a very high opinion of your capacity and ability, to that of course we must add the great value of your personality. You have my complete confidence in this matter.

As India's first High Commissioner in London, Krishna set patterns in India House that were not always known to the government and, when known, frequently not approved by them. India House, the Chancery, provided occupation for people Krishna wished to help, and parties were mostly for 'friends of India', where tea and spicy snacks were served. This was apparently Krishna's idea of official entertainment. He had been away from home many years and spoke no Indian language. His following came from supporters of the India League.

India House was a huge establishment, and everything there was on a grand scale including a fleet of staff cars—and a custom-built Rolls-Royce for the High Commissioner that had been ordered by Krishna. But nothing had been properly maintained. A woman, I think, is quicker to notice such things than is the average man. I made it known to the staff that this would not be tolerated, and for some time we had the kind of spring cleaning that had never been done before. At the end India House had had a face-lift and looked much younger.

Our embassy residence in Kensington Palace Gardens had been purchased by Sir Girja Shankar Bajpai from a rich American divorcée. It was a beautiful house. The main salon was panelled with boiserie from one of the famous French chateaux on the Loire. It was completely French, and there was no room to place Indian *objets d'art* or pictures, nor would they have fitted in with the French decor. There was an Italian fireplace in the dining room and two authentic Adam fireplaces in the bedrooms. Krishna had not wanted to live in this house and had had a bathroom added to a small room behind his office at the Chancery. This gave people the image of austerity he wished to create about himself, and he saved money because the Embassy remained closed and unstaffed.

Following Krishna Menon, Mr B.G. Kher, Chief Minister of Bombay and a leading figure of the national movement, was sent to London. Mr Kher, though one of our finest men, was not comfortable in diplomatic life. Coming after Krishna, who was more at home in England than in his homeland, it was an uphill task for him to get on any terms with the

British, official and otherwise. Being a strict vegetarian, he would not allow meat to be cooked in the Embassy kitchen, and when he entertained, which was very seldom, Indian food came from a restaurant. When I happened to be staying with him once on my way to the United Nations, both he and Mrs Kher told me how unhappy they were in such an ornate house. The bathrooms, lined with mirrors, were a cause of special embarrassment to them. This was an illustration of a fine and respected man doing a good job as Chief Minister being appointed to a post that he found uncongenial and for which he was not suited. The only people with whom he was really at ease were the Quaker group, many of whom he had long known personally.

The embassy residence had deteriorated a great deal by the time I went to London. The chandeliers alone were, unaffected by time and neglect. Everything else required attention, especially the beautiful panelling, which was dirty, and the parquet flooring, which needed expert polishing. London demanded a high standard of entertainment, and we were not equipped for this. After some futile attempts to persuade the ministry that an Embassy of this ranking must have better carpets, crockery, silver, and other equipment, I began using my own things, which were more suitable than anything our government had provided and which gave me pleasure to use. In India this gave rise to much talk of my luxurious living and extravagance. In fact, I am told that the wife of one of my successors in London complained that there was nothing in the Embassy because Mrs Pandit had removed everything when she left! There were as many incidents of the shortsighted policy of government here as in Washington, and unhappily for me I fell between two stools. The Ministry officials were afraid to sanction anything for fear of Parliament, and members of Parliament would not support any demand because I was the Prime Minister's sister. After the initial frustrations I decided to manage on my own and not trouble Bhai, as Foreign Minister, about what were after all trivialities. In the seven and a half years I spent in London I did not use anything provided by the government except the furniture and kitchen utensils.

For an envoy to a foreign country an Embassy is not only a home but a show window of the country he represents. To me India is a land of beauty and generosity, of traditional hospitality and the acceptance of many cultures. And therefore I tried to make 9 Kensington Palace Gardens a congenial setting where people of all backgrounds could meet and know one another, exchange serious talk, or relax.

In London there were several decisions to be taken by our government regarding protocol. One concerned the Western custom for women to curtsey to royalty. Bhai decided that we would namaskar the Queen and members of the royal family, as is our custom. Later all the Asian group—Sri Lanka, Burma, Thailand, Nepal, Indonesia—followed us in this. Pakistan used the Adab.

Presentation of credentials to the Court of St James's was a traditional and formal ceremony. The Ambassador or High Commissioner went to present credentials in a coach supplied by the Palace. There were no speeches, and the Queen spent a few minutes afterward chatting with the envoy. Queen Elizabeth is a simple and charming woman who performs her duties with dignity and without ostentation. The British royal family is not informal in the sense of Dutch or Scandinavian royalty, but even the House of Windsor has gradually shed much unnecessary protocol and grown closer to the people. It is not usual, I think, for a former envoy to speak or write about the royal family, but should Queen Elizabeth ever read my words she will understand that what I have told her so often in private conversation was not just a polite and insincere piece of small talk but a very genuine expression of my affection and admiration for her. The Queen Mother, too, has been gracious to me, and I have known many other members of the royal family. Early in my career as High Commissioner I had said to the Queen that she should remember my background as a rebel, and if I ever said or did anything that offended against protocol she must forgive me. I know there must have been many such occasions, but I also know that in spite of them the Queen and the Duke of Edinburgh have become my friends and I am not only very happy but privileged at the relationship.

Sometimes I do forget the demands of protocol, as for instance when the Prince of Wales was on his way to Nepal to attend the coronation of the king as his mother's representative. I was next to him at our President's banquet and said, 'Look here, young man, when are you going to get married?' Then realizing this was not proper, I added, 'Sir, do forgive me. I'm not curious—just selfishly interested because I would like to come to your wedding!' Prince Charles has a great sense of humour and we had a good laugh, to the amazement of some of the guests at the table.

Mr Churchill was Prime Minister when I arrived in London. On my first call at Downing Street at eleven o'clock he asked me if I would like some brandy. I politely declined and he said, 'This is something I do not understand about India, and you would feel much better if you had some.' I assured him I felt very well and happy at the honour of representing India at the Court of St James's. Churchill's manner of talking was enough to frighten any newcomer. Fortunately, having met him on my official U.N. visit, I was prepared. His next question was, 'Why are you called *Madame* Pandit—it's pure affectation.' 'I agree, Mr Prime Minister,' I answered, 'but I'm not responsible. The Americans call every foreign woman "madame."' 'Well,' he said, 'you are going to be Mrs Pandit here. Do you mind?' The first courtesy call was a short one, but he insisted on telling me the history of the Cabinet room in which we were sitting and making me look at the garden, lovely after a light fall of snow the previous night.

Among the various criticisms aimed against me by some groups in India during my term of office in London, one was that I knew only the aristocracy and had no contact with the people of the country. This caused my family some amusement, as my daughters are constantly accusing me of getting involved with the entire human race and taking on the responsibilities of all and sundry.

The British are supposed to be reserved and unemotional. I have found this to be one of those myths that somehow grow up about people and nations. I had had British friends before I went as High Commissioner, but soon I was on friendly terms with a great many people including the humble men and women with whom I dealt from day to day. I liked, whenever possible, to do my own shopping, and in this way to be able to talk to people an ambassador does not usually have an opportunity of meeting. At the corner of Kensington Street was a deaf old lady who sold flowers and whom I came to know well. She was so distressed when I was leaving after nearly eight years that I was touched to find that I had meant something to her. For larger receptions at the Embassy I sometimes went very early in the morning to Covent Garden to buy flowers, which I love, and soon I was known in the market. There was always a smile to welcome me, even from those whose stalls I did not visit. Once I wanted rather a lot of flowers that were expensive. I asked my vendor if I could not have a special rate. 'All right, laidy, all right.' Then turning to another customer he said, 'Look at 'er, the 'Igh Commissioner of India. She's me friend but always tries to beat me down. Comes 'ere in the morning and dines with Eden at night.' I did dine with Eden several times when he was Prime Minister, but I vividly remember an occasion when he came to dine with me. My cook chose that day to get drunk, and while the guests were waiting for dinner I was called to the kitchen by my frantic butler. Budhilal, in a high state of inebriation, was in the kitchen refusing to cook for a Prime Minister who had put Bibiji in jail! It took all my diplomatic experience to get through that evening.

Since I do not make friends according to their official labels, I knew and was fond of many men and women from all political parties, and with most of them I have kept in touch. Nye Bevan and Jennie Lee were friends from earlier days. It was a grief to all of us when Nye died. While he was very ill and Jennie was gallantly keeping the truth from him, Bhai and I visited them on their farm and spent the afternoon there. My last memory of him is his laughter as he cracked a joke with us. But apart from the political figures I was privileged to know, there were authors, artists, ballerinas, actors, and musicians who became my friends and whom my Embassy was proud to welcome. My home was open then as now to students and young people, whom I have always enjoyed meeting and from whom I have received more than my share of affection.

We had, represented in India House, departments of the various ministries of the Government of India. This was a legacy of British days. India House was heavily overstaffed—a legacy from Krishna Menon's days—and there were questions in Parliament over items of expenditure and staff. Apart from these, two problems were students and immigrant labour.

The Indian student community was a large one, and more admissions to universities were required every year. Most of the students were fully qualified, but in the case of several, their knowledge of English was not up to the standard set by earlier students. Once while visiting Cambridge Lord Adrian, then Master of Trinity, told me how distressed he was to see that the students then coming to the United Kingdom were below the standards of a generation ago. This distressed me also because I knew our boys and girls were not less able, but the educational system at home kept undergoing changes through the whims of government and became a hurdle to better accomplishment by our students. This point was not really understood in India, and members of Parliament asked questions about why more students could not gain admission to British universities.

During my term as High Commissioner I was honoured with honourary degrees by the Universities of London,

Edinburgh, Cardiff, Nottingham, and Loughborough.[17] Before I went to Cardiff Nye Bevan coached me in a couple of sentences in Welsh. I felt it was the right thing to do and many people appreciated my attempt.

Indian immigration was the other problem. As I have said earlier, there were in England Indians who had reached the top of their various professions, were highly respected, and happily settled down. This was before the scientific and technological brain drain from India began, and it was mostly medical men and some lawyers who came to England for their studies. Several of them married English women. These men were integrated into British society and became contributing members of the British economy. The problem began with what was known as unskilled labour—men who came from India and Pakistan after partition to seek economic opportunities and take factory jobs in the Midlands. Obviously they were confronted with a very different culture and standards of living and all the difficulties that arose out of this encounter. Their families grew as they sent for wives or relatives to join them. In order to save they economized to the greatest possible degree, sometimes several people sharing a room and cooking on a tiny gas ring, in a near-slum area that soon became worse. None spoke English to begin with, and they were slow to learn and therefore to integrate themselves with those among whom they now lived. We kept getting complaints from the areas where Indians were settled in large numbers, and I referred this matter to Delhi many times, fearing that deterioration of the situation would lead to some unpleasant incident.

I visited some of these areas and on two occasions I went to Liverpool and Manchester at the invitation of the mayors of those cities, who belonged to the Labour party and had been associated with the India League for a long time. I saw

17. Oxford University had also wanted to confer a degree, but it had to wait for some reason. It was conferred in 1964.

a number of dwellings occupied by Indian immigrants and was distressed beyond words—and also fearful of future consequences. The Indians and Pakistanis were happy to see me as they were very lonely, and my coming brought memories of home. I spoke to them about the necessity of learning the language, the need for cleanliness, and the attempt they must make to fit into foreign ways. But their efforts in this direction were slow even after the mayors had started special night classes to help them. The women took longer to adjust because their idea was to save enough money as quickly as possible to get back to their little farms at home, a natural enough urge, but their unfamiliarity with British ways led to many difficulties for India House and were the early beginning of the ugly situation that later led to discrimination and race riots. Today there are areas in London and its suburbs that are little Indias, Pakistans, and Bangladeshes, but there will have to be arduous and sustained efforts on both sides before these groups and the British can establish a mutually worthwhile relationship. The Asians who have decided to make England their home must become part of a new culture, combining their own with that of their adopted country, and the British must accept the fact that the Asian will seek wider fields away from home to earn a living. The Indian subcontinent has provided the basis of British prosperity and world domination for generations in the past. Perhaps it is time for the balance to be redressed and for the Asian to look farther afield to better his lot.

In the fall of 1956 I had permission from my government to go home on leave. It had been some time since I had had a holiday, and I was looking forward to being with the family for Diwali. During the summer I had acquired two new granddaughters, and Lekha and Tara were taking the babies and their older children to the family home in Anand Bhawan. Rita was coming from Tokyo with her son, who had been born there and spoke only Japanese, and the whole family was going to be reunited after several years. No sooner had I arrived in Allahabad, however, than I was summoned to Delhi and left by special plane. From Delhi I flew back to London. Suez had been attacked.

The Second World War had produced certain irreversible trends, chief among these being decolonization of parts of Asia. This was hardly a result of the generosity of the former great colonial countries but was forced on them by changed circumstances. Britain, by the sheer expenditure of human and material resources during the war, had been weakened, and France had suffered ignominious defeat at the hands of the Nazi war machine. The other significant change following the war was the emergence of two superpowers vastly superior in strength to any combination of powers in Europe. Despite these realities, old imperial habits die hard. Britain had depended greatly on India; during the heyday of the empire the backbone of the British presence in the Middle East and the Far East had been the Indian army, and Britain continued to have visions of a military role in these regions. France, in a much worse state, both physical and moral, than the United Kingdom, was determined to restore by every means at its disposal its former imperial authority.

The start of the Suez crisis may be dated to President Nasser's need for assistance to build the Aswan Dam. He had asked for aid and expected to be financed by the United States, Britain, and the World Bank. Nasser was at this time at the peak of his popularity, with his dream of Arab unity and his great desire to see the Arab world restored to some of its former glory. To the Western world, however, and especially to Britain and France, he was a dictator with ambitions toward greater territory and increasing influence in the Middle East. His acceptance of arms from Czechoslovakia and other east European countries had upset Dulles. The cold war was at its coldest, and as a sign of their displeasure the Americans withdrew their offer to build the Aswan Dam. The day after this happened, on July 26, Nasser made a speech in Alexandria saying that he was accepting aid from the Soviet

Union and threw a bombshell by announcing that he was nationalizing the Suez Canal. There was consternation in the Western world and especially in Britain and France. The latter was then engaged in war against Algerian and Indo-Chinese nationalism. Neither country seemed to have come to terms with the changed situation in the world, the rise of sentiment against colonial behaviour, or their diminishing positions as great European powers. It was evident that they viewed the Suez Canal as their rightful roadway and considered that they owned it. Equally they viewed that the Middle East, with its oil, was in their sphere of interest and influence as it had been in the past.

At this period our Ambassador in Cairo was a very able man, Nawab Ali Yavar Jung, who had been my colleague in the U.N. and who later went on to hold various posts of importance in India and abroad. As a result of the close relationship between Nehru and Nasser, there was constant dialogue between our Ambassador in Cairo and Nasser. Long before Independence was in sight, the Indian people had demonstrated their kinship with the Islamic world by supporting the Khilafat Movement in Turkey and the independence of the Egyptian monarchy from the British protectorate. There was now the intimate link between Nehru and Nasser. Both men sought, though by different means, to help other emerging countries to break away politically and economically from the domination of the European powers.

During the months preceding the Suez crisis Nasser was available at all times to the Indian Ambassador, who kept his Prime Minister informed and in touch with Nasser's thinking. The fiery speeches made by Nasser at this time were aimed at the Arab world as much as toward his own people, and on Nehru's advice he modified many of his statements.

Dulles had been aware of the Anglo-French belligerent aims toward Egypt and seemed to concur in wishing the end of Nasser—though not to the point of war. President Eisenhower, however, did not want any conflict on the eve of American elections. A conference was proposed for the principal maritime users of the Suez Canal and it was held in London in August of that year. Thereafter the Australian Prime Minister, Mr Robert Menzies, was asked to head a committee to speak with Nasser and suggest alternative plans for the working of the canal. These talks ended in failure. The concept of the Users Club to run the Suez Canal was attributed to Dulles, and great pressure was brought on Nehru for India to join it and to use his influence on Nasser. The idea was that an international authority of maritime powers should run the canal and pay Nasser a percentage of the fees collected. After nationalization, Britain and France had recalled their pilots from Port Said, expecting that without trained personnel the canal would cease to function and Nasser would have to depend on European know-how. This attitude was one that Indians knew of old. One of the arguments used against independence for India was that the country would disintegrate without the benevolent guidance of the British. In actual fact the head of the Suez Canal Authority had been training Egyptian pilots, and India sent pilots from the Calcutta port to help Egypt at this time. We refused to join the Users Club. We were a powerful force among nonaligned nations—most of Africa was still under the rule of colonial powers—and Nehru's voice in favour of Asians and Africans was a strong one.

We now know that Britain was determined to force the issue from the time the nationalization of the canal was announced and also that secret meetings were held by Britain, France, and Israel. At one such meeting at Sevres David Ben-Gurion, Guy Mollet, and Selwyn Lloyd came to an agreement to stop Nasser's 'expansionist ideas' and bring about his downfall. The Israelis did in fact attack the Sinai Peninsula on October 28 and carried on to Suez. The forces of Britain and France attacked on October 31, following a plan prepared well in advance. Port Said and Port Fuad were occupied and, according to information India received at that time, conditions were very bad, and we learned of heavy casualties among the Egyptian people.

It was interesting for me as High Commissioner in London to note that the British government had been in consultation with some of the Commonwealth countries before the Suez crisis broke out in the press, but that they had not informed the Asians in the Commonwealth of their intentions. The trend was obvious to us, and it was felt that Britain had not come to terms with her present position. India was then a member of the Security Council and strongly condemned the action.

When the trouble in Hungary began, India condemned Soviet action. At the same time, within days, the extraordinary Suez adventure had begun and Soviet troops, which had previously withdrawn from Budapest, returned to it. The grim situation that developed there engaged the attention of the world for a long time. In the conflict that took place between the Hungarian people and the Soviet army the Hungarians suffered terrible losses. Nobody could deny, and India certainly did not, that the people of Hungary wanted to be free of Soviet control. Bhai made a powerful speech in Parliament on the tragic events, giving the historical background of the past struggles for freedom of the Hungarians since the time of the Austro-Hungarian Empire. The present popular uprising was largely one of passive resistance to superior force, something Indians could well understand. The show of military strength in Hungary was a case of what could happen elsewhere in the world if military might was used against weak countries. This especially had an impact on government thinking in India and possibly other countries of Asia. But at that time we were also witnessing a show of combined military strength against Egypt. Whatever Britain and France may have thought of Nasser, he was the acknowledged leader of his people as well as of a large section of the Arab world. In Egypt the loss of life was considerable. As a result of the combined assault by Israel, Britain, and France, the casualties were estimated in the neighbourhood of seven or eight thousand for Egyptians as against the loss of a handful of the invaders. But financial and economic losses had also to be reckoned, and these continued over a period of years to be extremely grave and damaging to the economies of the countries concerned. India felt that the Suez crisis, which was intended to destroy Nasser and to keep Russia out of the Middle East, helped the Soviet Union to enter this area. Therefore, in the end, Western interests suffered more than those of Egypt.

In Hungary the Soviet army triumphed, but there is room for conjecture as to whether the Russians would have made the second assault on Hungary had Suez not flared up with the invasion and bombing of the canal area by the British and the French. Events in Hungary affected the prestige of Russia in many countries, especially those of the nonaligned world just as the Berlin airlift had influenced those who were in doubt of the real strength of the United States. Sending a thousand planes daily to feed and maintain Berlin was a great factor in establishing the powerful status of the United States in the eyes not only of Asia but also of the Soviet Union.

In our part of the world there was also the very real fear of possible atomic war if the balance of power was disturbed. Had the Soviet Union come to the aid of Egypt, or the Americans gone to help the Hungarians, this possibility could have become a reality and led to the Third World War, with unimaginable consequences for humanity. India, however, came to Nasser's defence in the case of Suez, sending our pilots, medical supplies, and, at a later stage, our forces, with the consent of the Egyptian government, to join the U.N. force in Suez. We were against Soviet action in Hungary in the Security Council though we did not approve of the language of the West. The Western world, which so wholeheartedly condemned Soviet action in Hungary, was not nearly so outspoken over British and French intervention in Suez.

Anthony Eden had been a seriously ill man for some time, and the strain imposed on him by the long-drawn-out

Suez crisis prevented his looking at things calmly. He was very nervous, and toward the end of his term retained no resemblance to the dashing young man of the forties who had resigned his post because of his convictions. Clarissa, Lady Eden, was an equally high-strung person. The whole Suez affair was hard on her, and she was almost as ill as her husband. Once, in a moment of exasperation, she told a friend that she felt the Suez Canal was flowing through her drawing room. Next day the remark was in the press and became the most quoted comment on the crisis at that time. Life is difficult for people in high places during abnormal times.

With the coming of Harold Macmillan to the prime ministership, No. 10 Downing Street was a different place. Both he and Lady Dorothy were calm, relaxed people. There seemed to be no sense of hurry or urgency about either. When I first met Harold Macmillan he seemed like a character out of Dickens or his favourite, Trollope, and he looked and acted older than he was. I liked his wit and dry humour—one could discuss political issues with him with far greater ease than with his predecessor, and he gave the impression that he had all the time in the world to listen. This attitude in a person who occupies a high and responsible position is conducive to an easy exchange of views, and after the hurried talks with Eden it was a great relief. Lady Dorothy was simple and charming. She was a daughter of the late Duke of Devonshire, and I thought her the nicest and most natural of the three sisters. I had commented once at a dinner party that the Prime Minister had scarcely eaten anything at several dinner parties, and she said laughingly, 'He doesn't like to make a fuss, but I usually make him some scrambled eggs when we get home!'

When the Prime Minister and Lady Dorothy visited India, I was unable to accompany them because I was ill. The visit was successful from all points of view and they enjoyed it.

The official world in the United Kingdom had been hoping that the Queen would visit India, and I knew she would be happy to accept if invited to do so, but, as there was some criticism in Parliament, Bhai felt it would offend against her dignity if there was even one dissenting voice against the visit. So we waited, and eventually, in 1959, the visit was arranged and proved a great success. The Indian people are contradictory in many ways, but they are not haters by nature. There was tremendous excitement when the Queen's visit was announced, and I was told of an old villager, whose memory was failing, inquiring when Queen Victoria was to pay us a visit!

All the plans went well—people loved the informality with which the visit had been planned, the simplicity of the Queen, and her warm manner toward all. Some of the elite were disappointed as they had expected her to wear fabulous jewels and a crown, which would havc given them an opportunity to bring out their own jewels and finery. I accompanied the Queen and the Duke in their aircraft and was with them throughout their Indian trip. In this way I came to know them both much better. Sometimes a part of the programme, carefully planned, would go wrong and, though somewhat embarrassing, would add humour to a formal occasion. One such incident took place in one of the former princely states. The Maharaja and Maharani were on the point of separation and the Maharani wanted the Queen to intervene in the marital dispute. She insisted on speaking to the Queen personally and, as the Queen was her guest, one could not keep her away. But chance intervened. There was a banquet at the palace that night and the Maharaja had sent for a retired controller of the household to come and supervise the party. This good man had been used, in the past, to arrange elabourate banquets for Viceroys, and the dinner menu was long and elabourate. The Queen had had a tiring day and was supposed to meet the Maharani after dinner. I suggested to the Maharaja that dinner might be advanced so she could retire early. He was very distressed and said he had arranged a surprise. The surprise came with the dessert in the shape of an ancient piper in full Highland regalia, somewhat motheaten, who went round and round the table playing his bagpipe offkey and taking great pride in his performance! I could not see the Queen's face as I was on the same side of the table as she was, but I could not help catching the Duke's eye. I thought that at any moment he would burst out laughing and I had the utmost difficulty in restraining myself. The piper would not stop, and with each round his tune was more off-key than the last. When he finally stopped the Queen and Duke thanked him as calmly and graciously as if he had given a wonderful performance. I was full of admiration for the strict training royalty receives to be able to act like this. The piper's day was made. He had been dragged out of retirement to remind the malika of the traditional observances of her own country! The result of the bagpipes was that there was no time for marital problems to be discussed between the Maharani and the Queen.

One of the advantages of the positions I have held has been that I have met unusual and interesting people. On the official plane relationships have remained formal, but of those I met informally many became my good friends and remain so. I recall my meeting with Viscount Montgomery of Alamein. He wanted to go to China but had no entrée as this was a period of near hostility between the People's Republic of China and Britain. He wrote to my brother asking for an introduction to Chairman Mao and inquiring if India would assist in arranging his visit. My brother instructed me to help Lord Montgomery, or Monty, as he was known. I had never met him and did not know anything about him apart from what was generally known from his days as an Allied commander. I asked Dickie Mountbatten for advice and inquired if it would be better for me to call on Monty or to invite him to a quiet lunch alone at my residence. Dickie advised asking him to lunch and warned me that he was very simple in his habits, to the point of austerity, that he ate lightly, and did not smoke or drink. Monty accepted my invitation, and I waited for him with some anxiety. The only other person present was my Deputy High Commissioner. While we had our fruit juice I found it difficult to start a conversation, but gradually the ice melted and by the time we sat down to lunch the situation had eased. I had ordered sole Florentine with salad and fresh fruit to follow and was relieved to see that my guest enjoyed the meal though he ate sparingly. He looked forward with great expectation to his visit to China, and we were able to help him in various ways including planning his itinerary. Fortunately, he had a very successful visit, met all the Chinese leaders, and came back full of enthusiasm for everything he had seen.

A short time after his return Monty and I were fellow guests at a City banquet, and both had to respond to the toasts that were made. 'City' means the City of London, and the banquets, given by different guilds, are annual functions. Monty spoke at great length of his experiences in China. He had found everything right and had no criticism to offer. In winding up his speech he said that people should not be afraid of revolutions. All revolutions were not bad, and by way of example he mentioned France, America, and China. He had exceeded his time, and when he sat down I had hardly five minutes in which to speak. After the initial remarks usual at such occasions, I said I was glad to know that the Field Marshal had approved of revolution—so did I. However, I was surprised that he had made no mention of the recent unique revolution in India by which the British had been made to leave. Also, I pointed to the example set by our revolution by which, after destroying an imperial system that had done great harm to humanity over a large part of the world, we retained friendship with those who had imposed it on us and were now happy to cooperate with them. I received thunderous applause!

I am old-fashioned enough to love tradition, and one reason I enjoyed England was that tradition was kept up in many ways, especially in famous homes. Among the most beautiful, and certainly the most charming, of them was 'Broadlands', the home of the Mountbattens. Many members of our family have spent happy weekends there through the years, although without Edwina it is not the same as it was.

The stately homes of England are famous, and I was lucky to be invited to several of them. Though the houses themselves were grand, it was the gardens—acres and acres of them—that I envied. The magnificent lawns looking smooth as billiard tables, the wonderful seasonal flowers, the great spreading trees giving dignity to the grounds—how I loved these things. Sometimes when Bhai and I were visiting together he would comment to me in Hindi that the British seemed to have an infinite number of ancestors—he never could get used to the large numbers of family portraits in every 'great' home. As a matter of fact, this also used to strike me as rather remarkable, and yet it was interesting to see the same features repeated century after century in the portraits done by well-known painters of the times. Once, staying with the Earl and Countess of Elgin in their beautiful Scottish home, I saw the face of an ancestress repeated through different generations, and to my surprise the present daughter of the house might well have posed for one of the early portraits we were shown. The Elgins were a family who had given two viceroys to India in 1862 and in 1894. They were said to be descended from the Bruce who used to be so well known in remote parts of the empire through the story told to the children of Bruce and the spider.

I came to know the late Duke of Wellington, Gerry to his friends, in a strange way. He came to see me one day because he wanted to get back a statue and a portrait of his ancestor that were in the Poona University. Two of the Duke of Wellington's ancestors had been deeply involved in Indian affairs. In 1798 Lord Mornington, who later became Marquis of Wellesley, had been appointed Governor General of Fort William in Bengal by the East India Company. He was an empire builder and with his brother Arthur, who later became

Duke of Wellington, he waged war in Mysore in the south of India and defeated Tipu Sultan, ruler of Mysore and a valiant fighter against the British.

This was a time in India, during the nineteen fifties, when members of the Indian Parliament were demanding the removal of the statues and pictures of Queen Victoria and subsequent kings and former viceroys, of which there were a great many all over the country. There was considerable heat on the subject. I knew that Bhai would have no objection to returning the two items asked for by the Duke of Wellington, but when approached he said that this could not be done immediately. The cost of transport would be heavy and Parliament was in no mood at present to sanction it. My own view of the removal of statues and pictures of former British rulers was quite different from the one popularly held in India. I wanted these to remain in the country because they were part of an important though unhappy period of our history, as important as the struggle through which we had achieved independence. They were different sides of the same coin. I felt then, and I still believe, that the children of India should know this period and understand that it came about largely through our own mistakes, our disunity, and our folly, and they should avoid the mistakes made by former generations. I do not approve of the habit of hiding one's head in the sand, ostrich fashion, and refusing to face up to what is unpleasant. Meanwhile, the Duke saw me several times on the matter of the return of the items he wanted and took me to see his home in London, which is now a museum. There were some very fine historic pieces shown to me, and in the end I arranged to exchange several things of value, one of them being the formal court dress worn by Tipu Sultan. Once this exchange was agreed upon by our government the formalities were completed in a short time and the Duke's ancestors returned to him.

Among my close and valued friends was Stella, Dowager Countess of Reading. During the period to which I refer, she spoke to me about getting back the statue of her late husband, the Earl of Reading, which stood in the courtyard of the Viceroy's House, now the President's House, in New Delhi. It was a matter of satisfaction to be instrumental in getting this done, and the last letter I received from Stella before she died was to tell me that the statue had been installed in Reading and she was happy to see it there.

The Secretary for Commonwealth Relations when I first went to the United Kingdom as High Commissioner in 1954 was Lord Home, now Sir Alec Douglas Home. With him and his wife, Elizabeth, I never felt an official barrier, for from the beginning they were people I liked and who I felt liked me. But I remember being surprised on the occasions I had to meet him as Commonwealth Secretary to see that his knowledge of India was more limited than it should have been. However, by then, I was accustomed to people not knowing much about my country, and I used to begin every official talk with a brief background about India. This was a time when the Western world was greatly preoccupied by the status of Kashmir, and even though Britain understood our position well enough, there was a deliberate denial of facts and a colonial habit of looking at the issue as a Hindu–Muslim question, which it was not. It was a straight political issue, yet in the traditional imperial manner every sort of red herring was dragged across the path of understanding in an attempt to make it seem a religious problem.

Alec possesses a dry sense of humour that is delightful—if one is not at the receiving end! When he announced that he would relinquish his title of earl in order to retain his seat in the House of Commons, a necessary prerequisite for anyone with political ambitions of being Prime Minister, Harold Wilson made a satirical comment referring to the 'Fourteenth Earl'. Alec's quick reply was that he thought somewhere in Harold Wilson's family tree there must have been a fourteenth Mr Wilson also! All unwittingly Alec nearly got me into trouble with my government by tempting me to bet at the Ascot races. I have loved horses and horse racing from the days of my youth. On one of the few occasions I allowed myself to be tempted was when, looking at the race card at Ascot, the name 'Pandit' met my eye. The horse was a rank outsider and the betting was nine to one, but because of the name I could not resist placing a small bet on him. To the delight of my friends he romped home! Months later an eminent Indian visitor to London said he had heard a rumour in Delhi that I had won nine thousand pounds at Ascot. I told him that I might have been able to do so if my government had not put so many bans on their envoys!

Perhaps of all the people I knew in London during my diplomatic career, my closest friend, not counting the Mountbattens, was Sir Walter Monckton (Lord Monckton). He and his wife were people with whom I had an affinity and of whom I was very fond. I spent many quiet evenings with them in their flat in the Temple talking about matters of mutual interest. He was a great lawyer and involved in many activities and, being a versatile man, his interests extended far beyond his profession. He was also a delightful talker with a restrained manner and a dry wit, which I enjoyed.

Margot Fonteyn became a close friend of mine, and when she married the Panamanian Ambassador, Senor Roberto Arias, he too joined the family circle. Tito, as he was called, was a most hospitable man, but after his marriage to Margot they were obliged to change the pattern of their entertaining to fit in with Margot's profession. They started to invite their friends to the ballet and then supper at home. It was always a lovely experience to see Margot dance, and the suppers afterward were very different from the usual diplomatic parties.

One evening after such a party I told Tito I had enjoyed myself even more than usual because the giant prawns served were my favourite dish. A few days later, as I was returning home from India House, the smell of fish was very noticeable and kept growing as we got to Kensington Palace Gardens.

My car turned into the gate and I saw a small van surrounded by my domestic staff. It appeared that Tito had sent me a present of prawns from Panama! My cook wanted to know how and where they were to be stored, since the amount was enormous, much too large for the facilities of the Embassy kitchen!

A charming memory of Margot always lingers with me. The Russian Bolshoi ballet with (Galina) Ulanova as prima ballerina was visiting London for the first time and the excitement and demand for tickets were quite phenomenal. The performances were breathtakingly beautiful, and Ulanova was the heroine of the hour. On the night of the last Bolshoi performance Margot, who had been as enthusiastic as anyone, gave a party in honour of Ulanova after the show. I was among those invited, and I happened to be in the little front courtyard through which one entered the house when Ulanova arrived. Margot, who was herself at the height of her fame at the time, received Ulanova with a deep curtsey. It was a graceful gesture of homage from one great artist to another.

Yehudi Menuhin and Diana, through the years that we have known them, have become members of the family. Bhai was very fond of them, and they were always guests in his home when they came to Delhi. Yehudi is much admired and loved in India, and received the Nehru Award a few years ago from the Nehru Foundation Committee for better understanding between nations. Among other personalities who have received this award have been Martin Luther King, Jr., posthumously, and Mother Teresa. In London there were so many men and women whose love and friendship have been meaningful that one cannot mention them all, but a beloved figure was Dame Sibyl Thorndike. She was devoted to India and Gandhi and, being herself a passive resister, she had faith in nonviolence. Whenever he was in London and she was acting, Bhai always found time to see the play.

While High Commissioner in London, I was accredited simultaneously to the Republic of Eire and later, also, to Spain.

With Ireland there was, as I have mentioned earlier, an emotional bond going back to 1916 and the Ulster uprising. This is strange because the Irish are by no means a nonviolent people, and their freedom struggle was as violent as it possibly could be. Yet in other ways their temperament and character are similar to ours, and it has been easy to make good and lasting friendships based on mutual understanding and admiration. At that time we had no Embassy of Ireland in New Delhi and the Irish Foreign Office felt a little guilty about this. They were a small nation and their first exchanges they felt must be with Roman Catholic nations. I found familiar faces in the Foreign Office, and a former Foreign Minister, Mr Seán Ó Ceallaigh, who had been with the U.N. for several years, was a friend and colleague.

When I presented my credentials to the President in Dublin it was Holy Week. The custom was for the President to give a luncheon immediately after the ceremony for the new Ambassador. Because of Holy Week meat could not be served, and we had a five-course fish luncheon beginning with caviar. Though every course was delicious I felt rather like a fish myself by the time the lunch was over! President Sean O'Ceallaigh, which is pronounced O'Kelly, had been a freedom fighter and had seen the inside of prison for a long period. He was a fine man, full of interesting talk and anecdotes, and a completely informal person. Throughout lunch, instead of the stiff conversation usual to an official occasion, everybody at the table exchanged stories of jail life, and before I left the President's Palace, I was accepted as a comrade. I think the Irish liked me as much as I liked them. I particularly enjoyed my visits to the Abbey Theatre and made friends with the artists. In my morning walks in Dublin it was quite usual to be stopped and greeted by men and women I did not know and asked about India's freedom struggle and Gandhiji. When I spoke about any incident of their own struggle, their faces would light up with delight that a foreigner was interested enough to have read their history and literature. I travelled a good deal and saw much of Ireland as there was little diplomatic work between our two countries at the time. In Cork especially I was greeted with great enthusiasm because my Embassy had, in their publicity, mentioned the fact that as a young girl I had won a gold medal for a national competition on 'The Meaning of Terence MacSwiney's Death'. MacSwiney had been Lord Mayor of Cork and had fasted in protest when he was jailed. In spite of appeals to the British government from people in all countries he was not released and he died in prison. For anyone in violent Ireland to practise satyagraha had made a great emotional appeal to India. This was in 1917, but when I visited Cork the memory of the sad incident was fresh in people's minds. When Mr de Valera became President I remained on the same good terms with him that I had enjoyed with his predecessor. I could not help admiring him because, in spite of rapidly failing eyesight, he was seriously studying Sanskrit and his hobby was mathematics. He never gave in to physical pain. When Bhai visited Ireland he said one day to the President, 'Why is it that the Irish, who seem so disinclined to work and so much addicted to fighting among themselves at home, become so successful when they go to America?' Mr de Valera replied, 'For exactly the same reason as your own countrymen, Mr Prime Minister!'

Spain was a strange assignment for me because we had not had ties of any sort with that country. During the Spanish Civil War India's sympathy had been with the Republicans, and in 1938 Bhai had paid a brief visit to the war front and the Congress had sent a token gift of wheat. Emotionally we had been deeply involved. The manner in which the Western democracies had behaved in supporting Franco while Hitler and Mussolini were building up their respective dictatorships had angered nationalist India, but now it was thought an exchange of envoys would be the proper thing. We had to build up a relationship between our countries, and that takes time. Meanwhile, I had to get to know the country and the people and have some contacts with the government.

Presentation of credentials in Spain was a very formal ceremony. A new envoy was driven in the glass coach of Queen Isabella I. It was a little jewel, but there was hardly room for me and the Chief of Protocol, a portly gentleman in full regalia, including a sword. We were squeezed in like a pair of sardines, and I was glad to be able to get out and breathe when we arrived at Franco's palace. This was imposing, and the guards in magnificent uniforms lining the steps were spectacular. Credentials were presented in a large ornate hall. Franco was in a military uniform and there were no speeches, but in the usual way we talked for a few minutes afterward. Franco had not been a leader we admired, but in the short time we talked he was absolutely straightforward with me and said that since there was no bond between our countries owing to our having been on different sides during the war years, we did not, perhaps, understand him or what his dreams were. He hoped we could come closer to the Spanish people, and he was glad to extend the hand of friendship to me.

I was able to travel and enjoy the beauty of Spain. I spent many hours in the Prado and I met a variety of people. The nature of my work in London was such that my visits to Madrid were short and infrequent, but a base for future political and trade relations was formed at that time.

Early in 1949 at the Commonwealth Prime Minister's Conference in London, Bhai had agreed to India's membership in the Commonwealth. He had always believed that any cementing force in world affairs should be retained if this could be done honourably. There were already too many disintegrating factors in the world. At a time when men and nations were recovering from the scars of war and people of goodwill and vision were working to lay the foundations of a new world order, every step to strengthen this effort became an obligation. India's remaining in the Commonwealth after becoming a sovereign democratic republic would be a unique gesture, signifying her ability to think in wider terms of world cooperation and mutual benefit. This would in no way nullify the pledges given to the Indian people during the freedom movement. The formula evolved to make India's membership possible was that, though India would not accept allegiance to the Crown, she would recognize the King as the symbolic head of the Commonwealth. There was an outcry among some Indians, and controversy raged in parts of the country opposing the idea of Commonwealth membership. The step, it was said, would be harmful to the national interest. It would cause a breach between our Asian and African neighbours, it would be going back on our pledges. However, both the All India Congress Committee, the executive of the Congress party, and the Constituent Assembly ratified the proposal. Far from causing a breach between India and her neighbours, as various countries of Asia and Africa became free of British domination most followed India's example. The British Commonwealth changed its character and now became the Commonwealth of Nations.

The first meeting between Kwame Nkrumah and my brother was amusing. They were both in London for the Commonwealth Prime Ministers' meeting in 1959, and Nkrumah was to call on Bhai at the High Commission Residence for breakfast. This was at a time when Nkrumah had given himself the title of Redeemer and had had stamps issued with a picture of his head. Bhai had been very upset about all this. I was waiting downstairs to receive Nkrumah, and as his car drew up my baby granddaughter was at the front door about to leave for her morning outing. Nkrumah was a colourful sight in his national robes, and as he smiled at the baby she leaped out of her nanny's arms into his. It was a sweet sight. While this was going on at the front door Bhai was coming down the stairs obviously lost in thought. He came toward Nkrumah and without a preliminary greeting said, 'What the hell do you mean by putting your head on a stamp?' Fortunately he recovered himself immediately, and in a moment both men were laughing and embracing each other. Breakfast turned out to be a pleasant meal!

I was sent to Ghana on two occasions on government work. The first time, Nkrumah had just married a young Egyptian girl. Neither could speak the other's language and she did not know much English. She was a very pleasant young woman but I thought she was very lonely. By the time of my second visit Nkrumah's popularity had declined, and he lived in fear of the threats made on his life. When I arrived in Accra he received me in his office and invited me to dinner. I had a car at my disposal, but he insisted on sending his own car to fetch me. An armed guard sat with the chauffeur, who took a circuitous route and we changed cars midway to the President's palace. I was most bewildered by these strange goings-on and more so when Nkrumah told me that he stayed in a different place every night. He was then a nervous man and showed me the steel vest he wore under his shirt. The evening passed in a tense atmosphere.

◆◆◆

38

Back to the Roots

At the end of my seven years in England I was restless. These years had been happy and fruitful in a personal sense as well as from the point of view of my assignment. I had enjoyed my work and been fulfilled by the friendship I had received. Yet there was something lacking, which disturbed my peace of mind. What I needed was to get back to my roots—to nourish and strengthen them and to revive my contacts with India, to use the knowledge gained and the experience acquired for the benefit of India.

Through fifteen years of experience in the important chancelleries of the world, I had learned that India's image abroad depended on her performance at home and that no ambassador, however skillful, could hope to present a glowing picture abroad unless this was a reflection of the situation at home. And so, after days and nights of serious thought, I decided I must turn homeward and devote myself to my country.

I knew that fifteen years' absence is a long time, especially when those years have been full of change at home and a whole new generation has been growing up. I was also aware of the immense problems facing the country, and because of this I thought every man and woman who could work would be welcomed and permitted to make some contribution to the patterns of new India.

When I said goodbye to London I was sad. After so long I felt almost as if I were leaving home, not going home, and yet I had a sense of purpose—a desire to identify myself once again with that India which Bhai, in one of his speeches, had described as 'a myth and an idea, a dream and a vision and yet very real and present and pervasive... Shameful and repellent, she is occasionally perverse and obstinate...this lady with a past. But she is very lovable and none of her children can forget her wherever they go...for she is part of them in her greatness as well as her failings.' And now she beckoned to me, and I had to go and fulfill myself in her and through her.

I had rented a flat in Bombay and I went to make a home there near my daughter Tara. At Santa Cruz airport I was surrounded by the press and a shower of questions. 'Why have you left your post? Have you any plans for work?' And suddenly—'Would you accept the Vice-Presidency if it was offered to you?' To this I replied that, besides the fact that it was a hypothetical question, I did not think I would be the right person. However, being honest, I added that obviously it would be a tremendous honour.

A day or two later I went to Delhi to stay with Bhai and Indira. I also called on the President. Dr Radhakrishnan was a valued friend. After some questions about London and mutual friends he said, 'I am glad you came to see me as soon as you arrived. I wanted to meet you before the Prime Minister had any talks with you.' He then said he was keen that I should be appointed Vice-President, a post that was vacant, and he had spoken about the matter to the Prime Minister, who seemed in agreement. 'He will probably mention this to you tonight,' he continued. 'If it is offered, don't refuse.' I told him about the questions at the airport, and he said that ever since it was known that I was leaving London there had been talk in various circles about the possibility of my becoming Vice-President, and that there had been indications that my name would be acceptable.

That night after dinner Bhai took me to his study. He told me right away that he would like me to be Vice-President but that he was looking carefully into the matter. I said I had no desire that he should do anything that might lead to public criticism of himself; as he was Prime Minister, my appointment as Vice-President could cause him embarrassment. In addition, I was not quite sure if I could handle the chairmanship of the Rajya Sabha—our Upper House—which is one of the functions of the Vice-President. This, he said, did not bother him at all, and the matter was left for the moment.

The following days were full of rumours and newspaper comments, and one evening the President sent for me. I found him somewhat disturbed and he told me, 'Pressure is being brought on the Prime Minister against your appointment. He must decide by tomorrow.' The next day was the festival of Holi, and that afternoon there was, as always on this occasion, a reception for members of Parliament in the Prime Minister's garden. I had often attended such functions, which were lively and full of fun. This time there was gaiety up to a point, but it was obvious that there was a great deal of whispering among the guests, and several of my friends asked me what decision the Prime Minister had made. The party ended and we had dinner. Bhai was unusually silent. As we left the dining room he linked his arm in mine and said, 'Come to my study for a moment.' I knew then that whatever decision he had made had been difficult for him. In the study he sat at his desk nervously moving various objects from one place to another. After some minutes I asked what he wanted to say to me. His reply, given almost apologetically, was, 'I have decided not to offer you the Vice-Presidency.' I went round to where he sat and kissed the top of his head—my usual practice when I wanted to reassure him. 'What's bothering you about it?' I asked. 'I know there was some feeling against it, and you have done the right thing.' 'On the contrary,' he replied, 'there was far more pressure in your favour than against, but I think we should have a Muslim in that position.' He did not mention a name, but it suddenly occurred to me that he might have Dr Zakir Husain in mind and I asked him if this was so. Dr Zakir Husain was a close friend of ours and had also known my husband well. I was fond of him and delighted at the news. 'You could not have made a better choice,' I told Bhai, and I genuinely meant what I said. As soon as the announcement had been made I went over to Dr Husain's house. He embraced me with tears in his eyes and said, 'My sister, *I* should have been congratulating *you.*' I assured him I was very happy at his appointment. My relationship with Zakir bhai became stronger and his eventual election as President of India was an honour for the country. He was a gentleman, a great scholar, and a man of integrity. He loved flowers and was an authority on roses. He died in office, but during his short term he raised India's prestige at home and her image abroad.

Some days later Bhai offered me the choice of the governorship of the state of either Mysore or Maharashtra. I was not at all interested in this sort of post.

'What am I supposed to do if I accept?' I asked him. 'Work,' he laughingly replied, and then told me to find out my duties from the Constitution. I was familiar with the Constitution but bothered by the many things that were not written regarding a governor's duties. I had been in political life for so long that I did not think I possessed the ingredients necessary for a governor under existing conditions. A governor of a state was more or less a figurehead. However, after thinking it over I decided to try, and told Bhai I would go to Maharashtra.

One December afternoon in 1962 I left my flat in Bombay, the capital of Maharashtra, and drove to Raj Bhawan, the residence of the Governor, where I took the oath of office before an assembly of Bombay's elite.

The Governor's residence in all states is a conventional large house, but in Bombay it was a collection of cottages thrown together without a plan. The furniture, belonging to the time of the Raj, had known better days, and the buildings themselves needed repair. The one really beautiful room was the study facing the Arabian Sea. It had been designed by Durga Bajpai, the talented architect son of Sir Girja Shankar Bajpai, who had been a former Governor. Part of my girlhood had been spent in the mountains and I fell in love with the sea. I would sit late on the veranda outside my study lost in the splendour of the ocean.

In British days a Governor was a very important person and had a definite role to perform. He represented the Viceroy and was an isolated figure seen on formal occasions. He was surrounded by protocol, pomp, and splendour, and the people he met were carefully screened because there were many hostile to the regime. An invitation to Government House was highly coveted by those who lived in happy submission to the British. But though that era had become a part of history, the Raj Bhawans largely functioned as Government Houses of the old days. Often there was little communication between the Governor and the people, and only the social elite figured in the list of Raj Bhawan parties.

One of the first things that I felt must be changed was the vast army of servants who were supposed to cater to the needs of the Governor. They must have been efficient in earlier days when the demands of the British were more exacting, but by the time I encountered them they were sloppy and ineffective. Some only came on duty for a few hours every day and I never knew what their functions were. I set about putting Raj Bhawan right by telling the servants their duties and having the whole place thoroughly cleaned and repaired. There was a furore in the State Assembly because it was thought that vast amounts of money were being spent by me to redecorate the place. It is customary in our country to apportion blame first and look for facts afterward, and talk of my so-called extravagance had preceded me! The truth was that our standards of maintenance are low, and the need to preserve symbols is not understood. I have always believed that imagination and initiative, not large sums of money, are required to create beauty around one, and I refuse to live in a state of drabness. So Raj Bhawan took on a more pleasing prospect.

Apart from the artificial walls that separated the Governor from the people there were barriers between the state government and the Governor. This was a leftover of the days when provincial autonomy was first introduced and the Congress ministers were suspicious of the British Governor and kept him at arm's length. Indeed, at times there was open hostility between the two. But in our changed circumstances this was unnecessary. In our Constitution the Governor has no political duties except in cases when the state government is dissolved and the Governor assumes powers until such time as a new government is elected. However, if the Chief Minister, the head of the government in the State Legislature, and his Cabinet share their trust and understanding with a Governor, as has been the case in some states, a worthwhile relationship can result and prove beneficial to the state. Unfortunately, this was not so in Maharashtra. Reading old files I soon discovered that all my predecessors—men of ability—had complained of being left out in the cold. They were never consulted or allowed to advise on state matters and were generally made to feel useless. This sense of frustration grew in me also as I realized that, though I was treated with courtesy, the state government made it clear that my duties were to inaugurate functions such as flower shows, to attend prize givings, and in general be a figurehead. As this was something I had never been it was difficult to accept. When my appointment as Governor had been announced the press had hailed it with enthusiasm, and the Marathi press in particular had been full of affection, referring to my coming there as 'the return of the daughter-in-law of Maharashtra'. I decided that I should devote myself to trying to bring the people closer to the office of Governor. I abolished the pretentious use of a motorcycle escort accompanied by a siren when I went out. And I used my own car for unofficial functions. I changed the pattern of official entertainment and included authors, artists, actors, and social workers in all parties. I felt that Raj Bhawan belonged to the people and they must not be excluded from it.

For the first time I also had the opportunity to take part in the varied social service activities of a large city like Bombay. In my earlier years in India I had been busy with political work, and though I had been a member of the All India Women's Conference, the Women's League for Peace and Freedom, and other women's organizations, my main interest had centred around political activities. Now I had the chance to see and associate myself with the splendid work being done by voluntary organizations for crippled children, the deaf and dumb, the retarded, and many other unfortunate and underprivileged citizens.

The political memories I have been recording would not be complete without a heartfelt tribute to my women colleagues who played such a noble part in the freedom struggle and then in the more difficult task of helping to build the new India. We have never had or needed a suffragette movement in India, and there was no antagonism between the sexes. Thanks to the wise leadership of Gandhiji, the Indian woman stepped out of her home into social and political life without opposition from men and functioned as a comrade with great efficiency. The names of those women who are holding responsible posts today in every field of activity are too many to be mentioned here. I am proud to have worked with many of them, and, as I see the new generation forging ahead, my heart is full of joy because it is my colleagues and I who built the road on which these girls can walk forward today.

While I was in Bombay I was asked by Mother Teresa to inaugurate a new area of her work in Santa Cruz, a suburb of Bombay. This wonderful woman is the nearest thing to a saint that I have ever met. She has worked in slum areas in Calcutta which the most dedicated would hesitate to approach, and purely by dint of her own noble example she has, through the years, collected around her a group of young nuns and voluntary workers in whom she has generated her own fine spirit. Her work spreads and is, without question, the highest form of service, for she picks up the abandoned, the incurables, and gives them love and the courage to die with dignity. I had known about Mother Teresa but had not met her until, one evening, when I was High Commissioner in London, I received a phone call from the Papal Nuncio asking me what I was doing that evening, and could I excuse the informality and have supper with him? I replied that unfortunately I had to go to an official dinner, but when he said that Mother Teresa was staying with him and wished to meet me before she left next day, I arranged for her to come to me immediately. I went to dress for my party, leaving word that I wanted to be informed the moment she arrived.

She had been shown into a small room next to the salon where I usually received visitors. For some reason only a side light had been put on, and when I entered the room I could not see that anyone was there. I switched on the chandelier and, in a comer of the room, sitting on the edge of a brocade chair, was a tiny woman wearing a coarse hand-spun white sari draped Bengali fashion. On her feet were thick ungainly sandals. She rose to greet me and a strange thing happened. Quite suddenly my surroundings seemed to recede as if I were looking at a fading film. The beautiful room and the glittering lights were no longer there; only the tiny figure in the white sari, with work-worn hands and lined face, seemed to dominate the room. I held out my hands and went toward her to clasp her own outstretched ones. I looked into the sad, kind eyes and as she smiled we were back in that little Embassy room once more and I was greeting a visitor. But I was a little dazed and told her that she had made me see truth and maya. 'My dear, what do you mean?' she asked, but I did not reply, for there was none to give. All I knew was that I had been through an experience—I might say a cleansing experience. Since that night it has been my good fortune to see Mother Teresa from time to time, and sometimes in some small way to help her work.

Bombay is the home of many of Ranjit's relatives, and my daughter Tara had lived there for many years, as had my sister Betty and her husband. During my stay in Raj Bhawan I had an opportunity, denied by the years of living abroad, to be in close touch with the family. Betty had the art of making friends and was always surrounded by them in whichever place she happened to be. Her home was always welcoming and well run, and her parties were famous. She had a flair for clothes and decoration. After her marriage she had not gone back to political activity, but, had there been scope in Indian life for a political hostess, she would have made an excellent one. She was a good talker and had a lively sense of humour. Both her sons were at Cambridge during my period as High Commissioner in London and they did well. Strangely enough, both were married from my house. The younger one, Ajit, married in London, and I had his wedding reception at 9 Kensington Palace Gardens. He is a young man of whom I am proud and it is a great satisfaction to me that he is making a name for himself in the banking world in the United States. Harsha, the elder, was married while I was Governor in Bombay, and the ceremony took place at Raj Bhawan. He too lives in the United States now. It is sad that, with so many talents, Betty was not at peace with herself as she grew older. She was always restless, and Bhai's death was a great blow to her. Her own death, a few days after her sixtieth birthday, was a tragedy—she had been visiting her sons in America and was on her way home when she died. She had seemed fit and full of *joie de vivre* and should have had many years still before her.

◆◆◆

39

A Parting

Bhai had been slowly going down in health since the Chinese attack. In January 1964, at the annual session of the Congress at Bhubaneswar in Orissa, he had a mild stroke from which he recovered enough to resume his daily tasks. He had been pained and disillusioned over the China incident, he had been deeply hurt by the knowledge that advisors whom he had trusted had misled him or not thought fit to give him correct advice. Many factors contributed to his already failing health, and he seemed to have no will left to live. Indira was, of course, with him in Delhi all the time. Betty came and went. I longed to stay near him as it was obvious that he was slowly dying and my heart was heavy. But when he saw me he always asked why I had taken a holiday from my duties, and, not wishing to irritate him or let him think we were worrying about his health, I went back to Bombay. Indu had promised to let me know truthfully how he was getting on.

Early in the morning of May 27 my bedside phone rang. I knew instinctively it was Indu with bad news. She told me, 'Papu is not at all well. Can you come immediately?' Bhai had just spent three days in Dehra Dun, which he liked, and had returned the previous evening looking much refreshed. He was suddenly taken ill in the early hours of the morning.

The commercial flight from Bombay to Delhi had left, and the Maharashtra government plane was being used that day by the Chief Minister, whom we could not reach. I phoned the President, Dr Radhakrishnan, and he was able to arrange a plane for me. This he did immediately, but the distance between Bombay and Delhi is considerable and precious time was lost. I left with Betty and Raja and my daughter Tara. When the plane was half an hour from Delhi the pilot broke the news to us that the Prime Minister of India had just died peacefully without recovering consciousness.

Lekha and some close friends were waiting for us at Delhi airport and we drove as fast as possible to the Prime Minister's house. The weeping crowds outside the gates were so dense that no car could get through them. We jumped out and with great difficulty made our way on foot. I rushed up the stairs to Bhai's room. His body was still warm and death had wiped away the lines of care from his face. He looked beautiful and serene and that is the face I carry in my heart. I could not cry—I knew my grief for him would have to take some other form. He had left behind a rich legacy; that others would have to carry it forward was evident from the well-known lines of Robert Frost he kept at his bedside.

The woods are lovely, dark and deep.
But I have promises to keep,
And miles to go before I sleep.
And miles to go before I sleep.

To those who have loved Bhai this was his message.

He often used to say that a good day to die would be on the Buddha Jayanti. He had always had a special feeling for the Buddha and his message. According to legend the Buddha was born, received enlightenment, and died on the day of the same full moon, which is celebrated as the Buddha Jayanti, and that was the day Bhai left us.

Some years ago Bhai had written to me on Buddha Jayanti:

May 24, 1956

Nan darling,

Today is Buddha Jayanti day and the full moon of Vaisakhi will rise again as it did 2500 years ago on the Buddha. We have celebrated it in India on a big scale for it seems to have a particular significance in this age of ours. It is curious—this homecoming of the Buddha to Indian minds and hearts after a long lapse. I am sending you this little note with my love and blessings. May we prove worthy of the greatest of our countrymen.

Love,
JAWAHAR

◆◆◆

40

At Peace with Myself

I am frequently asked which of my assignments I have enjoyed most. The answer is easy to give in one word—London. England was known to me. There was a British stamp on my upbringing, and I have never had difficulty in understanding the British people. I can talk with them, laugh with them, quarrel with and criticize them, and still remain friends with them, knowing that this is how they feel about me. It is a good relationship, and in the Western world England is my second home. I like the British people. I admire their guts, their highly developed sense of what is *not* done (more important in many ways than merely knowing what *is* done!), their habit of understatement, so typically their own—but above all, their ability to accept change. The two reasons that the Empire died gracefully were Gandhi and the British recognition that the time had come. No other colonial power did or could have done this even with a Gandhi to point the way. England no longer ranks among the great powers, and her influence in the world has diminished, but, with all her faults, England possesses certain moral qualities the world needs for they are basic to decent living, and it would be a sad day should these cease to exist.

My brother used to say he belonged to neither East nor West. I do not think he was correct in this assessment of himself. His was an unfettered involvement with humanity, and for one like him the words 'East' and 'West' are without meaning. It was his deep sensitivity that was responsible for the feeling that he belonged nowhere.

My own involvement, like that of most people, is a limited one. I have always felt equally at home in both worlds. I have no feeling of disloyalty when I make a small niche for myself in foreign lands and enjoy being there. My roots are deep in India, and however much I may love to travel, to live in other lands, to meet other people and adapt myself to other ways, India is my refuge and the place to which I turn in time of inner need.

The other question I am asked is how do I assess my work when I look back on it now. This is more difficult to answer because one is likely to be less objective than one should be. Fortunately my critical faculty has often been turned on myself and I am discerning enough to know my weaknesses and faults.

The early days of political work during the national struggle were a challenge in more than one way. My capacity to adjust to changing situations and enjoy them, to extract something from each happening, has stood me in good stead, and the Congress work into which I was plunged was interesting and demanding. For this reason I threw myself into it with enthusiasm and did well. As a minister of the Uttar Pradesh government I brought new ideas to the work and was able to see some of them implemented in the short period during which the Congress party remained in power. I had had no training for the work I was called upon to do, but, being eager to succeed, I taught myself a great deal by reading. Also, I was not too proud to learn from others. I think—no, I am sure—that, given the time, I could have done much more in the ministry.

The United Nations work was no problem because one works on a brief and to make speeches poses no difficulty for me as I enjoy speaking. I am not bad at negotiation, I like people, so my time in the U.N. was both constructive and effective. I can look back on it with satisfaction.

During my years as Ambassador there were ups and downs in India's relationship with the world, partly the result of the times we were passing through. In retrospect things tend to fall into place and assume their proper proportion, and the design looks clearer than when one sees it being evolved. My main qualifications are, I think, the ability to make friends, to build bridges, to be able to contribute to the easing of tensions. These qualities are needed in diplomacy and proved of value to my government, so I feel my record was not wholly undistinguished.

When I see the Moscow of today and the easy, friendly life our ambassadors are able to lead—the opportunities that are extended to them—I am a little envious that my time en poste was, because of the very different situation that prevailed then, unfruitful. By no stretch of the imagination could one call it anything else, though for me, personally, it was an experience worth having, and I am sorry I could not visit the Soviet Union again. The warmth of the people when not held in check gave evidence of friendship that would have meant much to me. The United States and the United Kingdom were on an entirely different level. There was need in both posts to adjust to different kinds of work and deal with different problems, but I knew both countries well, their backgrounds, their people, and this was an advantage to me when India's policies differed from those of the country to which I was posted. In the United States, for instance, I lived through a time of diplomatic stress during the period preceding the signing of the Japanese peace treaty, and the long-drawn-out

Korean War, when India's friendly advice was rejected and her motives suspect, when Nehru was dubbed Red, and our Ambassador in Peking, Mr K.M. Panikkar, was referred to as the Panniky Ambassador because he correctly predicted the consequences of America's crossing the thirty-eighth parallel. In the United Kingdom we had difficulties during the Suez crisis when we strongly opposed the combined Anglo-French action in support of Israel. But through all these events my personal integrity was never in doubt, and the friendship extended to me in my individual capacity never wavered in either America or England.

In the political field after Independence—as distinct from diplomatic representation—the story is different. I am not a politician. The ways of modern politics are not my métier; the slippery road of intrigue that politicians have to climb is not for mc, even though the prizes at the end may be considerable. I have never been more miserable than during the periods I was in Parliament and witnessed the distressing spectacle of undiluted personal ambition creating an unhealthful atmosphere in India, limiting the growth of our people, corroding their morals, and crippling their higher instincts. I feel I can look back on my career with some pleasure of work done honestly and with whatever ability I could bring to my various assignments. One should not really ask for more.

What has my family life been during these years? Since 1920 the changes that have taken place in my life have been rapid and mostly unexpected. After the coming of Gandhiji an established pattern was broken up and the pieces scattered; to pick them up and fit them to a new design more suitable for the change that had come, or that which would inevitably follow, was rather like doing a jigsaw puzzle. Traditional living had been an anchor, keeping our boat in a safe harbour. Now the anchor had gone and the boat was at the mercy of the wild waves on a stormy ocean. We had a skillful pilot in Gandhiji, but each one had to use his own judgment and summon up enough courage and determination to be able to reach the end of the voyage, whatever the outcome. There were not many at that time who believed India could be an independent nation in their lifetime.

My children were born in a period of uncertainty, and, in spite of our efforts, there was little security in their lives. Growing up in a home that was also the centre of the country's political activity, they were subjected to ideas that helped them to mature at an earlier age than if they had led a more normal life. They were toughened, it is true, but they also lost much of the tenderness that every child has a right to receive. Often when they wanted guidance there was no one there. Sometimes when a loving word was needed, the one to say it was absent, and emotionally they suffered. But the other side of the medal must not be forgotten. They learned very early in life the meaning of certain words—loyalty, integrity, courage. They learned responsibility, they were able to understand values and ideas and to commit themselves to ideals when still very young. Because of this they could identify with the freedom movement, recognize its perils, and accept them. They were able to share in what their parents were doing, so a bond was created between us. It kept us close in spite of physical separations, and we were comrades who shared, enjoying the good days, and, when problems arose, standing by one another.

My daughters have families of their own. The two eldest are grandmothers, and Rita will not have long to wait! Chandralekha and Rita have been foreign service wives, and since they married they have lived mostly abroad. Rita is most like me in temperament. She is an optimist and has been involved with people from her earliest years. She has an irrepressible vitality and a love of life. She has now embarked on a career of her own, and is director of public relations for the Oberoi Hotels. She is well suited to this work because it is much the same as that which she had to do in her embassies, and her capacity for friendship and languages is a great help to her. Her son, Gopal, is in Sweden, a gifted linguist, and her bright daughter, Jyoti, is at college in California. Jyoti is a determined young girl and in some ways reminds me of myself.

Chandralekha is gentle, generous, and loving, sensitive to her surroundings and with an instinctive awareness of people's needs. She is the sort of woman who holds things together, whatever the cost. Before she married she worked as a journalist. I hope that when she moves out of the artificial barriers of diplomatic life, after her husband retires, she will make a career for herself through writing. She has just finished writing a gem of a mystery novel. Her family consists of a son and two daughters. Minakshi, the elder daughter, who is sweet and gentle like her mother, is married to a fine young man, Rasheed Ibrahim. This has been one of those marriages that are helping to integrate the new India, for he is a Muslim by faith. Their four-year-old daughter, Farhana, who has made me a great-grandmother and a very proud one, is now my best friend and ally. Lekha's younger daughter, Manju, is a senior at Wellesley. She is a serious young woman, intensely aware of the world's pain and its problems. She is especially devoted to animals and concerned in their welfare. Arjun, Lekha's son, is a young man whose qualities of friendship and awareness of the political world would have stood him in good stead if he had been in the Foreign Service. He is a young business executive. My two sons-in-law, Ashok and Avtar, are very much part of my family, and their homes and Embassies have always welcomed me and extended the affection and care that one craves as the years pass.

Nayantara, who married immediately after coming home from the United States, has always made her home in India. She has a son and two daughters. Of the girls, Nonika is a typical product of the modern age, talented but restless. She is especially interested in clothes designing and methods of production for the foreign market, and she works in Delhi. Gita, the younger, has recently come home after graduating from London University. Gita is a crusader, deeply interested in politics and passionately dedicated to the cause of the underprivileged and to justice for the Third World. Tara's son, Ranjit, has followed his father in the business world and fits well into it. He is married to a charming Italian girl, Francesca. Their bonny baby boy, Gautam Giorgio, is my second great-grandchild.

Tara is a writer and is the author of nine books, including five novels. Nearly all these have been published in America and Britain besides India. She is also a political journalist. She possesses idealism and tremendous determination, the capacity to face a problem and not try to put it aside for another day. Combined with this are her good looks, which she shares with her sisters. Her marriage ended in divorce in 1967, and after this she devoted herself completely to her writing career, in which she has made a name for herself. She has surmounted many difficulties with great courage and made a new life for herself with E.N. Mangat Rai. Nirmal is a human being of great worth and gentleness and has had an outstanding career in the Indian Civil Service. Tara deserves the happiness that has come to her through him.

We are a close-knit and happy family. We share experiences and ideas with one another, and there is laughter and reminiscing when we are together. I am known as the Honourable Ancient One, and how wonderful it is to be on such terms with the young! The age gap between the grandchildren and me is a big one, but it is bridged by the fact that I try to understand the changing patterns of manners and morals even if I cannot always accept them. No grandchild of mine has ever complained that I have forgotten what it was like to be young, and I consider this a compliment. Indeed I have *not* forgotten, which is the reason that young people argue and disagree with me as much as they like but continue to trust me. This and the tenderness and love my daughters give me are my most valued possessions.

When the grandchildren were young they were often in Bhai's house and made much of by him. Having no maternal grandfather they called him Nanaji. During the Chinese invasion in 1962 the elder children, then in school in Dehra Dun, wrote to him on his birthday:

Dehra Dun
14th Nov. 1962

Darling Nanaji,

Today is your birthday, and we your grandchildren send you our love, and all good wishes for your health. We are very sad about the war and wish we could do something to drive out the Chinese. We would like to donate our pocket money to the National Defence Fund. We are sending you Rs. 80/from us all. I (Nonika) have a gold locket which Nani brought for me from Ghana. I would like to give you this and am asking Mummie to send it. Minakshi is sorry she has no real jewellery.

We shall be fighting by your side dear Nanaji. Lots of love and kisses.

Minakshi Noni
Ranjit Arjun
Gopal

While I was still in Parliament in 1967 my daughters had persuaded me to build a house in Dehra Dun. There were several reasons for choosing this location. It is in my home state of Uttar Pradesh. I have had close associations with the town since I was a girl, and we spent summers in the neighbouring mountain resort of Mussoorie, twenty miles away. My daughters went to school in Mussoorie, my grandchildren's schools were in Dehra Dun, my husband and my brother spent years in a Dehra Dun prison.

Dehra Dun is famous for its litchi orchards. This juicy fruit hangs from the trees in great red clusters. The skin is slightly prickly and the inside looks like a boiled egg. It has a faint rose aroma and a litchi makes delicious eating.

Dehra Dun has well-known schools, mostly started in British days, but some since then. There is the Indian Military Academy, which receives cadets from several Asian and African countries; the Forest Research Institute is considered the best in Asia, and the Oil and Natural Gas Commission is of growing importance to the country.

My home is actually in Rajpur, a village nine miles from

the town, in sylvan surroundings. It has also become the home of several hundred Tibetan refugees who now live and work there. The Government of India looks after them, and, apart from making very beautiful carpets, they have a number of cottage industries. These good people have now adapted themselves to India. The Dalai Lama lives in Dharamshala, another mountain resort higher in altitude than Dehra Dun. He is a remarkable young man who is self-educated and who thinks in modern terms of progress and the need for his small community in India to try to march in step with changing times. When I talked with him recently about the world situation he said smilingly: 'There is no room for a "living God" nor the need for one.' I remember the first time I met the Dalai Lama when he and his brother were ten and twelve years old on a visit to Delhi as my brother's guests. My brother wanted to give them some presents they would enjoy, and finally, as I recall, gave them each a camera and a bicycle. How excited the little Dalai Lama was, taking pictures with the new camera and behaving as any little boy does anywhere. He has, since those days, been through tragedy but has faced up to it and been moulded and matured because of it.

The Rajpur road is lined with jacaranda and laburnum trees. When the jacaranda are in flower the road seems to be covered in a delicate purple mist. Other seasons bring other flowers. I have a garden that some day will fulfill my dreams, and a little pool of waterlilies, pink and white, which add charm to the scene. To the northwest of my house is a hill, well wooded and nearly always green. Below it flows a stream that fills up in the monsoon rains, and the sound of running water is pleasant to hear. On this hillside live two friends who treat my garden as their personal property, coming and going at will. These are a pair of panthers whose main interest is the chicken farm across the road, which provides them with chicken dinners. My complaint is that these nocturnal meals are frequently eaten under the cassia tree on my lawn, and the heaps of white feathers left behind make extra work for my gardener, who already considers himself an overworked and underpaid man! Sometimes there are invasions of monkeys who destroy my vegetables and eat my fruit. My gardener will not try to scare them away or attack them because they are considered reincarnations of the monkey god, Hanuman. They may do what damage they please and know they are secure.

I like to observe festivals of all faiths in my home whenever possible. There is Diwali, with its lights and joys of the companionship of friends and family who can join me at this time; and Id, the Muslim festival of brotherhood and rejoicing; and the birthday of the Buddha with its message of compassion for mankind; and Christmas with the hope of peace. Even though Christ is betrayed again and again by the hatred in men's hearts and the ugliness of wars, truth and love are eternal, and to stop and think of them at certain times of the year makes for a cleansing of heart and mind.

During the summer I watch the sunrise while I drink my morning tea on the veranda, and in the evening the sunsets over the Siwalik hills in the west are breathtakingly beautiful, sometimes flaming red and gold, and at other times a mixture of soft shades of rose and pink and purple, all merging into one another. But what I love most are the serenity and silence. On nights when the garden is flooded with moonlight, the mountains look as if they have moved up to the edge of the lawn—good neighbours who know when *not* to speak. When there is no moon the darkness and the quiet of the night are soothing. One can see beyond the vision of the eye on such a night.

As I grow old, living alone is no problem. There are memories to gladden my heart and there are always things to do. My garden is demanding, cooking and experimenting with new dishes is a delightful hobby. There are visits by bus every week into town where I do my own shopping and exchange views on all possible subjects with my friends the shopkeepers. A great joy is reading, and there is so much to read! The small library in my house is my favourite room, and I live in the past or the present as I choose, enjoying both. Last, but most important, there are people—those whom I like and who care for me. I spend interesting hours with these friends whenever I wish and never feel lonely. So when I am asked what I do to pass the time I find the question quite absurd. There is not enough time to do all I want. I am always thinking ahead and planning.

Sometimes in the evenings I sit on my veranda and look at the high Himalayas facing me. There is strength in them and a sense of purpose that India needs. The world is passing through hard times, and India has faced tragedies in the recent past. Two years ago, when the Emergency ended, it seemed as if a new day had dawned. After the national election there was hope, there was determination, above all there was unity, and we thought we would face all difficulties together and conquer them. But the hopes of two years ago have not materialized, and the dream we dreamed is becoming a nightmare because the silver thread of unity seems to have snapped. Someone said to me recently, 'Order and safety and economic progress are what men need. Ideals do not fill an empty belly.' I was shaken. Have we reached a stage when we are prepared to bargain for bread against values? I do not believe it, and, while I am able, I shall fight this pernicious theory. Ours is a great country with a great civilization, and civilizations are built on values. But it is not good to look back too much. The past is useful only to understand the present; let us look ahead and go forward.

Governments change, men and women come and go, but India will remain and move from strength to strength for there will always be those who will truly serve her and will strive to keep her great. And no matter how many may desire the calm of despotism there will be thousands of others brave enough to launch out on 'liberty's boisterous sea'.

As I look at the mountains I give thanks for the abundance of God's blessings, above all for His having given me the strength to keep faith with my ideals. I am at peace with myself. I have lived most of my life in the sunlight and enjoyed it. Now that the twilight has come, I welcome it, for I know that the darkness that follows will be the beginning of another day.

Acknowledgements

For many years my daughters have been urging me to write this book. I have hesitated partly from laziness but mainly because I lacked confidence in my ability to do so. Or perhaps the time had not come? Even after I began I might never have reached the end but for the help given to me by my eldest daughter, Chandralekha Mehta. In spite of her duties as an ambassador's wife, she found time to do all the research needed for the book as well as the typing of the first draft and correcting the final one. Besides this, her infinite patience with all my moods and her clear memory were of the greatest assistance throughout. My daughter Nayantara Sahgal made time from her busy schedule of work as a member of the Indian delegation to the United Nations General Assembly in the fall of 1978 to edit the manuscript. My daughters and I understand one another and they know my feelings for them are too deep to require words of thanks.

My nephew Ajit Hutheesing has taken time off from his own professional responsibilities to advise me on matters I could not have dealt with alone. In India a nephew is like a son, so I do not have to be formal with him either.

The final draft of the book was typed by Shri Balbir Chand of the Indian Embassy in Mexico. I am grateful to him for the speed and efficiency with which he accomplished this task and, above all, for the devotion he put into it.

My thanks are due to Gertrude Chase for her earlier help with the book and my gratitude to Ruth Hagy Brod for her indefatigable efforts. To my publishers I would like to express my deep appreciation for their faith in an unknown author.

August 24, 1978 VIJAYA LAKSHMI PANDIT